The Way of the Lord

The Way of the Lord

Christological Exegesis of the Old Testament
in the Gospel of Mark

Joel Marcus

Westminster/John Knox Press
Louisville, Kentucky

Book design by The HK Scriptorium, Inc.

First Edition

This book is printed on acid-free paper that meets the American National Standards Institute Z39.48 standard. ⊗

Published by Westminster/John Knox Press
Louisville, Kentucky

PRINTED IN THE UNITED STATES OF AMERICA
9 8 7 6 5 4 3 2 1

Library of Congress Cataloging-in-Publication Data

Marcus, Joel, 1951–
    The way of the Lord : christological exegesis of the Old Testament in the Gospel of Mark / Joel Marcus. — 1st ed.
        p.   cm.
    Includes bibliographical references and indexes.
    ISBN 0-664-21949-7 (alk. paper)
    1. Bible. N.T. Mark — Relation to the Old Testament.   2. Bible. O.T. — Relation to Mark.   3. Jesus Christ — Person and offices. I. Title.
BS2585.2.M2395   1992
226.3'.06 — dc20   91-45741

Contents

Acknowledgments

I began work on this book during an eventful and stimulating research leave in Jerusalem during the 1988–1989 academic year. The leave was made possible by the generous financial support of Princeton Theological Seminary, for which I am extremely grateful. While in Jerusalem I studied at both the Ecole Biblique and Hebrew University, and I would like to thank both institutions for making their resources, especially their libraries, available to me. To my friend Doron Mendels of the Department of History at Hebrew University go special thanks for opening so many doors, including, in a way, the door to the beautiful apartment on the corner of Hanasi and Palmach. Thanks also for many kindnesses to the people at the Ecumenical Institute (Tantur), especially the director, Tom Stransky, and the chaplain, Vincent Martin.

Several people assisted me by reading and criticizing drafts of the material found here. Pride of place among them belongs to Bart Ehrman, whose generosity and sense of humor are matched only by the acuteness of his mind and the quantity of his red ink. I would also like to give special thanks to Nils Dahl for his detailed response to what became chapter 5. My editor at Westminster/John Knox, Jeff Hamilton, provided valuable comments on the whole work. Others who read drafts and offered helpful critiques of various chapters included Gary Anderson, Martin de Boer, Lou Martyn, Ulrich Mauser, and Marty Soards. Douglas Miller, the departmental assistant of the Princeton Seminary Biblical Department, gave valuable assistance in compiling the list of abbreviations.

A version of chapter 2 was presented at the regional meeting of the Catholic Biblical Association in March 1990, with a response by Robin Scroggs. A version of chapter 5 was presented at a symposium sponsored jointly by Princeton Theological Seminary, Union Theological Seminary, and Yale Divinity School, in New York City in the spring of 1988, with a response by Richard Hays. (I would also like to thank the editor of *Zeitschrift für die neutestamentliche Wissenschaft,* Erich Grässer, for permitting me to publish in this chapter a revised form of my article on Mark 9:11–13 that appeared there.) A version of chapter 6 was discussed at the New Testament Colloquium at Princeton Theological Seminary in the fall of 1990, with a response by Jim Hanson. A version of chapter 7 was presented in the Synoptic Gospels Section at the Annual Meeting of the Society of Biblical Literature in New Orleans in 1990, and the germ of chapter 9 was presented at the Passion Narratives Consultation at the Annual Meeting in Anaheim in 1989. I profited immensely from all these responses and discussions, and they have saved me from some embarrassing mistakes.

My wife, Gloria, has been a constant source of support and encouragement during the sometimes difficult years that this book has been gestating. I would also like to give proleptic thanks to Rachel for the way in which her presence with us since April 7, 1991 has lightened the final months of the preparation of the text; someday she will understand.

Lou Martyn was the first person who "saw" me as a New Testament scholar many years ago. Our relationship, and what it means to me, has continued to grow over the years. I dedicate this book to him.

Abbreviations

Ancient Sources

Apoc. Elijah	*Apocalypse of Elijah*
2 Apoc. Bar.	Syriac *Apocalypse of Baruch*
b. Ber.	Babylonian Talmud, *Berakot*
b. Ḥag.	Babylonian Talmud, *Ḥagiga*
b. Nid.	Babylonian Talmud, *Niddah*
b. Pesaḥ.	Babylonian Talmud, *Pesaḥim*
b. Sanh.	Babylonian Talmud, *Sanhedrin*
Barn.	*Barnabas*
Bib. Ant.	Pseudo-Philo, *Biblical Antiquities*

Dead Sea Scrolls

1QH	*Thanksgiving Hymns*
1QM	*War Scroll*
1QS	*Community Rule*
4Q500	*Benediction*
4QFlor	*Florilegium*
4QpsDanA[a]	pseudo-Daniel
4QPs[f]	Psalms Scroll
4QpPs37	*Pesher on Psalm 37*
11QPs22	*Apostrophe to Zion*
CD	*Damascus Document*

Cant. Rab.	*Canticle of Canticles Rabbah*
Deut. Rab.	*Deuteronomy Rabbah*
Eccl. Rab.	*Ecclesiastes Rabbah*
Ep. Arist.	*Epistle of Aristeas*
Exod. Rab.	*Exodus Rabbah*

Gos. Thom.	Gospel of Thomas
LXX	Septuagint
Me'il.	Me'ila
Midr. Psalms	Midrash Psalms
Midr. Cant.	Midrash Canticle of Canticles
MT	Masoretic Text
Pesiq. Rab. Kah.	Pesiqta de Rab Kahana
Pss. Sol.	Psalms of Solomon
Ruth Rab.	Ruth Rabbah
Sib. Or.	Sibylline Oracles
Sipre Deut.	Sipre Deuteronomy
Sipre Num.	Sipre Numbers
T. Benj.	Testament of Benjamin
T. Sol.	Testament of Solomon
Tg. Isa.	Targum of Isaiah
Tg. Psalms	Targum of Psalms
Tg. Cant.	Targum of Canticle of Canticles

Modern Works

AB	Anchor Bible
AnBib	Analecta Biblica
ANRW	Aufstieg und Niedergang der römischen Welt: Geschichte und Kultur Roms im Spiegel der neueren Forschung, edited by H. Temporini and W. Haase. Berlin and New York: Walter de Gruyter.
APOT	Apocrypha and Pseudepigrapha of the Old Testament, edited by R. H. Charles. 2 vols. Oxford: Clarendon Press, 1913.
ATANT	Abhandlungen zur Theologie des Alten und Neuen Testaments
AUSS	Andrews University Seminary Studies
BAGD	Bauer, W., F. W. Gingrich, and F. W. Danker. A Greek-English Lexicon of the New Testament and Other Early Christian Literature. 2nd ed. Chicago: University of Chicago Press, 1979.
BASOR	Bulletin of the American Schools of Oriental Research
BDB	Brown, F., S. R. Driver, and C. A. Briggs. A Hebrew and English Lexicon of the Old Testament. Oxford: Clarendon Press, 1952.

BDF	Blass, F., A. Debrunner, and R. W. Funk. *A Greek Grammar of the New Testament and Other Early Christian Literature*. Chicago: University of Chicago Press, 1961.
BETTA	Beiträge zur Evangelischen Theologie. Theologische Abhandlungen
BHT	Beiträge zur historischen Theologie
Bib	*Biblica*
BJRL	*Bulletin of the John Rylands University Library of Manchester*
BJS	Brown Judaic Studies
BKAT	Biblischer Kommentar: Altes Testament
BR	*Biblical Research*
BZ	*Biblische Zeitschrift*
CBQ	*Catholic Biblical Quarterly*
CBQMS	Catholic Biblical Quarterly Monograph Series
CGTC	Cambridge Greek Testament Commentaries
CNT	Commentaire du Nouveau Testament
ConBNT	Coniectanea biblica, New Testament
ConBOT	Coniectanea biblica, Old Testament
ConNT	Coniectanea neotestamentica
CRINT	Compendia rerum iudaicarum ad novum testamentum
EKKNT	Evangelisch-katholischer Kommentar zum Neuen Testament
ExpT	*Expository Times*
FB	Forschung zur Bibel
FRLANT	Forschungen zur Religion und Literatur des Alten und Neuen Testaments
GKC	*Gesenius' Hebrew Grammar*, edited by E. Kautzsch, translated by A. E. Cowley. 2nd ed. Oxford: Clarendon Press, 1910.
HNT	Handbuch zum Neuen Testament
HSM	Harvard Semitic Monographs
HTKNT	Herders theologischer Kommentar zum Neuen Testament
HTR	*Harvard Theological Review*
HTS	Harvard Theological Studies
IDB	*Interpreter's Dictionary of the Bible*, edited by G. A. Buttrick. Nashville: Abingdon Press, 1962.
IDBSup	*Interpreter's Dictionary of the Bible, Supplementary Volume*, edited by K. Crim. Nashville: Abingdon Press, 1976.
Int	*Interpretation*

IRT	Issues in Religion and Theology
JBL	*Journal of Biblical Literature*
JJS	*Journal of Jewish Studies*
JSNT	*Journal for the Study of the New Testament*
JSNTSup	Journal for the Study of the New Testament— Supplement Series
JSOT	*Journal for the Study of the Old Testament*
JSOTSup	Journal for the Study of the Old Testament— Supplement Series
JTS	*Journal of Theological Studies*
LCL	Loeb Classical Library
LQ	*Lutheran Quarterly*
MeyerK	H. A. W. Meyer, Kritisch-exegetischer Kommentar über das Neue Testament
NCB	New Century Bible
NICNT	New International Commentary on the New Testament
NovT	*Novum Testamentum*
NovTSup	Novum Testamentum, Supplements
NTAbh	Neutestamentliche Abhandlungen
NTOA	Novum Testamentum et Orbis Antiquus
NTS	*New Testament Studies*
OBO	Orbis biblicus et orientalis
OTL	Old Testament Library
OTP	*The Old Testament Pseudepigrapha*, edited by J. H. Charlesworth. 2 vols. Garden City, N.Y.: Doubleday & Co., 1983, 1985.
RB	*Revue biblique*
RNT	Regensburger Neues Testament
RSV	Revised Standard Version
SANT	Studien zum Alten und Neuen Testament
SB	Stuttgarter Bibelstudien
S-B	Strack, H. L., and P. Billerbeck. *Kommentar zum Neuen Testament aus Talmud und Midrasch*. 6 vols. Munich: Beck, 1922–1961.
SBB	Stuttgarter biblische Beiträge
SBLDS	SBL Dissertation Series
SBLMS	SBL Monograph Series
SBLSCS	SBL Septuagint and Cognate Studies
SBLSP	SBL Seminar Papers
SBLSS	SBL Semeia Studies
SBM	Stuttgarter biblische Monographien
SBT	Studies in Biblical Theology

SEÅ	*Svensk exegetisk årsbok*
SJLA	Studies in Judaism in Late Antiquity
SJT	*Scottish Journal of Theology*
SNTSMS	Society for New Testament Studies Monograph Series
STDJ	Studies on the Texts of the Desert of Judah
StudNTUmwelt	Studien zum Neuen Testament und seiner Umwelt
SVTP	Studia in Veteris Testamenti pseudepigrapha
TBei	*Theologische Beiträge*
TBl	*Theologische Blätter*
TBü	Theologische Bücherei
TDNT	*Theological Dictionary of the New Testament,* edited by G. Kittel and G. Friedrich. 10 vols. Grand Rapids: Wm. B. Eerdmans Publishing Co., 1964–1976.
THKNT	Theologischer Handkommentar zum Neuen Testament
TLZ	*Theologische Literaturzeitung*
TRE	*Theologische Realenzyklopädie*
TU	Texte und Untersuchungen
VTSup	Vetus Testamentum, Supplements
WBC	Word Biblical Commentary
WUNT	Wissenschaftliche Untersuchungen zum Neuen Testament
ZAW	*Zeitschrift für die alttestamentliche Wissenschaft*
ZNW	*Zeitschrift für die neutestamentliche Wissenschaft*
ZTK	*Zeitschrift für Theologie und Kirche*

1

Introduction

Mark's Old Testament Usage: Overview

In a programmatic statement at the very beginning of his Gospel, the author of Mark announces his conviction that his story about the good news of Jesus Christ takes place "as it has been written in Isaiah the prophet." He then goes on to buttress this claim with a conflated citation from Exodus, Malachi, and Isaiah (Mark 1:1–3). A few verses later, at the climactic moment in Jesus' baptism, a divine voice comes forth from heaven to hail Jesus with words drawn from Psalm 2, Isaiah 42, and perhaps Genesis 22 (1:11).

The situation is similar at the end of the Gospel: citations of the Old Testament occupy positions of extraordinary prominence. At the most critical moment of the trial scene in chapter 14, for example, Jesus answers the high priest's question about his identity with a response that melds a quotation from Daniel with an allusion to Psalm 110 (14:61–62). This response leads ineluctably to Jesus' condemnation and death on the cross, where he expires with the first words of Psalm 22 on his lips (15:34) after being stripped and mocked in ways that recall the same psalm (15:24, 29).

In between this scriptural beginning and this scriptural ending, citations of and allusions to the Old Testament continually pop up in the Markan narrative, usually on the lips of Jesus himself.[1] Mark's initial claim that the good news is as it has been described by Isaiah the prophet is matched by Jesus' assertion that Isaiah prophesied the bad news of the scribes' and Pharisees' hypocrisy (7:6), and in 4:12 Jesus uses another Isaian text to present the spiritual condition of his opponents, the "outsiders," as one of

---

[1] To see some of them at a glance, consult R. G. Bratcher's useful handbook *Old Testament Quotations in the New Testament*, Helps for Translators Series, 2nd ed. (London, New York, and Stuttgart: United Bible Societies, 1984), pp. 12–17.

1

divinely willed blindness.[2] Jesus, moreover, frequently debates with these opponents about the meaning of the scriptures[3] or uses Old Testament texts as weapons with which to attack them,[4] and he sums up his condemnation of one group with the charge that they "know neither the scriptures nor the power of God" (12:24). The eschatological discourse in chapter 13, moreover, is full of Old Testament citations and allusions, especially from Daniel, and the latter half of Mark's Gospel is studded with assertions by Jesus that his path to suffering and death has been foretold in the scriptures of Israel (9:12; 14:21, 27, 41; cf. 8:31; 9:31; 10:33).

Recent Research on Mark's Old Testament Use

In spite of this wealth of references to the Old Testament in the Markan narrative, Mark's use of the Old Testament has been a relatively neglected subject in recent scholarship. For many years, the only full-length monograph of major importance was the dissertation of A. Suhl, which was published in 1965.[5] This work aims to be a comprehensive redaction-critical study of the Markan Old Testament citations and allusions. Taking his point of departure from W. Marxsen's thesis that Mark's Gospel is primarily an address to the author's community rather than an account of past events, Suhl argues that Mark is not interested in the past for its own sake or in its continuity with the present, and hence that his use of Old Testament texts cannot be described as a matter of "proof from Scripture" or even of "promise and fulfillment." He merely uses Old Testament language and "coloring" to show that the same God who spoke in the Old Testament is also behind the events involving Jesus; he quotes the Old Testament only to make the general assertion that the gospel message is in accordance with the scriptures (cf. 1 Cor. 15:3–4).

Despite its detailed and sometimes insightful analysis of individual pericopes, Suhl's work has been rightly criticized for being determined by a dogmatic application of the thesis of his doctoral advisor Marxsen. In a penetrating review, E. Grässer has pointed out that Suhl never sufficiently grapples with the fact that Mark uses *precisely Old Testament texts* as a paint

---

[2] On the identity of the outsiders, the use of Isa. 6:10, and other exegetical questions about Mark 4:10–12, see J. Marcus, *The Mystery of the Kingdom of God*, SBLDS 90 (Atlanta: Scholars Press, 1986), chapter 3.

[3] See 7:9–13; 10:1–12; 12:18–27, 35–37; cf. 12:28–34, which is a scriptural discussion with a friendly interlocutor.

[4] See 11:17; 12:10–11; cf. 8:18, where an allusion to Jer. 5:21 is used for an attack on the disciples.

[5] A. Suhl, *Die Funktion der alttestamentlichen Zitate und Anspielungen im Markusevangelium* (Gütersloh: Gerd Mohn, 1965).

box for important sections of his Gospel.[6] Mark does *not* content himself, as Paul does in 1 Cor. 15:3–4, with the broad assertion that what happened to Jesus was "according to the scriptures";[7] he also quotes and alludes to specific Old Testament passages and evidently interprets at least some of them as prophecies that have now been fulfilled in Christ.

This understanding is established already by the very first of the Old Testament citations in Mark, the conflated citation in 1:2–3, which is introduced by the phrase "as it has been written in Isaiah the prophet." Grässer rightly challenges Suhl's assertion that Mark merely juxtaposes the Old Testament prophecy with the New Testament event without implying that the one is the fulfillment of the other, and he counters Suhl's apodictic declaration that καθώς ("as") "does not as yet tell us very much" about Mark's attitude toward the Old Testament.[8] On the contrary, Grässer argues, καθώς, coupled with the designation of Isaiah as "the prophet" and the position of this Old Testament citation at the very head of Mark's Gospel, tells us a great deal about Mark's view: the forward-looking expectation of "Isaiah" is of crucial importance for him, and he thinks that this expectation was being realized in the series of events that began with John's prophesied appearance in the wilderness. Grässer makes a similar point about the attitude toward the scriptures implied in 7:6; 14:21; and 14:49.

Suhl's study, then, is not the last word on the use of the Old Testament in Mark, nor did it seem to stimulate other major investigations of the subject. True, Suhl's subject matter had been anticipated in an article by S. Schulz in 1961, and in the years that followed individual articles on Mark's use of the Old Testament continued to appear.[9] U. Mauser, moreover, studied one aspect of the subject in his monograph on the wilderness theme in Mark; L. Hartman looked at the use of the Old Testament in Mark 13, H. C. Kee at its use in Mark 11–16, and D. J. Moo at its use in the Gospel passion narratives in general.[10] In addition, wide-ranging studies of the use of the

---

[6] E. Grässer, review in *TLZ* 91 (1966), 667–669; see also H. Anderson, "The Old Testament in Mark's Gospel," in *The Use of the Old Testament in the New and Other Essays: Studies in Honor of William Franklin Stinespring*, ed. J. M. Efird (Durham, N.C.: Duke University Press, 1972), pp. 280–306, esp. pp. 285–286; H.-J. Steichele, *Der leidende Sohn Gottes: Eine Untersuchung einiger alttestamentlicher Motive in der Christologie des Markusevangeliums*, Biblische Untersuchungen 14 (Regensburg: Pustet, 1980), pp. 27–36.

[7] Though see 9:12; 14:21, 41. Even here, however, Mark probably has specific passages in mind; see chapter 5 below.

[8] Suhl, *Zitate*, pp. 136–137.

[9] S. Schulz, "Markus und das Alte Testament," *ZTK* 58 (1961), 184–197. See, e.g., Anderson, "Old Testament," in *Use of the Old Testament*, ed. Efird, pp. 280–306; W. S. Vorster, "The Function of the Use of the Old Testament in Mark," *Neotestamentica* 14 (1980), 62–72; M. D. Hooker, "Mark," in *It Is Written: Scripture Citing Scripture: Essays in Honour of Barnabas Lindars*, ed. D. A. Carson and H. G. M. Williamson (Cambridge: Cambridge University Press, 1988), pp. 220–230.

[10] U. Mauser, *Christ in the Wilderness: The Wilderness Theme in the Second Gospel and Its Basis in the Biblical Tradition*, SBT 39 (Naperville, Ill.: Alec R. Allenson, 1963); L. Hartman,

Old Testament in the New were published, and some of them devoted space to Markan scriptural exegesis.[11]

It cannot be said, however, that the spark lit by Suhl was fanned into anything resembling a flame until the 1980s. At the beginning of that decade, H.-J. Steichele published his dissertation, a study of some Old Testament motifs in Markan christology. In the middle of the decade, J. D. M. Derrett came out with a two-volume commentary on Mark that attempted to show that the entire Gospel was based on an Old Testament "grid" provided in the main by Exodus, Numbers, and Joshua. Near the end of the decade, similarly, W. Roth claimed to have "cracked the code of Mark" and to have discovered that it was based on the paradigm of the Elijah/Elisha narratives of 1 Kings 17 to 2 Kings 13. As the 1990s began, D. and P. Miller published a monograph describing Mark as a midrash on earlier literature, including the Old Testament.[12] These recent publications reflect a burgeoning interest in the general area of the use of the Old Testament in later writings, including the New Testament,[13] and, more broadly still, in the phenomenon of "intertextuality."[14]

Prophecy Interpreted: The Formation of Some Jewish Apocalyptic Texts of the Eschatological Discourse Mark 13 Par., ConBNT 1 (Lund: Gleerup, 1966); H. C. Kee, "The Function of Scriptural Quotations and Allusions in Mark 11–16," in *Jesus und Paulus: Festschrift für Werner Georg Kümmel zum 70. Geburtstag,* ed. E. E. Ellis and E. Grässer (Göttingen: Vandenhoeck & Ruprecht, 1975), pp. 165–188; D. J. Moo, *The Old Testament in the Gospel Passion Narratives* (Sheffield: Almond Press, 1983).

[11] See, e.g., D. M. Smith, "The Use of the Old Testament in the New," in *Use of the Old Testament,* ed. Efird, pp. 40–43; R. N. Longenecker, *Biblical Exegesis in the Apostolic Period* (Grand Rapids: Wm B. Eerdmans Publishing Co., 1975), pp. 137–139.

[12] Steichele, *Leidende Sohn;* J. D. M. Derrett, *The Making of Mark: The Scriptural Bases of the Earliest Gospel,* 2 vols. (Shipston-on-Stour: P. Drinkwater, 1985); W. Roth, *Hebrew Gospel: Cracking the Code of Mark* (Oak Park, Ill.: Meyer-Stone Books, 1988); D. and P. Miller, *The Gospel of Mark as Midrash on Earlier Jewish and New Testament Literature,* Studies in the Bible and Early Christianity 21 (Lewiston, N.Y.: Edwin Mellen Press, 1990).

[13] Earlier works on this subject include C. H. Dodd's classic *According to the Scriptures: The Sub-structure of New Testament Theology* (London: Nisbet, 1952); B. Lindars, *New Testament Apologetic: The Doctrinal Significance of the Old Testament Quotations* (Philadelphia: Westminster Press, 1961); A. T. Hanson, *Jesus Christ in the Old Testament* (London: SPCK, 1965); R. T. France, *Jesus and the Old Testament: His Application of Old Testament Passages to Himself and His Mission* (Downers Grove, Ill.: Inter-Varsity Press, 1971); and Longenecker, *Biblical Exegesis.* The 1980s saw the publication of M. Fishbane, *Biblical Interpretation in Ancient Israel* (Oxford: Clarendon Press, 1985); J. L. Kugel and R. A. Greer, *Early Biblical Interpretation,* Library of Early Christianity (Philadelphia: Westminster Press, 1986); D. Juel, *Messianic Exegesis: Christological Interpretation of the Old Testament in Early Christianity* (Philadelphia: Fortress Press, 1988); M. J. Mulder, ed., *Mikra: Text, Translation, Reading and Interpretation of the Hebrew Bible in Ancient Judaism and Early Christianity,* CRINT 2.1 (Assen and Maastricht: Van Gorcum; Philadelphia: Fortress Press, 1988); see also *It Is Written,* ed. Carson and Williamson.

[14] See, e.g., R. B. Hays, *Echoes of Scripture in the Letters of Paul* (New Haven, Conn.: Yale University Press, 1989); S. Draisma, ed., *Intertextuality in Biblical Writings: Essays in Honour*

The recent works on Mark's biblical exegesis mentioned in the previous paragraph are of differing value to exegetes of Mark. Neither the commentary by Derrett nor the monograph by Roth enters into detailed discussion with secondary literature on Mark, and both tend to force the Markan evidence arbitrarily into the grid provided by the particular Old Testament passages that each author considers important.[15] It must be questioned, moreover, why Derrett and Roth come up with such different grids and why neither grid corresponds to sections of the Old Testament that are extensively utilized in Mark's overt Old Testament citations. The monograph by D. and P. Miller, which considers every section of Mark to be a midrash on a particular Old Testament theme, contains some illuminating suggestions but also does not engage much of the secondary literature on Mark and often suffers from a lack of scholarly control.[16] The monograph by Steichele, on the other hand, is a valuable study of the way in which Mark uses certain Old Testament themes to express his understanding of the identity of Jesus, and it takes careful account of previous scholarship on Mark's christology. It is not, however, a comprehensive work, since it takes up Old Testament motifs in only three passages (albeit crucial ones): 1:1–11; 9:2–13; and 15:20–41.

Recent Research on Markan Christology

Like Steichele's work, the present study will concentrate on the way in which Mark uses the Old Testament specifically for his christology, though it will attempt to be more comprehensive than Steichele's monograph and to look at nearly all of the passages in which we can observe Mark making christological use of Old Testament texts.[17] It would be ideal if we could study not just Mark's christological exegesis but *all* of his Old Testament citations and allusions, but such an exhaustive study would be of prohibitive length. This is especially true because, as we shall see, Mark's narrative has been influenced by the Old Testament more than is generally thought. Some limitation of focus, therefore, is necessary, and a limitation to christology

---

of *Bas van Iersel* (Kampen: Kok, 1989); D. Boyarin, *Intertextuality and the Reading of Midrash* (Bloomington, Ind.: Indiana University Press, 1990).

[15] See the reviews of Derrett's book by Q. Quesnell in *CBQ* 48 (1986), 559–560, and of Roth's book by H. C. Kee in *JBL* 109 (1990), 538–539.

[16] The Millers' contentions, for example, that Mark 1:1–45 is a "midrash on Elijah and the crowds of old Israel" and that 2:1–3:12 is a "midrash on Levi-Moses and the crowds of old Israel" are not convincingly sustained in the exegesis of the individual pericopes, and their view that Mark treats Jesus as merely *a* son of God, à la Wisd. Sol. 2:6–20, rather than as God's unique Son (*Midrash*, 38, 58, 207–208, etc.), is highly questionable.

[17] Some of these passages, admittedly, will be treated only in passing; see, e.g., the references to Mark 6:34 (cf. Num. 27:17; Ezek. 34:5) in chapter 2, the reference to Mark 11:9–10 (cf. Ps. 118:25–26) in chapter 6, and the reference to Mark 13:26 (cf. Dan. 7:13–14) in chapter 8.

makes particularly good sense in light of the leading role played by christology in Mark's thought and of the interest this subject commands in
contemporary discussion of Mark.

That Mark's Gospel was written primarily to establish a particular understanding of Jesus' identity is scarcely disputed, even in the many recent
works that have concentrated on another aspect of the Gospel, its theme
of discipleship.[18] What *is* disputed is the best way to gain access to that
Markan understanding.

One popular approach has been to study Mark's usage of different
christological titles such as "Christ," "Son of God," and "Son of man."[19] Among
scholars who adopt this approach, the 1980s have seen a retreat from the
theory popularized by N. Perrin that Mark intended to correct a "Son of
God" christology by means of a "Son of man" christology;[20] in a well-received
recent monograph, for example, J. D. Kingsbury has argued to the contrary
that "Son of God" is Mark's central christological category.[21]

Closely connected with the issue of "corrective christology" is that of
the background of Mark's Gospel in the history of religions. Perrin and his
school contend that Mark's cross-centered theology is a reaction against
a theology of glory rampant in his community; according to this theology,
Jesus is θεῖος ἀνήρ, a "divine man." Although this view has ebbed since the
1970s, partly because of accumulating evidence that θεῖος ἀνήρ is not a fixed
concept in Hellenism and partly because of attention to the dynamics of

---

[18] On the interrelationship between Mark's christology and his theme of discipleship, see
M. E. Boring, who speaks of Mark as a narrative about "Jesus-in-relationship to the disciples"
("The Christology of Mark: Hermeneutical Issues for Systematic Theology," *Semeia* 30 [1984],
143–144). Other representative studies of Markan discipleship include K. Stock, *Boten aus
dem Mit-Ihm-Sein: Das Verhältnis zwischen Jesus und den Zwölf nach Markus,* AnBib 70 (Rome:
Biblical Institute Press, 1975); R. C. Tannehill, "The Disciples in Mark: The Function of a
Narrative Role," in *The Interpretation of Mark,* ed. W. Telford, IRT 7 (Philadelphia: Fortress
Press; London: SPCK, 1985), pp. 134–157 (orig. 1977); E. Best, *Following Jesus: Discipleship
in the Gospel of Mark,* JSNTSup 4 (Sheffield: JSOT Press, 1981); C. Breytenbach, *Nachfolge
und Zukunftserwartung nach Markus: Eine methodenkritische Studie,* ATANT 71 (Zurich:
Theologischer Verlag, 1984); C. C. Black, *The Disciples according to Mark: Markan Redaction
in Recent Debate* (Sheffield: JSOT Press, 1989); and J. D. Kingsbury, *Conflict in Mark: Jesus,
Authorities, Disciples* (Minneapolis: Fortress Press, 1989), pp. 89–117.

[19] The epitome of this approach to christology is the still-useful volume of F. Hahn, *Christologische Hoheitstitel: Ihre Geschichte im frühen Christentum,* FRLANT 83 (Göttingen: Vandenhoeck & Ruprecht, 1963).

[20] N. Perrin, "The Christology of Mark: A Study in Methodology," in *Interpretation,* ed.
Telford, pp. 95–108 (orig. 1971, 1974). Perrin drew on the work of T. J. Weeden ("The Heresy
That Necessitated Mark's Gospel," *Interpretation,* ed. Telford, pp. 64–77 [orig. 1968]; also *Mark:
Traditions in Conflict* [Philadelphia: Fortress Press, 1971]); see the account of the history of
research in J. D. Kingsbury, *The Christology of Mark's Gospel* (Philadelphia: Fortress Press,
1983), pp. 25–33.

[21] Kingsbury, *Christology,* passim.

Mark's story,[22] the issue of the history-of-religions background of the Gospel has not gone away. The thesis of P. Vielhauer, that Mark's presentation of Jesus as Son of God is modeled on an Egyptian coronation ritual, has been of particular importance here, especially in German scholarship. According to Vielhauer, the divine voice at the baptism (1:11) corresponds to the Egyptian king's exaltation and adoption by the god; the voice at the transfiguration (9:7) to his presentation before the other gods; and the centurion's confession at the crucifixion (15:39) to his enthronement.[23] Although there are problems with the thesis that this particular Egyptian ritual is *the* background for Mark's christology,[24] Vielhauer's emphasis on royal traditions foreshadows recent studies that see the Markan Jesus as a kingly figure whose contours have been shaped by the Davidic traditions of the Old Testament and postbiblical Judaism.[25]

Besides the challenge to "corrective christology" from the side of the history of religions, another and in some ways more radical challenge has arisen among scholars who have questioned whether a one-sided focus on christological titles is the best way to gain access to Mark's christological convictions. Some of these scholars have advocated instead a "narrative" approach to the subject, one that sees Jesus' identity as being revealed through the flow of Mark's story itself rather than solely through what the Gospel has to say about titles. Partisans of the narrative approach also prescind in principle from the diachronic attempt to separate the traditions available to Mark from his own editorial contributions, preferring to concentrate on the synchronic task of coming to grips with the Gospel as it presently stands as a narrative whole.[26] This approach to Mark and to the New Testament in general is a growing force in the scholarship of the

---

[22] For a summary of the literature, see J. D. Kingsbury, "The 'Divine Man' as the Key to Mark's Christology—The End of an Era?" *Int* 35 (1981), 243–257.

[23] P. Vielhauer, "Erwägungen zur Christologie des Markusevangeliums," in *Zeit und Geschichte: Dankesgabe an Rudolf Bultmann zum 80. Geburtstag,* ed. E. Dinkler (Tübingen: J. C. B. Mohr [Paul Siebeck], 1964), pp. 165–169.

[24] Vielhauer never explains the tradition-historical connection between Mark and the putative Egyptian coronation ritual (which is itself a reconstruction of E. Norden). How is Mark (and the other New Testament writers who are thought to reflect it) supposed to have found out about it? Further, in Vielhauer's scheme Jesus' baptism corresponds to the moment of exaltation, but Mark links the motif of exaltation not with Jesus' baptism but with his resurrection (12:35–37; 14:61–62). See further the criticisms of Steichele, *Leidende Sohn,* pp. 292–294.

[25] See, e.g., D. Juel, *Messiah and Temple: The Trial of Jesus in the Gospel of Mark,* SBLDS 31 (Missoula, Mont.: Scholars Press, 1973); Steichele, *Leidende Sohn; F. J. Matera, The Kingship of Jesus: Composition and Theology in Mark 15,* SBLDS 66 (Chico, Calif.: Scholars Press, 1982); Kingsbury, *Christology.*

[26] E.g., R. C. Tannehill, "The Gospel of Mark as Narrative Christology," *Semeia* 16 (1979), 57–95; Boring, "Christology," pp. 125–153. Kingsbury's book *Christology* embraces a narrative approach to Markan christology while at the same time giving primary attention to the christological titles.

English-speaking world, where it is challenging the hegemony of the historical-critical approach and where its popularity has fed and been fed by that of the "narrative theology" of Hans Frei.[27]

The Approach of This Study

This study will attempt to exploit the strengths of the methods described above while avoiding the pitfalls of a unilateral concentration on any one of them. It will give detailed attention to the meanings of such titles as "Christ," "Son of David," "Son of man," and "Son of God," since all of these titles have roots in Old Testament texts cited by Mark. It will examine history-of-religions backgrounds closely, especially the trajectory of inter-pretation of the Old Testament texts Mark has used. It will also pay atten-tion to the narrative flow of Mark's Gospel as well as to the narrative context of the Old Testament passages that he cites.

To be more specific about the method employed here, it will have five main features. First, as should be obvious already, the point of entry into the question of Markan christology will be the Markan passages in which christological points are scored by means of references to Old Testament texts. In order to gain some control of the subject, we will begin each chapter with a look at passages that are accompanied by citation formulas ("as it has been written," etc.) and/or that contain significant overlaps in vocabulary with Old Testament texts. Once this safe point of departure has been estab-lished, we will be able to branch out to investigate the possibility of more subtle allusions in the larger context. In this way we hope to avoid the arbitrariness that besets some of the recent studies of the Old Testament background of Mark.

Second, in identifying Old Testament citations and allusions used by Mark and inquiring about their importance for Markan christology, we will ask questions concerning Mark's use of his sources and try to give some provi-sional answers. This study will assume that there can be no turning back from the insight of form, source, and redaction criticism that the writers of the Gospels incorporate traditions that have previously been handed down in either oral or written form. This being the case, the question arises as to how much of Mark's "messianic exegesis," to borrow D. Juel's term, is inherited from his traditions and how much is his own contribution. If it could be shown, for example, that all of the Old Testament allusions in Mark came down to him unchanged from his oral and written sources, there would

---

27 H. W. Frei, *The Eclipse of Biblical Narrative: A Study in Eighteenth and Nineteenth Century Hermeneutics* (New Haven, Conn.: Yale University Press, 1974). For an illuminating overview of the rise and varieties of the narrative approach, see S. D. Moore, *Literary Criticism and the Gospels: The Theoretical Challenge* (New Haven, Conn.: Yale University Press, 1989).

at least be room to wonder whether or not such allusions were of great importance to him. If, on the other hand, it could be established with reasonable certainty that all of these allusions were the result of Markan redactional activity, the opposite conclusion would inevitably follow. As we shall see, the truth probably lies somewhere between these two extremes. We should recognize, of course, that even Old Testament references taken over from tradition might have great significance in Mark's eyes. We would feel more certain about this conclusion, however, if it could be shown that Mark sometimes introduced such references into the material transmitted to him or otherwise highlighted them. This does indeed turn out to be the case.

We are hampered, of course, in not having Mark's sources available to us *except as they have been incorporated into his Gospel*,[28] so that we must first deconstruct their Markan form in order to arrive at a putative pre-Markan form, then turn our attention to the Markan editing that has just been peeled off in order to see what effect it has had on the pre-Markan tradition. This is a procedure that is full of methodological dangers, and C. C. Black has recently documented the disturbing tendency of some redaction critics to produce widely differing source analyses that conveniently support their own theological agendas.[29] But in spite of the fact that redaction criticism, like other critical methods, is subject to abuse, distinguishing source material from redactional additions can sometimes be done with reasonable certainty, and if so it is worth the effort. This study will try to differentiate cases in which the reconstruction is highly probable from those in which it is more uncertain, and in the latter cases especially it will not base too much of the exegesis on the reconstruction.

Although this study will not lay aside the redaction-critical arsenal of scholarly weapons, it will also try to accommodate the concern of the "narrative" approach by paying primary attention to the function of Mark's Old Testament citations in their overall Markan context.[30] The third feature of the work, then, will be an interpretation of Mark's biblical usage that is

---

[28] This assumes that Mark is the first Gospel, a contention that has been challenged by W. Farmer and the members of his school of neo-Griesbachians, though the defenders of Markan priority are still in the majority. For a good summary of the contemporary debate, see A. J. Bellinzoni, ed., *The Two-Source Hypothesis: A Critical Appraisal* (Macon, Ga.: Mercer University Press, 1985); for a convincing refutation of the Farmer position, see C. M. Tuckett, *The Revival of the Griesbach Hypothesis: An Analysis and Appraisal*, SNTSMS 44 (Cambridge: Cambridge University Press, 1983).

[29] C. C. Black, "The Quest of Mark the Redactor: Why Has It Been Pursued, and What Has It Taught Us?" *JSNT* 33 (1988), 19–39; idem, *Disciples*.

[30] Thus this study allies itself with a type of redaction criticism that does not focus solely on an author's alteration of putative sources; rather, it views the work as a whole as the primary context for interpreting any part of it. For the overlap between this "composition criticism" and narrative criticism, see Moore, *Literary Criticism*, pp. 4–7.

accountable to the whole of his narrative. The theme of "the way," which appears in the citations in Mark 1:2–3, for example, will be brought into connection with the expression of that theme elsewhere in the Gospel, and the concept of Jesus as God's royal son, which is first articulated through the allusion to Ps. 2:7 in Mark 1:11, will be related to the ubiquitous Markan theme of the kingdom of God.

A fourth focus of this study will be early Jewish and Christian interpretations of the Old Testament passages used by Mark. We cannot simply assume, of course, that Mark knew these other interpretations, but in many cases we will see compelling reasons for presuming that he did and so for thinking that they provide important background to his Old Testament exegesis. Some interpretations of Old Testament passages are so common as to be virtually ubiquitous. There is a widespread tendency in postbiblical Jewish exegesis, for example, to interpret Old Testament texts eschatologically, and this pattern is followed in New Testament appropriations of the Old Testament. Some trajectories of ancient biblical exegesis, moreover, explain otherwise puzzling gaps in the Markan narrative. Such exegeses of Old Testament texts must be used with caution to illuminate the Markan treatments of the same texts, especially when they postdate Mark; but when so used they can be of invaluable assistance in uncovering new directions for the understanding of Mark's exegetical work.[31]

Eschatologically oriented Jewish interpretations of Old Testament texts are especially illuminative of the Markan intention in appropriating those same texts because Mark and his community seem to be in touch with the Great Revolt of Palestinian Jews against Roman rule (A.D. 66–74), which was probably strongly influenced by a form of apocalyptic eschatology and which was either still in process or had recently ended when the Gospel was written. This brings us to the fifth and final emphasis of our study, the life setting of Mark and of his community in the environment created by the Jewish Revolt and the light this setting throws on his Gospel, not least on his Old Testament exegesis.

In a forthcoming article I will present a detailed argument for situating Mark and his community in the Roman province of Syria shortly after the destruction of the Temple in A.D. 70.[32] The argument includes the following main points, some of which will be elaborated further in the course of the present study: (1) the close correspondence between the phrasing

---

[31] See the responsible yet imaginative usage of Jewish Old Testament exegesis in Juel's *Messianic Exegesis.*

[32] J. Marcus, "The Jewish War and the *Sitz im Leben* of Mark," *JBL* (forthcoming); cf. G. Theissen, *Lokalkolorit und Zeitgeschichte in den Evangelien: Ein Beitrag zur Geschichte der synoptischen Tradition,* NTOA 8 (Freiburg: Universitätsverlag; Göttingen: Vandenhoeck & Ruprecht, 1989), pp. 246–284.

of Mark 13:1–2 and the actual fate of the Temple (cf. Josephus, *Jewish War* 7.1), and between the Markan account of the triumphal entry and cleansing of the Temple (Mark 11:1–18), on the one hand, and events that occurred during the Jewish War, on the other (*Jewish War* 4.574–78); (2) the probability that both "abomination of desolation" in 13:14 and "den of brigands" in 11:17 are references to the occupation of the Temple by Zealots beginning in the winter of A.D. 67–68 (*Jewish War* 4.151–57); (3) the linkage between the "false Christs" of 13:6, 21–22 and the messianic expectation that apparently catalyzed the revolt (see, e.g., *Jewish War* 6.313), and the way in which this linkage illuminates the ambivalent attitude toward Davidic messianism displayed in 10:47–48; 11:9–10; and 12:35–37; and (4) the plausible sociological connection between the Jew–Gentile tension in Syria, which fed, and fed on, the revolt, and Mark's championship of Gentiles and vilification of Jewish leaders.

As we move on to a study of individual pieces of Markan Old Testament exegesis, we will see that the postulated situation of tension with Jewish revolutionary groups provides a plausible setting not only for Mark's Gospel in general but also for his exegesis of certain Old Testament passages in particular. Some of the same scriptural prophecies that appear to have galvanized the anti-Roman revolutionaries turn up in Mark's Gospel as testimonies to a different sort of holy war with different enemies and a different sort of Messiah as its standard-bearer. Mark's exploitation of these testimonies is probably in part a polemical response to their use by the Jewish revolutionaries; his Old Testament exegesis appears to be forged in the fires of a warfare that is both military and theological.

This study, then, will combine attention to the Old Testament texts themselves, a reconstruction of Mark's role in transmitting them, an examination of the way in which he expresses similar themes elsewhere in his Gospel, glances at the interpretation of the same texts elsewhere in his world, and an appraisal of the message they convey to a community living in the crisis-filled atmosphere created by the Jewish War.

Having outlined our game plan, we can now proceed to a study of the individual Markan passages. The very beginning of Mark is a good place to start.

2

Mark 1:2-3

The Gospel According to Isaiah

1:2a As it has been written in Isaiah the prophet:
1:2b   *Behold, I am sending my messenger before your face*
1:2c   *who will prepare your way;*
1:3a *a voice of one crying in the wilderness:*
1:3b   *Prepare the way of the Lord,*
1:3c   *straight make his paths!*[1]

The Old Testament Texts

After the superscription in the first verse of his work, Mark immediately turns to the Old Testament, introducing his citation with the words, "As it has been written in Isaiah the prophet." Despite this introductory formula, what follows it is not simply a quotation from Isaiah but a conflation of three passages, Ex. 23:20; Mal. 3:1; and Isa. 40:3. Such conflation of Old Testament texts is familiar from postbiblical Judaism and is especially common in the Dead Sea Scrolls.[2] The accompanying chart displays the different versions of the Old Testament texts conflated by Mark.[3]

---

[1] All translations of Markan passages at the heads of chapters are my own; I have underlined the sections that are Old Testament citations or allusions. Elsewhere biblical citations are either from the RSV or adapted by me from it; translations of modern languages are my own.

[2] See H. C. Kee, "The Function of Scriptural Quotations and Allusions in Mark 11–16," in *Jesus und Paulus: Festschrift für Werner Georg Kümmel zum 70. Geburtstag,* ed. E. E. Ellis and E. Grässer (Göttingen: Vandenhoeck & Ruprecht, 1975), p. 181: "Thus the most significant parallel between Markan exegesis and the exegetical method employed at Qumran is the juxtaposing of scriptures that in their origins had little or nothing to do with each other, but which in the hands of the exegete are shown to be mutually illuminating and to give rise to theological perceptions that were not anticipated in any of the original components and that thus define the eschatological community, its hopes and obligations."

[3] For the texts in Greek and Hebrew and a helpful discussion, see K. Stendahl, *The School of St. Matthew and its use of the Old Testament,* 2nd ed. (Philadelphia: Fortress Press, 1968; orig. 1954), pp. 47–54.

Mark 1:2 conflates Ex. 23:20 ("behold I send out my messenger before your face" [alt.]) with Mal. 3:1 ("who will prepare your way" [alt.]). The conflation has precedent in Jewish tradition[4] and is natural enough, since in both passages God promises the addressee that he will send an angel or messenger[5] before him. The conflated text seems not to be wholly dependent on the Septuagint, since the verb used in the Synoptics, κατασκευάζειν ("to prepare"), diverges from the verb used in the Septuagint of Mal. 3:1, ἐπιβλέπεσθαι ("to survey").[6] Both verbs can translate the Hebrew פנה found in the Masoretic Text; the Septuagint apparently takes פנה as a *qal*, while the Synoptic version takes it as a *piʿel*. Rather than being taken from the Septuagint, then, Mark 1:2 seems to reflect an independent rendering of the Hebrew text into Greek.[7]

As can be seen from the chart of parallels, this conflated text is already present in Q (Matt. 11:10 = Luke 7:27), where it appears, however, in a context different from its Markan one — namely, Jesus' praise of John the Baptist — and on the lips of Jesus rather than as the narrator's comment. The sole textual divergence of the Markan passage from the one in Q is the absence in Mark of the words "before you" at the end.[8]

Unlike the Old Testament passages quoted in Mark 1:2, Isa. 40:3, which is quoted in Mark 1:3, is cited by Matthew and Luke in a context similar to the Markan one, namely, the narrator's introduction of John the Baptist (Matt. 3:3//Luke 3:4). Also unlike Mark 1:2, the citation of Isa. 40:3 in the Synoptics seems to be dependent on the Septuagint, since it follows the Septuagint in connecting "in the wilderness" with the crying voice rather than with the imperative "Prepare!"[9] This dependence is perhaps further

---

[4] *Exod. Rab.* 32.9 and *Deut. Rab.* 11.9; see S-B 1:597; Stendahl, *School*, pp. 49–53; R. H. Gundry, *The Use of the Old Testament in St. Matthew's Gospel*, NovTSup 18 (Leiden: E. J. Brill, 1967), pp. 11–12; R. Pesch, *Das Markusevangelium*, HTKNT 2, 2 vols. (Freiburg: Herder, 1976–77), 1:78; K. R. Snodgrass, "Streams of Tradition Emerging from Isaiah 40:1-5 and Their Adaptation in the New Testament," *JSNT* 8 (1980), 34. Stendahl, drawing on the work of J. Mann, points out that Mal. 3:1-8, 23–24 was the *haphtarah* reading for Ex. 23:20 (*seder* 61a). Pesch notes that in the Septuagint the two passages are conformed to each other by small changes in wording from the Masoretic Text.

[5] In both Hebrew and Greek, the same word means both "angel" and "messenger" (מלאך; ἄγγελος).

[6] See Stendahl, *School*, p. 49; R. N. Longenecker, *Biblical Exegesis in the Apostolic Period* (Grand Rapids: Wm. B. Eerdmans Publishing Co., 1975), p. 138 n. 12.

[7] Stendahl, *School*, p. 51. The root meaning of פנה is "to turn"; in the *qal* one of its nuances is "to turn and look" and hence "to look," whereas in the *piʿel* it can mean "to turn away" or "make clear," as in clearing away obstacles, hence "to prepare" (BDB, p. 815).

[8] Not apparent in the English text of the chart is the insignificant difference between Matt. 11:10 and Luke 7:27 caused by the presence of the word ἐγώ in the former.

[9] Stendahl, *School*, p. 48; C. E. B. Cranfield, *The Gospel According to Saint Mark*, CGTC (Cambridge: Cambridge University Press, 1974; orig. 1959), p. 40. This dependence has recently been disputed by Gundry (*Use*, pp. 9–10) and Pesch (*Markusevangelium* 1:77 n. 12), who claim

Mark 1:2	Matthew 11:10 = Luke 7:27	Exodus 23:20 LXX	Malachi 3:1 MT	Malachi 3:1 LXX
behold I send out (ἀποστέλλω) my messenger before your face	behold I send out (ἀποστέλλω) my messenger before your face	behold I send out (ἀποστέλλω) my messenger before your face	behold I send my messenger	behold I send out (ἐξαποστέλλω) my messenger
who will prepare (κατασκευάσει) your way	who will prepare (κατασκευάσει) your way before you	to guard you on the way	and he will clear/survey (פנה) a way before your face	and he will survey (ἐπιβλέψεται) a way before your face

Mark 1:3 = Matthew 3:3 = Luke 3:4	John 1:23	Isaiah 40:3 MT	Isaiah 40:3 LXX
the voice of one crying in the wilderness	I am the voice of one crying in the wilderness	the voice of one crying	the voice of one crying in the wilderness
prepare (ἑτοιμάσατε) the way of the Lord	straighten (εὐθύνατε) the way of the Lord	in the wilderness clear/survey (פנה) the way of the Lord	prepare (ἑτοιμάσατε) the way of the Lord
straight make (εὐθείας ποιεῖτε) his paths		straighten (ישר) in the desert a highway for our God	straight make (εὐθείας ποιεῖτε) the paths of our God

Note: Scripture quotations are RSV (alt.).

attested by the fact that both the Synoptic passage and the Septuagint use a periphrastic construction (εὐθείας ποιεῖτε) to express the command "make straight."

Matthew and Luke agree against Mark, however, in citing Isa. 40:3 immediately *after* John the Baptist has been introduced rather than immediately *beforehand*. Because they agree also, as we have seen, in omitting Ex. 23:20//Mal. 3:1 in this context, because they both contain the expression περίχωρος τοῦ Ἰορδάνου ("region about the Jordan," Luke 3:3; Matt. 3:5), which is absent from Mark, and because Q probably contained some introduction to the figure of John the Baptist before Matt. 3:7–12//Luke 3:7–18, it seems likely that Matthew and Luke are following Q rather than Mark in their parallels to Mark 1:2–6.[10]

There are several good grounds for thinking that Mark himself is responsible for all three of the Markan variations from Q: the introduction of Ex. 23:20//Mal. 3:1 into its present context (Mark 1:2), the elimination of the words "before you" from Mal. 3:1, and the movement of the entire block of Old Testament citations to its present position before John the Baptist is introduced. First, the movement of Isa. 40:3 from the more "natural" position it occupies in Q, after John the Baptist has been introduced,[11] to its Markan position before John's introduction, makes sense as the editorial work of a writer who, like many New Testament authors, wishes to place Old Testament quotations or allusions at the beginning of his work.[12] Second, the introduction of Ex. 23:20//Mal. 3:1 into the present context makes sense as Mark's work, since the fusion of two or more scriptural passages into one conflated citation is a characteristic Markan method of biblical usage.[13]

---

that the Targum, the Peshitta, and the Vulgate also connect the voice with the wilderness. All three of these versions, however, contain the parallelism "in the wilderness/in the desert," and it is only the absence of this parallelism in the Septuagint which enables "in the wilderness" to be taken with "the voice of one crying." On the other hand, later rabbinic traditions do frequently connect "in the wilderness" with the crying voice; see, e.g., the passages cited in S-B 1:96–97.

[10] See H. Schürmann, *Das Lukasevangelium*, HTKNT 3/1 (Freiburg: Herder, 1969), p. 161 and n. 105. Mark 1:2–3 is thus probably an instance of an overlap between Mark and Q; on these overlaps in general, see W. G. Kümmel, *Introduction to the New Testament* (Nashville: Abingdon Press, 1975), p. 70. There is therefore no necessity for the assumption, which lacks any manuscript evidence, that Mark 1:2 is a later gloss; see J. A. Fitzmyer, *The Gospel According to Luke*, AB 28, 28A, 2 vols. (Garden City, N.Y.: Doubleday & Co., 1981, 1985), 1:461.

[11] See R. A. Guelich, "'The Beginning of the Gospel': Mark 1:1–15," *BR* 27 (1982), 8–9.

[12] Cf. Matt. 1:1–17; "in the beginning" in John 1:1 (cf. 1 John 1:1), as well as numerous other Old Testament allusions in the Johannine prologue; Rom. 1:2; Heb. 1:1 and indeed the whole of Hebrews 1.

[13] See Kee, who cites, besides 1:2–3, also 1:11 (Isa. 42:1/Ps. 2:7); 11:1–11 (Zech. 9:9/Ps. 118:25–26); 11:17 (Isa. 56:7/Jer. 7:11); 12:1–12 (Isa. 5:1–2/Ps. 118:22–23); 13:24–26 (Isa. 34:4/Josh. 2:10/Ezek. 32:7–8/Dan. 7:13–14); and 14:62 (Dan. 7:13/Ps. 110:1) ("Function," in *Jesus und Paulus*, ed. Ellis and Grässer, pp. 175–178).

Third, if Mark has prefixed Ex. 23:20/Mal. 3:1 (Mark 1:2) to Isa. 40:3 (Mark 1:3) but neglected to change the ascription from "as it has been written in Isaiah the prophet," the technically inaccurate ascription is plausibly explained.[14] Fourth, the formal parallelism of 1:2 and 1:3, which we think has been created by their attachment to each other and by the elimination of the words "before you" from 1:2, is appropriate for a passage that is being given a place of prominence at the very beginning of a literary work. Finally, the elimination of "before you" accents the parallelism between "your way" (1:2) and "the way of the Lord" (1:3), and the resultant emphasis on the theme of "the way" coheres with the stress laid on this theme throughout Mark's Gospel (see below).

If, as we have argued, Mark is responsible for the combination of Ex. 23:20/Mal. 3:1 with Isa. 40:3, important consequences for our picture of him and of his relationship to his community ensue. The combination of Mal. 3:1 with Isa. 40:3 reflects a knowledge of the Hebrew or Aramaic text; in the Masoretic Text and the Targum, but *not* in the Septuagint, the two passages contain exactly the same expression for "prepare the way" (פנה אורח/פנה דרך). Since, however, Mark 1:2 and 1:3 retain *different* Greek translations of the Hebrew or Aramaic expression, we may suggest that Greek versions of Ex. 23:20/Mal. 3:1 and Isa. 40:3 were already part of the scriptural testimony treasured by Mark's community,[15] and that Mark brought the two passages together partly on the basis of his knowledge that they contained the identical expression in the Hebrew or Aramaic text.[16] Mark, then, would seem to be writing for a Greek-speaking community, though he himself has a rather good knowledge of the Hebrew or Aramaic

---

[14] See Schürmann, *Lukasevangelium*, 1:161 n. 105. In the present instance, then, there is no need for a "testimony hypothesis" to explain the incorrect ascription. In support of this hypothesis, see R. Harris, *Testimonies*, 2 vols. (Cambridge: Cambridge University Press, 1916, 1920); more recently J. A. Fitzmyer, "'4Q Testimonia' and the New Testament," in *Essays on the Semitic Background of the New Testament*, Sources for Biblical Study 5 (Missoula, Mont.: Scholars Press, 1974; orig. 1957), pp. 59–89; for a skeptical opinion, see Stendahl, *School*, pp. 216–217.

[15] These passages both seem to have had a long history of transmission as independent logia related to John the Baptist. Exodus 23:20/Malachi 3:1 seems to predate even Q, since it is disruptive in its Q context (see R. Bultmann, *History of the Synoptic Tradition* [New York: Harper & Row, 1963; orig. 1921], p. 165), and Isa. 40:3 is referred to John the Baptist independently of the Synoptics in John 1:23 (see Stendahl, *School*, p. 52).

[16] Contra Stendahl (*School*, pp. 51–52) and Longenecker (*Biblical Exegesis*, p. 138 n. 12), who think that Ex. 23:20/Mal. 3:1 and Isa. 40:3 were combined with each other already in a Semitic milieu by the method of *gezerah shavah*. Why, however, would the person who subsequently translated the text into Greek have rendered פנה first with κατασκευάζειν, then a few lines later with ἑτοιμάζειν? Of course, a desire for stylistic variety cannot be ruled out, but then one would have thought that the author would have done something about the repetition of ὁδόν.

text of the Old Testament.[17] His ad hoc use of the Septuagint and Semitic versions of the Old Testament in 1:2–3 is reminiscent of the formula quotations in Matthew and demonstrates a similarly sophisticated kind of exegetical reflection on the Old Testament texts.[18]

Mark himself, then, emerges from our analysis as the person responsible for the present form of 1:2–3. He is the one who has seen, on the basis of his knowledge of the Hebrew text, that Mal. 3:1 and Isa. 40:3 are linked by the phrase פנה דרך, and he has consequently prefaced the citation of Isa. 40:3 with the conflation of Ex. 23:20 and Mal. 3:1.[19] With such a knowledge of the Hebrew text, he has probably retained the ascription of the passage to Isaiah not out of ignorance that the first part is from Exodus and Malachi[20] but out of some sort of theological intention — exactly *what* sort, we shall presently explore. He has shaped the conflation literarily by eliminating the phrase "before you" from its end, thus highlighting the theme of the way and the parallel between "your way" and "the way of the Lord." Finally, he has accented the importance of the Old Testament citations by moving the entire block of them from their position after the introduction of John the Baptist to their present place between the Gospel's superscription and the description of John.

"As It Has Been Written in Isaiah the Prophet"

The movement just described already suggests that the Old Testament plays an important role in the Markan proclamation of the good news of Jesus Christ. Its importance comes into sharper focus when we consider the formula introducing the conflated Old Testament citation, καθὼς γέγραπται ("as it has been written," Mark 1:2a). Recently, R. A. Guelich has argued persuasively that in the New Testament καθὼς γέγραπται always plays a transitional role; its function is to act as a bridge between a previously mentioned fact or event and the Old Testament citation that follows and

---

[17] The frequency of Aramaic words in the Gospel supports the contention that Mark knew that language; see M. Hengel, who cites 3:17–19; 5:41; 7:11; 8:34; 10:46; 11:9–10; 14:1, 32, 36, 45; 15:22, 34, and comments: "I do not know any other work in Greek which has as many Aramaic or Hebrew words and formulae in so narrow a space as does the second Gospel. They are too numerous and too exact to be explained as the conventional barbarisms (ῥῆσις βαρβαρική) of the miracle worker and magician. . . . Most of these foreign-sounding words are omitted by Matthew and Luke" (*Studies in the Gospel of Mark* [Philadelphia: Fortress Press, 1985]).

[18] See Stendahl, *School*, pp. 53–54.

[19] Snodgrass asserts that there is some slight evidence that Mal. 3:1 and Isa. 40:1–5 were already conflated in Judaism ("Streams," p. 35), but upon investigation the evidence turns out to be negligible. The Jewish texts he cites refer to Mal. 3:23, not 3:1, and they link it with other Isaian passages that speak of comfort, not with Isa. 40:1–5.

[20] Contrary to the testimony hypothesis; see n. 14 above.

confirms it.²¹ The transitional function of καθὼς γέγραπται is established
by its one occurrence in the Septuagint (2 Kings 14:6; cf. Dan. 9:13 [Theodo-
tion]), by later Jewish parallels (Qumran, rabbinic traditions),²² and by its
numerous usages in the New Testament. It is especially striking that in 1QS
8:13–14 the corresponding formula is used transitionally to link a previous
statement with a citation of Isa. 40:3, thus forming a close analogue to Mark
1:1–3 and parallels.

In the present instance, the transitional usage of καθὼς γέγραπται means
that the conflated citation in 1:2b–3 is to be understood as a comment on
the superscription in 1:1. We may, therefore, follow Guelich²³ and translate
the first few words of the Gospel thus:

> The beginning of the gospel of Jesus Messiah, Son of God, as written
> by Isaiah the prophet, "Behold, I send my messenger before your face. . . ."

In such a case, the reference to "Isaiah" is meant as an elaboration of Mark's
central theme, for it provides the proper context for understanding the
gospel's beginnings.

The Gospel and Deutero-Isaiah

This assertion that the gospel announced in v. 1 and the "Isaiah" passage
quoted in vv. 2–3 are closely linked is supported by an important observation from the history of religions: the word "gospel" itself, as it is used in
the New Testament, has its most important background in Deutero-Isaiah.
P. Stuhlmacher points out the Isaianic context of the use of εὐαγγέλιον
("gospel") in the Q logion Matt. 11:5//Luke 7:22, which he considers to be
an authentic saying of Jesus.²⁴ He traces this usage back to the Old

---

²¹ See Guelich, "Beginning," p. 6; contra V. Taylor, who demurs on the grounds that in Luke
11:30; 17:26; John 3:14; 1 Cor. 2:9 καθὼς stands at the beginning of a sentence (*The Gospel
According to Saint Mark*, 2nd ed. [Grand Rapids: Baker Book House, 1981; orig. 1950], p. 153).
Of these examples, however, only 1 Cor. 2:9 introduces an Old Testament citation, the other
three passages illustrating the construction καθὼς . . . οὕτως ("as . . . so"). As for 1 Cor. 2:9,
here the formula καθὼς γέγραπται is preceded by the word ἀλλά ("but"), which creates a dis-
junction between the Old Testament citation following and the preceding sentence, a dis-
junction not present in Mark 1:2, which lacks the ἀλλά.

²² See Guelich, "Beginning," p. 6. The Qumran formula is כאשר כתוב ("as it is written"),
found in 1QS 5:17; 8:14; CD 9:19; 4QFlor 1:12, etc. In rabbinic traditions we find לפי שכתוב
("according as it is written") and similar formulas; see W. Bacher, *Die älteste Terminologie der
jüdischen Schriftauslegung*, 2 vols. (Leipzig: Hinrichs, 1899, 1905), 1:91–94.

²³ Guelich, "Beginning," p. 14 n. 26; D. and P. Miller, *The Gospel of Mark as Midrash on
Earlier Jewish and New Testament Literature*, Studies in the Bible and Early Christianity 21
(Lewiston, N.Y.: Edwin Mellen Press, 1990), p. 34.

²⁴ P. Stuhlmacher, *Die paulinische Evangelium*, vol. 1, *Vorgeschichte*, FRLANT 95 (Göttingen:
Vandenhoeck & Ruprecht, 1968), pp. 109–179, 218–225.

Testament root בשׂר ("to announce"), which is rendered with the εὐαγγελ-
word group in the Septuagint. Rabbinic traditions and the Targum know
this root in the form of the substantive בשׂורה ("announcement"), and
εὐαγγέλιον in Rev. 14:6 seems to reflect this Semitic usage. Stuhlmacher
singles out the *pi'el* participle מבשׂרת/מבשׂר in Isa. 40:9; 41:27; and 52:7
as especially important background for the New Testament εὐαγγέλιον. He
remarks that, by their implicit dualism between the sphere of God and that
of human beings and their expectation that the distance between these two
spheres is about to be bridged, such passages demonstrate that Deutero-
Isaiah is "the father of apocalyptic."[25]

It is especially significant that, according to Stuhlmacher, one of the fountainhead verses for the concept of εὐαγγέλιον is Isa. 40:9, which is the continuation of the passage quoted in Mark 1:3. A look at Isa. 40:9–10a (alt.)
is instructive:

> Get you up to the high mountain,
> O herald of good tidings to Zion (מבשׂרת ציון);[26]
>
> lift up your voice with strength,
> O herald of good tidings to Jerusalem (מבשׂרת ירושלם);
>
> lift it up, fear not;
> say to the cities of Judah, "Behold your God!"
>
> Behold, the Lord God comes with might,
> and his arm rules for him. . . .

The theme of the coming of Yahweh shows that these verses are linked with
40:3 not only by their proximity but also thematically; the announcement
of Yahweh's coming completes the admonition to prepare a way before him.
But Isa. 40:9–10 also has strong thematic links with the opening section
of Mark's Gospel. The first, as we have noted, is the word "gospel" itself;
the Septuagint here uses the substantive participle ὁ εὐαγγελιζόμενος to
translate מבשׂרת. This is not just a formal link, since the good news in Isaiah,
as in Mark, is a revelation of God's coming in power: "Behold your God!"
To this Isaian announcement of a revelation of the divine advent we may
compare the revelatory picture painted in Mark 1:9–11 (clouds opening,
vision of dove, voice from heaven), and the entire course of events in 1:14–15:

---

[25] Ibid., pp. 116–122.

[26] Here I choose the reading from the RSV margin rather than that in the RSV text, "O
Zion, herald of good tidings." The problem is whether to render the second word in the phrase
מבשׂרת ציון as an appositive or an indirect object; see Stuhlmacher, *Evangelium*, pp. 119–120.
The same ambiguity is present two lines later in the phrase מבשׂרת ירושלם. I choose to take
the place-names as an indirect object because of the parallelism with "the cities of Judah."

Jesus *comes*[27] into Galilee at the critical moment in history[28] preaching the good news of God and announcing that God's kingly power has drawn near.[29] Jesus' proclamatory activity (κηρύσσων), furthermore, has an analogy in the Isaian admonition "Lift up your voice!" The link between the Markan context and the Isaian one, as traditionally interpreted, is cemented by the Markan reference to the βασιλεία τοῦ θεοῦ ("kingdom of God"), for the Targum on Isa. 40:9 significantly translates "Behold your God" with אתגליאת מלכותא דאלהכון, "the kingly power of your God has been revealed."[30]

In view of all this evidence, it is difficult not to agree with Guelich's conclusion that when Mark refers to Isaiah by name in 1:2a, he is not just identifying the source for what follows in 1:3, but rather is hinting more broadly that his whole story of "the beginning of the gospel" is to be understood against the backdrop of Isaian themes.[31] Guelich points to other examples of such themes in Mark 1:1–15: the wilderness (1:4, 7–8, 12–13; cf. Isa. 40:3 and numerous other Isaian passages); the splitting of the heavens (1:10; cf. Isa. 64:1); the content of the heavenly voice (1:11; cf. Isa. 42:1); and living at peace with the animals (1:13b; cf. Isa. 11:6–8; 65:25).[32] Guelich's list can be augmented by the observation that the forgiveness of sins (Mark 1:4) is a major emphasis of Deutero-Isaiah.[33]

---

[27] F. Mussner notes that ἦλθεν in 1:14, coming as it does after instances of the same verb in vv. 7 and 9, has an almost epiphanic ring ("Gottesherrschaft und Sendung Jesu nach Mk 1,14f.: Zugleich ein Beitrag über die innere Struktur des Markusevangeliums," in *Praesentia Salutis: Gesammelte Studien zu Fragen und Themen des Neuen Testaments* (Düsseldorf: Patmos, 1967), p. 82.

[28] Cf. the solemn introduction, "After John the Baptist was handed over. . . ."

[29] On the translation of ἡ βασιλεία τοῦ θεοῦ as "God's kingly power," see J. Marcus, "Entering into the Kingly Power of God," *JBL* 107 (1988), 663–675.

[30] There are other contacts between the Isaiah Targum and the opening part of Mark's Gospel. B. D. Chilton notes that *Tg. Isa.* 53:1, like Mark 1:15, combines the term "good news" (בשורה) with a phrase about belief (*God in Strength: Jesus' Announcement of the Kingdom*, StudNTUmwelt, Serie B, Band 1 [Freistadt: Plöchl, 1979], p. 95). *Tg. Isa.* 41:27, moreover, like Mark 1:1–2, links the good news with the words of the prophets.

[31] Contrary to Guelich ("Beginning," pp. 5–12), "the beginning of the gospel" in Mark 1:1 probably has a wider reference than just the Markan prologue in 1:1–13 or 1:1–15. See Taylor (*Mark*, p. 152), Pesch (*Markusevangelium* 1:75–76), J. Marcus (*The Mystery of the Kingdom of God*, SBLDS 90 [Atlanta: Scholars Press, 1986], p. 231 n. 9), and F. J. Matera ("The Prologue as the Interpretative Key to Mark's Gospel," *JSNT* 34 [1988], n. 15), who argue that 1:1 is the superscription to Mark's whole work. This conclusion is supported, in a way, by Guelich's own study, since Mark's use of Isaian themes is not restricted to the prologue. See, for example, the reference to Isaiah in 7:6–7; this is the only other time in Mark's Gospel in which γέγραπται is used in conjunction with the name of a biblical author. As we shall see, moreover, the Deutero-Isaian themes of "the way of the Lord" and the wilderness are conspicuously influential later in Mark's story.

[32] Guelich, "Beginning," pp. 8–10.

[33] See B. W. Anderson, "Exodus Typology in Second Isaiah," in *Israel's Prophetic Heritage:*

Such expansion of the field of vision opened up by an Old Testament citation in the New Testament is not without its dangers. Critics of C. H. Dodd, for example, have questioned his contention that New Testament citations of the Old Testament, like some citations of the Old Testament in rabbinic literature, refer to the larger context of the Old Testament citation.[34] Yet there are instances where one is forced by the evidence of the text itself to assume such a context.[35] In the present case, such a procedure is justified not only by the confluence of allusions to Isaiah in Mark's beginning but also by the two secure links that were noted at the head of this section: the literary link between "gospel" in 1:1 and "Isaiah the prophet" in 1:2, and the history-of-religions link between "gospel" and Deutero-Isaiah.[36]

"Streams of Tradition" in Interpreting Isaiah 40:3

The conclusion that Mark has in mind more than the particular Isaian verse he quotes in 1:3 is supported by an important recent study by K. R. Snodgrass. The title of Snodgrass's article is itself suggestive: "Streams of Tradition Emerging from Isaiah 40:1–5 and Their Adaptation in the New Testament." Snodgrass notes, as others have before him, that the Old Testament citations in Mark 1:2–3 are introduced without explanation and are initially somewhat puzzling[37]— unless, he adds, a context for understanding them is presumed. He finds such a context in the consistent tendency of

---

Essays in Honor of James Muilenburg, ed. B. W. Anderson and W. Harrelson (New York: Harper & Row, 1962), p. 191.

[34] C. H. Dodd, According to the Scriptures: The Sub-structure of New Testament Theology (London: Nisbet, 1952), pp. 126–127; criticisms in A. C. Sundberg, "On Testimonies," NovT 3 (1959), 268–281; D. M. Smith, "The Use of the Old Testament in the New," in The Use of the Old Testament in the New and Other Essays: Studies in Honor of William Franklin Stinespring, ed. J. M. Efird (Durham, N.C.: Duke University Press, 1972), pp. 29–30; D. Juel, Messianic Exegesis: Christological Interpretation of the Old Testament in Early Christianity (Philadelphia: Fortress Press, 1988), pp. 19–22. Though Sundberg is generally dubious that the larger context is in view, he does admit that this is occasionally the case. On the rabbinic method of implying the continuation of a given quotation, see Stendahl, School, p. 88 n. 1 and the literature cited there; also E. E. Ellis, "Midrash, Targum, and the New Testament Quotations," in Prophecy and Hermeneutic in Early Christianity: New Testament Essays (Grand Rapids: Wm. B. Eerdmans Publishing Co., 1978; orig. 1969), pp. 195–197.

[35] Cf. the similar conclusions with regard to Luke and Paul of J. T. Carroll ("The Uses of Scripture in Acts," in Society of Biblical Literature 1990 Seminar Papers, ed. D. J. Lull [Atlanta: Scholars Press, 1990], pp. 515–520) and R. B. Hays (Echoes of Scripture in the Letters of Paul [New Haven, Conn.: Yale University Press, 1989]) respectively.

[36] On the latter, see now Miller and Miller, Mark as Midrash, p. 39.

[37] Neither the speaker ("I"), the addressee ("you"), nor the messenger is identified. See Snodgrass, "Streams," pp. 35–36; cf. J. A. Fitzmyer, "The Use of Explicit Old Testament Quotations in Qumran Literature and in the New Testament," in Essays, p. 35; H. Anderson, "The Old Testament in Mark's Gospel," in Use of the Old Testament, ed. Efird, p. 283.

Jewish interpreters to view Isa. 40:1–5 as a divine promise of eschatological comfort. The original prophecy of a return from Babylonian exile is reinterpreted in Jewish sources from later centuries (Dead Sea Scrolls, Apocrypha and Pseudepigrapha, rabbinic traditions) to refer to a return of the exiles at the end of days, a return accompanied by spiritual renewal of the people and indeed of the cosmos itself. As Snodgrass says, Isa. 40:1–5 "was a classic statement of the consolation that comes from God and was understood specifically in the context of God's eschatological comfort."[38]

The existence of this stream of tradition for interpreting Isa. 40:3 means that the citation of that verse in Mark 1:3 cannot simply be reduced, as it often is by New Testament commentators, to a scriptural testimony concerning the relative positions of John the Baptist and Jesus (forerunner, fulfiller)[39] or to the fact that John appeared in the wilderness.[40] Certainly the wilderness is an important theme in Mark 1, and Guelich has done a fine job of showing the way in which Mark has highlighted this theme in the opening verses of his Gospel.[41] But the wilderness theme in Mark is not an end in itself; rather, as the ascription of 1:2–3 to "Isaiah the prophet" already indicates, the wilderness motif in Mark primarily points to the Isaian picture of the wilderness as the staging ground for Yahweh's future victory over the power of evil.

Isaiah 40 and the Revolutionary Ferment in Palestine

The eschatological significance of Isa. 40:3 and of the wilderness theme in general in Mark is supported by the probability that both the passage and the theme played an important role in the events leading up to and including the Jewish Revolt against the Romans in A.D. 66–74, which form the background for Mark's Gospel.

It is particularly significant for our purposes that several of the uprisings that foreshadowed or accompanied the Great Revolt involved a retreat to

[38] Snodgrass, "Streams," p. 31.

[39] Contra D. E. Nineham, *Saint Mark*, Pelican New Testament Commentaries (Middlesex: Penguin, 1963), p. 57; E. Schweizer, *The Good News According to Mark* (Atlanta: John Knox Press, 1970), p. 31.

[40] Contra Fitzmyer, "Use," in *Essays*, pp. 35–36; with U. Mauser, *Christ in the Wilderness: The Wilderness Theme in the Second Gospel and Its Basis in the Biblical Tradition*, SBT 39 (Naperville, Ill.: Alec R. Allenson, 1963), p. 81.

[41] Guelich, "Beginning," pp. 8–10. Only Mark of all the Synoptics says specifically that John appeared "in the wilderness" (1:4), and only he repeats the wilderness location, mentioned in 1:12, in 1:13a; this repetition is a clear indication of redactional emphasis. The notice in 1:13b about Jesus' being with the wild animals (different in Matthew and Luke) also implies a wilderness location.

the wilderness, and that this retreat seems to have been based not only
on the obvious tactical advantages that such a location afforded but also
on the importance of the wilderness as the staging ground for God's
eschatological holy war in the religious traditions of Israel. In a recent article,
D. R. Schwartz has studied the reports in Josephus concerning Theudas
(A.D. 45), unnamed "impostors" in the time of Felix (around A.D. 57), an
Egyptian prophet at about the same time, another "impostor" in the time
of Festus (A.D. 60–62), and Jonathan the Weaver in Cyrene in A.D. 73.[42]
All of these revolutionary leaders led their followers out to the wilderness
with the promise that they would there see miraculous signs of God's
redemption. Schwartz shows that although Josephus deliberately plays down
the religious basis of these actions, they were probably in large measure
motivated by the hope that God would fulfill the ancient promises of
eschatological victory in the wilderness contained in the scriptures, notably
in Isaiah 40. Schwartz's hypothesis is supported by 1QM 1:2–3, a passage
that shows that the biblical connection between Isaiah 40 and holy-war
traditions was not lost in anti-Roman Jewish circles in the first century. This
passage from the Qumran *War Scroll* is a probable allusion to Isa. 40:3,
and it refers to the returned exiles (= the members of the Qumran community) who pitch camp in the desert of Jerusalem in preparation for war.[43]

Mark's use of the Deutero-Isaian prophecy of an eschatological manifestation in the wilderness, therefore, does not appear in a vacuum. It continues,
rather, the use of a passage that apparently fired Jewish hopes for an
apocalyptic holy war that would begin in the Judean wilderness and climax
in the liberation of Zion. Mark accepts this basic pattern of expectation
but introduces into it his own ideas on the identity of the human leader
in the holy war, the nature and identity of the enemies against whom the
battle is to be directed, and the way in which the victory is to be attained.

The Wilderness Motif in Mark

For Mark, as for the traditions of Jewish exegesis described in the previous
pages, God's revelation of his saving purpose begins in the wilderness. In
a careful study, U. Mauser has shown that, when the Markan Jesus leaves
the desert in 1:14, this is not the end of the wilderness theme for Mark,
since in 1:35, 45; 6:31–32, 35 Jesus is again in "a desert place" (ἔρημος τόπος;

---

[42] D. R. Schwartz, "Wilderness and Temple: On Religion and State in Judea in the Second
Temple Period," in *Priesthood and Kingship* (Jerusalem: Zalman Shezer Center for the History
of Israel, 1987 [Hebrew]), pp. 61–78. See also M. Hengel, *The Zealots: Investigations into the
Jewish Freedom Movement in the Period from Herod I Until 70 A.D.* (Edinburgh: T. & T. Clark,
1989; orig. 1961), pp. 249–255. See Josephus, *Antiquities* 20.97–99, 167–168, 169–172, 188;
Jewish War 2.261–263; 7.437.

[43] Snodgrass, "Streams," p. 28; cf. Schwartz, "Wilderness and Temple," p. 71 n. 36.

cf. ἐπ᾽ ἐρημίας in 8:4). Mauser rightly asserts that ἔρημος τόπος is Markan redactional vocabulary, calling attention to the striking repetition of the phrase in the feeding story in 6:31–32, 35. This story links up with the saga of the wilderness wanderings of the Israelites not only by its desert location and by the motif of a miraculous feeding but also by the arrangement of the people in groups of hundreds and fifties (Mark 6:40; cf. Ex. 18:21 and the recollection of the exodus arrangement in 1QS 2:21–22). Mauser also notes the background of the "sheep without shepherd" motif (Mark 6:34) in the wilderness tradition of Num. 27:17.[44]

The primary background for the Markan wilderness theme, however, is not the story of the first exodus but the hope for a second exodus at the end of days. Mauser traces back to Hosea (2:14), Ezekiel (20:35–38), and Deutero-Isaiah (40:3; 48:20–21) the expectation that Israel will move into the desert a second time in order to experience a new encounter with God, and he sees this expectation evident in the presence of the Qumran community in the wilderness as well as in Mark 1:35–37; 1:45; and 6:33, where notices about Jesus' withdrawal to the desert are followed by descriptions of people flocking to him there.[45] Mauser follows E. Lohmeyer, moreover, in observing that the statement in 1:5 that *all* the country of Judea and *all* the people of Jerusalem went out to John the Baptist to be baptized is, from a historical point of view, an exaggeration, but that it makes sense in light of the prophecies in Deutero-Isaiah of an end-time exodus to the wilderness on the part of the people of God. He notes, in addition, that the "sheep without shepherd" motif in 6:34 echoes not only Num. 27:17 but also Ezek. 34:5, where the reference is to a *new* wilderness action of God.[46] He also calls attention to the unusually vivid and somewhat paradoxical detail in Mark 6:39 that Jesus, in his desert feeding of the five thousand, makes the people sit down "on the green grass,"[47] and he connects this detail with the theme of an eschatological transformation of the wilderness into a place of amazing fertility.[48]

Such highlighting of the wilderness theme in Mark 1 and the two feeding stories is a valuable contribution to Markan exegesis. This study, however, parts company with Mauser over the relative importance of the first and

---

[44]   Mauser, *Wilderness*, pp. 104–105, 135.

[45]   Ibid., pp. 45–52, 58–61, 107, 137.

[46]   Ibid., p. 50 n. 1, pp. 92, 135.

[47]   As Mauser notes, the unusualness of finding green grass in a wilderness is somewhat attenuated by the fact that, in the biblical tradition, the concept of "wilderness" can include pastures sufficient for the grazing of flocks. Yet, as he further remarks, "the vivid description is so striking that a reason for it must be extant" (*Wilderness*, p. 136).

[48]   Ibid., pp. 136–137, citing Ezek. 34:26–29, though it seems to me that a passage such as Isa. 51:3 is more immediate background for Mark 6:39.

second exoduses.[49] Mauser sometimes irons out the differences between various expressions of the wilderness theme in the Old Testament and in Mark, forcing them to conform to his primary type, the exodus under Moses. For example, in commenting on the conflation of Ex. 23:20 and Mal. 3:1 in Mark 1:2, he says that these combined sayings "really melt into one in which Exod 23:20 is the predominant part."[50] The verbal similarity to Mal. 3:1, however, is actually greater than that to Ex. 23:20, since the latter contains no counterpart to Mark 1:2c. The attribution of the conflated text to "Isaiah the prophet" in 1:2a, moreover, suggests that Mark means it to be understood in a prophetic rather than a Pentateuchal context.[51] Mark 1:2, then, offers not only a comparison with but also a contrast to Jewish traditions that link Ex. 23:20 and Mal. 3:1 in such a way that the latter becomes merely a pendant to the former.[52]

Another example of Mauser's tendency to emphasize the first exodus to the detriment of the second occurs in his discussion of Deutero-Isaiah.[53] Here he claims that this writing, like Hosea and Ezekiel, follows in the footsteps of the Pentateuch by using the wilderness theme to express both the threat of judgment and the promise of hope. Certainly, however, as Mauser's own survey brings out, the aspect of hope is overwhelmingly predominant in the Deutero-Isaian use of the theme, whereas judgment is mentioned

---

[49] It is also difficult to go along with Mauser when he widens the scope of his inquiry by linking the wilderness theme closely with the themes of the mountain (Mark 3:13; 6:46; 9:2; 13:3) and of the sea (numerous Markan passages), so that all of these passages comprise a complex in which the wilderness plays the central role (*Wilderness*, pp. 108–119, 124–128). This hypothesis is based on the association of Sinai with the wilderness in the Old Testament and the kinship there between ideas about the wilderness and those about the sea. Since *Mark*, however, never links these three themes explicitly — for example, by associating either the mountain or the sea with the ἐρημ- word group — Mauser's conclusion that Mark's whole Gospel is based on a wilderness typology remains speculative.

[50] Mauser, *Wilderness*, p. 81.

[51] See W. Roth, *Hebrew Gospel: Cracking the Code of Mark* (Oak Park, Ill.: Meyer-Stone Books, 1988), p. 94.

[52] See, for example, *Exod. Rab.* 32.9, an elaboration of the promise that God, who preserved the fathers, will also preserve the children. There follow citations of biblical passages in which God aided "the fathers" by means of angels; one of these passages is Ex. 23:20. A little further on we read: "And it will be similar in the future, when he will reveal himself, and redemption will come for Israel, as it is said, 'Behold, I send my messenger, and he will clear a way before your face' (Mal. 3:1)." Here the primary concentration is on what God did in the past. Similarly, the fact that Mal. 3:1 was part of the *haphtarah* reading for Ex. 23:20 does not mean, contra Stendahl (*School*, p. 50), that the sermon was given on the Malachi text, but that Malachi would have been brought in to supplement and elucidate Exodus; see B. Z. Wacholder in the prolegomenon to the new edition of J. Mann, *The Bible as Read and Preached in the Old Synagogue* (New York: KTAV, 1971; orig. 1940), p. xxiv.

[53] Mauser, *Wilderness*, pp. 50–52.

only as a shadow that has now been dispersed (see, e.g., 40:1–2).[54]

At another juncture, however, Mauser makes an important remark about the *discontinuity* between the Deutero-Isaian presentation of the wilderness theme and that in the Pentateuch:

> Passages such as 43:16f. and 48:20f. display unmistakable memories of the Exodus stories; but it is also clear that *the second exodus is not simply a repetition of the first* [emphasis added]. It will surpass the leaving of Egypt in that there will be no haste, no flight in fear as before (52:12; cf. Exod 12:39). The destination of the journey, Jerusalem, was made a desert through the destruction by the Babylonians. This wilderness, however, will be changed into a paradise (51:3).[55]

As noted above, another way in which the second exodus will supersede the first is the far greater predominance of grace over judgment. In the Deutero-Isaian picture of the wilderness sojourn, little room is left any longer for human disobedience; it has been crowded out by the titanic proportions of the divine victory.[56] This observation is especially important for our study because, as we have already noted, Mark 1:2a indicates that it is the Deutero-Isaian use of the theme that is determinative for Mark.

Our investigation, then, affirms Mauser's central thesis of the importance of the wilderness theme for Mark, while at the same time adding that it is specifically the Deutero-Isaian form of this theme, with its hope of eschatological victory in the wilderness, that is crucial for Mark.

Deutero-Isaiah and Apocalyptic Eschatology

The Markan usage of this Deutero-Isaian theme can rightly be labeled an apocalyptic one, as its cosmic backdrop suggests. Mauser himself cites with approval J. M. Robinson's remark that the Markan exorcism and controversy stories carry the cosmic struggle into historical settings, and he

---

[54] See B. W. Anderson, "Exodus Typology," in *Israel's Prophetic Heritage*, ed. Anderson and Harrelson, pp. 191–192.

[55] Mauser, *Wilderness*, p. 51. B. W. Anderson makes this point even more emphatically, pointing out that in one passage, 43:18–19, the sense of discontinuity is so strong that the prophet, "speaking with necessary paradox" (cf. 46:8–11), can urge the people not to remember "the former things," for Yahweh is doing a new thing that overshadows and supersedes the old ("Exodus Typology," in *Israel's Prophetic Heritage*, ed. Anderson and Harrelson, pp. 191–192). See also W. Zimmerli, "Der 'neue Exodus' in der Verkündigung der beiden grossen Exilspropheten," in *Gottes Offenbarung: Gesammelte Aufsätze zum Alten Testament*, TBü 19 (Munich: Chr. Kaiser Verlag, 1963), pp. 192–204.

[56] See B. W. Anderson, "Exodus Typology," in *Israel's Prophetic Heritage*, ed. Anderson and Harrelson, p. 191: "Unlike the old exodus, there will be no terrors or dangers along the way, and the people, instead of murmuring, will march with a faith that breaks forth into hymns of praise. . . ."

adds that the settings in wilderness, mountain, and sea also do the reverse, referring the historical setting back to the cosmic struggle. "Wilderness, mountain and sea are reminders of a deeper level of history undergirding the historically tangible events of Christ's ministry."[57]

The deepening effect of the wilderness setting in Mark reproduces its effect in the Old Testament original. As F. M. Cross has demonstrated in his groundbreaking book *Canaanite Myth and Hebrew Epic*, the Deutero-Isaian picture of Yahweh's victory march through the wilderness is a proto-apocalyptic one. In a chapter significantly entitled "The Divine Warrior," Cross shows that Isa. 40:3–6 and related passages describing Yahweh's "processional way" through the wilderness combine old Israelite holy war traditions with notions of cosmic battle derived from Canaanite mythology. In another chapter, Cross describes the resultant picture of preparation for a war of liberation with cosmic dimensions:

> The setting is in the heavenly council in which Yahweh addresses his heralds, "Comfort ye, comfort ye, my people." . . . Their proclamation announces the imminence of Yahweh's appearance in acts of redemption and, more specifically, directs preparations for the construction of a desert highway on which Yahweh will march through a transformed wilderness at the head of his people. This herald proclamation in verses 3 and 4, to level hills and raise valleys, is directed to supernatural beings, to the council of Yahweh, as is indicated by the cosmic scale of the project.[58]

Yet this cosmic operation takes place not in heaven but on an earthly stage, and the divine warrior's triumphant march through the wilderness is also the historical return of Israel to Zion. Precisely the same overlaying of the historical and the mythological planes in a vision of the end is characteristic of later Jewish apocalyptic eschatology and justifies Cross's reference to the Deutero-Isaian processional way as a "proto-apocalyptic theme."

This is not the place for a detailed review of the discussion in recent scholarship of the term "apocalyptic."[59] It will suffice to pass along M. C.

---

[57] Mauser, *Wilderness*, p. 142. E. Best disagrees with Robinson and Mauser, arguing that the cosmic struggle is essentially over after the temptation narrative in 1:12–13, when Satan is decisively defeated (*The Temptation and the Passion: The Markan Soteriology*, SNTSMS 2 [Cambridge: Cambridge University Press, 1965], pp. 18–27). Best, however, is unable to explain convincingly the Markan references to Satanic activity later in Jesus' ministry (8:33) and even in the postresurrectional period (4:15; see pp. 28–30, 182–83).

[58] F. M. Cross, *Canaanite Myth and Hebrew Epic: Essays in the History of the Religion of Israel* (Cambridge, Mass.: Harvard University Press, 1973), pp. 106–108, 188. Cross cites, besides Isa. 40:3–6, also 35:8–10; 44:24–28; 51:9–11; and 62:10–12. See more recently C. R. Seitz, "The Divine Council: Temporal Transition and New Prophecy in the Book of Isaiah," *JBL* 109 (1990), 229–247.

[59] This paragraph is dependent on the excellent discussion of apocalyptic eschatology in

de Boer's observation that even some of those who proffer a restrictive definition of the literary genre "apocalypse" recognize that ideas characteristic
of it are found also in other genres.[60] Thus it makes sense to speak of
"apocalyptic eschatology" even in a literary work such as Mark, which is
not, strictly speaking, an apocalypse. As the term itself implies, the two
most important elements in apocalyptic eschatology are revelation ("apocalyptic," from the Greek word ἀποκαλύπτειν, "to reveal") and the dualism of
the two ages ("eschatology").[61] Both elements are pronounced in Isa. 40:1–11.
The context is strikingly revelatory: the reader is granted insight into the
secret deliberations of the council of Yahweh. What is revealed is the birth
of a new epoch in cosmic changes (flattening of mountains, raising of valleys)
so dramatic that only the strongly discontinuous category "the new age"
does justice to their result. As the same biblical author puts it a few chapters
later in a passage related to ours by the theme of the wilderness way and
marked by an emphasis on perception and radical newness:

> *Remember* not the former things,
>   nor *consider* the things of old.
> Behold, I am doing *a new thing;*
>   now it springs forth, *do you not perceive it?*
> I will make *a way in the wilderness*
>   and rivers in the desert. (Isa. 43:18–19)

---

the article by M. C. de Boer, "Paul and Jewish Apocalyptic Eschatology," in *Apocalyptic and
the New Testament: Essays in Honor of J. Louis Martyn,* ed. J. Marcus and M. L. Soards, JSNTSup
24 (Sheffield: Sheffield Academic Press, 1989), pp. 169–190. C. C. Black, questioning the use
I make of the term "apocalyptic" with reference to Mark in my dissertation (see *Mystery,* p. 61
n. 173), asserts that "the telltale indicators of Marcan apocalyptic—determinism, the revelation of divine mysteries with cosmic consequences, a dualistic perception of reality—also
characterize the Fourth Gospel, whose eschatology has customarily been regarded as rather
different from Mark's" (*JBL* 107 [1988], 544). Though in general I find Black's criticism very
helpful, in this case I think it important to point out that I spoke not of "a dualistic perception of reality" but of "the doctrine of the two *ages.*" *That* doctrine seems to distinguish Mark
somewhat from John, since in John the linear, horizontal dualism implied when one speaks
of two *ages* has in large measure (though not totally) been replaced by a vertical dualism (e.g.,
"of this world/not of this world" and "from below/from above" in John 8:23).

    [60] See P. D. Hanson, "Apocalypse, Genre" and "Apocalypticism," *IDBSup,* pp. 27–34; J. J.
Collins, *The Apocalyptic Imagination: An Introduction to the Jewish Matrix of Christianity* (New
York: Crossroad, 1984), p. 2.

    [61] See J. H. Charlesworth, who writes that the characteristic tone of apocalyptic literature
"derives from the author's certainty of having received a *new revelation* that contains a perspective in discontinuity with *Heilsgeschichte*" (*The New Testament Apocrypha and Pseudepigrapha:
A Guide to Publications, with Excursuses on Apocalypses,* ATLA Bibliography Series 17
[Metuchen, N.J.: Scarecrow Press; London: The American Theological Library Association,
1987], p. 23).

Note the prominence of verbs of perception ("remember," "consider," "perceive") and the announcement that "a new thing" is happening.

If, as we have contended, the larger Deutero-Isaian context is in view in Mark 1, John the Baptist and Jesus are set firmly within the context of Jewish apocalyptic eschatology by the citation of Isa. 40:3 in Mark 1:3. Their appearance on the scene fulfills the prophecies of old because it heralds eschatological events,[62] because it is the preparation for and the beginning of the fulfillment of that end so eagerly yearned for since Old Testament times: the triumphant march of the holy warrior, Yahweh, leading his people through the wilderness to their true homeland in a mighty demonstration of saving power.

The Way of the Lord—An "Ethical" Way?

The apocalyptic nature of Mark's wilderness hope and his retention of the Deutero-Isaian context have important consequences for the interpretation of "the way of the Lord" in 1:3, for they suggest that the genitive κυρίου ("of the Lord") should be taken as a subjective rather than an objective genitive. In Isaiah "the way of the Lord" means Yahweh's own way through the wilderness,[63] his victory march, which indeed carries the returning people in its wake and so has implications for human action, but in which his own mighty demonstration of saving power is the center of attention and the source from which all "ethics" flow. A similar interpretation may be suggested for the Markan use of the phrase.

This suggested interpretation differs from the usual one; "the way of the Lord" in Mark 1:3 is most often interpreted "ethically" to mean the way in which the Lord wants people to walk. Snodgrass, for example, asserts that the Synoptic use of Isa. 40:3 has its forerunner in the Qumran interpretation (1QS 8:12–16 and 9:17–20), in which the members of the community "viewed their right living in the wilderness as the means of preparation for the soon coming of God."[64] The Synoptics use the passage in a similar "ethical" way, according to him, as is evident from the way in which they link Isa. 40:3 with John the Baptist's preaching of repentance.

To turn first to Snodgrass's point about Qumran, examination of the use of Isa. 40:3 in 1QS reveals that it is not so one-sidedly "ethical" as he claims. He translates 1QS 8:12–16 as follows:

[62] See Guelich, "Beginning," pp. 10–12; and J. D. Kingsbury, The Christology of Mark's Gospel (Philadelphia: Fortress Press, 1983), pp. 56–57.
[63] Although דרך/ὁδός sometimes means the road upon which one walks, it often denotes an action, the "way" that one takes, one's course or journey; see BDB, pp. 202–203; W. Michaelis, "ὁδός, κτλ.," TDNT (1968; orig. 1954), 5:43.
[64] Snodgrass, "Streams," p. 30.

And when these become a community in Israel according to all these
rules, they will separate from the dwelling of perverse men in order to
go to the desert to prepare there the way of Him even as it has been
written. "In the wilderness prepare the way of . . . , make straight in the
desert a highway for our God." This is the study of Torah which he commanded by the hand of Moses to do according to all that has been revealed
time and again and even as the prophets revealed by the Holy Spirit.[65]

Contrary to this translation, however, it is probable that the *niph'al* verb
יבדלו in 8:13 should be translated not as a reflexive ("they will separate")
but as a passive ("they will be separated"),[66] in which case an important
part of the context of the passage is God's action of separating for himself
an elect community from out of the *massa perditionis*. Such an interpretation is supported by the other important *niph'al* verb in the passage, נגלו
("that has been revealed"), which has God as its implied subject. It is God's
own revelation of "the mysteries of wonder and truth" to the community's
leader that makes possible the study of the Torah that occurs in the community. Similarly, the other Qumran passage that cites Isa. 40:3 explicitly,
1QS 9:17–20, does so in a context that speaks of "walking *in all that has
been revealed*" by God. Thus, though human action is certainly in view in
the Qumran passages that speak of "the way of the Lord," this action takes
place within God's *own* revelation and preparation of the way, and the latter
aspect cannot be excluded from the meaning of "the Way" as a designation
of the Qumran community or its life (1QS 9:17–21; 10:21).

Yet it must be admitted that the *dominant* note sounded by the Qumran
use of Isa. 40:3 is that of human action; the *pesher*, after all, takes that passage
as a prophecy of the community's Torah study, although even here the study
is on the basis of the new revelation of the Teacher of Righteousness. The
Qumran use of the passage, however, is not necessarily determinative for
the Markan one. The question remains whether or not human action is also
the dominant note sounded by Mark 1:3 in its context. Snodgrass thinks
that it is, writing that Mark and the other Synoptics "emphasize the ethical
content of [John the Baptist's] message by emphasizing the theme of
repentance."[67] Here he refers to Mark 1:4, which immediately follows the
citation of Isa. 40:3 in 1:3 and describes John's appearance in the wilderness
"preaching a baptism of repentance for the forgiveness of sins" (κηρύσσων
βάπτισμα μετανοίας εἰς ἄφεσιν ἁμαρτιῶν). This, to Snodgrass and most

[65] Ibid., pp. 28–29.
[66] See A. Dupont-Sommer, *The Essene Writings from Qumran*, trans. G. Vermes (Gloucester,
Mass.: Peter Smith, 1973); cf. E. Lohse, *Die Texte aus Qumran: Hebräisch und Deutsch* (Munich:
Kösel, 1964). Both the reflexive and the passive are biblical alternatives for translating the
niph'al of בדל; see BDB, p. 95.
[67] Snodgrass, "Streams," p. 33.

exegetes, is transparently a description of a preacher with an "ethical" message.

But is that really so? E. Lohmeyer presents a different analysis of Mark 1:4, noting that what we have been calling the "ethical" interpretation would require the sentence to say, "John preached repentance in baptism," not "John preached a baptism of repentance." According to the actual wording, however, John preaches not *repentance* but *baptism*.[68] Baptism is evidently regarded here not as a human action but as a divine one, something that can be *proclaimed;* elsewhere in the New Testament κηρύσσειν almost always has as its subject either John, Jesus, or the apostles and as its object an action of God (the gospel, the kingdom of God, etc.).[69] This divine gift of baptism, according to Lohmeyer, leads to repentance, which is God's reversal of the direction of a human life, putting it back on the way of his own righteousness (cf. Matt. 21:32). In this eschatological sacrament, forgiveness of sins is granted ("for the forgiveness of sins" modifies "baptism" rather than "repentance").

Lohmeyer's interpretation of 1:4 is certainly supported by the allusion to the baptism in the Holy Spirit (1:8) and by the description of Jesus' own baptism (1:9–11), which follow in short order, for here it is unmistakable that baptism is understood as an eschatological action of divine grace. John the Baptist, moreover, is presented in 1:2–3 as Jesus' forerunner, and as we shall see below this forerunning probably includes the anticipation of Jesus' message in John's. In Jesus' own initial proclamation of the gospel (1:15) the announcement of a divine action precedes the call for a human orientation to that action, so it makes sense that the divine action should have a similar priority in John's preaching.[70] Thus the link between Mark 1:3 and 1:4 by means of the phrase "in the wilderness" actually supports the theocentric reading of "the way of the Lord" we have been proposing, since it connects the way of the Lord with the divine gift of baptism.[71]

The Way of the Lord in Mark—
Entering God's Basileia

Our proposed reading of "the way of the Lord," which puts the main emphasis on the Lord's own creation of a way, and only a secondary emphasis

---

[68] E. Lohmeyer, *Das Evangelium des Markus*, MeyerK, 11th ed. (Göttingen: Vandenhoeck & Ruprecht, 1951), pp. 13–15.

[69] Lohmeyer mentions three exceptions: Mark 5:20; Acts 15:21; and Rom 2:21 (*Evangelium*, p. 13 n. 3).

[70] On Mark 1:15, see J. Marcus, "'The Time Has Been Fulfilled!' (Mark 1:15)," in *Apocalyptic and the New Testament*, ed. Marcus and Soards, pp. 49–68.

[71] The phrase "the way of the Lord" recurs in Mark 12:14, where it clearly does have an "ethical" meaning. Here, however, the phrase is placed in the mouth of Jesus' enemies!

on the human walk along that way, is further supported by a look at some
of the usages of ὁδός ("way") elsewhere in Mark's Gospel. Of these the most
significant are the seven references (8:27; 9:33–34; 10:17, 32, 46, 52 — half
of the Markan total) clustered in the Gospel's central section, 8:22–10:52,
which describes Jesus' journey up to Jerusalem.[72] As E. Best notes, this
section is the center of Mark's instruction to his readers on the meaning
of Christ and their own discipleship,[73] and it would be no exaggeration to
say that the phrase "on the way," which appears at its beginning, middle,
and end (8:27; 9:33–34; 10:32, 52), could well stand as its title. Of the seven
references to the ὁδός here, the majority, if not all, are redactional, and they
structure the whole carefully constructed journey account, which is probably also a Markan creation.[74] This predominantly redactional use of ὁδός
sets Mark's central section off from the rest of the Gospel.[75]

Some significant scholarly work has been done on the Old Testament
background for the theme of the ὁδός in this central section. In his dissertation, W. Kelber links this redactional use of ὁδός with the theme, also prominent in this section, of entrance into the kingdom of God (9:47; 10:15,
23–25). The model for this entrance, says Kelber, drawing on the work of
H. Windisch, is the Deuteronomic motif of the entrance into the land, and
"the Markan entrance formula is ultimately derived from a translation of
Deuteronomy's entrance tradition into an eschatological key."[76] The journey
of Jesus and his disciples, therefore, constitutes for Kelber a second entry

---

[72] Cf. E. Best, who identifies the literary unit as 8:27–10:45, but notes that it is preceded
and followed by stories of healing the blind (*Following Jesus: Discipleship in the Gospel of
Mark*, JSNTSup 4 [Sheffield: JSOT Press, 1981], p. 15).

[73] Ibid.

[74] Ibid., pp. 15–17; L. Schenke, *Die Wundererzählungen des Markusevangelium*, SBB 5 (Stuttgart: Katholisches Bibelwerk, 1974), p. 355; D.-A. Koch, *Die Bedeutung der Wundererzählungen
für die Christologie des Markusevangeliums* (Berlin and New York: Walter de Gruyter, 1975),
p. 114 n. 4, p. 131. The phrase ἐν τῇ ὁδῷ ("in the way") binds together the whole literary unit.
In 8:27; 9:33–34; and 10:32 it is part of the Markan frame and occurs in close connection
with the three passion predictions. Its final usage, in 10:52, only makes sense within the larger
Markan context of 8:27–11:1. As for the other usages of ὁδός in the section, the notice in 10:17
that Jesus was going out εἰς ὁδόν ("on the way") when he was encountered by the rich young
man is not really vital to the story, though it is not disruptive of it either. It is most likely
redactional, however, since in the Markan context it serves to contrast the rich man who rejects
Jesus' call to "the way" with blind Bartimaeus, who accepts it (10:46, 52). Contrary to Best,
however, I would estimate that παρὰ τὴν ὁδόν ("along the way") in 10:46 is probably traditional, since it seems to be an intrinsic part of the story.

[75] With Best (*Following*, p. 17 n. 8), who rightly disputes J. Schreiber's contention that ὁδός
is almost *always* redactional in Mark. According to Best, it is probably traditional in 2:23;
4:4, 14–15; 11:8; and 12:14, probably redactional in 6:8, perhaps redactional in 8:3. "Thus it
is principally in 8:27–10:52 that the word is used redactionally."

[76] W. Kelber, "Kingdom and Parousia in the Gospel of Mark" (Ph.D. diss., University of
Chicago, 1970), p. 109.

into the promised land, and Jesus' ministry is in the view of W. Swartley, who follows Kelber, "the ὁδός to the kingdom of God."[77]
The work of Kelber and Swartley is important, but it needs to be modified in several respects. Kelber's phrase about the "translation of Deuteronomy's entrance tradition *into an eschatological key*" should be taken more seriously than Kelber himself seems to do. Windisch, upon whom both Kelber and Swartley draw, already notes that the history-of-religions background for the "entering" statements includes not only the Deuteronomic traditions about entry into the land but also the cultic *tôrôt* of entry found in the Psalms. These two *Sitze im Leben* are fused and eschatologically transfigured in Deutero-Isaiah, as F. M. Cross observes:

> The old Exodus-Conquest route, the way through the wilderness, becomes at the same time the pilgrimage way to Zion. The march of the Conquest abruptly shifts into the festal, ritual procession to Zion. The procession to Zion and the feast on the holy mountain . . . have recast, so to speak, or redirected the route of the Exodus and Conquest to lead to Zion.[78]

I have shown elsewhere that these Deutero-Isaian passages form the most direct background for the Synoptic sayings about entering the βασιλεία τοῦ θεοῦ (usually translated "kingdom of God").[79] The return of Yahweh is presented as an extension of his kingly power, and its effect is described by means of the old shout from the cult, "Yahweh has become king!" (יהוה מלך). As in the processions described in the psalms, Yahweh's entry into the city encompasses the entry of the people, so in Deutero-Isaiah Yahweh's return to Zion carries in its wake the people's return. Read with this background in mind, the Synoptic sayings about entering the βασιλεία conceive of the βασιλεία not as a *place* but as God's eschatological extension of his kingly power into a lost world, and human beings are invited to *enter into*—that is, participate in—this divine extension of power. As in Old Testament holy war traditions, the motive power is that of God, but human beings can be incorporated into his forward momentum (βασιλεία). The central section of Mark's Gospel, then, is not, as Kelber and Swartley would have it, about the human way *to* the βασιλεία but rather about God's way, which *is* his βασιλεία, his own extension of kingly power.

[77] W. M. Swartley, "The Structural Function of the Term 'Way' in Mark," in *The New Way of Jesus: Essays Presented to Howard Charles*, ed. W. Klassen (Newton, Kans.: Faith and Life Press, 1980), pp. 78–79.
[78] Cross (*Canaanite Myth*, p. 108), citing Isa. 35:8–10; 40:3–5; 44:24–28; 51:9–10; 62:24–28. The last citation is an error; probably Cross means 62:10–12. I would include here also Isa. 52:1–12.
[79] Marcus, "Entering," pp. 101–113.

The Healing of the Blind

Not only the Markan theme of the ὁδός of the Lord but also the inter-related theme of his βασιλεία draws on a Deutero-Isaian background. The link between the Markan ὁδός and the Deutero-Isaian picture of eschato-logical triumph is confirmed by the important passage 10:46–52, in which Bartimaeus receives his sight from Jesus and follows him "on the way."

It has long been surmised that significant background to the stories of Jesus' healing of blind people in the Gospels lies in Isaian prophecies that in the new age the blind will receive their sight.[80] What has apparently not been noticed is the traditional link between this theme of the healing of blindness and the theme of Yahweh's "way" through the wilderness. That march, as we recall, is accompanied in Isaiah by an eschatological trans-formation of nature; as part of that transformation the blind receive their sight. For example, Isa. 35:1–7 opens with a prophecy of the blooming of the wilderness (35:1–2) and the coming of Yahweh to save his people (35:4). At this time "the eyes of the blind will be opened" (35:5–7), and this removal of blindness is linked to the picture of the holy highway upon which the redeemed of the Lord return to Zion with exultant singing. Thus, the bloom-ing of the wilderness, the opening of blind eyes, and the way of the Lord are interrelated themes.

Similarly impressive background to Mark 10:46–52 is provided by Isa. 42:10–16. The passage begins with a call for the whole earth, including the desert places, to praise Yahweh (vv. 10–12). This call is followed by tradi-tional holy war imagery: "The Lord goes forth like a mighty man," and so on (vv. 13–15). One effect of Yahweh's holy war on behalf of his people is the enlightenment of the blind:

> And I will lead the blind
> in a way that they know not,
> in paths that they have not known
> I will guide them.
> I will turn the darkness before them
> into light,
> the rough places into level ground. (Isa. 42:16)

The passage speaks not only of God enlightening the blind but also of his *leading* them *in a way;* compare the picture of Bartimaeus, his blindness

[80] See, e.g., H. van der Loos, *The Miracles of Jesus*, NovTSup 9 (Leiden: E. J. Brill, 1965), p. 415; K. Kertelge, *Die Wunder Jesu im Markusevangelium: Eine redaktionsgeschichtliche Unter-suchung*, SANT 23 (Munich: Kösel, 1970), p. 160; Koch, *Bedeutung*, p. 130 n. 18, p. 174; J. Ernst, *Das Evangelium nach Markus*, RNT (Regensburg: Pustet, 1981), p. 312. The Isaian passages cited include 29:18; 35:5; 42:7, 16, 18.

healed, *following* Jesus *in the way*.[81] The enlightenment, moreover, is accompanied in Isa. 42:16 by a smoothing out of rough places, a motif associated with "the way of the Lord" not only here but also in Isa. 40:3–4.[82] Thus, as in the Markan story of Bartimaeus, the enlightenment of the blind is linked in Deutero-Isaiah with the motif of the way, and this is done in a manner that recalls the initial Markan reference to the way, the Old Testament citation in 1:2–3. The link of the Bartimaeus story with the Deutero-Isaian motif of the wilderness way coheres with the story's setting in Jericho, which is on the edge of the Judean wilderness.[83]

The Way Up to Jerusalem

Thus the climactic instance of ὁδός in Mark 8:22–10:52 reflects the Deutero-Isaian picture of Yahweh's triumphant processional march, and it seems likely that the remaining six instances in this section should be read in the same light. This supposition gains credence when we recall that Mark has placed the Deutero-Isaian passage about the way of the Lord programmatically at the head of his Gospel (1:3).[84] He has, moreover, prefaced this reference to the Lord's way with the conflated citation that speaks of the way of Jesus (1:2), thus hinting to his readers that the way of the Lord *is* the way of Jesus.[85] When, therefore, those readers encounter in 8:22–10:52 the picture of Jesus and his disciples *on the way* up to Jerusalem, they will probably be led to surmise that this way of Jesus is the Deutero-Isaian "way of the Lord."

But in Mark the Deutero-Isaian picture of the Lord's triumphal way has suffered a strange reversal from its intersection with the theology of the cross. The usage of ὁδός in 10:32–34 is a crucial illustration of this point:

> And they were *on the way* (ἐν τῇ ὁδῷ) *going up* (ἀναβαίνοντες) *to Jeru-salem*, and Jesus was *going before* them, and they were amazed, and *those who were following* were afraid. And taking the twelve again he began to tell them the things that would happen to him: "Behold, *we are going*

---

[81] The Septuagint version of the passage confirms the verbal link with the phrasing of Mark 10:46–52: καὶ ἄξω τυφλοὺς ἐν ὁδῷ ᾗ οὐκ ἔγνωσαν.

[82] Another link of Isa. 42:16 with 40:3 is the parallelism of "way" and "paths."

[83] On Jericho's wilderness location, see Mauser, *Wilderness*, p. 19.

[84] See Best, *Following*, p. 15.

[85] Contra M. A. Tolbert (*Sowing the Gospel: Mark's World in Literary-Historical Perspective* [Philadelphia: Fortress Press, 1989], pp. 239–248), the "messenger before your face" of 1:2 is John the Baptist, not Jesus, and "your way" is Jesus' way, not the way of the reader. Verses 2–3 are immediately followed by a passage in which the Baptist speaks of Jesus coming after him (1:7), and Tolbert's reference to 13:14 does little to dilute the force of the objection that if the way of Mark's readers were in view the pronoun σου ("you") would need to be a plural rather than a singular.

up (ἀναβαίνομεν) *to Jerusalem,* and the Son of man will be handed over
to the chief priests and the scribes, and they will condemn him to death
and hand him over to the Gentiles, and they will beat him and spit on
him and scourge him and kill him; and after three days he will rise."

To understand this remarkable passage properly, it is necessary to recall
that the strikingly repeated ἀναβαίνει ("to go up") is a technical term for
the festal ascent to the holy city.[86] In Deutero-Isaiah, however, as we have
seen, this theme of the festal procession to Zion has been fused with that
of the holy war of conquest. This *traditionsgeschichtlich* observation
confirms our suggestion that the "way" described in Mark 10:32–34 (ἐν τῇ
ὁδῷ, 10:32) is the way of the Lord, the preparatory stage of the divine invasion of the holy city and hence the cosmos. In Deutero-Isaiah this divine
invasion carries in its wake the return of the people to Zion; so too in Mark
10:32–34 Jesus is followed by an elect group who have been taken up into
his forward momentum and thereby catapulted into the front lines of the
divine assault on the world.[87]

An ironic twist, however, has inverted the normal way of painting the
Deutero-Isaian picture of victorious holy war. Jesus announces to his companions that he is going up to Jerusalem not in order to triumph over his
enemies in a conventional way but in order to be killed by them. Nothing
could be more antithetical to conventional notions of victory than Jesus'
long prophecy of his own betrayal, condemnation, mockery, physical abuse,
and execution (10:33–34). Yet, it must be forcefully added, this prophecy
is not a *denial* of the Deutero-Isaian hope for a holy war victory; it is, rather,
a radical, cross-centered *adaptation* of it. For those with eyes to see (see
4:9, 23), the fearful trek of the befuddled, bedraggled little band of disciples
is the return of Israel to Zion, and Jesus' suffering and death there *are* the
prophesied apocalyptic victory of the divine warrior. The same spirit that
will later shape the Markan passion narrative infuses Mark 8:22–10:52, a
unitary redefinition of apocalyptic eschatology that paradoxically hears in
Jesus' cry of dereliction the triumph song of Yahweh's return to Zion, that
paradoxically sees in his anguished, solitary death the long-awaited advent
of the kingdom of God.

This strange development of apocalyptic eschatology would have a special
significance for Mark's community. That community, as we have already
noted, is one rent by internal strife and threatened by persecution from
without, including persecution from Jewish revolutionaries who probably
see their own movement as a fulfillment of the Deutero-Isaian prophecy

---

[86] See J. Schneider, "βαίνω, κτλ.," *TDNT* (1964; orig. 1933), 1:519.
[87] On the influence of the concept of the divine warrior on Mark's picture of Jesus, see
B. A. Stevens, "'Why "must" the Son of Man suffer?' The Divine Warrior in the Gospel of
Mark," *BZ* 31 (1987), 101–110.

of victorious holy war. Mark's use of the passage, therefore, may in part be polemical: the true fulfillment of the prophecy of Yahweh's triumphant march through the wilderness lies not in the military campaigns of the revolutionaries but in the weary trek of Jesus and his disciples up to Jerusalem.

The members of Mark's community would easily read themselves into this portrait of the disciples on their way up to Jerusalem. Cued by the placement of the key ὁδός passage at the beginning of the Gospel and by the statement that the gospel was as Isaiah had prophesied it (1:2–3), they would know that the subsequent ὁδός passages were meant to be interpreted in the light of this first one, and hence that their own path of suffering and death was overlaid with the end-of-days picture of Yahweh's march through the wilderness with his chosen people in tow. They would recognize, therefore, that the eschatological power of God was powerfully present among them even in their time of weakness, failure, suffering, and death. All appearances to the contrary, they would perceive, their journey up to Jerusalem was the victory march of the divine warrior, casting down every obstacle as he made his triumphant way to Zion, causing the blind to see and the desert to bloom about him (see 6:39; 8:22–26; 10:46–52).

The Way of Jesus and the Way of the Lord

Mark 1:2–3 is an important passage not only for discussion of Mark's use of the Old Testament but also for discussion of his christology.[88] All of our work up to the present has had christological implications; now it is time to try to define them more precisely.

We have mentioned several times the parallel between "your way" in Mark 1:2 and "the way of the Lord" in Mark 1:3. Our redactional analysis has shown this parallel to be a Markan creation, since it is Mark himself who has prefaced 1:2 to 1:3 and eliminated the phrase "before you" from the end of 1:2. The christological question that remains is exactly what the parallel between "the way of Jesus" and "the way of the Lord" implies about Mark's view of the relationship between Jesus and God. This is a difficult question because the change from the second person address in 1:2 ("your way") to the third person reference in 1:3 ("the way of the Lord") makes the relationship between these persons initially unclear.[89]

In consequence of this lack of clarity, contemporary scholars draw widely differing christological conclusions from the juxtaposition in Mark 1:2–3. One significant stream of interpretation sees the parallel between "your way" and "the way of the Lord" as evidence that Mark wishes to identify

---

[88] See Mauser, *Wilderness*, p. 80.
[89] See Kingsbury, *Christology*, p. 56.

Jesus with the κύριος ("Lord"). K. Stendahl, followed by R. Pesch, notes that the end of Mark 1:3 reads, "Straight makes *his paths*," an alteration of the Septuagint reading of Isa. 40:3, "Straight make the paths *of our God.*" The elimination of the explicit reference to God suggests to Stendahl and Pesch that "here as in so many other cases the LXX's κύριος is not the M.T.'s Yahweh but Christ. . . ."[90] An opposing line of interpretation, however, says that the κύριος in 1:3 must be God in distinction from Christ, asserting that elsewhere in Mark κύριος is never used as a christological title.[91] A third position asserts that the question of the identity of the κύριος in 1:3 is insoluble.[92]

The pessimism of this last position is unwarranted; Mark's picture of the relationship between Jesus and the title κύριος is subtle and complicated, but not totally obscure. We may begin with a literary observation: the close relationship between Jesus and the Lord is underlined not only by the parallel between "your way" and "the way of the Lord" but also by the repetition of the "ou" sounds throughout 1:2–3: ἰδού . . . μου . . . προσώπου σου . . . σου. It is obvious from the Markan context, moreover, that John the Baptist, the messenger who prepares the way of Jesus (1:2), is also the voice that speaks of preparing the way of the Lord (1:3). One path, therefore, seems to be described in 1:2–3 under two names: "your [Jesus'] way" and "the way of the Lord." A very close connection between Jesus and the Lord is thus implied by 1:2–3.

This close connection is visible also elsewhere in the Gospel. In 2:28, for example, Jesus says, "The Son of man is κύριος even of the sabbath." In 11:3 he instructs his disciples that anyone who challenges them about their appropriation of the colt is to be told, "ὁ κύριος has need of it, and will send it back here immediately." Finally, in 12:36–37 Jesus quotes Ps. 110:1 to show that the Messiah is David's κύριος. Although in all of these cases κύριος can be read in its secular meaning of "master," "owner,"[93] the attentive Markan reader would probably discern a deeper nuance, especially in view of the widespread and early Christian transference to Jesus of κύριος as a divine

---

90 Stendahl, *School,* p. 48; cf. Pesch, *Markusevangelium* 1:77. Snodgrass, disagreeing, suggests that the substitution of "his paths" for "the paths of our God" arises instead from an attempt to avoid the divine name, and he compares 1QS 8:13, where an intensified form of the third person pronoun replaces the tetragrammaton of the Masoretic Text ("Streams," p. 34). As this parallel shows, however, it is the title "the Lord," not the designation "our God," which might cause a problem and have to be replaced; yet the Synoptic version of Isa. 40:3 lets κυρίου stand. "His paths" in Mark 1:3 is not explainable as a euphemism.

91 See, e.g., Snodgrass, "Streams," p. 34; D. Lührmann, *Das Markusevangelium,* HNT 3 (Tübingen: J. C. B. Mohr [Paul Siebeck], 1987), p. 34.

92 H. Anderson, "Old Testament," in *Use of the Old Testament,* ed. Efird, p. 283.

93 On the secular meaning of κύριος, see BAGD, p. 459 (1).

designation.[94] In any event, a connection between the terms "Jesus" and κύριος is established by Mark 2:28; 11:3; and 12:36–37.

Yet the passage last mentioned, 12:36–37, also presents another κύριος, who is in fact called ὁ κύριος, *the* Lord, and who seems to be distinct from Jesus, yet standing in the closest possible connection with him, since Jesus sits at his right hand. This combination of close connection with distinction recalls certain features of the juxtaposition of "your [Jesus'] way" and "the way of the Lord" in 1:2–3. Here, too, as we have seen, there is a very close connection between the figures; yet Mark seems to draw back from *identifying* Jesus with the κύριος. Stendahl moves in the opposite direction and does identify Jesus with the κύριος but provides evidence of this reserve, noting that "your way" in Mark 1:2 does not agree completely with "his way" in 1:3, though both are in disagreement with the Masoretic Text and the Septuagint. "This lack of agreement," he remarks, "is striking if the fusion is original to Mark and a christological adaptation to the context is presumed."[95] He views this lack of agreement as evidence that the fusion is *not* original to Mark and that it perhaps reflects the post-Markan interpolation of 1:2.[96] We have rejected the interpolation theory, however,[97] and have argued that Mark intentionally prefaced 1:2 to 1:3. If he did not smooth out the discrepancy between "your way" and "his way," perhaps this roughness reflects a desire to preserve, along with a strong impression of the relatedness of Jesus to God, also a measure of acknowledgment of the distinction between them. This distinction coheres with several Markan passages that imply Jesus' subordination to God (10:18, 40; 13:32; 14:36; and 15:34).[98]

The Markan view of the relation between Jesus and the κύριος, then, subtly combines a recognition of the separateness of the two figures with a recognition of their inseparability.[99] Perhaps the best way to express this

[94] On the κύριος title, see J. A. Fitzmyer, "The Semitic Background of the New Testament Kyrios-Title," in *A Wandering Aramean: Collected Aramaic Essays*, SBLMS 25 (Missoula, Mont.: Scholars Press, 1979), pp. 115–142.

[95] Stendahl, *School*, p. 51. Apparently Stendahl thinks that if Mark were responsible for 1:2–3 he would conform the pronouns to each other in some such way as this: "Behold, I send my messenger before his face, who will prepare his way; the voice of one crying in the wilderness: Prepare the way of the Lord, make straight his paths."

[96] Later in his book, Stendahl suggests an alternate theory: the fusion of the two passages might have taken place in groups gathered around John the Baptist (*School*, p. 215). This theory, however, in no way solves the problem of the lack of agreement of the pronouns, and it is, as Stendahl admits, speculative.

[97] See n. 10 above in this chapter.

[98] See Marcus, *Mystery*, pp. 183–184.

[99] Lührmann tips Mark's delicate christological balance too far in the direction of distinctiveness when he says that in Mark 1:3, as in the Old Testament, the κύριος is God himself *in distinction from* the Son, who is referred to in 1:2 (*Markusevangelium*, p. 34; emphasis added).

complex relationship is to say that, in Mark, where Jesus acts, there the Lord is also powerfully at work.[100] This view of the relationship is borne out by numerous Markan passages. In Mark 5:19, for example, Jesus instructs the Gadarene demoniac to go home and tell his friends "what great things ὁ κύριος has done for you." Jesus identifies the man's benefactor as "the Lord"; yet he himself has been the direct agent of the demoniac's healing, and in the redactional v. 20 the man goes out and announces the things that *Jesus* has done for him.[101] Jesus, then, acts with the power and authority of the κύριος. Later in the Gospel, therefore, when they read about Jesus' triumphal entry into Jerusalem, Mark's readers will know that, as often happens in the Gospel, there is a deeper meaning to the crowd's acclamation than they are aware of themselves.[102] "Blessed is he who comes *in the name of the Lord!*" (11:9) is not just an invocation of the Lord's blessing on Jesus, but also an unwitting acknowledgment that his advent is a revelation of God himself.[103] Other passages that lack the phrase ὁ κύριος imply the same view: where Jesus acts, God is acting. For example, the scribes' outraged question in 2:7, "Who can forgive sins but God alone?," is answered in 2:10: "the Son of man has authority on earth to forgive sins." The forgiveness of sins which Jesus exercises in his capacity as Son of man reflects God's own prerogative.

The view that where Jesus acts, there God is acting, is exactly what we would expect from our previous analysis of the Markan theme of "the way of the Lord." We have seen that throughout Mark's Gospel, and particularly in the central section (8:22–10:52), Jesus' "way" is painted in the familiar biblical colors of the Deutero-Isaian "way of the Lord." The main point of this portrayal is to show that Jesus' journey up to suffering and death in Jerusalem is, in the strange logic of a cruciform apocalyptic theology, the victorious assault of the divine warrior on the resistant cosmos.[104] Mark thus establishes an identity between the two ways, that of Jesus and that of the

---

[100] A. J. Hultgren characterizes Mark's christology as "theopractic," which means that it is God who acts in Christ (*Christ and His Benefits: Christology and Redemption in the New Testament* [Philadelphia: Fortress Press, 1987], pp. 61–63). Cf. J. A. Fitzmyer's conclusion that the early church's christological use of the title κύριος implied a comparison, but not an identification, of Jesus with God ("*Kyrios*-Title," in *Wandering Aramean*, p. 130).

[101] Mark 5:20 is a "framework" verse and therefore redactional; see the scholars cited by E. J. Pryke, *Redactional Style in the Marcan Gospel: A Study of Syntax and Vocabulary as Guides to Redaction in Mark* (Cambridge: Cambridge University Press, 1978), p. 14.

[102] On Markan irony, see D. Juel, *Messiah and Temple: The Trial of Jesus in the Gospel of Mark*, SBLDS 31 (Missoula, Mont.: Scholars Press, 1973), pp. 44–46 and passim; D. Rhoads and D. Michie, *Mark as Story: An Introduction to the Narrative of a Gospel* (Philadelphia: Fortress Press, 1982), p. 60; Marcus, *Mystery*, pp. 111–117.

[103] See W. Lane, *The Gospel of Mark*, NICNT (Grand Rapids: Wm. B. Eerdmans Publishing Co., 1974), pp. 397–398.

[104] See O. Betz, "Jesu heiliger Krieg," *NovT* 2 (1957–1958), 116–137.

Lord, without simply identifying Jesus with God, for the distinction between them is maintained in that Jesus' apparent defeat is the occasion for God's victory (cf. 15:33–39).[105]

The christology of Mark's Gospel, then, is a topic that cannot be comprehended in isolation but necessarily involves consideration of Mark's eschatology and theology.[106] Indeed, of those three topics, Markan christology is the third, not in order of importance but in logical order of discussion. Apocalyptic eschatology, with its expectation and hope of a divine act at once shattering and salvific, is the indispensable framework within which Mark's christology operates. To paraphrase Rudolph Otto: Mark's christology, like Jesus himself, is carried forward by the tidal wave of the divine victory.[107] Apocalyptic eschatology by itself, however, is an insufficient explanation of Mark's thought, for it undergoes an almost alchemical transformation when it collides with the theology of the cross.[108] Mark takes the raw ore of Jewish apocalyptic conceptions and subjects them to a christological neutron bombardment, thereby producing a powerful, disturbing, unpredictable new form of apocalyptic eschatology.

Preparing the Way

We have spoken a great deal about the way and have concluded that for Mark it is both God's own way and the way of Jesus; but what does it mean to *prepare* the way?

In Mark 1:2, Mal. 3:1 is quoted to identify John the Baptist as the preparer of the way. Mark probably understands this preparation in a double sense. As N. Perrin has noted, Mark's Gospel portrays a progression of witness and suffering from John to Jesus to the church: first John preaches and is delivered up (1:7, 14); then Jesus preaches and is delivered up (1:14; 9:31; 10:33); and finally the Christians preach and are delivered up (3:14; 13:9–13).[109] John thus prepares Jesus' way both by his preaching and by his martyrdom. This exegesis is borne out by the observations that Mark applies the verb χηρύσσειν ("to preach") to John in 1:4, 7, then to Jesus in 1:14, and

---

[105] Contra Stevens ("Divine Warrior," pp. 101–110), Mark does not identify Jesus as the divine warrior. That role is still fulfilled by God, though Jesus' activity is brought into close connection with it.

[106] On *theo-logy* proper, see J. R. Donahue, "A Neglected Factor in the Theology of Mark," *JBL* 101 (1982), 563–594.

[107] R. Otto, *The Kingdom of God and the Son of Man: A Study in the History of Religion* (1934; reprint, Boston: Starr King, 1957), p. 103.

[108] There is, however, a foreshadowing of this transformation in the inclusion of the Servant Songs in the "proto-apocalyptic" Deutero-Isaiah; see the discussion of the Servant Songs in chapter 8 below.

[109] N. Perrin and D. C. Duling, *The New Testament: An Introduction: Proclamation and Parenesis, Myth and History*, 2nd ed. (New York: Harcourt Brace Jovanovich, 1982), pp. 110, 238.

that John's arrest and execution are described in more detail than any other Markan event not directly involving Jesus (6:17–29). John's arrest seems in Mark's view to pave the way for Jesus' ministry proper, for in 1:14 we read: *"after John was delivered up,* Jesus came into Galilee preaching the gospel of God" (alt.).[110]

The reference of χατασχευάζειν ("to prepare") in Mark 1:2 seems fairly clear: John prepares Jesus' way by preaching and dying a martyr's death. More difficult is the attempt to divine the reference of ἑτοιμάζειν (another word for "to prepare") in 1:3, even though the words are virtually synonymous. Here John, the preparer of the way according to 1:2, seems to be calling on *others* to prepare the way, and the importance of this preparation is emphasized by the synonymous parallelism of 1:3bc. But who are these others? Because of the link between 1:3, where we hear of a proclamation in the wilderness, and 1:4, where John preaches in the wilderness, it seems clear that the addressees of 1:3 are the objects of John's proclamation in 1:4–8, the Jewish crowds who stand generally for the potential disciples of Jesus.[111] Yet it is difficult to make sense of this identification in the overall context of Mark's theology. Do human beings prepare the Lord's way, in Mark's eyes? Why, then, is Mark's picture of the disciples painted in such dark colors?[112] Even the minor characters who sometimes seem to display greater faith than the "official" disciples[113] do not so much *prepare* the Lord's way as *recognize* its link with Jesus' way and follow him in it. Indeed, in an important sense, Mark pictures exactly the opposite of human beings preparing the Lord's way; the earthly Jesus, acting in the power of God, *goes before* the disciples (10:32, 52) and prophesies that this precedence will continue even after his resurrection (14:28; cf. 16:7). Christian discipleship is a matter of following Jesus in the way of the cross (8:34;

---

[110] See Best, *Following,* p. 16.

[111] Though the word ὄχλος ("crowd") is not used in 1:5, the assemblage described there should probably be identified with the crowd that appears subsequently in the Gospel. A marked emphasis on the group's largeness, and thus a linkage with the "crowd" motif, is conveyed by the repetition of the word πᾶς (*"all* Judea and *all* the Jerusalemites"). On the crowd in Mark as "the vague amorphous mass of men which is the object of evangelization," see E. Best, "The Role of the Disciples in Mark," *NTS* 23 (1977), 392.

[112] On the blindness of the disciples in Mark, see J. B. Tyson, "The Blindness of the Disciples in Mark," *JBL* 80 (1961), 261–268; K.-G. Reploh, *Markus, Lehrer der Gemeinde,* SBM 9 (Stuttgart: Katholisches Bibelwerk, 1969), pp. 83–86; Marcus, *Mystery,* pp. 99–103; F. J. Matera, *What Are They Saying About Mark?* (Mahwah, N.J.: Paulist Press, 1987), pp. 38–55.

[113] E.g.. the litter-bearers of the paralytic (2:4–5), the woman who touches Jesus' garment (5:27–28, 34), the Syrophoenician woman (7:24–30), the father of the epileptic boy (9:24), Bartimaeus (10:46–52), the woman who anoints Jesus (14:3–9), the centurion at the cross (15:39), and Joseph of Arimathea (15:43–46).

10:52) or of being with him (cf. 3:14),[114] not of going before him or of preparing his way.[115]

One possible way of treating the command in 1:3 to prepare the Lord's way is to view it as an instance in which Mark simply follows the tradition that has come down to him and by so doing creates some tension with the leading line of his own thought.[116] If, as we have argued, he himself is responsible for prefacing 1:2 to 1:3, it is probable that 1:2 reveals his predominant thought, namely, that John the Baptist, in his eschatological role as forerunner, prepares Jesus' way.

Yet the commands in 1:3 cannot simply be dismissed. Mark is not the sort of author to leave standing without obvious comment a tradition that is totally opposed to his own view.[117] He must, therefore, be able to understand the exhortations in 1:3 in a manner that is compatible with his theology, even if they do not represent the leading line of his own thought. A few exegetical possibilities for understanding 1:3bc in a Markan context follow.

1. Mark may understand the preparation of the Lord's way in a rather prosaic manner as the arrangements that people make for Jesus' ministry in the course of the Gospel narrative. For example, in 3:9 Mark has the disciples prepare a boat for Jesus, and in the two stories of miraculous feeding the Markan Jesus delegates to the disciples the tasks of finding out how much food is present, making the people sit down, and dividing the food that he has multiplied (6:38–39, 41; 8:6–7). In 11:1–6, he sends them to appropriate a colt for his triumphal entry. Later in the same pericope, in 11:8–10, the people of Jerusalem literally prepare the way for his entry, strewing garments and clothes in the road; they also precede Jesus (and

---

[114] On the theme of being with Jesus in Mark, see K. Stock, *Boten aus dem Mit-Ihm-Sein: Das Verhältnis zwischen Jesus und den Zwölf nach Markus*, AnBib 70 (Rome: Biblical Institute Press, 1975).

[115] In 3:14; 6:7 Jesus sends out (ἀποστέλλειν) the Twelve, but there is no suggestion that they are laying the groundwork for a missionary journey of his own. In 6:45 Jesus commands the disciples to get into the boat and *precede* him to the other side (this is altered in Matt. 8:23). In the continuation of the story, however (6:46–51), the disciples prove to be incapable of carrying out this command and are helpless until Jesus begins to go before them (6:48: ἤθελεν παρελθεῖν αὐτούς) and his presence is restored to them.

[116] See E. Best, "Mark's Preservation of the Tradition," in *The Interpretation of Mark*, ed. W. Telford, IRT 7 (Philadelphia: Fortress Press; London: SPCK, 1985), pp. 119–133.

[117] Contrast T. J. Weeden, according to whom Mark incorporates into his Gospel traditions with which he violently disagrees in order to battle against their proponents, his enemies within the Markan community ("The Heresy That Necessitated Mark's Gospel," in *Interpretation*, ed. Telford, pp. 64–77; idem, *Mark: Traditions in Conflict* [Philadelphia: Fortress Press, 1971]). The recognition that Mark's narrative is too unified to be construed in this way is one of the valuable contributions of recent literary studies of the Gospel; see Matera, *What Are They Saying*, pp. 75–92. On the other hand, the principle of literary unity can be carried too far; see chapter 7 n. 38 below.

follow him) in festal procession. In 14:15, 16 Jesus commands the disciples to prepare the Passover, and they do so; in both verses the verb is ἑτοιμάζειν, the identical verb that appears in 1:3. Finally, according to 15:41 a group of women serve Jesus during the entire course of his Galilean ministry. It is possible that in some of these cases the human actions depicted symbolically allude to actions that take place in the Markan community,[118] but if such nuances are present, they are subtle indeed.

2. Another possibility is that characters in the Gospel pave Jesus' way by making preparations for his death. In 14:8-9 Jesus emphasizes the importance of the action of the woman who has poured ointment over his head (it will be mentioned wherever the gospel is proclaimed) and says that she has anointed his body beforehand for his burial. The nuance of temporal precedence implied by προέλαβεν ("to do beforehand") ties this scene with the theme of preparation. Similarly, in 15:42-47 Joseph of Arimathea takes pains to arrange Jesus' body for burial, and the narrator notes that these arrangements occur on "the day of *preparation*" (παρασκευή; see the cognate verb κατασκευάσει in 1:2). This second exegetical possibility, which links the preparation of the way in 1:3 with the preparation for Jesus' death, has the advantage of being consonant with our conclusion above that John prepares Jesus' way by preceding him to martyrdom.

3. A third possibility appears when we reflect that Jesus' way does not end for Mark with his death and resurrection. Although no Markan instance of ὁδός specifically ties "the way" with Jesus' postresurrectional existence, the whole genius of Mark's Gospel is to overlay the story of Jesus' earthly ministry with the postresurrectional story of Mark's church, and this overlay implies that Jesus' "way" continues in the time of the church.[119] Mark 14:8 and 16:7, moreover, speak specifically of Jesus going before the disciples in the post-Easter period; the image of a road is thereby suggested. It is possible that Mark thinks that post-Easter disciples in some way prepare this road—for example, by not concerning themselves with what they are to say under interrogation, in order that the Holy Spirit may speak through them (13:11).

4. A final possibility is suggested by Mark 13:26, which speaks of a movement of Jesus at the parousia; at the eschaton everyone will see him *coming* on the clouds of heaven. Yet this coming, according to 13:10, must be preceded by the church's worldwide proclamation of the gospel. In a sense,

---

[118] Thus the disciples' preparation for the two feeding miracles and the Passover may suggest the celebration of the Eucharist in Mark's community; see Q. Quesnell, *The Mind of Mark: Interpretation and Method through the Exegesis of Mark 6:52*, AnBib 38 (Rome: Pontifical Biblical Institute, 1969), passim.

[119] On this overlaying technique in Mark, see Marcus, *Mystery*, pp. 69-71.

therefore, one might say that the church's preaching of the gospel fills up the eschatological measure and thus "prepares the way" for Jesus' return.[120] Perhaps all four of these exegetical possibilities can be combined. We may say that in Mark certain people heed John's exhortation and prepare the way for Jesus by aiding him in his earthly ministry, a ministry that ends in his death. By faithful obedience human beings also — in a very qualified sense — prepare the way for Jesus' continuing manifestation of himself in the post-Easter period, and for his return. It should be emphasized again, however, that none of this human preparation of Jesus' way carries for Mark the theological weight that Jesus' own creation of a way does. Jesus' coming is the advent of the βασιλεία τοῦ θεοῦ, the kingly power of God. Human beings do not create this end-time display of saving power or even in a true sense lay the groundwork for it, but merely enter into it. Crucial for Mark are the depiction of Jesus blazing a new trail into the cosmos and the conviction that this trail is the way of the Lord, the highway along which God himself moves as the invisible but powerfully present comforter of the afflicted, liberator of the captives, and enlightener of the blind.

Conclusions:
Mark 1:2–3 and the Markan Community

Mark's community, on the evidence of our findings in this chapter, is one that contains at least some readers who have a deep interest in and knowledge of the Old Testament.[121] Their scriptural study may not be as formalized as that of Qumran, where no assemblage of ten community members at any time of night or day took place unaccompanied by exegesis (1QS 6:6–7), but they still live in an atmosphere steeped in the scriptures, and they can be expected to fill in from those scriptures Mark's bare-bones descriptions of the ministries of John the Baptist and Jesus. They will know, for example, that Isaiah 40, a verse of which is quoted in Mark 1:3, is a *locus classicus* for the concept of gospel, and thus Mark can anticipate that they will be able to make the link between 1:1, where the word "gospel" occurs, and

---

[120] On the concept of the eschatological measure and its use in Mark, see R. Stuhlmann, "Beobachtungen und Überlegungen zu Markus 4.26–29," *NTS* 19 (1973), 153–162; idem, *Das eschatologische Mass im Neuen Testament*, FRLANT 132 (Göttingen: Vandenhoeck & Ruprecht, 1983); Marcus, *Mystery*, pp. 188–189, 192–194.

[121] Mark's community probably contains members with a variety of levels of acquaintance with and interest in the Old Testament. The consequent differences in their responses to Mark's Old Testament citations and allusions corresponds to the difference discussed by contemporary literary theorists between maximal and minimal readers. See, for example, the discussion of Fielding's differentiation between the "mere English reader" and "the classical reader" in W. Iser, *The Implied Reader: Patterns of Communication in Prose Fiction from Bunyan to Beckett* (Baltimore: Johns Hopkins University Press, 1974), pp. 32, 38.

1:2–3. He also can expect these biblically literate Christians to be aware of other themes associated with Isa. 40:3 in the larger Isaian context: the wilderness, the way of the Lord, the enlightening of the blind, the festal procession to Jerusalem. Aided by Mark's hint in 1:2a that the beginning of the gospel is "as it has been written by Isaiah the prophet," they will be able to understand these themes in their Isaian context when they come to prominence later in Mark's Gospel. If Mark's understated, terse, enigmatic narrative is "freighted with background,"[122] that background is in large measure supplied by the narratives and poetry of the Old Testament.

This does not necessarily mean that most of the members of Mark's community are Jews; the distancing (and inaccurate) statement in 7:3 that all Jews are scrupulous handwashers seems to rule out this possibility.[123] Some of them at least, however, have certainly imbibed from Jews or Jewish Christians a reverence for the holy writings, an awareness of the need to study them continually, and some Jewish traditions and methods of biblical interpretation. They seem to be aware, for example, of the Jewish stream of tradition that interprets Isa. 40:3 in an eschatological context and of the contextual association of this passage with the theme of the kingdom of God. They may have become aware of this trajectory of exegesis partly through the use made of Isaiah 40 in the events leading up to and including the Jewish Revolt of A.D. 66 and following, and Mark's own interpretation of the passage may in part be directed against this use: people are taken up into the forward momentum of Yahweh's wilderness way not by bearing arms against the Romans but by bearing the cross of Jesus.

It is indeed significant, then, that Mark chooses to open his work with a series of Old Testament citations. The gospel is "as it has been written in Isaiah the prophet," for Isaiah prophesies a new action of God, who will make his victorious way through the wilderness and lead his people back to the promised land in a saving act of holy war. Mark identifies this act with Jesus' way, his progress through the world, his movement up to death and resurrection in Jerusalem. That movement is repeated by the Markan community, a band of disciples that recognizes itself to be following in Jesus'

---

[122] Borrowing E. Auerbach's characterization of the Genesis narrative of the sacrifice of Isaac (*Mimesis: The Representation of Reality in Western Literature* [Princeton, N.J.: Princeton University Press, 1953], p. 12).

[123] On the related question of whether or not Mark himself is a Jew, see Marcus, *Mystery*, p. 83 nn. 31 and 33; idem, "The Jewish War and the *Sitz im Leben* of Mark," *JBL* (forthcoming), n. 111. As our study has already shown, Mark seems to have some knowledge of the Hebrew and/or Aramaic Old Testament and of Jewish exegetical traditions, and this knowledge points in the direction of a Jewish upbringing. The technical inaccuracy of "all the Jews" in 7:3 does not negate this conclusion, since this statement may be the result not of ignorance but of generalizing for a Gentile audience, as in *Ep. Arist.* 305; see Hengel, *Studies*, p. 148 n. 51; and R. A. Guelich, *Mark 1–8:26*, WBC 34A (Dallas: Word Books, 1989), p. 364.

footsteps (see 10:32), carrying his cross (see 8:34), and dying his death (see 13:12). It is of vital importance to this community—literally a matter of life and death—to know through its inspired exegesis that this suffering way of Jesus is also the victorious way of the Lord.

It would be no exaggeration, then, to say that "the way of Jesus/the way of the Lord" is not only the double theme of Mark's Gospel but also the controlling paradigm for his interpretation of the life of his community.[124] In the chapters that follow we will see how this theme is enriched in the rest of the Gospel by christological transformations of other motifs grounded in the Old Testament and in ancient Jewish biblical interpretation.

---

[124] See Kingsbury, who terms 1:2–3 the "epigraph" of Mark's story (*Christology,* pp. 56–57).

3

Mark 1:9-11

The Beloved, Well-pleasing Son

1:9a *And it came to pass in those days*
1:9b   that Jesus came from Nazareth in Galilee
1:9c   and was baptized in the Jordan by John.
1:10a And immediately on *coming up out of the water* he perceived
1:10b   *the heavens being torn open*
1:10c   and *the Spirit* like a dove *coming down upon him*
1:11a   and a voice from the heavens:
1:11b   *"You are my beloved Son,*
1:11c   *with you I have been pleased."*

Our discernment of a Deutero-Isaian background for Mark's prologue and indeed for the central theme of his entire Gospel (the way of the Lord), is confirmed by the next Markan passage containing clear biblical echoes, the account of Jesus' baptism in 1:9–11. That Mark is conscious of and wishes to highlight the scriptural background of this passage is indicated by the solemn biblical formula that introduces it, "And it came to pass in those days."[1] Much of the passage thus introduced has, as we shall see, a Deutero-Isaian background. Yet the identification formula "You are my Son" points toward a different biblical background in Psalm 2. In our passage, then, Mark diversifies his biblical palette in order to depict a Jesus whose coming is not only the fulfillment of the prophecies of Deutero-Isaiah but also the revelation of the Son of God.

---

[1] Cf., e.g., the Septuagint versions of Ex. 2:11; Judg. 18:31; and 1 Kgdms. 28:1 (cited by R. Pesch, *Das Markusevangelium*, HTKNT 2, 2 vols. [Freiburg: Herder, 1978], 1:88–89).

The Old Testament Texts

The main subject of the Markan baptismal pericope is the heavenly vision/ audition experienced by Jesus, which consists of his perception[2] of three divine actions: (1) the opening of the heavens, (2) the descent of the Spirit/dove, and (3) the sounding forth of the heavenly voice. Of the visionary events, the third is climactic because of its position at the end,[3] the change from sight to sound, and its role in interpreting the first two.[4] All three of these events have significant Old Testament background, as the accompanying chart shows.

The description of the open heaven has struck many as an allusion to Isa. 63:19 (LXX 64:1): "O that you would rend the heavens and come down!" (alt.) (לוא־קרעת שמים ירדת). Here Mark, in contrast to the Matthean and Lukan parallels, does not use the usual biblical verb for the opening of heaven, ἀνοίγειν ("to open"), but the unusual and rather harsh σχίζειν ("to rip"). The Hebrew counterpart to this verb, קרע, appears in the Masoretic Text of the theophany of Isa. 63:19, but Mark's verb σχίζειν does not appear in the Septuagint, which instead employs ἀνοίγειν. If Mark 1:10b, then, is dependent on a version of Isa. 63:19, that version is not the Septuagint but the Masoretic Text.[5]

R. Pesch has questioned such dependence, pointing out that *Joseph and Aseneth* 14:2 uses ἐσχίσθη ὁ οὐρανός in a description of a vision that bears no relation to Isa. 63:19.[6] Isaiah 63:19, however, is not the only verse from Isaiah 63 that has contacts with Mark 1:10. In a short but important article, I. Buse has enumerated other contacts between the two passages;[7] these can be seen in the chart of parallels. Isaiah 63:11 (MT) speaks of *bringing up from the sea* the shepherd of the flock; compare the Markan Jesus' ascent from the water. In the same verse, the Isaian author says that God *put his Holy Spirit in* this shepherd, and in the Septuagint of Isa. 63:14 we read

---

[2] That Jesus alone perceives the visionary events in Mark is indicated by the word εἶδεν ("he saw") in 1:10 and the fact that the voice in 1:11 addresses him alone; see Pesch, *Markusevangelium* 1:90, 92.

[3] See J. D. Kingsbury, *The Christology of Mark's Gospel* (Philadelphia: Fortress Press, 1983), p. 65.

[4] F. Lentzen-Deis rightly claims that the function of 1:11 is to interpret what has preceded it (*Die Taufe Jesu nach den Synoptikern*, Frankfurter Theologische Studien 4 [Frankfurt: Knecht, 1970], pp. 249–76), but he is incorrect in claiming that it interprets the baptism itself (1:9) rather than the visionary events that follow it (1:10); see A. Vögtle's review of Lentzen-Deis in *BZ* N.F. 17 (1973), 115–123.

[5] The *Isaiah Targum* uses a different verb from either the Masoretic Text or the Septuagint, the *aph'el* form of רכן ("to cause to sink").

[6] Pesch, *Markusevangelium* 1:90–91.

[7] I. Buse, "The Markan Account of the Baptism of Jesus and Isaiah LXIII," *JTS* n.s. 7 (1956), 74–75.

Mark 1:10 (alt.)	Isaiah 63:11 MT	Isaiah 63:14 LXX	Isaiah 63:19 MT
and immedi- ately coming up	where is he who brought up		
out of the water	from the sea (LXX: from the earth) the shepherd of his flock		
he saw the heavens ripping			O that you would rip the heavens
and the Spirit	where is he who put within him (LXX: in [εἰς] him)	a spirit from the Lord	
like a dove descending upon (εἰς) him	his Holy Spirit	descended	and descend

specifically of a *descent of the Spirit;* compare the Spirit's descent upon (εἰς) Jesus.[8] In most cases Mark's contacts are closest with the Masoretic Text; see 63:11 "from the sea" in contrast to the Septuagint's "from the land"; "within *him*" in contrast to the Septuagint's "within *them*"; 63:19 "*rip* the heavens" in contrast to the Septuagint's "*open* the heavens." In one case, however—the descent of the Spirit in 63:14—the contact is present only vis-à-vis the Septuagint.[9]

The words of the heavenly voice in Mark 1:11bc borrow the phrasing of Ps. 2:7 for the first part of the pronouncement "You are my son," as is indicated by the near identity with the Septuagint.[10] The slight difference

---

[8] In *koine* Greek εἰς can be equivalent to ἐπί (see BDF, §207 [1]; Pesch, *Markusevangelium* 1:91; Kingsbury, *Christology*, pp. 62–63). An allusion to Isa. 63:11 may be a factor in the choice of εἰς over ἐπί in Mark 1:10c (contrast the Matthean and Lukan parallels); it is unnecessary to bring in, as F. Hahn does (*Christologische Hoheitstitel: Ihre Geschichte im frühen Christentum*, FRLANT 83 [Göttingen: Vandenhoeck & Ruprecht, 1963], p. 342), "Hellenistic" conceptions of the Spirit uniting itself with Jesus.

[9] The Masoretic Text of this verse reads, "Like cattle that go down into the valley, the Spirit of the Lord gave them rest." The Septuagint has sundered the motif of descent from the cattle and connected it with the Spirit.

[10] As H.-J. Steichele points out, the predication formula "You are . . ." occurs frequently in the Old Testament, but it is linked with the title "Son of God" only in Ps. 2:7 (*Der leidende Sohn Gottes: Eine Untersuchung einiger alttestamentlicher Motive in der Christologie des Markusevangeliums*, Biblische Untersuchungen 14 [Regensburg: Pustet, 1980], p. 147). A derivation from Ps. 2:7 is supported by the Western reading of the Lukan parallel, Luke 3:22, which cites also the continuation of the psalm verse ("This day I have begotten you"; cf. Heb. 1:5),

in wording from the Septuagint (the Markan tradition moves "you are" to the beginning of the declaration) is probably insignificant.[11]

The word ἀγαπητός ("beloved") at the end of 1:11b, however, is not transparently from Ps. 2:7, though R. H. Gundry has pointed out that the (admittedly late) *Tg. Psalms* 2:7 imports the word "beloved" (חביב) into the divine acclamation: "You are beloved to me as a son to a father."[12] It might be claimed, moreover, that the special relationship indicated by the word "beloved" is already implied in the original psalm by the emphatic אני: "*I myself* have begotten you."[13] There are also, however, several other theories on the scriptural source of the word "beloved" in Mark 1:11b:

1. ἀγαπητός may be explained as an allusion to Isa. 42:1, "Behold my servant, . . . *my chosen one*" (בחירי MT; cf. LXX ὁ ἐκλεκτός μου).[14] As we shall see in a moment, Mark 1:11c seems to reflect the continuation of this verse. Although the Septuagint does not use ἀγαπητός in Isa. 42:1, it does use it in the parallel and related passages Isa. 41:8–9 and 44:2, and a comparison of the Markan/Matthean version of the transfiguration voice (Mark 9:7; Matt. 17:5) with the Lukan version (Luke 9:35) demonstrates the close linguistic relationship between ἀγαπητός and Luke's word ἐκλελεγμένος ("one who has been chosen"), which is a cognate of ἐκλεκτός. John 1:34 is relevant also, for here ἐκλεκτός is used in the Johannine version of the baptismal voice.[15] The strongest piece of evidence for an allusion to Isa.

---

and by patristic references to the baptism, which quote Ps. 2:7 alone; see B. Lindars, *New Testament Apologetic: The Doctrinal Significance of the Old Testament Quotations* (Philadelphia: Westminster Press, 1961), p. 140; P. G. Bretscher, "Exodus 4:22–23 and the Voice from Heaven," *JBL* 87 (1968), 301; F. J. Matera, *The Kingship of Jesus: Composition and Theology in Mark 15*, SBLDS 66 (Chico, Calif.: Scholars Press, 1982), p. 77.

[11] J. M. Robinson (*Das Geschichtsverständnis des Markus-Evangeliums*, ATANT 30 [Zurich: Zwingli Verlag, 1956], p. 23); R. H. Gundry (*The Use of the Old Testament in St. Matthew's Gospel*, NovTSup 18 [Leiden: E. J. Brill, 1967], p. 30 n. 2), and A. Vögtle ("Die sogenannte Taufperikope Mk 1, 9–11: Zur Problematik der Herkunft und des ursprünglichen Sinns," in *EKKNT: Vorarbeiten* 4 [Zurich: Benziger Verlag, 1972], p. 135) think that the switch is due to a desire to identify *Jesus* as the one to whom the declaration of Ps. 2:7 applies: "*You*, and not another, are my son." Steichele, however, rightly denies this, comparing Mark 8:29 σὺ εἶ ὁ Χριστός (*Leidende Sohn*, pp. 136–137 n. 104); here the emphasis is on Χριστός, in spite of its placement at the end of the identification.

[12] Gundry, *Use*, pp. 30–31; contra B. D. Chilton, who asserts that ἀγαπητός corresponds best to יחיד, not to חביב, in Hebrew and Aramaic (*A Galilean Rabbi and His Bible: Jesus' Own Interpretation of Isaiah* [London: SPCK, 1984], p. 130). As Gundry points out, although ἀγαπητός is sometimes used in the Septuagint to render יחיד ("single, sole"), this is not a strictly accurate rendering; יחיד is more accurately rendered in other Septuagint passages with μονογενής.

[13] See H.-J. Kraus, *Psalmen*, BKAT 15, 2 vols. (Neukirchen-Vluyn: Neukirchener Verlag, 1960), 1:11.

[14] See C. R. Kazmierski, *Jesus, the Son of God: A Study of the Markan Tradition and Its Redaction by the Evangelist*, FB 33 (Würzburg: Echter Verlag, 1979), pp. 48–53.

[15] On ἐκλεκτός as the original reading in John 1:34, see R. E. Brown, *The Gospel According to John*, AB 29, 29A, 2 vols. (Garden City, N.Y.: Doubleday & Co., 1966, 1970), 1:57.

42:1, however, is that the version of this verse cited in Matt. 12:18 speaks
of "my beloved one," using precisely the word ἀγαπητός.

2. The word may recall the Aqedah narrative, the story of Abraham's
aborted sacrifice of Isaac, in which God and the angel refer to Isaac as
Abraham's beloved son (Gen. 22:2, 12, 16 LXX: τὸν υἱόν σου τὸν ἀγαπητόν/τοῦ
υἱοῦ σου τοῦ ἀγαπητοῦ).[16]

3. ἀγαπητός may reflect πρωτότοκος ("firstborn") in Ex. 4:22–23, "Israel
is my firstborn son."[17]

Of these theories, the last may be quickly dismissed, since even its
originator does not claim that it explains the *Markan* form of the baptismal
voice, only its putative original form, which he finds reflected above all in
2 Peter 1:17.[18] Of the remaining three Old Testament backgrounds, Isa. 42:1
has the best claim to be the source for Mark's ἀγαπητός. Admittedly, the
passages from Genesis 22 are closest in word choice and word order to
Mark's phrase "my beloved son," but there is no second-person address here,
as there is in Ps. 2:7, and the rest of Mark's Gospel shows little trace of
Aqedah theology. The echo of the Aqedah story in Mark 1:11, therefore, is
very faint if present at all. The link between Ps. 2:7 and the word "beloved,"
moreover, is tenuous; the strongest evidence for it, the introduction of this
word into the Targum, probably reflects a later rabbinic attempt to weaken
the force of the original, perhaps in view of Christian exploitation of the
verse.[19] The best alternative seems to be to see ἀγαπητός as a reflection
of Isa. 42:1 that has been interpolated into the text of Ps. 2:7, especially
since the continuation of the Isaian verse is cited in Mark 1:11c ("in whom
I have been pleased"). The main objection to this alternative is the absence
of ἀγαπητός from all versions of Isa. 42:1 except Matt. 12:18, where the citation of Isa. 42:1, it is asserted, may reflect the baptismal voice rather than
the other way around.[20] The close linguistic relationship between ἐκλεκτός/
ἐκλελεγμένος and ἀγαπητός, however, weakens the force of this argument,
and even if it is true, Matt. 12:18 at least reveals that *Matthew* sees a link
between ἀγαπητός in the baptismal voice and Isa. 42:1. The primary

---

[16] See G. Vermes, *Scripture and Tradition in Judaism: Haggadic Studies*, SPB 4 (Leiden:
E. J. Brill, 1961), pp. 222–223; Kazmierski, *Son of God*, pp. 53–56.
[17] Bretscher, "Exodus 4:22–23," pp. 301–311.
[18] Since Ex. 4:22 LXX differs from Mark 1:11b both in grammatical structure (third-person
identification rather than second-person address, lack of definite article) and in the adjective
applied to the "son" (πρωτότοκος, "firstborn," rather than ἀγαπητός, "beloved"), it is difficult
to see it as significant background for the *Markan* version of the pronouncement. Indeed,
Bretscher himself acknowledges that the σὺ εἶ ("you are") of Mark 1:11 moves the allusion
away from Ex. 4:22 and toward Ps. 2:7.
[19] See Kazmierski, *Son of God*, p. 40.
[20] See Steichele, *Leidende Sohn*, pp. 128–133.

background of ἀγαπητός, therefore, is probably Isa. 42:1, though there is perhaps a secondary reference to Genesis 22 as well. The final clause of the heavenly voice, "in you I have been pleased," probably reflects the oracle in Isa. 42:1: "Israel my chosen one, my soul has accepted him" (alt.); the divine speaker goes on to promise that he will put his Spirit upon this chosen figure (cf. Mark 1:10).[21] Matthew 12:18 renders Isa. 42:1 ὁ ἀγαπητός μου εἰς ὃν εὐδόκησεν ἡ ψυχή μου, a locution that is strikingly similar to the phrasing of the baptismal voice. Though Matthew's verb εὐδόκησεν disagrees with that of the Septuagint in this passage (προσεδέξατο), it agrees with that used by Theodotion and Symmachus.[22]

This background in Deutero-Isaiah is confirmed by the evidence of the *Isaiah Targum*, which, as B. D. Chilton has pointed out, contains passages that are strikingly similar to Mark 1:10-11 in form and content:[23]

> *Tg. Isa.* 41:8-9:   You, Israel my servant, Jacob in whom I have been
>   pleased with you. . . . You are my servant, I have
>   been pleased with you and I will not cast you off.
> *Tg. Isa.* 42:1:   Behold my servant, . . . my chosen in whom my
>   Memra has been pleased; I will put my Holy Spirit
>   upon him.
> *Tg. Isa.* 43:10:   . . . my servant the Messiah in whom I have been
>   pleased with him.

As Chilton notes, these passages are linked with Mark 1:9-11 in its Markan context by (1) the identification of the servant as the Messiah (*Tg. Isa.* 43:10); (2) the use of the precise phrase "I have been pleased" (אתרעיתי) in (3) a solemn second-person address (*Tg. Isa.* 41:8-9); we may add (4) the reference to the impartation of the Spirit. The divine voice in Mark 1:11bc, then, is a mixture of Ps. 2:7 and Isa. 42:1,[24] with the influence of Ps. 2:7 being predominant in 1:11b and the influence of Isa. 42:1 being predominant in 1:11c.

---

[21] The advent of the Spirit in Mark, then, reflects not only Isaiah 63 but also Isaiah 42.

[22] Kazmierski, *Son of God*, p. 40. Steichele, in opposing an allusion to Isa. 42:1 (*Leidende Sohn*, pp. 131–135), argues that εὐδοκεῖν occurs frequently in the Old Testament, that its use in 2 Kingdoms 22:20 and Isa. 62:4 is a closer parallel to Mark 1:11 than its use in Isa. 42:1, and that the impartation of the Spirit is also a common biblical motif. Mark, therefore, is, according to him, simply employing "biblical language" here; he does not have a specific passage in mind. These observations are valid if each motif is taken singly, but the *combination* of εὐδοκεῖν with the impartation of the Spirit and the ἀγαπητός motif points to Isa. 42:1.

[23] Chilton, *Galilean Rabbi*, pp. 128–130; translations slightly altered from this work and from Chilton's *The Isaiah Targum: Introduction, Translation, Apparatus and Notes*, The Aramaic Bible 11 (Wilmington, Del.: Michael Glazier, 1987).

[24] This opinion is shared by E. Klostermann, K. Stendahl, O. Kuss, and J. M. Robinson; see the references in Steichele, *Leidende Sohn*, p. 122 n. 46; see also H. C. Kee, "The Function of Scriptural Quotations and Allusions in Mark 11–16," in *Jesus und Paulus: Festschrift für Werner Georg Kümmel zum 70. Geburtstag*, ed. E. E. Ellis and E. Grässer (Göttingen: Vandenhoeck & Ruprecht, 1975), p. 177.

Are any of these Old Testament allusions the result of Mark's own editorial activity? It is probable that the allusion to Ps. 2:7 in 1:11b, "you are my son," belongs in this category. In the previous chapter we have argued that conflation of two or more biblical texts is a typical Markan strategy,[25] and it is just such a conflation that results from the introduction of Ps. 2:7 into the context otherwise provided by Isa. 42:1. As the accompanying chart illustrates, moreover, John 1:32–34 contains a version of the baptismal tradition whose eclectic combination of similarities to and differences from the Synoptic versions suggests that John reflects an independent form of the tradition,[26] a form that was known to Matthew and Luke, though they also knew Mark's edited version of it.[27] In this form of the tradition, Jesus was probably spoken of in the third person ("this is") rather than being addressed in the second person ("you are").[28] In addition, he was probably referred to as God's "chosen one"[29] rather than as his "son."[30] Thus, the wording of the voice corresponded closely to Isa. 42:1. Mark's editorial work, according to this reconstruction, would include the restriction of the vision to Jesus, which would necessitate the change to a second-person address, and the substitution of the title "beloved son" for "chosen one of God," which would bring Ps. 2:7 into the picture. The substitution of "beloved son" could be plausibly explained as reflecting the importance of the title "Son of God" in Mark's overall story,[31] and the restriction of the vision to Jesus as reflecting

---

[25] On Mark's technique of conflation, see chapter 2 n. 13 above. Steichele mentions, but rightly discounts, the scant evidence that Ps. 2:7 and Isa. 42:1 were already linked in Judaism (*Leidende Sohn*, p. 125). In *Midr. Psalms* 2, par. 9 (14b), they are merely part of a list of scriptural texts used to show that Israel is God's son.

[26] John has probably edited this tradition, however; such features as the "remaining" of the Spirit on Jesus and the highlighting of the role of the Baptist reflect Johannine themes (see Brown, *John* 1:66).

[27] See Brown, *John* 1:65–66. The existence of variant traditions of Jesus' baptism within one community is not intrinsically unlikely, given the importance of baptism in the life of the early church. Though the exact relation between the accounts of Jesus' baptism and the practice of baptism in the early church is obscure—and it is unlikely that the Christian practice gave rise to the accounts (see R. Bultmann, *History of the Synoptic Tradition* [New York: Harper & Row, 1963], pp. 252–253; Vögtle, "Taufperikope," pp. 127–130)—it is probable that early Christians made some link between the two baptisms, if only because of the similarity in practice and the common element of the impartation of the Spirit; see Bultmann, *History*, p. 250.

[28] Note the agreement on this point between Matthew and John against Mark.

[29] On "chosen one" as the original text of John 1:34, see Brown, *John* 1:57.

[30] There is no discernible motive for John, if he is aware of it, to change the identification of Jesus from "Son of God" to "the chosen one of God," since the title "Son of God" (or "the Son"), which occurs approximately thirty times, is far more important in his Gospel than "the chosen one of God," which occurs only here.

[31] Aside from its possible use in the superscription to the Gospel (see B. M. Metzger, *A Textual Commentary on the Greek New Testament* [London and New York: United Bible Societies, 1971], p. 73) and its use by the demons in 3:11 (cf. 1:24), the title appears in 14:61–64, where

Mark 1:10	Matthew 3:16	Luke 3:21–22a	John 1:32–34
(and was baptized . . .)	and when Jesus was baptized	and Jesus having been baptized, and while he was praying	
and immediately coming up from the water	immediately he came up from the water		
he saw the heavens ripping	and behold opened were the heavens	opened was the heaven	I have seen
and the Spirit like a dove descending upon (εἰς) him	and he saw the Spirit of God descending like a dove upon (ἐπί) him	and the Holy Spirit descended in bodily form like a dove upon (ἐπί) him	the Spirit descending like a dove from heaven and it remained upon (ἐπί) him

Mark 1:11	Matthew 3:17	Luke 3:22b	John 1:34
and a voice from the heavens:	and behold, a voice from the heavens, saying:	and there was a voice from heaven:	and I have seen and borne witness that
"You are my beloved son, in you I have been pleased"	"This is my beloved son, in whom I have been pleased"	"My son you are, in you I have been pleased"	this is the chosen of God

Note: Scripture quotations are RSV (alt.).

the messianic secret motif: until Jesus' death on the cross, no human being may know his true identity as Son of God.[32]

---

it provides the basis for Jesus' condemnation, and in three revelatory scenes, "the pillars on which [Mark's] Gospel rests" (A. M. Ambrozic, *The Hidden Kingdom: A Redaction-Critical Study of the References to the Kingdom of God in Mark's Gospel*, CBQMS 2 [Washington, D.C.: Catholic Biblical Association, 1972], p. 23), which are strategically placed at the beginning, middle, and end of the Gospel (1:11; 9:7; 15:39). J. Zmijewski also reaches the conclusion that "my son" in 1:11 represents Markan redaction ("Die Sohn-Gottes-Prädikation im Markusevangelium: Zur Frage einer eigenständigen markinischen Titelchristologie," *StudNTUmwelt* 12 [1987], 21–28), though some of his arguments differ from those presented here.

[32] See H. Greeven, "περιστερά," *TDNT* (1968; orig. 1959), 6:68 n. 57. On this "salvation-historical" interpretation of the messianic secret in Mark, see the description of the views of W. Wrede, E. Percy, G. Strecker, H. Conzelmann, and E. Schweizer in C. Tuckett, ed., *The Messianic Secret*, IRT 1 (Philadelphia: Fortress Press, 1983), pp. 15–17; see also D. Senior, *The Passion of Jesus in the Gospel of Mark*, Passion Series 2 (Wilmington, Del.: Michael Glazier, 1984), p. 144.

This seems to be a plausible scenario, but it is even more important to observe the crucial role played by *both* Deutero-Isaiah *and* Psalm 2 in the present Markan form of the baptismal narrative. Most of the biblical background for the passage, we have seen, is to be found in Deutero-Isaiah, but a significant, indeed climactic, position is granted to the quotation of Ps. 2:7, which begins the words of the heavenly voice.

Mark 1:10:
Jesus' Baptism as Apocalyptic Theophany

Three features of Mark 1:10 tie the verse with Isaiah 63, where we read: "Where is he who *brought* [him] *up from the sea*? . . . Where is he who *put within him* his *Holy Spirit*? . . . O that you would *rip the heavens!*" (vv. 11, 19, alt.). These features are the ripping of the heavenly fabric, Jesus' ascent from the water, and the use of εἰς ("in" or "within"). As we have seen in the previous chapter, Mark is strongly conscious of the Isaian background of "the beginning of the gospel of Jesus Christ" (1:1–3). Although we have uncovered no evidence that he himself is responsible for the reminiscences of Isaiah 63 in 1:10, it is quite probable that he has them in mind as he retells the story of Jesus' baptism.

This being the case, the Markan account of the baptism of Jesus should probably be viewed as a description of an eschatological *theophany,* like the pertinent passages from Isaiah 63. As E. Lohmeyer points out, the violent tearing of the heavens, emphasized by the Markan verb σχίζειν, points to a background in apocalyptic dualism:

> [The tearing of the heavens] is rooted in the view that heaven and earth are shut up against each other, so that God can no longer associate with his people in an unmediated manner, or they with him, as once happened. It is therefore a sign of unusual grace when the heaven opens. This occurs in a miracle that embraces the entirety of the people or of the world; not accidentally, the motif is found almost solely in apocalypses.[33]

Other apocalyptic features of the passage, according to Lohmeyer, are the advent of the Spirit, the ὡς language ("*as* a dove"; cf. Rev. 5:6), and the voice from heaven (cf. Rev. 14:3). F. Hahn, moreover, notes that the opening of the heavens and the voice from heaven are combined in the prototypical apocalypse (Rev. 4:1).[34]

---

[33] E. Lohmeyer, *Das Evangelium des Markus,* MeyerK, 11th ed. (Göttingen: Vandenhoeck & Ruprecht, 1951), pp. 21–22; see also W. Lane, *The Gospel of Mark,* NICNT (Grand Rapids: Wm. B. Eerdmans Publishing Co., 1974), p. 55.

[34] Hahn, *Hoheitstitel,* pp. 340–341; on the apocalyptic features of the passage, see also Steichele, *Leidende Sohn,* pp. 113, 119.

Lohmeyer's apocalyptic interpretation of the Markan baptismal account is borne out by a comparison with Mark 15:38–39, a passage whose vocabulary and context are strikingly similar to those of 1:10–11:

> And the curtain of the Temple was ripped (ἐσχίσθη) into two from top to bottom. The centurion standing opposite him, seeing (ἰδών) that he gave up the spirit (ἐξέπνευσεν) in this manner, said, "Truly this man was the Son of God!"

The common features include employment of the verbs σχίζειν (in the passive voice)[35] and ἰδεῖν ("to see"), reference to spirit (ἐξέπνευσεν/πνεῦμα), and use of an identification formula ("this man was"/"you are") that points to Jesus' divine sonship. Both passages, moreover, speak of a descending divine action (the *descent* of the Spirit, the tearing of the Temple veil *from top to bottom*). In accordance with this movement from above and other features of its context, Mark 15:38–39 can be termed an apocalyptic theophany, and it is probable that the structurally similar Markan baptismal account should be described in the same terms.[36]

What is described in Mark 1:9–11, therefore, is not just a red-letter event in the biography of Jesus, a vision that he receives along with his personal endowment by the Spirit, but rather the eschatological occurrence of the Spirit's advent.[37] In spite of the word εἶδεν, the account of Jesus' baptism belongs not primarily to the category of personal vision[38] but to that of apocalyptic occurrence, of theophany.[39]

But why is perception of the theophany restricted to Jesus if Mark 1:9–11 is not simply a personal vision experienced by him? The answer is related to the way in which Mark's apocalyptic eschatology is qualified by the motif of the messianic secret or, more accurately stated, by the motif of Jesus' suppression of publicity about his divine sonship. Aside from 1:11 and the

---

[35] Mark 1:10 and 15:38 are the only occurrences of σχίζειν in the Gospel.

[36] Mark 15:38–39 is embedded in a pericope (15:33–39) whose apocalyptic features include the division into hours, the darkening of the earth, the call for Elijah, and the tearing of the Temple veil so that the glory of God begins to flood the earth; see J. Marcus, *The Mystery of the Kingdom of God*, SBLDS 90 (Atlanta: Scholars Press, 1986), pp. 148–149. On 1:9–11 and 15:33–39 as related theophanies, see Senior, *Passion*, p. 146.

[37] See Lohmeyer, *Evangelium*, p. 23.

[38] See Bultmann, *History*, p. 248.

[39] See Kingsbury, *Christology*, p. 61; Vögtle, "Taufperikope," pp. 135–136. The theophany designation is opposed by Lentzen-Deis (*Taufe*, pp. 100–102) because the effects of the Spirit's advent in Mark 1:9–11 are so different from those usually described in Old Testament theophanies (mountains melting, rivers drying up, etc.). The different kinds of effects, however, are due to the messianic secret motif, as we shall see, not to the fact that Mark 1:9–11 is not a theophany. As has been shown by Vögtle in his review of Lentzen-Deis and by Steichele (*Leidende Sohn*, p. 150 n. 159), Lentzen-Deis's own characterization of Mark 1:9–11 as an "interpretative vision" fails to convince.

textually questionable 1:1, the title "Son of God" occurs four times in Mark's Gospel: 3:11; 5:7; 9:7; 15:39; cf. 1:24 ("holy one of God") and 14:61 ("the Son of the Blessed"). In three of these cases (1:25; 3:12; 9:9), the revelation of Jesus' divine sonship is followed by an injunction to silence. In the other three cases (5:7; 14:61; 15:39), the injunction is absent, but the motif of the "messianic secret" is not thereby compromised. The absence of the injunction after 5:7 is probably to be explained by the fact that the exorcism does not take place in the presence of a crowd, but in the relative seclusion of a mountainous region.[40] Its absence after 14:61 and 15:39 is more significant: with Jesus' passion and death, the time for maintaining the secrecy of his identity is at an end.[41] Not by any exorcism or miracle that he has performed, nor by his powerful preaching and teaching, but precisely *by his suffering and death,* is Jesus revealed as the Son of God.

In the light of this review, it may be claimed that the restriction to Jesus of perception of the heavenly voice and of the events associated with it functions in a manner analogous to the commands to silence elsewhere in the Gospel. Until Jesus' passion, death, and resurrection, no one can understand in exactly what way he is the Son of God; therefore, knowledge of this sonship is hidden from the public and granted only to God, Jesus, and the demons, who have in common a supernatural insight that transcends that granted to human beings.[42]

Contrary to Lentzen-Deis, therefore, it is correct to term Mark 1:9–11 a theophany and to see its model in the theophany described in Isaiah 63. The splitting of the heavens at Jesus' baptism is a sign that God is about to answer the ancient prayer that he "rend the heavens and come down" (Isa. 63:19), that he is about to fulfill his prophetic promises and set the end-time events in motion. He will do this by putting his own Spirit, the life-giving power of the new age, within the world by imparting it to "the shepherd of his flock" (cf. Isa. 63:11). As Lohmeyer puts it, the baptism is an eschatological miracle that embraces the entirety of the people and the world — although, we may add, most of those thereby embraced *do not know it yet.* By the references to Isaiah 63 in Mark 1:9–11, Mark's community is let in on the vital secret that in Jesus' baptism the eschatological theophany foretold in the Old Testament has occurred.[43]

---

[40] The crowd enters only in 5:14. True, there are pig herders in the *vicinity* when the exorcism takes place (5:14), but it is not clear that they hear the words of demonic confession in 5:7, only that they see the stampede of the pigs in 5:13. See Kingsbury, *Christology,* p. 86.

[41] See the literature cited in this chapter in n. 32.

[42] Cf. 9:7, in which the disciples hear the divine voice identifying Jesus as the Son of God, but fail to understand it; see Kingsbury, *Christology,* pp. 99–100.

[43] Kazmierski claims that "in his re-telling of the [baptismal] story Mark has stressed not its apocalyptic but its Christological significance" (*Son of God,* p. 30). This is certainly a false dichotomy from the Markan point of view; see chapter 2, pp. 40–41 above.

Trajectories in the Interpretation of Psalm 2

The impression of Mark's hearers that Jesus' baptism was an eschatological theophany would have been reinforced when they heard 1:11b, "You are my Son," words that, as we have seen, were probably introduced into the baptismal context by Mark himself. Psalm 2, the passage from which this pronouncement is taken, was consistently understood in the Judaism of Jesus' and of later times, and in early Christianity, as a prophecy of eschatological events: the rebellion of Yahweh's enemies against him and his Messiah, and the latter's decisive defeat of those enemies.

In order to justify this assertion, we will look at some relevant trajectories in the interpretation of Psalm 2 within the Old Testament itself, later Judaism, and early Christianity.

THE ESCHATOLOGICAL-MESSIANIC INTERPRETATION

Although the original version of Psalm 2 understands Yahweh's "anointed one" to be the reigning Davidic monarch, the security of whose realm is assured against all challengers, already by the time of its incorporation into the Psalter it is probably being reinterpreted in an eschatological sense. The Davidic monarch becomes the future scion of the Davidic line, a figure later identified, because of v. 7, by means of the term "Messiah." The attacks of the surrounding kings become the long-awaited eschatological battle in which Yahweh's reign over the world is definitively established for all time.[44]

This same eschatological/messianic interpretation is developed further in intertestamental Judaism. As E. Lövestam notes, this interpretation has two foci: the rebellion against God and his anointed one described in vv. 1–2 and the decisive defeat of that rebellion described in vv. 7–9.[45] Both foci are evident in the use made of Psalm 2 in *Psalms of Solomon* 17:21–46. Psalm 2 is one of the main elements in the tapestry of biblical allusions that are used here to portray the victory of "the Lord's Messiah"; see, for example, vv. 21–25:

> See, Lord, and raise up for them their king,
>   the son of David, to rule over your servant Israel
>   in the time known to you, O God.

---

[44] See H. Klein, "Zur Auslegung von Psalm 2: Ein Beitrag zum Thema: Gewalt und Gewaltlosigkeit," *TBei* 10 (1979), 68. Klein's assumption of the psalm's eschatological reinterpretation by the time of its inclusion in the Psalter is based on the destruction of Judean sovereignty that had intervened. See also A. A. Anderson, who points out that one of the reasons that royal psalms survived in the postexilic period was that they could be reinterpreted in a messianic sense (*Psalms*, NCB, 2 vols. [London: Oliphants, 1972], 1:40).

[45] E. Lövestam, *Son and Saviour: A Study of Acts 13,32–37*, ConNT 18 (Lund: Gleerup, 1961), pp. 22–23.

Undergird him with the strength to destroy the unrighteous rulers,
   to purge Jerusalem from gentiles
   who trample her to destruction;
   in wisdom and in righteousness to drive out
   the sinners from the inheritance;
to smash the arrogance of sinners
   like a potter's jar;
To shatter all their substance with an iron rod;
   to destroy the unlawful nations with the word of his mouth;
At his warning the nations will flee from his presence;
   and he will condemn sinners by the thoughts of their hearts.[46]

These verses seem to be a commentary on Psalm 2 and Isaiah 11;[47] the elements that specifically echo the psalm are those that speak of the destruction of the foreign oppressors (see Ps. 2:8–9) by a Davidic king whose royal power flows from his relationship with God (see Ps. 2:6–7). The passage also implies the sinful rebellion which precipitates that victory (trampling Jerusalem to destruction, the arrogance of sinners, unlawful nations; see Ps. 2:1–3).

An eschatological interpretation of the psalm is given also in 4QFlor 1:18–2:3, where its first two verses are interpreted as referring to "the end of days" (אחרית הימים).[48] The absence of a messianic component in this text is not necessarily significant,[49] because the text is fragmentary and may well have gone on to portray a messianic figure.

The Jewish interpretation of Psalm 2 in an eschatological context continues into the rabbinic period. The major outlines of this interpretation are well summarized by M. A. Signer. As background for his discussion of Rashi's interpretation of the psalm, Signer first describes the tradition of interpretation available to Rashi:

> The major focus of the rabbis was on the first four verses within an apocalyptic or redemptive context: the war of God and Magog, the victory of Israel over the wicked idolators, or Israel's triumph at the sea over Pharaoh. . . . Rashi had before him a tradition of interpretation which

---

[46] Translation by R. B. Wright in *OTP*. Unless otherwise noted, all translations of Old Testament pseudepigrapha are from this work.

[47] S-B 3:675; M. A. Chevallier, *L'Esprit et le Messie dans le bas-Judaïsme et le Nouveau Testament* (Paris: Presses universitaires de France, 1958), pp. 5, 10–17; Klein, "Auslegung," p. 68.

[48] Steichele, *Leidende Sohn*, p. 145.

[49] Contra J. A. Soggin, "Zum zweiten Psalm," in *Wort-Gebot-Glaube: Walter Eichrodt zum 80. Geburtstag*, ed. H. J. Stoebe, ATANT 59 (Zurich: Zwingli Verlag, 1970), p. 205; with Steichele, *Leidende Sohn*, p. 145.

held David as the author of the Psalm, a dialogue between God and the
wicked, and an apocalyptic tradition of Israel triumphant.[50]

Although v. 7 of the psalm was not the major focus of rabbinical interest,[51]
it was still so commonly assumed that this verse referred to the Messiah
that Rashi was obliged to refute this identification as an act of defensive
exegesis against Christian use of the term "Son of God."[52]

Jewish sources from the biblical period on, therefore, overwhelmingly
interpret Psalm 2 as a reference to an eschatological victory by God, a victory
sometimes won through the instrumentality of the Messiah. The consistency
of this eschatological interpretation in the extant Jewish sources makes it
likely that representatives of the "fourth philosophy"—that is, the religiously
inspired activists who supported the Jewish Revolt of A.D. 66–74—also put
to good use the psalm's prophecy that the anointed one would dash into
pieces the hostile foreign nations arrayed against him.[53]

This eschatological and messianic interpretation continues, though with
a christological sharpening, in the New Testament. The most commonly
cited verse of the psalm is v. 7 (in contrast to rabbinic interpretation, which
concentrates on vv. 1–4). Outside of the baptismal scenes, all the references
to this verse in the New Testament relate it to the resurrection,[54] an event
that belongs, of course, to the eschatological order. As in the Jewish sources
referred to above, the other focus of interpretation is the eschatological
Völkerkampf described in Ps. 2:1–2. Examples of this usage include the clear

---

[50] M. A. Signer, "King/Messiah: Rashi's Exegesis of Psalm 2," *Prooftexts* 3 (1983), 274; on
rabbinic interpretations, see also S-B 3:675–677; P. Volz, *Die Eschatologie der jüdische Gemeinde
im neutestamentlichen Zeitalter nach den Quellen der rabbinischen, apokalyptischen und
apokryphen Literatur,* 2nd ed. (Tübingen: J. C. B. Mohr [Paul Siebeck], 1934), p. 176.

[51] Signer remarks, "Classical rabbinic literature never explained Psalm 2 as a continuous
narrative in which all verses related to one another" ("King/Messiah," p. 274); v. 7, in other
words, was not usually related to vv. 1–4, which were the main focus of interest. This observation might at first seem to damage our thesis that the quotation of v. 7 in Mark 1:11 brings
into view the entire psalm. A Jewish hesitancy to refer to Ps. 2:7, however, is understandable
in light of the Christian exploitation of the title "Son of God" in the verse and probably goes
a long way toward explaining the lack of a unitary rabbinic interpretation of the psalm.

[52] Signer quotes Rashi: "Our rabbis expounded the subject of this psalm as king/messiah.
However, according to its context in the narrative of Scripture and as an answer to the Christians it would seem correct to explain it about David himself" ("King/Messiah," p. 274).

[53] See the references to Psalm 2 in the studies of the revolt by M. Hengel (*The Zealots:
Investigations into the Jewish Freedom Movement in the Period from Herod I Until 70 A.D.* [Edin-
burgh: T. & T. Clark, 1989], pp. 240, 246) and R. A. Horsley and J. S. Hanson (*Bandits, Prophets,
and Messiahs: Popular Movements at the Time of Jesus,* New Voices in Biblical Studies [San
Francisco: Harper & Row, 1985], p. 133 n. 15).

[54] J. A. Fitzmyer ("'Now This Melchizedek . . .' [Heb 7:1]," in *Essays on the Semitic Background
of the New Testament,* Sources for Biblical Study 5 [Missoula, Mont.: Scholars Press, 1974],
p. 224), citing J. Dupont and E. Lövestam, who in their turn cite Acts 13:33, 36; Heb. 1:5; and 5:5.

use of these verses in Acts 4:25–26[55] and Rev. 19:19, and the allusions in Rev. 11:15 ("the kingdom of this world" versus the kingdom of "the Lord and his anointed one"); 12:10 ("the kingdom of our Lord and the authority of his anointed one"); and 17:18 ("the kings of the earth").[56]

THE COSMIC BATTLE

Another feature of Psalm 2 and of its history of interpretation into the intertestamental period also suggests that it should be understood in a context of eschatology, and specifically of apocalyptic eschatology. This is the great stress laid on the opposition to God and to his Messiah, an opposition that is sometimes interpreted as transcending the realm of the merely human.

"Why do the nations rage?"—already in the original psalm, the revolt of the hostile kings and Yahweh's response to it are painted with the vivid mythological colors of the primeval battle against the surging forces of chaos.[57] The rebellious nations are the political expression of these demonic forces, the memory of whose losing battle against God was probably preserved in the liturgy of the Israelite autumn festival.[58] The rhetorical question that opens the psalm expresses the central dilemma that would so preoccupy later apocalyptic thinkers: How could the anti-God forces, which were supposed to have been defeated by God at the creation, dare to rear their ugly heads again and challenge God's sovereignty?[59]

The psalm's concentration on the gravity of the opposition to God and his Messiah is continued in later Jewish exegesis. As we have noted above, the first few verses of the psalm are one of the foci of that exegesis, and these verses, as Lövestam points out, are associated with the idea of opposition, rebellion, and hostile attack upon God, the Messiah, and Israel.[60] Developing hints already present in the original psalm, Jewish exegesis sometimes portrays this opposition as one that transcends the realm of the merely human. The mention of Belial in 4QFlor 2:2, for example, suggests

---

[55] See Soggin, "Zweiten Psalm," in *Wort-Gebot-Glaube*, ed. Stoebe, p. 206.

[56] See H. B. Swete, *The Apocalypse of St. John: The Greek Text with Introduction Notes and Indices* (London: Macmillan Publishers, 1906), pp. 139, 152, 253.

[57] See H.-J. Kraus, *Die Königsherrschaft Gottes im Alten Testament*, BHT 13 (Tübingen: J. C. B. Mohr [Paul Siebeck], 1951), p. 68; V. Sasson, "The Language of Rebellion in Psalm 2 and in the Plaster Texts from Deir 'Alla," *AUSS* 24 (1986), 147–154.

[58] J. Gray, *The Biblical Doctrine of the Reign of God* (Edinburgh: T. & T. Clark, 1979), pp. 79–80. Gray mounts a good case for the existence of the autumn festival on pp. 7–38 of the same book. Skepticism about the festival is expressed by Kraus (*Königsherrschaft*, passim; *Psalmen* 1:201–205), but Kraus is unable to explain satisfactorily the enthronement motif and vivid language in Psalm 47.

[59] See Soggin, "Zweiten Psalm," in *Wort-Gebot-Glaube*, ed. Stoebe, p. 201.

[60] Lövestam, *Son and Saviour*, pp. 22–23.

that the citation of Ps. 2:1–2 in 4QFlor 1:18–19 is understood as a reference
to the demonic power that stands behind the hostile nations.[61] The rabbinic
interpretation of these verses as referring to the wars of Gog and Magog
also points to the opposition's superhuman dimension.[62] This demonic interpretation of Ps. 2:1–2 continues in several New Testament passages. The seer of the Apocalypse describes the forces arrayed
against Christ and his followers in the final eschatological war as "the beast
and the kings of the earth with their armies" (Rev. 19:19). The phrase "the
kings of the earth" is taken from Ps. 2:2, and the mention of the beast, which
precedes this phrase, indicates the demonic dimension of these kings' hostility. "The kings of the earth" are also mentioned in Rev. 17:18, where they
are linked with the monstrous image of the great harlot drunk with the
blood of the saints (cf. 17:1–6). The same conception of a supernatural
opposition standing behind the human opposition to Jesus is probably
implied by the phrase "the rulers of this age" in 1 Cor. 2:6, 8;[63] this locution, too, seems to be at least partially dependent on Psalm 2.[64]

Thus, several of the New Testament usages of Psalm 2 take up the psalm's
concentration on the grave threat posed by the opposition to God and to
his anointed one, developing further the hints already found in the psalm
and in Jewish exegesis that this opposition is larger than its human representatives. The "kings of the earth" set themselves against Yahweh and his
anointed one, not entirely on their own initiative, but as the exponents of
a world-embracing kingship opposed to that of God.

Kingship in Psalm 2

The subject of kingship was central to Psalm 2 from the beginning and
is even built into its structure. A. Weiser, for example, divides the psalm

---

[61] See Kee, "Function," in *Jesus und Paulus,* ed. Ellis and Grässer, p. 181.

[62] See K. G. Kuhn ("Γὼγ καὶ Μαγώγ," *TDNT* [1964; orig. 1933], 1:789–791), according to
whom the use of the double name "Gog and Magog" in intertestamental Judaism (*Sib. Or.*
3:319, 512), the New Testament (Rev. 20:8–9), and rabbinic traditions "reflects the mythicising of the whole conception" that is derived from Ezekiel 38–39; see S-B 3:834, which speaks
of "Satanic influence" on Gog and Magog in the Apocalypse and in rabbinic traditions.

[63] The most thorough recent study of 1 Cor. 2:6, 8 claims that the "rulers" there are human
beings (M. Pesce, *Paolo e gli arconti a Corinto: Storia della ricerca [1888–1975] ed esegesi di
I Cor 2, 6.8* [Brescia: Paideia, 1977]). See, however, the good criticism of G. B. Caird (*JTS* 29
[1978], 543–544), who argues convincingly that demonic powers must also be included in
the referent; see already M. Dibelius, *Die Geisterwelt im Glauben des Paulus* (Göttingen:
Vandenhoeck & Ruprecht, 1909), pp. 88–92.

[64] Psalm 2 certainly does present a picture of "the rulers of this age" (cf. "the kings of the
earth") who are headed toward destruction. T. Ling notes, in favor of a background in Psalm
2, that Acts 4:26 uses the word ἄρχων ("ruler") in the context of a quotation from Psalm 2,
and that the psalm, like 1 Cor. 2:6, 8, implies that the hostile rulers lack wisdom (Ps. 2:10)
("A Note on I Corinthians II,8," *ExpT* 68 [1956–67], 26).

into four strophes: (1) vv. 1–3, the kings of the earth; (2) vv. 4–6, the heavenly king; (3) vv. 7–9, the king in Zion; and (4) vv. 10–12, the warning.[65] The first and third of Weiser's headings are obvious; v. 2 mentions "the kings of the earth," and v. 6 speaks of "my [God's] king." Weiser's second heading is also justified, since the description in v. 4 of God as "the one sitting in heaven (יושב בשמים)" implies kingly enthronement.[66] The royal authority exercised by the Israelite ruler (later the Messiah), then, is one that he receives from the heavenly king and exercises in his name; to obey him is to obey God, while to revolt against him is to throw off God's yoke. As T. Mettinger points out, this congruence between the two kingships is brought out by various literary features of the psalm:

> The suffixes in Ps 2 serve to express the close relationship between the king and his God. Thus "YHWH and his anointed" are treated as a unity in v 2; and v 3 speaks of "their bonds" and "their cords." When God speaks of the king he refers to him as "my king" (v 6) and "my son" (v 7). And God refers to the king's capital, Zion, as "my holy hill" (v 6).[67]

Therefore, the heavenly king and his earthly representative possess an inseparable royal authority, both in their view and in the view of their opponents. Correspondingly, in vv. 10–11 the human king in Zion enjoins the foreign rulers to fear not him but God. H.-J. Kraus comments on v. 11: "There is no difference; to subject oneself to Yahweh means to be subject to the king in Jerusalem."[68]

The theme of kingship continues to be central in postbiblical usage of Psalm 2. Sirach 47:11, for example, speaks of "the decree of the kingdom" (ממלכת מלכות) given to David, and 4QPatriarchal Blessings 2 of "the covenant of kingship" (ברית המלכות), both apparently with reference to the "decree" (חק) of Ps. 2:7.[69] The inseparability of the royal authority of the human king who reigns in Zion (now understood as the Messiah), on the one hand, and that of God, on the other, also continues to be emphasized. We have already seen that *Pss. Sol.* 17:21–46 is largely dependent on Psalm 2 for its portrait of the Messiah. The insightful remarks of G. L. Davenport on the inseparability of the two kingships in the *Psalms of Solomon* passage reveal something about postbiblical exegesis of Psalm 2:

---

[65] A. Weiser, *The Psalms*, OTL (Philadelphia: Westminster Press, 1962), pp. 109–116.

[66] See Kraus, *Königsherrschaft*, p. 69; P. C. Craigie, *Psalms 1–50*, WBC 19 (Waco, Tex.: Word Books, 1983), p. 66.

[67] See T. Mettinger, *King and Messiah: The Civil and Sacral Legitimation of the Israelite Kings*, ConBOT 8 (Lund: Gleerup, 1976), p. 262; cf. Gray, *Reign of God*, p. 79.

[68] Kraus, *Königsherrschaft*, p. 71.

[69] See L. C. Allen, "The Old Testament Background of (ΠΡΟ)'ΟΡΙΖΕΙΝ in the New Testament," *NTS* 17 (1970–71), 104.

Any consideration of the plea for God to raise up a new king for his people [*Pss. Sol.* 17:21] must take full account of the affirmation with which the psalm begins and ends: the Lord himself is king (vv 1, 46)! Consequently, the one who will occupy the throne of David will be king in a qualified sense only. He will reign under the authority of the true King, the Lord himself. The use of the appositive *your servant* (v 21) further reminds us that ultimately the people are not subjects of the earthly monarch, but of God. Their subjection to the earthly king is the means of their subjection to God, and, conversely, by their rejection of the Davidic dynasty the usurpers have rejected God's kingship.[70]

Here, then, we observe exactly the same relationship that pertains in the original psalm, an equivalence on the one hand between subservience to the kingship of God and subservience to the kingship of the Messiah, and on the other hand between revolt against God's kingship and revolt against the kingship of his anointed one.

This trajectory of interpretation of Psalm 2 continues in the New Testament. Revelation 11:15, for example, reflects the parallelism of God's kingship and that of the Messiah in a locution dependent on Ps. 2:2: *"The kingdom of this world* has become *that of our Lord and of his Christ,* and he shall reign forever and ever"* (alt.). Here both the phrase "the kingdom of this world" and the phrase "[the kingdom] of our Lord and of Christ" reflect the psalm (*"the kings of the earth* set themselves *against the Lord and against his Anointed"*). In the second phrase the single word βασιλεία ("kingdom") is modified by two parallel genitives, τοῦ κυρίου ἡμῶν ("of our Lord") and τοῦ Χριστοῦ αὐτοῦ ("of his Christ"); the inseparability of the two kingships could not be more graphically expressed. Similar remarks apply to Rev. 12:10, in which "the βασιλεία of our God" and "the ἐξουσία [authority] of his Christ" are paralleled.

This same parallelism is found also in Luke 22:29. Here Jesus says to his disciples, "I confer (διατίθεμαι) on you, as my father conferred on me, βασιλεία" (alt.). This passage too seems to be dependent on Psalm 2; it alludes to the father–son relationship between Jesus and God, speaks of Christ's βασιλεία, and implies God's own kingship, since he confers βασιλεία on Jesus. Colossians 1:13 also speaks of Christ's βασιλεία and contains language strikingly similar to that of Mark 1:11 ("son of his love"); it also seems to be at least partly dependent on Psalm 2.[71]

---

[70] G. L. Davenport, "The 'Anointed of the Lord' in Psalms of Solomon 17," in *Ideal Figures in Ancient Judaism: Profiles and Paradigms,* ed. J. J. Collins and G. W. E. Nickelsburg, SBLSCS 12 (Chico, Calif.: Scholars Press, 1980), pp. 71–72.

[71] On the connection of Col. 1:13 with Psalm 2, see E. Schweizer, *The Letter to the Colossians: A Commentary* (Minneapolis: Augsburg, 1982), p. 52. I have not seen reference to Psalm 2 in the secondary literature on Luke 22:29.

In some later interpretations of Psalm 2, as we have seen in the previous section, this joint kingship of God and his Messiah is opposed by an unholy alliance of the kings of the earth with the demonic ruler or rulers from whom they derive their power. Thus we may say that some interpretations of Psalm 2 within Judaism and early Christianity suggest the existence of two opposed supernatural kingships, each represented by an earthly kingship corresponding to it.

Mark's Appropriation of the Trajectories

These trajectories in the interpretation of Psalm 2 have striking points of contact with the worldview of Mark, and specifically with 1:9–11 in its immediate context.

The eschatological dimension of Psalm 2 is strongly emphasized in the Markan context.[72] We have already noted eschatological features in the baptismal pericope prior to the divine voice (the splitting of the heavens and the descent of the Spirit). This eschatological emphasis is continued in the passages that immediately follow the baptism. First Mark presents a short account of the temptation of Jesus by Satan (1:12–13). Here the one who has just been anointed by the Spirit (1:10) is exposed to demonic opposition but triumphs as a result of divine succor, just as in the psalm the anointed king is attacked by God's enemies but triumphs over them because of God's support.

The temptation scene is followed by the important transitional pericope in which Jesus comes into Galilee announcing good news: the time of the dominion of Satan is at an end, and God's kingly power (βασιλεία τοῦ θεοῦ) has come near (1:14–15).[73] The βασιλεία τοῦ θεοῦ, however, is the theme not only of Mark 1:14–15 but also of Psalm 2. The psalm, we have observed, depicts the most intimate connection imaginable between the kingly rule of God and that of the Messiah, along with an antithetical relationship between their combined rule and the hostile βασιλεία of the earthly kings.

Mark includes both of these dimensions in his conception of the βασιλεία τοῦ θεοῦ. The opposition between God's kingly power and a hostile βασιλεία is already suggested by the juxtaposition of its announcement in Jesus' proclamation (1:14–15) with the temptation narrative (1:12–13), and it is expressly

---

[72] See Steichele, who relates the messianic-eschatological interpretation of Psalm 2 to the eschatological features of the baptism itself, of 1:1–8, and of 1:14–15 (*Leidende Sohn*, pp. 147, 152–153).

[73] On this interpretation of Mark 1:14–15, see J. Marcus, "'The Time Has Been Fulfilled!' (Mark 1:15)," in *Apocalyptic and the New Testament: Essays in Honor of J. Louis Martyn*, ed. J. Marcus and M. L. Soards, JSNTSup 24 (Sheffield: Sheffield Academic Press, 1989), pp. 49–68.

confirmed in 3:22–27 (the βασιλεία of Satan versus that of Jesus and God).⁷⁴
As the latter passage already hints, the parallelism of the kingly power of
God with the kingship of Jesus is also a Markan motif, for each of the three
crucial instances of "Son of God" in Mark (1:11; 9:7; 15:39) occurs in close
proximity to a reference to the kingdom of God.⁷⁵ The probably redactional
use of the title in the baptismal pericope (1:11), for example, is closely
followed by the redactionally placed notice about Jesus' inaugural announcement of the kingdom of God (1:14–15).⁷⁶ Similarly, in 9:1, a verse that Mark
has placed at the introduction to the transfiguration narrative,⁷⁷ Jesus promises his disciples that some of them will see God's βασιλεία coming in power
before they die. Immediately afterward, three of the disciples are made
witnesses to a numinous vision in which Jesus himself becomes the con-
duit of God's eschatological power and is acclaimed "Son of God" by the
voice out of the cloud (9:7). In 15:39, finally, the centurion, seeing how Jesus
dies, is the first human being to apply the title "Son of God" to him. Shortly
thereafter, in a statement that is probably ironic, the narrator describes
Joseph of Arimathea as "one waiting for the kingdom of God"; Joseph does
not realize that, in Jesus' death, the kingdom has begun to arrive. The
implication of this series of juxtapositions seems to be that the arrival of
the kingdom of God is coterminous with the revelation of Jesus' messianic
kingship, his status as the royal "Son of God."⁷⁸
    We have seen points of contact, then, but is there any direct influence
of Psalm 2 on the development of the Markan juxtaposition of the kingship
of Jesus with the kingdom of God? Both the use made of Psalm 2 in early
Christianity and considerations of Markan redaction point to an affirmative
answer. With regard to the former, it is probable that there is a link between
the early church's memory of Jesus' proclamation of the kingdom of God
and its application to him of the royal title "Son of God," *with Psalm 2 func-
tioning as a middle step.* P. C. Craigie writes:

> When Jesus began his ministry of preaching, his central theme was the
> kingdom of God (Mark 1:14–15), and from the perspective of the Gospel
> writers, it is clear that Jesus was in some sense the king in this newly

---

⁷⁴ On the antithesis between God's kingdom and that of Satan in Mark, see further Marcus,
Mystery, pp. 217–218.
⁷⁵ See Ambrozic, *Hidden Kingdom,* p. 23; Marcus, *Mystery,* p. 54.
⁷⁶ Ambrozic (*Hidden Kingdom,* pp. 4–6) thinks that 1:14–15 is redactionally constructed,
but B. D. Chilton (*God in Strength: Jesus' Announcement of the Kingdom,* StudNTUmwelt,
Serie B, Band 1 [Freistadt: Plöchl, 1979], pp. 29–64) mounts a good case for the presence
of tradition in 1:15. He too, however, thinks that 1:14, and thus the *placement* of the announcement of the kingdom's advent, is redactional.
⁷⁷ See E. Nardoni, "A Redactional Interpretation of Mark 9:1," *CBQ* 43 (1981), 365–384.
⁷⁸ See Ambrozic, *Hidden Kingdom,* p. 23.

announced kingdom. It is precisely the proclamation of the kingdom of God in the teaching of Jesus which permits the terminology of royalty in Psalm 2 to be incorporated into the New Testament language about Jesus.[79]

Craigie's suggestion that Psalm 2 played a crucial role in ascribing divine sonship to Jesus is supported by several New Testament passages that reflect that psalm. Revelation 11:15 and 12:10 parallel the βασιλεία of Jesus with that of God, and Luke 22:29 implies the same parallelism and links it with Jesus' divine sonship; Col. 1:13, moreover, speaks of the son's βασιλεία. Though Craigie's theory may not be the whole story in the ascription of the title "Son of God" to Jesus,[80] it is plausible that *one* line of development of early Christian thought was from a memory of Jesus' proclamation of the kingdom of God to the kingship psalms, including Psalm 2,[81] to the identification of Jesus as the "Son of God" on the basis of that psalm. If this is so, it is not unlikely that Mark is utilizing the same link in 1:11–15 and other passages.

This conclusion is supported by redactional considerations, for we have seen that Mark is probably responsible both for the introduction into the baptismal pericope of the title drawn from Psalm 2, "beloved son," and for the insertion a few verses later of a reference to the kingdom of God (1:15). Especially in view of the traditional connection between the two themes in Psalm 2 and its later exegesis, it seems likely that the psalm is the common denominator in these two redactional insertions.

Mark's use of Psalm 2, then, is not limited to the direct citation of it in 1:11. Rather, the whole series of short pericopes in 1:9–11, 12–13, and 14–15 reflects the basic "plot" of the psalm, and its influence may extend even

---

[79] Craigie, *Psalms 1–50*, pp. 68–69.

[80] D. Juel (*Messianic Exegesis: Christological Interpretation of the Old Testament in Early Christianity* [Philadelphia: Fortress Press, 1988], pp. 77–81 and passim), following up on the work of N. A. Dahl ("The Crucified Messiah," in *The Crucified Messiah and Other Essays* [Minneapolis: Augsburg, 1974], pp. 10–36), argues that the main source of the attribution to Jesus of "Son of God" and other messianic titles was Jesus' death as a messianic pretender. Early Christians, reflecting on this event in the light of scriptures considered messianic in Judaism (especially 2 Samuel 7, but also Psalm 2), came to the conclusion that Jesus was the Son of God. Juel's theory does not necessarily exclude other converging lines of early Christian exegesis.

[81] In terms of genre, Psalm 2 is a royal psalm, a type usually considered to be distinct from the psalms celebrating the kingship of Yahweh; see Anderson, *Psalms* 1:33–35, 39–40. As J. H. Eaton points out, however, "the event of the Davidic king's installation is here enclosed in a presentation of God's kingship. . . . The autumnal festival contained a dramatically conceived assertion of God's Creator-kingship; this psalm strongly suggests that the basic rites of the Davidic kingship were involved in it" (*Kingship and the Psalms*, 2nd ed. [Sheffield: JSOT Press, 1986], p. 113). A rigid distinction between the two forms, therefore, would seem to be out of place.

further into Mark's story. The enemy forces, concretizations of primeval chaos, array themselves against the Lord and against his anointed, shouting in defiance, "What have you to do with us?" (see Mark 1:24) and throwing against them all their hostile might (see Ps. 2:1–3). The one enthroned in heaven, however, shrugs off this display of impotent rage and majestically brings forth his earthly executive, an executive whose purpose and power are so deeply congruent with his own that he can be called his son, and that the revelation of his kingship can simultaneously represent the earthly manifestation of the kingly power of God (see Ps. 2:4–7). In the continuation of Mark's story, and beyond its end, this figure will shatter God's enemies and be given worldwide dominion, receiving the nations for his inheritance and setting them on the road toward trust in God (see Ps. 2:8–11).[82] Of course, this plot will be given a typical Markan twist by the fact that the scene of messianic victory will be the cross.[83]

The Meaning of "Son of God"
in Psalm 2:7 and in Mark 1:11

The influence of Psalm 2 on the Markan narrative has important ramifications for the meaning of "Son of God" in Mark 1:11, for it suggests that a good starting place for interpretation of the title is its meaning within the psalm.[84] The most obvious nuance of the title there is royal. As we have seen in the preceding section, the psalm and its subsequent history of interpretation emphasize the congruence between the royal rule of God and that of the king/Messiah. At his coronation, the earthly monarch has been invested with the kingly authority that has up to this point belonged exclusively to his royal "father."[85] This congruence is an important dimension of the monarch's divine sonship. The king who sits enthroned in heaven imparts his own worldwide dominion to the one whom he calls "my king"

---

[82] On shattering God's enemies, see the exorcism stories and 13:26; on receiving worldwide dominion that includes the Gentiles, see 7:24–30; 13:10, 27; on trust in God, see the Markan theme of faith (1:15; 2:5, etc.).

[83] See Steichele, who rightly emphasizes that 1:11 does not express *everything* that Mark means by the title "Son of God": "Above all there is no mention here of the suffering and the cross of Jesus" (*Leidende Sohn*, pp. 160–161).

[84] The tendency of older scholarship to interpret "Son of God" as a reflection of a Hellenistic "divine man" Christology has faded in recent years; see J. D. Kingsbury, "The 'Divine Man' as the Key to Mark's Christology—The End of an Era?" *Int* 35 (1981), 243–257.

[85] See E. Lipinski, who compares formulas of investiture from Mesopotamia and Egypt to Psalms 2:7–8 and 110 (*La Royauté de Yahwé dans la Poésie et le Culte de l'Ancien Israël* [Brussels: Paleis der Academiën, 1965], pp. 338–347).

and sets on the throne in Zion, his holy hill; the king is thus God's "son" in sharing in his kingly rule.[86]

As we have seen, this idea of the congruence of the two reigns continues in Jewish interpretations of Psalm 2 and in the New Testament. It is no surprise, therefore, to find that in the New Testament the title drawn from Ps. 2:7, "Son of God," is linked with the idea of Christ's universal and everlasting royal dominion (see, e.g., Rom. 1:4; Heb. 1:5; 5:5).[87] This linkage is found also in Luke 22:29 and Col. 1:13, passages that are partly dependent on Psalm 2. Colossians 1:13, moreover, contains language strikingly similar to that of Mark 1:11 ("son of his love"). It is probable, then, that in Mark 1:11 also one important implication of the title "Son of God" is the royal dominion of Christ. This royal interpretation of "Son of God" is especially likely in view of the proximity between 1:9–11, in which Jesus is called God's son, and 1:14–15, in which he proclaims the kingdom of God.

But it is not sufficient merely to call "Son of God" a royal title. It is also important to investigate what *sort* of kingly dominion is implied by the title and what its basis is. Here again a look at the original psalm is a helpful point of departure.

Rooted in quite literal ancient Near Eastern (especially Egyptian) conceptions of the king's descent from God,[88] the divine announcement of Ps. 2:7, "You are my son; today I have begotten you," retains in the faith of Israel an ineradicable substratum of meaning in which the Israelite king, like the ark of the covenant, is considered to be the bearer of the personal presence of Yahweh himself.[89] Psalm 2:7 goes beyond the oracle 2 Sam. 7:14[90] and indicates more than that the king is "adopted" by God as his royal executive.[91] As H. Gese points out, if adoption into a particular role were all that was in view, the first part of the divine oracle, "You are my son," would be sufficient.[92] The oracle continues, however, "today I have begotten you." This power-laden announcement, as E. Zenger points out, implies a new birth,

---

[86] See Soggin, "Zweiten Psalm," in *Wort-Gebot-Glaube*, ed. Stoebe, p. 201; see also O. Keel, who points to Egyptian examples in which kingly power is the consequence of divine sonship (*The Symbolism of the Biblical World: Ancient Near Eastern Iconography and the Book of Psalms* [New York: Seabury Press, 1978], p. 248).

[87] See Lövestam, *Son and Saviour*, pp. 26–27; Fitzmyer, "This Melchizedek," in *Essays*, p. 224.

[88] On the Egyptian parallels see Klein, "Auslegung," p. 64; Keel, *Symbolism*, p. 248.

[89] See Kraus, *Königsherrschaft*, p. 69.

[90] See H. Gross, "Der Messias im Alten Testament," in *Bibel und Zeitgemässer Glaube, Band I, Altes Testament*, ed. K. Schubert (Vienna: Klosterneuburger, 1965), pp. 247–248; Matera, *Kingship*, p. 141.

[91] Contra Soggin ("Zweiten Psalm," in *Wort-Gebot-Glaube*, ed. Stoebe, p. 194) and Mettinger (*King and Messiah*, pp. 261–262); with Keel (*Symbolism*, p. 248), who says that the term "adoption" is too juridical, that sonship has emotional as well as legal aspects.

[92] H. Gese, "Natus ex virgine," in *Vom Sinai zum Zion: Alttestamentliche Beiträge zur biblischen Theologie*, BETTA 64 (Munich: Chr. Kaiser Verlag, 1974), p. 137.

a change in essence, not just in office.[93] The resultant openness of the title "Son of God" to a high interpretation that transcends the boundaries of juridical adoption is probably the main reason for its relative disuse as a messianic title in Judaism.[94] T. Mettinger, therefore, somewhat misses the mark when he claims, "The utterance [of Psalm 2:7] points forward: not with regard to his descent but with regard to his future task, the king is proclaimed 'son' of God."[95] On the contrary, it is not just the king's task but also the superhuman power necessary to *accomplish* that task that is in view in the bestowal of the title "Son of God."

This interpretation of "Son of God" is supported by the observation that, if we take the title's context in Psalm 2 seriously, it is intrinsic to it that the kingship delegated to Yahweh's anointed one is opposed and threatened by a hostile kingship of cosmic dimensions. This seems to be Mark's view, too. F. Matera points out that the exact form of the title that appears in 1:11, "beloved son," resurfaces in the parable of the vineyard (12:1–12), a story that emphasizes the opposition to Jesus and echoes Psalm 2 also in the use of the term κληρονομία ("inheritance"; cf. Ps. 2:8 LXX). Though in this particular case the human opposition to Jesus is at the center of focus, in Mark's Gospel as a whole it is clear that the human opposition reflects a supernatural one.[96] Correspondingly, in the interpretations of Psalm 2 that are most crucial for New Testament exegesis (as well as implicitly in the original psalm), the hostile kingship that opposes and is overcome by the kingship of God consists not only of human enemies but also of their supernatural puppet masters. The "Son of God" who brings about their defeat, therefore, must also be a figure of more than human stature, and the concept of legal adoption is inadequate to express the meaning of his sonship. In Mark 1:11, then, Jesus is the Son of God because he is granted substantial participation in God's holiness, God's effective opposition to the powers of evil (see 1:21–28, in which Jesus' exorcism of the demon is linked with the title "Holy One of God").[97]

---

[93] E. Zenger, "'Wozu tosen die Völker . . .': Beobachtungen zur Entstehung und Theologie des 2. Psalms," in *Freude an der Weisung des Herrn: Beiträge zur Theologie der Psalmen: Festgabe zum 70. Geburtstag von Heinrich Gross*, ed. E. Haag and F.-L. Hossfeld (Stuttgart: Katholisches Bibelwerk, 1986), p. 502 n. 22; cf. Klein, who points to the new name given to the king at his enthronement (2 Sam. 12:25; 2 Kings 23:34; 24:17) and to the series of purification rites and robing ceremonies that probably precede it ("Auslegung," p. 65).
[94] On this disuse, see the excursus at the end of this chapter.
[95] Mettinger, *King and Messiah*, pp. 261–262.
[96] The finest study of this aspect of Mark's theology is still J. M. Robinson, *The Problem of History in Mark and Other Marcan Studies* (1957; reprint, Philadelphia: Fortress Press, 1982), pp. 81–94.
[97] On Jesus' holiness as including his effective opposition to the demons, see O. Procksch, "ἅγιος, κτλ.," *TDNT* (1964; orig. 1933), 1:101–102.

In Markan Christology, therefore, there can be no dichotomy between a royal interpretation of Jesus' divine sonship and a concept of that sonship that sees Jesus as participating in some way in God's very power and being.[98] Along with his stress on Jesus' participation in God's power and being, however, Mark still maintains a sense of Jesus' distinction from God. This distinction is already present in the original psalm; "Yahweh" and "his anointed one" are two separate characters, and in v. 11 the rebellious kings are urged to fear Yahweh, not the earthly king.[99] Psalm 2 thus implies the same combination of identification with God and distinction from him that we saw implied in Mark 1:2–3. Contrary to Acts 2:36, which appears to allude to Ps. 2:2, "against the Lord and against his anointed," and to apply *both* titles to Jesus,[100] Mark emphasizes the inseparable link between God and Jesus while at the same time maintaining the distinction between them. Jesus is God's *son*, not God himself. As son, however, he shares in God's βασιλεία, his kingly power, and becomes the instrument of its extension into every corner of the creation through his defeat of the demonic cosmic forces that twist and destroy human life.

"In You I Have Been Pleased"

After the weighty intervention of the reference to Ps. 2:7 in Mark 1:11b, Mark returns in 1:11c to the Deutero-Isaian background that has been so important in this introductory section of the Gospel and that he probably found in the source for 1:9–11, alluding with the concluding words of the divine voice, "in you I have been pleased," to Isa. 42:1 (MT and LXX: "my soul has been pleased with/accepted him"). This verse begins the first of the Deutero-Isaian Servant Songs (Isa. 42:1–4), and in retaining the allusion Mark may wish already to suggest that Jesus is Yahweh's Suffering Servant,[101] an identification which will assume importance later in the Gospel and which we will explore in subsequent chapters.[102]

For now we wish to concentrate on the fact that Mark has retained the aorist εὐδόκησα from the version of Isa. 42:1 that has come down to him. The most natural way of taking such an aorist is as a reference to a *past*

98 Some scholars who interpret the Markan title "Son of God" in terms of "royal messianism" seem to assume such a dichotomy; see, e.g., D. Juel, *Messiah and Temple: The Trial of Jesus in the Gospel of Mark*, SBLDS 31 (Missoula, Mont.: Scholars Press, 1973), pp. 108–114; Matera, *Kingship*, pp. 140–145, 149.

99 See H. Gross, "Messias," in *Bibel und Zeitgemässer Glaube*, ed. Schubert, pp. 247–248; Zenger, "Tosen," in *Freude*, ed. Haag and Hossfeld, p. 502 n. 22.

100 Lövestam, *Son and Saviour*, p. 25.

101 See C. Maurer, "Knecht Gottes und Sohn Gottes im Passionsbericht des Markus-evangeliums," *ZTK* 50 (1953), 32–34; Zmijewski, "Sohn-Gottes-Prädikation," pp. 25–28.

102 See chapter 5 below on Mark 9:11–13, and chapter 8, on the passion narrative.

event— "in you I *have been* pleased."[103] Over against those who interpret εὐδόκησα as an aorist expressing what has just happened or as corresponding to the Hebrew stative perfect, and who therefore, for one reason or another, translate 1:11c as "in you I *am* pleased,"[104] B. W. Bacon and R. H. Gundry seem to be on the right track when they argue that the aorist speaks of God's past election of Christ.[105] Two converging lines of analysis support this interpretation.

The first is Isa. 42:1 itself. If we have been correct in concluding that this verse is in the background of Mark 1:11c, the perfect רצתה ("was pleased with") of the Masoretic Text and the aorist προσεδέξατο ("accepted") of the Septuagint provide the model for Mark's aorist εὐδόκησα. Contrary to V. Taylor, רצתה in Isa. 42:1 MT is not simply a stative perfect.[106] The Old Testament passage in its context within Isaiah and within the traditions of Israel in general speaks of the election of Israel, a past event[107] that is now being made the surety for the new thing that God is about to do, namely, putting his Spirit on Israel. The past choice of Israel and the impending bestowal of the Spirit in Isa. 42:1 correspond perfectly to the past choice of Jesus and the present bestowal of the Spirit in Mark 1:10–11.[108] By a common New Testament transposition, what is ascribed to Israel in the Old Testament is transferred to Jesus,[109] and therefore the divine election of Israel for an eschatological task becomes in Mark 1:11 the divine election of the Messiah to his eschatological role. The tenses of the verbs in Isa. 42:1, therefore, do not dissolve into a homogeneous mush, and neither, it may be presumed, do they in Mark's use of the verse.

This interpretation of εὐδόκησα is supported by other New Testament usages of the verb εὐδοκεῖν ("to be well pleased") and the cognate noun

---

[103] Because of the difference between Greek and English tense usage, the Greek aorist must sometimes be translated as an English perfect; see E. D. W. Burton, *Syntax of the Moods and Tenses in New Testament Greek* (Grand Rapids: Kregel, 1976; orig. 1900), §52.

[104] For these options, see J. H. Moulton et al., *A Grammar of New Testament Greek*, 4 vols. (Edinburgh: T. & T. Clark, 1908–65), 1:134–35; V. Taylor, *The Gospel According to Saint Mark*, 2nd ed. (Grand Rapids: Baker Book House, 1981), pp. 64, 161–162; Steichele, *Leidende Sohn*, pp. 150–151.

[105] B. W. Bacon, "Notes on New Testament Passages," *JBL* 16 (1897), 136–139; idem, "Supplementary Note on the Aorist εὐδόκησα, Mark i. 11," *JBL* 20 (1901), 28–30; Gundry, *Use*, pp. 31–32.

[106] See K. Elliger, *Jesaja II (41,17–42,9)*, BKAT (Neukirchen-Vluyn: Neukirchener Verlag, 1971), p. 202.

[107] See, e.g., Isa. 41:8–9; 43:10; 44:1–2; 48:12; these passages develop further the Deuteronomic concept of the election of Israel as the people of God (e.g., Deut. 4:37; 7:6; 10:15; 14:2). See G. Quell et al., "ἐκλέγομαι," *TDNT* (1967; orig. 1942), 4:153 n. 42; p. 163.

[108] That in Isaiah the bestowal of the Spirit is future whereas in Mark it is present is easily explained: in Mark 1:10–11 the ancient prophecy is being fulfilled.

[109] See C. H. Dodd, *According to the Scriptures: The Sub-structure of New Testament Theology* (London: Nisbet, 1952), pp. 89–103, 116–119.

εὐδοχία ("goodwill"). Already at the turn of the century B. W. Bacon published two short studies that brought this New Testament evidence to bear on the problem of εὐδόχησα in Mark 1:11. He showed that in most of the New Testament instances in which εὐδοχεῖν and εὐδοχία are attributed to God, they are used of the deity's sovereign, inscrutable decree; that which is otherwise unaccountable is declared to be "the good pleasure of God."[110] Of these passages, the fundamental one for comparison with Mark 1:11 par., according to Bacon, is Eph. 1:4–9, since it collocates the terms εὐδοχία and ἠγαπημένος ("the one who has been beloved"). This collocation is not accidentally similar to the collocation of εὐδόχησα and ἀγαπητός ("beloved") in Mark 1:11: Eph. 1:4–9 is an indirect reference to Christian baptism, interpreted as incorporation into Jesus' own baptism.[111] It is especially significant for interpretation of εὐδόχησα in Mark 1:11, then, that Eph. 1:4–9 clearly speaks of a premundane choice of Christ, "the beloved," and uses εὐδοχία to do so. The evidence is strong, therefore, that the aorist εὐδόχησα in Mark 1:11 is a true past tense that speaks of a divine choice of Jesus that occurred *before* his baptism.

While Bacon's interpretation is basically persuasive, it is in need of qualification. Drawing on an observation of E. Lohmeyer, we may specify that in the New Testament the εὐδοχ- word group speaks not simply of a divine choice but of a divine choice *for an eschatological work.*[112] This eschatological dimension to εὐδοχεῖν is borne out in the Markan case by the observation that something christologically significant happens at the baptism — namely, the advent of the Spirit — and that this advent is conceived of as an eschatological event.[113] There is in Mark, moreover, no explicit reference to Jesus' preexistence on the lines of John 1:1 or Col. 1:15–17. Indeed, if we were to ask ourselves at what point Mark thinks that Jesus becomes the Messiah, the most likely answer would be, at the baptism; it would, at least, be very easy to interpret the coming of the Spirit upon

---

[110] Bacon, "Notes," p. 137. For εὐδοχεῖν, see, besides the baptismal passages, the Matthean citation of Isa. 42:1 (Matt. 12:18) and the descriptions of the transfiguration in Matt. 17:5 and 2 Peter 1:17; also Luke 12:32; 1 Cor. 1:21; Gal. 1:15; Col. 1:19. The remaining New Testament instances are judgment passages that speak of the things God does *not* delight in: 1 Cor. 10:5; Heb. 10:6, 8, 38. For εὐδοχία, see Matt. 11:26//Luke 10:21; Eph. 1:5, 9; Phil. 2:13; Luke 2:14?.

[111] Bacon, "Supplementary Note," p. 29; cf. J. Coutts, who cites (a) the phrase "in the beloved" in Eph. 1:6; (b) the reference to adoption in Eph. 1:5; (c) the usages of εὐδοχία in Eph. 1:5, 9; (d) the reference to forgiveness of sins in Eph. 1:7; and (e) the references to sealing, and to hearing and believing the word, in Eph. 1:13–14 ("Ephesians I.3–14 and I Peter I.3–12," *NTS* 3 [1956–57], 124–127).

[112] Lohmeyer, *Evangelium*, p. 24. This characterization fits all of the passages cited in n. 110 except the judgment passages.

[113] Steichele, *Leidende Sohn*, pp. 157–159.

Jesus in 1:10 as an anointing.[114] It seems, therefore, that Mark 1:11c, like some Jewish traditions, implies God's preexistent *choice* of the Messiah,[115] without deciding the question of exactly when Jesus *becomes* Messiah. Mark *may* think that that event occurs at the baptism, though he certainly is not clear on the subject.[116]

Although Bacon has rightly emphasized the pastness of the divine choice indicated by εὐδόκησα, this pastness does not mitigate the eschatological newness of what occurs at the baptism. In good apocalyptic fashion, Mark 1:9–11 brings together primordial time and end time.[117] The heavens that have been shut up since the youth of humanity are reopened; the Spirit that hovered over the primeval waters once more descends to liberate the earth from the stranglehold of chaos;[118] and a voice unheard for age upon age sounds forth, announcing a decision made long ago in the eternal counsel. The words of that decision lay mysteriously hidden and uncomprehended in the scriptures of Israel, but now, with their fulfillment in Jesus' baptism, they can be understood by Mark's readers, who are privileged to witness the epiphany of 1:9–11. The good pleasure of God, his delight in his creation, his life-giving conviction that "it is very good" (see Gen. 1:31), is reborn in the baptismal waters, rises from them in the person of Jesus, and goes out with him to embrace the world and do battle against the forces of negation that crush the hopes of humanity.

Conclusions: Mark 1:9–11 and the Markan Community

Mark's readers have known since the start of his Gospel that his theme is "the way of the Lord" (1:2–3) and that this way is a way of victory. This Deutero-Isaian background, with its vision of an eschatological theophany,

---

[114] See D. E. Nineham, who cites Acts 10:38, which speaks of Jesus' anointing with the Spirit, and Isa. 61:1, which brings together the verb מָשַׁח ("to anoint") and the noun רוּחַ ("Spirit") (*Saint Mark*, Pelican New Testament Commentaries [Middlesex: Penguin, 1963], p. 62). Nineham also mentions that in the Old Testament anointing is often followed by Spirit-possession; see, e.g., 1 Sam. 10:1, 6, 10.

[115] See S-B 2:334–335, which refers to *1 Enoch* 48:3, 6 and rabbinic traditions that speak of the name of the Messiah as one of the things that was created before the world.

[116] See the guarded remarks of M. Dibelius, *From Tradition to Gospel* (Cambridge: James Clarke & Co., 1971; orig. 1933), p. 273; and Steichele, *Leidende Sohn*, pp. 158–159.

[117] On *Urzeit* and *Endzeit* in apocalyptic eschatology, see D. S. Russell, *The Method and Message of Jewish Apocalyptic* (Philadelphia: Westminster Press, 1964), pp. 282–284; for the application of this typology to Mark 1:9–11, see Lohmeyer, *Evangelium*, p. 25.

[118] Cf. Taylor's interpretation of the phrase "like a dove" in Mark 1:10, which stresses the parallel to the Spirit hovering like a dove over the primeval waters (*Mark*, p. 161). A tradition ascribed to Ben Zoma (second-generation Tanna) in *b. Ḥag.* 15a supports this exegesis.

continues to play an important role in the Markan description of Jesus' baptism. But the Isaian vision of God's magnificence is so overwhelming that it tends to swallow up death and every other contrary reality in the divine victory (cf. Isa. 25:8),[119] leaving scant room for the opposition that is such an important factor in the day-to-day life of Mark's community. By conflating Isa. 42:1 with Ps. 2:7, the Markan version of the baptismal voice brings into sharper focus the hostile powers that oppose that vision, while still maintaining the emphasis on God's ultimate triumph.

Mark accomplishes this shift by altering the first words of the divine voice that sounds forth at the baptism, displacing a reference to Isa. 42:1 with a reference to Ps. 2:7. He does so partly, of course, because the title "Son of God" is so important to his picture of Jesus. The use of "my son" in 1:11, however, also brings along with it the larger context of opposition, of the collision of the kingdoms, which is intrinsic to its use in Psalm 2. It is thus no accident that immediately after the divine identification of Jesus as "Son of God" the severity of the opposition is revealed in a naked challenge to Jesus' power on the part of Satan (1:12–13).

The Markan community is one that knows firsthand the brutal force of this challenge to God's sovereignty and to Jesus' role in extending it. Set in the midst of a tribulation unparalleled since time began (13:19), witnessing the disintegration of close natural ties and suffering betrayal to death on that account (13:12), hated by all for Jesus' name (13:13), the members of that community might well wonder whether primeval chaos had returned, might well join in the psalmist's complaint that the nations were in uproar and the peoples devising a deadly form of vanity (Ps. 2:1). Delivered for judgment to rulers and monarchs (Mark 13:9), including perhaps Jewish revolutionary leaders[120] who themselves invoke Psalm 2 to justify their holy war against the Romans, the Markan Christians might well protest that the kings of the earth were setting themselves against the Lord and against his anointed (Ps. 2:2)—and seeming to get away with it!

The continuation of the psalm, however, invites Mark's community to lift its eyes from the surging chaos that seems to engulf it and to fix them instead on the magnificent vision of the one enthroned in heaven, the monarch omnipotent against every storm of life. In the light of this vision, the wild opposition of demons and human beings is seen not to be the deadly serious

---

[119] On the close relationship between the Isaian apocalypse in Isaiah 24–27 and the work of Deutero-Isaiah, see G. W. Anderson, "Isaiah xxiv–xxvii Reconsidered," in *Congress Volume: Bonn, 1962*, VTSup 9 (Leiden: E. J. Brill, 1963), p. 125; W. R. Millar, *Isaiah 24–27 and the Origin of Apocalyptic*, HSM 11 (Missoula, Mont.: Scholars Press, 1976), p. 118.

[120] J. R. Donahue calls attention to Josephus's report (*Jewish War* 3.335–344) that the Zealots held trials when they took over Jerusalem, and he compares the trials described in Mark 13:9, 11–13 (*Are You the Christ?* SBLDS 10 [Missoula, Mont.: Society of Biblical Literature, 1973], pp. 217–224).

thing that it first appears to be, but rather a phenomenon that is worthy only of a disbelieving shake of the head. How do the "rulers" dare to set themselves against the living God? Do they not know who it is they oppose? Do they not fear his righteous zeal to act on behalf of those who are his own? Mark's depiction of the invincible power of Jesus as he spearheads the battle against the demonized world enables his community not only to conquer its fear of its enemies but even to join in the divine laughter that sounds forth in the psalm. Let the enemy forces do their worst, striking even—as they think—unto the death. The joke will be on them; "one little word will fell them."[121]

The phrasing of the divine voice assures Mark's community that the one for whose sake its members now find themselves hated on all sides (13:13), the one for whom they have suffered the loss of all things (8:33–36; 10:28–29), the one whose inglorious end seemed to prove that he was at best an unsuccessful royal pretender, at worst an object of divine wrath (see 15:16–39), is actually the beloved son of the heavenly father, the one in whom he took delight from the beginning of his way (see Prov. 8:22). No experience of hostility, suffering, or even death can erase the words that first sounded forth at the baptism; indeed, at the climax of Mark's Gospel, when contradiction reaches its apex, practically the same words will be heard, this time pronounced by a human tongue (15:39). Mark's community is thereby put on notice that, even when called to take up Jesus' cross and to participate in his death, it will find itself empowered to proclaim the astonishing and liberating message that, through Jesus, God is on the march in the suffering world (see 13:11). No one can retract the word "son" that God has addressed to Jesus and, through him, to humanity; nor can anyone stop "beloved" from expressing the ultimate significance and goal of his irresistible commitment to his world.

Excursus: The Disuse of the Title "Son of God" in Ancient Judaism

H.-J. Steichele mentions the tendency of ancient Jewish sources to avoid the title "Son of God."[122] Especially striking, as Steichele points out, is the

---

[121] As most will recognize, the quotation is from Luther's hymn "A Mighty Fortress Is Our God." See N. Frye on Milton's *Paradise Lost:* "The devils have no strength against God at all. It is difficult not to feel that the entire war in heaven is a huge practical joke to the Father, all the more of one because of the seriousness with which the devils take it" ("The Story of All Things," in *Paradise Lost*, ed. S. Elledge, Norton Critical Edition [New York: W. W. Norton & Co., 1975; orig. 1965], p. 418).

[122] Steichele, *Leidende Sohn*, pp. 139–147.

absence of the title from *Psalms of Solomon* 17, in spite of the evident use of Psalm 2 there; only the *people* is called the son of God (17:30), whereas the Messiah is called many things (the leader, the Son of David, the anointed of the Lord, the king) but not "the Son of God." The quotation of Ps. 2:7 in the *Mekilta* demonstrates a similar collectivizing tendency, applying divine sonship not to the Messiah but to the Israelites oppressed by Pharaoh.[123]

As for the Qumran texts, even in 4QFlor 1:10–13, where the words of 2 Sam. 7:14, "I will be his father, and he will be my son," are referred to the Davidic Messiah, the *title* "Son of God" is not present.[124] The title "Son of God" *may* be used in 4QpsDanA^a, but the text is too fragmentary for secure conclusions to be drawn from it, and the reference could also be to a pagan king.[125] G. Vermes, after reviewing the Qumran messianic texts, concludes that "any claim to an equality or interchangeability of [the epithet Son of God and the title Messiah] exceeds the evidence."[126]

Similarly negative results emerge from study of *1 Enoch* and *4 Ezra*, in neither of which the title "Son of God" is original.[127]

As Steichele notes, a few rabbinic traditions *do* use "Son of God" as a messianic title, but others polemicize against the Christian misunderstanding of the title in a physical sense. Not directly relevant for our purposes are the talmudic traditions cited by Vermes in which Ḥanina ben Dosa (first-generation Tanna) and R. Meir (third-generation Tanna) are called "my son" by God.[128] Apart from the problem of dating, these traditions do not use "son" in a titular sense to denote God's unique son.

Reviewing some of this evidence, Steichele hypothesizes that the avoidance of the title "Son of God" in ancient Jewish texts may be due to a fear

---

[123] *Mekilta, Shirata* 7; see Vermes, *Jesus the Jew*, p. 262 n. 26.

[124] See Juel, *Messiah and Temple*, pp. 110–111. Even more drastic weakenings are visible in the Targums on 2 Sam. 7:14 and 1 Chron. 7:13; see J. Marcus, "Mark 14:61: Are You the Messiah-Son-of-God?" *NovT* 31 (1988), 138–141.

[125] See J. A. Fitzmyer, "The Contribution of Qumran Aramaic to the Study of the New Testament," in *A Wandering Aramean: Collected Aramaic Essays*, SBLMS 25 (Missoula, Mont.: Scholars Press, 1979), pp. 90–94, 105–107; idem, "The Aramaic Language and the Study of the New Testament," *JBL* 99 (1980), 14–15.

[126] Vermes, *Jesus the Jew*, p. 199. Even Vermes's statement, "All that may be said of the Scrolls in this connection is that they indicate that the epithet, *son of God*, can accompany the title, 'Messiah,'" is a bit inaccurate, since it is not the epithet that occurs but a quotation of 2 Sam. 7:14, "he shall be my son."

[127] See E. Lohse et al., "υἱός, υἱοθεσία," *TDNT* (1972), 8:361: the reference to the Messiah as "my son" in the Ethiopic version of *1 Enoch* 105:2 is probably not original, since it is not present in the Greek, and the references to him as God's *filius* in 4 Ezra 7:28; 13:32, 37, 52; 14:9 are probably mistranslations of the Greek παῖς corresponding to the Hebrew עבדי. On 4 Ezra, see J. Jeremias, "παῖς θεοῦ," *TDNT* (1967; orig. 1954), 5:681 n. 196; M. E. Stone, "Features of the Eschatology of IV Ezra" (Ph.D. diss., Harvard University, 1965), pp. 71–75.

[128] *Contra* Vermes, *Jesus the Jew*, pp. 206–210.

that it could be misunderstood in a physical manner. This hypothesis, however, challenges Steichele's own contention that the title in Mark 1:11 should be understood in an adoptionistic, juridical sense; if it was for the most part avoided in Judaism because of its connotations of quasi divinity, it is reasonable to assume that Mark, in adopting it, was attracted to precisely those connotations.

4

Mark 9:2-8

The Transfigured Son of God

9:2a And *after six days*
9:2b   Jesus takes Peter and James and John
9:2c   and leads them up to *a high mountain*
9:2d   privately, by themselves.
9:2e And *he was transfigured* before them,
9:3a   and his garments became dazzling, extremely white,
9:3b   so white that no bleacher on earth can whiten them thus.
9:4a And there appeared to them *Elijah with Moses,*
9:4b   and they were conversing with Jesus.
9:5a And answering, Peter says to Jesus:
9:5b   Rabbi, it is good for us to be here,
9:5c   and let us make three tabernacles,
9:5d   one for you and *one for Moses and one for Elijah.*
9:6a For he did not know what to answer,
9:6b   for they were afraid.
9:7a And there came *a cloud overshadowing them,*
9:7b   and there came a *voice from out of the cloud:*
9:7c   This is my beloved son,
9:7d   *listen to him!*
9:8a And suddenly, looking around,
9:8b   they no longer saw anyone
9:8c   except Jesus alone with them.

The Old Testament Text
and the Old Testament Allusions

There are no word-for-word citations of Old Testament texts in the Markan transfiguration narrative. The concluding words of the heavenly voice,

80

however, "Listen to him!" (ἀκούετε αὐτοῦ), are so close to the exhortation
of Deut. 18:15, "To him you shall listen" (אֵלָיו תִּשְׁמָעוּן, αὐτοῦ ἀκούσεσθε),[1]
that we may speak of a virtual citation.
The heavenly voice of which these words are the conclusion represents
the climax of the entire narrative, the point toward which it all builds,[2] for
it interprets all the major events that have preceded it: Jesus' transformation, the appearance of Moses and Elijah, and the arrival of the overshadowing cloud. Peter's suggestion in v. 5 and the editorial comment on it in v. 6[3]
introduce a note of incomprehension and dramatic tension that is not resolved until the voice sounds forth. Immediately upon its being heard, the
vision ends.

In its Old Testament context, the exhortation "to him you shall listen"
is part of Moses' instructions to the children of Israel to obey the prophet
who will arise after his death:

> Yahweh your God will raise up for you a prophet like me from among
> you, from your brethren—*to him you shall listen.* . . . And Yahweh said
> to me, . . . "I will raise up for them a prophet like you from among their
> brethren; and I will put my words in his mouth, and he shall speak to
> them all that I command him." (Deut. 18:15–18, alt.)

If the larger context of this passage is in view in the words "listen to him!"
in Mark 9:7, then the Markan transfiguration narrative identifies Jesus as
this "Prophet-like-Moses," who became an important figure in the eschatological expectation of postbiblical Judaism.[4]

---

[1] In both Hebrew and Greek, the second person of the future (Hebrew imperfect) is an
alternate way of expressing a command; see GKC §107n; J. H. Moulton et al., *A Grammar
of New Testament Greek*, 4 vols. (Edinburgh: T. & T. Clark, 1908–65), 3.86; BDF §362; see
also H.-J. Steichele, *Der leidende Sohn Gottes: Eine Untersuchung einiger alttestamentlicher
Motive in der Christologie des Markusevangeliums*, Biblische Untersuchungen 14 (Regensburg:
Pustet, 1980), p. 168 n. 219.
[2] See H. C. Kee, "The Transfiguration in Mark: Epiphany or Apocalyptic Vision?" in
*Understanding the Sacred Text: Essays in Honor of Morton S. Enslin on the Hebrew Bible and
Christian Beginnings*, ed. J. Reumann (Valley Forge, Pa.: Judson Press, 1972), p. 139.
[3] On 9:6 as Markan redaction, see J. M. Nützel, *Die Verklärungserzählung im Markus-
evangelium*, FB 6 (Würzburg: Echter Verlag, 1973), pp. 125, 138; M. Horstmann, *Studien zur
markinischen Christologie: Mk 8,27–9,13 als Zugang zum Christusbild des zweiten Evangeliums*,
NTAbh 6, 2nd ed. (Münster: Aschendorff, 1973), pp. 81–83; J. Gnilka, *Das Evangelium nach
Markus*, EKKNT 2, 2 vols. (Zurich: Benziger Verlag, 1978, 1979), 2:53; B. D. Chilton, "The
Transfiguration: Dominical Assurance and Apostolic Vision," *NTS* 27 (1980), 118–120; E. Best,
Following Jesus: Discipleship in the Gospel of Mark, JSNTSup 4 (Sheffield: JSOT Press, 1981),
p. 56.
[4] On the Prophet-like-Moses in Judaism, see H. M. Teeple, *The Mosaic Eschatological Prophet*,
SBLMS 10 (Philadelphia: Society of Biblical Literature, 1957); J. Jeremias, "Μωυσῆς," TDNT
(1967), 4:867–873; W. A. Meeks, *The Prophet-King: Moses Traditions and the Johannine Christology*, NovTSup 14 (Leiden: E. J. Brill, 1967), passim. On the use made of this expectation in

That this larger Mosaic context is indeed in view is confirmed when we observe that the citation in 9:7 is only the most visible manifestation of a complex tissue of allusions in the transfiguration narrative to the Pentateuchal accounts of Moses. Already in 1840 David Friedrich Strauss noted the essential points of similarity between the transfiguration accounts in the Synoptic Gospels and the stories of Moses on Sinai in the Old Testament. As Strauss observed, the primary parallels extend over two different passages, Ex. 24:1–2, 9–18 (Moses' ascent of the mountain with Aaron, Nadab, and Abihu) and Ex. 34:29–35 (the transfiguration of Moses' face), but the "earlier ascent of the mountain . . . might easily be confounded with the later one."[5] Indeed, there is evidence that the two ascents were confounded in the Judaism of Mark's time; Pseudo-Philo, who was nearly a contemporary of Mark, places the events of Ex. 34:29–35 immediately after those of 24:15–18 (*Bib. Ant.* 11:15–12:1).[6]

The parallels first noted by Strauss have been succinctly enumerated by J. Jeremias,[7] and can be presented in tabular form:

Mark		*Exodus*
9:2a	six days	24:16
9:2a	three disciples	24:1, 9
9:2b	ascent of mountain	24:9, 12–13, 15, 18
9:2b–3	transfiguration	34:29
9:7b	God reveals self in veiled form through cloud	24:15–16, 18
9:7b	voice out of cloud	24:16

We may add to this list a verse in a passage that follows shortly, Mark 9:15, in which the crowd, seeing Jesus, is astonished at him.[8] Since no adequate

---

early Christianity, see H.-J. Schoeps, *Theologie und Geschichte des Judenchristentums* (Tübingen: J. C. B. Mohr [Paul Siebeck], 1949), pp. 87–98; R. N. Longenecker, *The Christology of Early Jewish Christianity*, SBT n.s. 17 (Naperville, Ill.: Alec R. Allenson, 1970), pp. 32–38; T. F. Glasson, *Moses in the Fourth Gospel*, SBT 40 (London: SCM Press, 1963); J. L. Martyn, *History and Theology in the Fourth Gospel*, 2nd ed. (Nashville: Abingdon Press, 1979; orig. 1968), pp. 102–111; D. P. Moessner, *Lord of the Banquet: The Literary and Theological Significance of the Lukan Travel Narrative* (Minneapolis: Fortress Press, 1989).

   [5] D. F. Strauss, *The Life of Jesus Critically Examined* (Philadelphia: Fortress Press, 1972; orig. 1840), pp. 544–545.

   [6] See E. Schweizer, *The Good News According to Mark* (Atlanta: John Knox Press, 1970), p. 181. For the text of Pseudo-Philo, see D. J. Harrington, *OTP* 2:297–377.

   [7] Jeremias, "Μωυσῆς," n. 228; cf. Gnilka, *Evangelium* 2:32.

   [8] Steichele points to differences in detail between the Sinai accounts in Exodus and the Markan transfiguration (*Leidende Sohn*, pp. 173–181). These observations are accurate but beside the point. The common details do not have to function in exactly the same way in the two narratives for Mark's account to reflect that of the Old Testament, and the number of convergences in theme and vocabulary is simply too large to be fortuitous; see W. R. Stegner,

motivation for such astonishment can be found within the story line itself,[9] and since the astonishment is so similar to the awe of the Israelites when they beheld Moses' transfigured face in Ex. 34:29–35, it is probable that the Moses typology is at work in this detail as well.[10]

The thesis that Mark's transfiguration narrative is stamped with a Moses typology seems at first glance to be called into question by the way in which Mark 9:4 lists Elijah's name before Moses' ("there appeared to them *Elijah with Moses*"). To complicate matters further, it is at least possible that Mark himself is responsible for this order. The reverse order, Moses–Elijah, is reflected not only a verse later in Mark's own narrative (9:5) but also in an agreement of Matthew and Luke over against Mark in their parallel to 9:4 (Matt. 17:3; Luke 9:30). They also agree against Mark in having Jesus' face as well as his clothes shine (Matt. 17:2; Luke 9:29). This shining conforms their transfiguration narratives more closely than Mark's to Ex. 34:29–30, in which Moses' face shines as he descends Sinai with the two tablets of the law. Either Matthew and Luke, independently of each other, realized that the Markan story reflected a Moses typology and decided to make the likeness to the Old Testament narrative even closer by illuminating Jesus' face and switching the order of the names of his companions, or they knew, besides Mark, something like Mark's putative source, an independent version of the transfiguration in which Jesus' face shone and in which his visitors were listed as "Moses and Elijah." The order Moses–Elijah in Mark 9:5 tips the scales a little bit in the direction of this order having been present in the pre-Markan version of 9:4 and thus supports the second hypothesis slightly.[11]

The order Elijah–Moses, however, does not really lessen the Mosaic typology of Mark's transfiguration narrative; instead it ensures that that typology will be interpreted *eschatologically*. In many Jewish traditions

---

Narrative Theology in Early Jewish Christianity (Louisville, Ky.: Westminster/John Knox Press, 1989), pp. 87–91. The phrase "after six days" in 9:2 is particularly striking, as Steichele himself acknowledges (pp. 181–182); this is the only definite time indication outside of the passion narrative, and Steichele can come up with no convincing alternative to seeing it as a reminiscence of the Sinai story in the Old Testament.

[9] Contra, e.g., V. Taylor, *The Gospel According to Saint Mark*, 2nd ed. (Grand Rapids: Baker Book House, 1981), p. 396: "The amazement is due to the unexpected appearance of Jesus."

[10] See Nützel, *Verklärungserzählung*, pp. 160–161. W. Lane objects that "the charge of 9:9 would be senseless if Jesus' appearance called attention to what had taken place upon the mountain" (*The Gospel of Mark*, NICNT [Grand Rapids: Wm. B. Eerdmans Publishing Co., 1974], p. 330 n. 48), but this is probably demanding too much rationalism of Mark's narrative.

[11] Supporting one or the other element of this reconstruction are E. Lohmeyer, *Das Evangelium des Markus*, MeyerK, 11th ed. (Göttingen: Vandenhoeck & Ruprecht, 1951), p. 175 n. 1; Taylor, *Mark*, p. 389; Nützel, *Verklärungserzählung*, pp. 97–98; Horstmann, *Christologie*, pp. 85–88; Gnilka, *Evangelium* 2:32; Chilton, "Transfiguration," pp. 117–118; Best, *Following*, p. 57.

Elijah but not Moses was expected to return just prior to the end in order to pave the way for the Messiah,[12] and Mark's awareness of this expectation is clear from the immediately following passage, 9:9–13 (see the next chapter of this study). The appearance of "Elijah with Moses," then, indicates that what is pictured in the transfiguration narrative is not a timeless mythic pageant but a vision related to the advent of "the great and terrible day of the Lord" (cf. Mal. 4:5). The radiance of Jesus' garments fits with this eschatological context, since Old Testament, Jewish, and New Testament traditions speak of the radiance with which the righteous will be clothed at the eschaton (Dan. 12:3; 2 *Apoc. Bar.* 51:1–3; Matt. 13:43; Rev. 7:13–14), and 2 Cor. 3:7–18 compares this eschatological glory with Moses' radiance in a passage that, like Mark 9:2, uses the verb μεταμορφοῦν.[13]

Despite the upstaging of Moses by Elijah in the list of 9:4, therefore, the Mosaic typology is central to the transfiguration. What significance does this typology have for Mark? Three dimensions of the Mosaic image in post-biblical Judaism are significant here: Moses' enthronement, his translation to heaven at his death, and his divinization. We will consider each in turn.

Moses' Enthronement

The first postbiblical trajectory in the presentation of Moses that is relevant for the Markan transfiguration narrative has to do with Moses' enthronement at Mount Sinai. In his thorough study of the traditions about Moses that circulated in intertestamental and rabbinic Judaism, Wayne Meeks has concluded that Moses' ascent of Sinai was often portrayed in this way.[14] The interpretation of the Sinai event as an enthronement is found already in the work of the second-century B.C. Jewish poet Ezekiel the Tragedian. In his *Exagōgē*, Ezekiel has Moses describe a visionary dream in which he receives the tokens of kingship from God on Sinai:

> On Sinai's peak I saw what seemed a throne
> so great in size it touched the clouds of heaven.
> Upon it sat a man of noble mien,
> becrowned, and with a scepter in one hand
> while with the other he did beckon me.

---

[12] As W. Michaelis says, "In the strict sense the precursor motif applies only to Elijah. Messianically Moses is a type or countertype of the Messiah, a predecessor rather than a precursor" ("σκηνή, κτλ.," *TDNT* [1971], 7:380). The only rabbinic text found by S-B (1:757) that speaks of Moses as the Messiah's precursor is *Deut. Rab.* 3, but, as Nützel points out, this text is very late (*Verklärungserzählung*, pp. 115–116).

[13] Kee, "Transfiguration," in *Understanding the Sacred Text*, ed. Reumann, pp. 143–144.

[14] Meeks, *Prophet-King*, passim; idem, "Moses as God and King," in *Religions in Antiquity: Essays in Memory of Erwin Ramsdell Goodenough*, ed. J. Neusner, Studies in the History of Religions [Supplements to *Numen*] 14 (Leiden: E. J. Brill, 1968), pp. 354–371.

I made approach and stood before the throne.
He handed o'er the scepter and he bade
me mount the throne, and gave to me the crown;
then he himself withdrew from off the throne.
                                   (lines 68–82)[15]

In this account, which has some striking similarities to the vision described
in Dan. 7:13–14,[16] the ascent of Sinai ("he beckoned me . . . I approached")
is linked with Moses' reception of a kingly scepter and of a crown, and with
his mounting of a throne. Jethro's interpretation of the dream goes on to
predict that Moses will "cause a mighty throne to rise, and you yourself will
rule and govern men" (lines 85–86), thus cementing the royal interpretation of the Sinai ascent.

A similar interpretation of the Sinai event as an enthronement of Moses
is found in a writing of Philo. In the *Life of Moses* the events on Sinai are
described in these terms:

> If, according to the proverb, "friends' things are common," and the prophet
> [Moses] was declared the friend of God, then it follows that he would
> share also his possessions, according to what was needful. . . . What then?
> Did he not also enjoy an even greater partnership with the Father and
> Maker of the universe, being deemed worthy of the same title? For he
> was named god and king (θεὸς καὶ βασιλεύς) of the whole nation. And
> he was said to have entered into the darkness where God was, that is,
> into the formless and invisible and incorporeal archetypal essence of
> existing things, perceiving things invisible to mortal nature. (1.155–158)[17]

Here Moses' ascent of Mount Sinai (his entry into the darkness where God
was; cf. Ex. 20:21) is interpreted as an enthronement ("he was named . . .
king"). It should also be noted that Moses is called a prophet, an epithet
reminiscent of Deut. 18:15, the verse quoted in Mark 9:7.

Meeks amply demonstrates that the views of Ezekiel and Philo are not
idiosyncratic. The New Testament itself shows an awareness of the relationship between the Moses typology and the kingship theme. In John
6:14–15 the people recognize Jesus as "the prophet who is coming into the
world" — that is, the Prophet-like-Moses of Deut. 18:15–18 — and then

---

[15] Meeks, "Moses," in *Religions in Antiquity*, ed. Neusner, pp. 358–359. On the date of
Ezekiel's *Exagōgē*, see R. G. Robertson in *OTP.*

[16] See Robertson, who remarks that in both passages a figure is chosen by God to represent him as divine vizier (*OTP* 2:811); note also the clouds of heaven and the approach to
the heavenly throne.

[17] Translation from Meeks, "Moses," in *Religions in Antiquity*, ed. Neusner, p. 355.

attempt to seize him and make him king.[18] Rabbinic and Samaritan traditions regularly speak of Moses' kingship, and they often connect it with his
ascent of Sinai. In some of these traditions Moses' beaming face (Ex.
34:29) is interpreted as his reception of God's crown of light, and it is also said
that he receives a royal robe of light from God.[19]

Not only does Moses become a king, however; his enthronement also
implies his participation in *God's* kingship. This point is already clearly made
in Ezekiel's *Exagōgē*, in which God invests Moses with the symbols of his
own kingship, handing over to him his crown and scepter and even, extraordinarily, abdicating his throne in favor of him. It is implicit also in the passage
from Philo's *Life of Moses* quoted above; Moses can be called a king because
God is a king and because God grants him a share of his own kingship,
on the principle that "friends share things in common."

As Meeks demonstrates, although Philo does not explicitly say that God
is a king, this supposition is absolutely essential for his argument, and the
fact that there is a missing link in the reasoning suggests that he is drawing
on a preexisting exegetical tradition. This missing link is supplied in a
passage from the tannaitic midrash *Tanḥuma* (4:51–52), in which Moses'
kingship is exegetically derived from God's on the principle that God shares
his glory with those who fear him; this derivation is then confirmed by a
citation of Deut. 33:5. Although there is no specific reference to the Sinai
ascent here, it is implied by the proof text from Deut. 33:5 and by a reference
elsewhere in the homily to Ex. 34:29.[20] Other rabbinic traditions about
Moses that do not specifically relate to Sinai also link his kingship with that
of God, and one at least uses the well-known rabbinic phrase "taking upon
oneself the yoke of the kingdom of heaven."[21]

For the reader of Mark, the connection between Moses' transfiguring
experience on Sinai and his reception of God's kingship is strikingly reminiscent of the fact that the account of Jesus' transfiguration immediately
follows 8:38–9:1, in which the coming of the kingdom of God (9:1) is

---

[18] See Meeks, *Prophet-King*, p. 1; John 6:14–15 is the point of departure for Meeks's entire
book.
[19] See Meeks, "Moses," in *Religions in Antiquity*, ed. Neusner, pp. 355–359; idem, *Prophet-
King*, pp. 181–196, 227–238.
[20] Meeks, *Prophet-King*, pp. 185, 192–195; idem, "Moses," in *Religions in Antiquity*, ed.
Neusner, pp. 355–357. Various Samaritan traditions also imply that God granted Moses a share
of his kingship on Sinai (Meeks, "Moses," pp. 357–358).
[21] See Meeks, *Prophet-King*, pp. 184–185, citing *Mekilta*, Beshallah 6 (J. Z. Lauterbach, *Mekilta
de-Rabbi Ishmael*, 3 vols. [Philadelphia: Jewish Publication Society, 1961; orig. 1933–35], 1:235])
and *Sipre Num.* par. 80. The latter links Jethro's taking upon himself the yoke of the kingdom
(i.e., becoming a proselyte) with his being the father-in-law of Moses, the king.

paralleled to Jesus' own coming as Son of man (8:38).[22] Mark 9:1, a redactionally placed "hinge" verse, links the parousia prophecy of 8:38[23] with
the transfiguration narrative of 9:2–8;[24] Mark thus implies that Jesus' transfiguration is a prolepsis of "the kingdom of God come in power." Like Moses,
then, Jesus ascends the mount and there is seen to be a king, a sovereign
whose kingship partakes of God's own royal authority over the universe
(βασιλεία τοῦ θεοῦ). This implication is further accentuated by the fact that
the divine voice in 9:7 hails Jesus as "Son of God," a title which, as we have
seen, has its roots in the royal traditions of Israel.[25] In line with this royal
context, the transfiguration of Jesus' clothing, like Moses' transfiguration
in some Jewish traditions, is probably symbolic of a royal robing.

For biblically literate readers, therefore, one of the chief functions of the
Mosaic typology in the transfiguration narrative would be to drive home
the association between Jesus' kingship and the coming of God's kingdom.

Moses' Translation at His Death

In Mark the transfiguration narrative is not an end in itself; rather, it points
beyond itself to an eschatological event, Jesus' resurrection from the dead.
The royal Mosaic features of the transfiguration narrative, therefore, fore-
shadow the enthronement of Jesus that occurs at his resurrection. This
association of enthronement with an after-death experience also has Mosaic
precedent.

The linkage of the transfiguration narrative with the resurrection is
established redactionally by its juxtaposition with 9:9–10 and is underlined
in an intriguing manner by the larger context of the Old Testament passage
cited in 9:7. In 9:9, which is a redactional verse,[26] the Markan Jesus
establishes a link between the transfiguration narrative and the resurrection

---

[22] Note the parallel terminology: "when he *comes* in his father's *glory*"; "the kingdom of
God *coming* in *power.*" Cf. the parallelism in 11:9–10 between *he who comes* in the name of
the Lord and *the coming kingdom* of David. On the relation of the traditions of Moses'
enthronement to the Markan transfiguration narrative, see Kee, "Transfiguration," in *Understanding the Sacred Text,* ed. Reumann, pp. 147–149.

[23] Which uses the imagery of Dan. 7:13–14, as does Ezekiel's *Exagōgē;* see above, p. 85.

[24] E. Nardoni, "A Redactional Interpretation of Mark 9:1," *CBQ* 43 (1981), 365–384; see
also J. Marcus, *The Mystery of the Kingdom of God,* SBLDS 90 (Atlanta: Scholars Press, 1986),
p. 52.

[25] The reference to God's kingdom in 9:1 is thus linked conceptually with the reference
to the kingly title "Son of God" in 9:7, and this linkage is congruent with the association of
that title with the kingdom of God that we observed in our study of 1:9–15 (see chapter 3
above).

[26] See Gnilka, *Evangelium* 2:40: Mark 9:9–10 are redactional, since the theme of resurrection is not specifically handled in vv. 11–13 but relates to the transfiguration narrative and
to 8:31.

by ordering the disciples not to tell anyone what they have seen on the mountain until the Son of man is raised from the dead (ἐκ νεκρῶν ἀναστῇ; cf.
τὸ ἐκ νεκρῶν ἀναστῆναι, "the rising from the dead," in 9:10). It is striking
that the vocabulary of raising found in Mark 9:9–10 is found also in the
larger context of Deut. 18:15, the "Prophet-like-Moses" passage cited in Mark
9:7. Here the imperative to listen to Moses' successor is based on the promise that Yahweh will *raise up* (יָקִים; ἀναστήσει)[27] such a successor from among
Moses' brethren. Although in the original text the verb "to raise" is used
in the sense of "to bring upon the scene,"[28] in later times the verb came
to be associated with the idea of the raising of the dead.[29] One suspects
that the larger context of the passage from Deuteronomy is in Mark's mind
and that he interprets the Deuteronomic reference to raising up Moses'
successor as a hint of Jesus' resurrection.

This possibility is strengthened when it is recalled that in Second Temple
Judaism, the New Testament, and rabbinic traditions, Moses, like Enoch
(Gen. 5:24) and Elijah (2 Kings 2:11), was believed to have ascended to
heaven at his death, and this ascent was believed to have been foreshadowed
by the ascent of Sinai. Philo, for example, takes it for granted that Deut.
34:6, "no one knows his grave," means that Moses was translated, stating
matter-of-factly that Enoch, Moses, and Elijah all obtained the reward of
heavenly translation (*Questions on Genesis* 1.86).[30] As Meeks points out,
moreover, Philo's descriptions of Moses' translation parallel his descriptions
of his ascent on Sinai, and this parallelism is found also in some rabbinic
midrashim that link Deut. 34:5 ("and Moses died *there*") with Ex. 34:28
("and he was *there* with the Lord").[31] This parallelism between Sinai and
translation provides a plausible background for the redactional linkage made
in Mark 9:2–10 between the events on the mountain and the reference to
resurrection, since resurrection and ascension to heaven are related
concepts, although admittedly they have different history-of-religions
backgrounds.[32]

It must be acknowledged that the notion of Moses' translation contradicts
the plain sense of Deut. 34:5: "So Moses the servant of the Lord died there

---

[27] Cf. Deut. 18:18, where the first person of the same verbs is used: אָקִים; ἀναστήσω.
[28] BDB, p. 879.
[29] See D. C. Duling, "The Promises to David and Their Entrance into Christianity— Nailing
Down a Likely Hypothesis," *NTS* 68 (1973), 55–77.
[30] Meeks, *Prophet-King*, p. 124.
[31] Ibid., pp. 122–125, 210. In discussing the rabbinic traditions Meeks notes that the connection between Deut. 34:5 and Ex. 34:28 is strained; "one can only conclude that Moses'
final ascension was already connected with his ascent on Sinai and that the exegetical
connection by the coincidence of the word שָׁם 'there,' was secondary" (p. 210).
[32] See G. W. E. Nickelsburg, Jr., *Resurrection, Immortality, and Eternal Life in Intertestamental
Judaism*, HTS 26 (Cambridge, Mass.: Harvard University Press, 1972).

in the land of Moab." That notion is, moreover, explicitly denied by Josephus (*Antiquities* 4.326) and the *Mekilta* (*Baḥodesh* 4 [Lauterbach 2:224]). The very strength of these protests, however, suggests that in some circles Moses' translation to heaven at his death was an important article of faith.[33] Indeed, as J. D. Tabor points out, Josephus's own references to Moses' death are somewhat contradictory;[34] in another passage (*Antiquities* 3.96) he mentions that there is a difference of opinion about it, with some claiming that rather than dying Moses returned to the divinity. In the very passage in which Josephus denies that this is true, *Antiquities* 4.326, he also introduces features not present in the biblical account that would seem to support it:

> And while he said farewell to Eleazar and Joshua and was still communing with them, a cloud suddenly descended upon him and he disappeared in a ravine. But he has written of himself in the sacred books that he died, for fear that any might say that by reason of his surpassing virtue he had gone back to the divinity.[35]

If Josephus wants to *deny* that Moses "returned to the divinity" at his death, Tabor asks, why does he import the cloud/translation motif? The most convincing explanation is that this motif is a feature of a widespread account of Moses' death whose tendency to divinize Moses frightens Josephus.[36] For our purposes, the fact that the disappearance of Moses is linked with the descent of a cloud is particularly interesting, since this is exactly what happens in Mark 9:7-8. The cloud in the Markan verse serves not only as a stage prop for the sounding forth of the heavenly voice but also as a foreshadowing of the cloud upon which Jesus will, presumably, be taken up to heaven at his resurrection (see Acts 1:9)[37] as well as of the clouds upon which he will return at the parousia (Mark 13:26; 14:62).

Jewish traditions related to the Markan transfiguration narrative, then, link Moses' enthronement on Sinai with his translation to heaven at his death. Mark himself, furthermore, has framed the transfiguration narrative with the kingship motif of 9:1 and the resurrection motif of 9:9-10. These converging lines of evidence point to a Markan view that Jesus assumes a status of kingship at his resurrection. As we shall see in chapter 7 below,

---

[33] See Meeks, *Prophet-King*, p. 205.

[34] J. D. Tabor, "'Returning to the Divinity': Josephus's Portrayal of the Disappearances of Enoch, Elijah, and Moses," *JBL* 108 (1989), 225-238.

[35] Translation of H. St. J. Thackeray in LCL.

[36] This thesis of Tabor is already anticipated by Meeks (*Prophet-King*, pp. 140-141), who remarks, "The polemic presupposes practice."

[37] The fact that no account of this exaltation is narrated in Mark's Gospel is no evidence against this presumption, since Mark assumes much action beyond the end of his Gospel that the Gospel does not specifically narrate; see J. L. Magness, *Sense and Absence: Structure and Suspension in the Ending of Mark's Gospel*, SBLSS (Atlanta: Scholars Press, 1986).

this view is confirmed by Mark's application of Psalm 110:1 to Jesus' resurrection in 12:35–37.

In Mark's eyes, however, Jesus' resurrection and his crucifixion constitute a unitary event, and so it is not surprising that, as we shall see in chapter 8, there are already strong suggestions of kingship in the account of Jesus' crucifixion in Mark 15. One of these, the mocking investiture of Jesus with a royal robe by the soldiers in 15:17, forms a christologically significant counterpart to the transfiguration. Readers of chapter 15 who hear of the way in which Jesus' tormentors clothe him with a cloak of royal purple, place a crown of thorns on his head, and hail him sarcastically as King of the Jews will know that this is the same Jesus who, a few short chapters back, appeared before the entranced disciples robed with a royal cloak of supernatural light. They will therefore be able to gather that the soldiers' actions unwittingly express a central truth about Jesus, his royal identity, the identity into which he is inducted by the death and resurrection to which the soldiers are driving him.

Moses' Divinization and Jesus' Divine Sonship

But what exactly is involved in that royal identity? Here again a comparison with Moses traditions is illuminating. In *Life of Moses* 1.158, which was quoted above, Philo implies that the enthronement of Moses on Sinai involved his becoming a god: "For he was named god and king of the whole nation." A similar notion of Moses' divinity is found in a commentary in *Pesiqta de Rab Kahana* on the phrase from Deut. 33:1, משה איש האלהים, "Moses the man of God." Here the phrase is read as "Moses, a man, God":

> "A man, god": "A man" when he ascended on high; "god" when he descended below. "And Aaron and all the sons of Israel saw Moses and behold! his face emitted beams of light." (Ex. 34:30)[38]

In this exegesis Moses' transfigured appearance is interpreted as a sign that he has attained a divine status by his sojourn on Sinai. Elsewhere Philo, rabbinic traditions, and Samaritan traditions derive the notion of Moses' godlikeness from Ex. 7:1, "See, I have made you a god to Pharaoh" (alt.).[39]

Such ideas of the divinization of Moses were in some tension with the monotheism of Judaism. In other passages Philo himself explains that Moses'

---

[38] *Pesiq. Rab Kah.*, *pisqa'* 32; cf. *Deut. Rab.* 11.4; Midrash on Psalms 90:1; cited by Meeks, "Moses," in *Religions in Antiquity*, ed. Neusner, p. 357; idem, *Prophet-King*, p. 195.

[39] Philo, *Allegorical Interpretation* 1.40; *On the Sacrifices of Abel and Cain* 9; *The Worse Attacks the Better* 161–62; *On the Migration of Abraham* 84; *On the Change of Names* 19; *On Dreams* 2.189; see Meeks, "Moses," in *Religions in Antiquity*, ed. Neusner, p. 355. On the rabbinic and Samaritan traditions, see Meeks, *Prophet-King*, pp. 193, 195, 234–236.

divinity is to be understood only figuratively,[40] and Josephus and rabbinic traditions both use the biblical account of Moses' death and burial to ward off the conclusion that he did not die and may thus become an object of worship. Such polemic implies a practice against which it is directed, and thus it is probable that already in the first century there were Jews who went so far as to worship Moses as a god.[41]

This history-of-religions background has some relevance for the question of how "high" a title "Son of God" is in Mark 9:7. Certainly, as we have noted, it is a royal title, but the Philonic association of "king" with "god" in *Life of Moses* 1.158 should warn us against seeing royalty and divinity as necessarily separate categories, a point we have already made in our study of Jesus' divine sonship in Mark 1:11. The persistent Jewish traditions about Moses becoming a god on Sinai, coupled with the evident Sinai/Mosaic typology of Mark's transfiguration narrative, suggest the possibility that the divine voice in Mark 9:7 is attributing to Jesus a status that transcends the human.

Such an interpretation of the title "Son of God" in 9:7 is supported by the immediate context of the transfiguration. We have already pointed to the fact that the transfiguration is preceded by 8:38–9:1, in which the coming of the kingdom of God is paralleled to the coming of the Son of man. It is now appropriate to add that in 8:38 the Son of man is more precisely designated as one who will come *"in the glory of his Father with the holy angels."* Although the title "Son of God" does not explicitly appear here, it is certainly implied ("in *his Father's* glory"). This Son of man/Son of God, moreover, will bear his father's δόξα ("glory") when he comes, and the latter term, which goes back to the Old Testament, denotes "the divine mode of being," as G. Kittel puts it. Kittel, moreover, speaks of the decisive step taken in some New Testament passages, including Mark 8:38, of using in relation to Christ a word that was used almost exclusively in relation to God in the Old Testament and Jewish sources.[42] The association of the Son of man with the divine δόξα in 8:38, then, implies a high conception of Christ's status and links 8:38 with the picture of the glorified Jesus in 9:2–8. The high Christology of 8:38 is further evidenced by the fact that this glorified Son of man will come *with the angels;* he is thus at least on a par with, and probably superior to, those heavenly denizens.[43]

Thus, in some of the Jewish traditions about Moses, the Markan Jesus'

---

[40] See Meeks, *Prophet-King*, p. 105.

[41] Ibid., p. 211.

[42] The one exception noted by Kittel in the latter sources, significantly, is that Moses is sometimes spoken of as participating in the divine glory on the basis of Ex. 34:29–35 ("δοκέω, κτλ.," *TDNT* [1964; orig. 1935] 2:246–248).

[43] See Kittel on the δόξα of the angels in the Old Testament, intertestamental Judaism, and the New Testament ("δοκέω," p. 251).

participation in God's kingship is understood in a very realistic way. Listening to Jesus is like listening to God (9:7); seeing the transfigured Jesus is like seeing the glory of God (8:38; 9:2–3); perceiving the arrival of Jesus as eschatological Son of man is like perceiving the arrival of God's kingly power (8:38–9:1). Although Mark does portray Jesus as being subordinate to God, his Jesus is one whose identity approaches the category of divinity. The title "Son of God," therefore, is a perfect one for the Markan Jesus, since it bespeaks both his unique familial likeness to God and his subordination to the one whom he calls "Father" (see 8:38; 13:32; 14:36).

Conclusions: Mark 9:2–8 and the Markan Community

Mark's transfiguration narrative, which is strategically situated near the very center of his Gospel, adds some Mosaic features to the scriptural outline of Jesus' identity that has been sketched so far in the Gospel. Jesus is the figure spoken of by the very fountainhead of Judaism, Moses, as destined to appear at the end of days to claim the obedience of the people of God, just as Moses himself had done when the people was born. Like the Moses of Jewish legend, Jesus is a king—indeed, a king who participates in God's own rule. Like Moses in some Jewish traditions, he is not bound by death and attains a status close to that of God himself. These Mosaic features of Jesus' identity are reinforced by the deliberate echoes of Exodus 24 and 34 in the narrative.

Yet, as we have noted, Mark combines this Mosaic typology with a reversal of the names of Moses and Elijah in 9:4. The emphasis on Elijah makes clear that Mark's readers are not to understand Jesus in precisely the same way as Philo understands Moses, as a man divinized because of his virtue and therefore made immortal. He is above all, rather, an *eschatological* figure, one who shows to those with eyes to see not only what humanity can be but also *what the world is becoming* in the eschatological era inaugurated by the raising of the dead.[44] The God whose Son he is, similarly, is not just the invisible essence behind the changing appearances of the cosmos but a holy warrior whose triumph means the liberation of the captive universe. The βασιλεία of God in which the Son participates is more than God's invisible control over the course of events in an unchanging world; it is God's active movement *into* the world, the way of the Lord, which is at the same time the way of Jesus.[45]

---

[44] Note the alternation between the personal reference to Jesus' resurrection from the dead in 9:9 and the more general phrasing of 9:10, τὸ ἐκ νεκρῶν ἀναστῆναι, "the resurrection of the dead."

[45] See our treatment of these two ways in 1:2–3 in chapter 2 above. In 1:2–3, moreover, as in 9:2–8, the eschatological dimension shapes the entire understanding of the Old Testament background; see chapter 2 above, pp. 24–26.

For the members of the Markan community, the images of Jesus robed in light, conversing with Moses and Elijah, and being proclaimed Son of God by a heavenly voice probably function as a counter to other, profoundly unsettling images: images of dark days of tribulation fallen upon the church (see 13:19); images of beatings in synagogues, perhaps on the grounds of apostasy from the tradition symbolized by Moses (see 13:9; 7:5; 10:4); images of eloquent and militant personalities who are persuading many, even within the community, that *they* are the successors of Moses whose coming was prophesied of old (see 13:6, 22).[46] Which set of images truly shows where the Markan community stands? The radiant Jesus or the darkness of the tribulation? The Jesus who is attested by Moses and Elijah or the Jesus who is rejected by Moses' disciples? The Jesus singled out by a divine voice as God's unique son or the Jesus whose claims have been dwarfed by the plausible-sounding claims of other Messiahs?

The context in which Mark places his transfiguration narrative provides some insight into the way in which he attempts to resolve the tension between these images. As has often been noted,[47] in the Markan context the word that the disciples are called to hear at the transfiguration (9:7) is above all the word he has just uttered in 8:31, the word that prophesies his rejection, suffering, and death, as well as his resurrection. This saying, moreover, is followed by others that link these events with the life and fate of the disciples (8:34–35). Those who lose their lives for Jesus' sake will save them; the members of Mark's community can expect to experience an outpouring of the power of God even as they are called to suffer with Jesus (see 13:11). Thus the unearthly radiance of the transfiguration and the darkness of the Markan present are seen finally to cohere with each other, but only because they are tied together by the eschatological figure of the dying and rising Christ, in whose sufferings—but also in whose glory!—the Markan community participates as it follows him on the way.

Mark supports this interpretation by following his transfiguration narrative with an exegetical discussion about John the Baptist, a figure who paves the way for Jesus by going before him in the way of suffering and death (9:9–13). It is to this discussion that we now turn.

---

[46] In the Pentateuch Moses is not only a lawgiver but also a military leader. In some Jewish revolutionary circles in the first century, therefore, the "Prophet-like-Moses" was probably expected to be a military leader as well; M. Hengel, *The Zealots: Investigations into the Jewish Freedom Movement in the Period from Herod I Until 70 A.D.* (Edinburgh: T. & T. Clark, 1989), p. 230; R. A. Horsley and J. S. Hanson, *Bandits, Prophets, and Messiahs: Popular Movements at the Time of Jesus,* New Voices in Biblical Studies (San Francisco: Harper & Row, 1985), pp. 137–138. On the merging of the expectations for the Prophet-like-Moses and the Messiah, see Martyn, *History and Theology,* pp. 104–111.

[47] See, e.g., Lohmeyer, *Evangelium,* pp. 180–181; Schweizer, *Mark,* p. 183; Horstmann, *Christologie,* pp. 137–139.

5

Mark 9:11–13

The Suffering Son of Man and His Forerunner[1]

9:11a   And they asked him saying,
9:11b   Why do the scribes say that *Elijah must come first?*
9:12a   And he said to them,
9:12b   *Elijah, when he comes first, restores all things?*
9:12c   And how has it been *written of the Son of Man that he should suffer many things and be rejected?*
9:13a   But I say to you that Elijah has come
9:13b   and *they did to him whatever they wanted,*
9:13c   as it has been written concerning him.

The Old Testament Texts

In contrast to the passages studied thus far, Mark 9:11–13 offers no specific citations or even virtual citations of Old Testament texts. Mark 9:11b, 12b, however, the scribes' expectation that Elijah must come before the Messiah,[2] is a clear allusion to Mal. 3:22–23 LXX (3:23–24 MT; 4:5–6 Eng.):

> And behold, I am sending you Elijah the Tishbite before the great and manifest day of the Lord comes. And he will restore (ἀποκαταστήσει)[3] the heart of a father to his son and the heart of a man to his neighbor, lest I come and strike the earth utterly (alt.).

---

[1] This chapter is a revised version of my article "Mark 9,11–13: As It Has Been Written," *ZNW* 80 (1989), 42–63.

[2] Verse numbers will be cited according to the Septuagint in what follows. For the debate about whether or not there was in first-century Judaism an expectation of Elijah coming before the Messiah, see the excursus at the end of this chapter.

[3] This word, to which ἀποκαθιστάνει ("restores") in Mark 9:12b corresponds, establishes the dependence of the Markan text on the Septuagint of Malachi, since the Masoretic Text has differently והשיב, "and he will cause to turn."

It is more difficult to decide exactly what Old Testament texts are in view in 9:12c, where the Markan Jesus says that it has been written that the Son of man should suffer many things and be rejected. It is generally agreed that we are dealing not with a direct citation of a specific Old Testament text, nor with a Jewish exegetical tradition, but with a Christian interpretation of several Old Testament passages.[4] Exegetes differ about which Old Testament texts are more important, but most think that both the picture of Yahweh's suffering servant in Isaiah 52:13–53:12 and the Psalms of the Righteous Sufferer are in the background.[5] That these two bodies of literature provide part of the background of Mark 9:12c and related Markan passages[6] will be confirmed below in chapter 8, where it will be shown that there are numerous allusions to both of them in the Markan passion narrative.

Neither of these bodies of literature, however, mentions the Son of man. As C. H. Dodd suggested long ago, the identity of the sufferer as the "Son of man" probably brings into view at least Daniel 7—which also plays a role in the Markan passion narrative (14:62)—and perhaps Psalm 80 as well.[7] In the former, the "one like a son of man" is linked with "the people of the saints of the Most High" who undergo tribulation before their final, eschatological vindication (Dan. 7:13–14, 18, 21, 25, 27). In the latter, the Son of man, Yahweh's right-hand man, is linked with Israel, the plundered vine (Ps. 80:14–17). In both cases, as in the Psalms of the Righteous Sufferer and Isaiah 53, there is a corporate dimension to the figure of the suffering Son of man.[8] The transfer of the attributes of these corporate figures to Jesus, as Dodd showed, reflects a Christian exegetical tradition which thinks of Jesus as the inclusive representative of the people of God. "It has been written of the Son of man, that he must suffer many things and be rejected,"

---

[4] A. Suhl denies that any specific Old Testament passages are in view; 9:12c is a bald assertion that Jesus' suffering is "scriptural" (*Die Funktion der alttestamentlichen Zitate und Anspielungen im Markusevangelium* [Gütersloh: Gerd Mohn, 1965], p. 44). It strains credulity, however, to assert that readers at all familiar with the Old Testament could read the statement that "the Son of man must suffer many things" without thinking of figures such as the Suffering Servant of Isaiah and the Righteous Sufferer of the Psalms.

[5] See, e.g., C. E. B. Cranfield, *The Gospel According to Saint Mark*, CGTC (Cambridge: Cambridge University Press, 1974), p. 277; R. Pesch, *Das Markusevangelium*, HTKNT 2, 2 vols. (Freiburg: Herder, 1978), 2:79; D. J. Moo, *The Old Testament in the Gospel Passion Narratives* (Sheffield: Almond Press, 1983), passim; M. Black, "The Theological Appropriation of the Old Testament by the New Testament," *SJT* 39 (1986), 1–17. Cranfield cites Isa. 52:13–53:12 and Psalms 22; 118:10, 13, 18, 22; also Dan. 7:21, 25; Zech. 13:7. Pesch adds Pss. 69:33 and esp. 89:39 [LXX 88:39]: καὶ ἐξουδένωσας . . . τὸν χριστόν σου.

[6] Mark 8:31; 9:31; 10:33, 45; 14:21, 41.

[7] See C. H. Dodd, *According to the Scriptures: The Sub-structure of New Testament Theology* (London: Nisbet, 1952), pp. 116–119.

[8] On the corporate aspects of the Danielic "one like a son of man," the Righteous Sufferer of the Psalms, and the Suffering Servant of Isaiah, see further chapter 8 below.

is not so much a biblical citation or even an allusion, as a creative exegesis that brings together a number of passages.

We have already seen Mark doing something similar in 1:2–3, where he brings together three passages, Ex. 23:20, Mal. 3:1, and Isa. 40:3, yet introduces them all with the formula, "as it has been written in Isaiah the prophet." Here, it is true, he conflates several passages rather than, as in Mark 9:12c, paraphrasing them. It is nevertheless significant, as we have seen, that Mark includes all three Old Testament passages under the rubric "Isaiah." This inclusion itself comes close to being an exegetical conclusion: in Mark's eyes, Mal. 3:1 and Isa. 40:3 prophesy the same event, and that event is an eschatological recapitulation of the first exodus, to which Ex. 23:20 refers.[9] Nor is Mark alone among New Testament authors in using the formula καθὼς γέγραπται ("as it has been written") to designate exegetical conclusions. In Gal. 4:22, for example, Paul uses this formula to "summarize a quantity of Old Testament material spread over a number of chapters in Genesis."[10] Similarly, John 7:38 uses the formula "as the scripture has said" to introduce what is probably an exegetical conclusion from several scriptural passages.[11]

These New Testament instances in which "as it has been written" and similar formulas designate an exegetical conclusion rather than a quotation draw on contemporary Jewish practice. Recently M. Black has pointed to the "peshering" of Hos. 3:4 in CD 20:15–17, "As He [God] said, 'There shall be no king, no prince, *no judge, no man to rebuke with justice. . . .*'"[12] As Black notes, the italicized words have no counterpart in the original Hebrew text, yet the formula "He said" is usually used for biblical citations. The italicized words therefore represent "a targum-type expansion or explication" of the original text, an expansion which is itself cited as holy scripture. A similar phenomenon confronts us at every turn in the *Temple Scroll*, where the Qumran community's *halakot*, themselves derived by exegesis of the Old Testament,[13] are interspersed with direct citations from the Pentateuch itself, and Pentateuchal citation and Qumran exegesis alike are

---

9   See chapter 2 above, pp. 20, 24–25.

10   C. K. Barrett, "The Allegory of Abraham, Sarah, and Hagar in the Argument of Galatians," in *Rechtfertigung: Festschrift für Ernst Käsemann*, ed. J. Friedrich et al. (Tübingen: J. C. B. Mohr [Paul Siebeck], 1976), pp. 1–16, esp. p. 9.

11   The parallel in John 7:38 was suggested to me orally by M. C. de Boer; on it, see R. E. Brown, *The Gospel According to John*, AB 29, 29A, 2 vols. (Garden City, N.Y.: Doubleday & Co., 1966, 1970), 1:320–323.

12   Black, "Theological Appropriation," pp. 3–4.

13   See L. H. Schiffman, *The Halakhah at Qumran*, SJLA 16 (Leiden: E. J. Brill, 1975), pp. 19, 75–76. Schiffman's work was published before the *Temple Scroll*, but his conclusion has, if anything, been strengthened by the publication of the latter.

"set out as direct divine speech (in the first person) addressed to Moses. . . ."[14] It is not so unusual, then, that Mark 9:12c uses the formula "it has been written" to denote an exegetical conclusion. This part of our passage (9:12c) may very well be a piece of Markan editing designed to bring Mark's theology of the cross to the fore.[15] Mark 9:13 follows smoothly after 9:11-12b, since both deal with the scriptural witness to the returning Elijah, but 9:12c is disruptive, suddenly bringing in the intrusive theme of the sufferings of the Son of man.[16] Without it, 9:11-13 is a straightforward pericope addressing what was surely a problem for the early church: if Jesus was the Messiah, where was his reputed predecessor, Elijah? The answer: John the Baptist was Elijah. In addition to 9:12c, it is also likely that the phrase "as it has been written of him" in v. 13c is Markan redaction.[17]

The Violent Fate of Elijah
and Scriptural Contradictions

Mention of Mark 9:13c brings up the other major difficulty with our passage: *Where* is it written that "they" will do violence to the returning Elijah?[18] This is a problem because there is simply no Old Testament passage which prophesies that the eschatological Elijah figure will suffer violence. Nor, indeed, does there seem to be an established postbiblical Jewish expectation of this sort.[19] Commentators therefore sometimes take Mark

---

[14] J. Maier, *The Temple Scroll: An Introduction, Translation, and Commentary*, JSOTSup 34 (Sheffield: JSOT Press, 1985), p. 3. Cf. Maier's further comment: "Many biblical quotations appear in a modified, abbreviated or expanded form and it is not uncommon to find several Biblical passages which deal with similar subject matter, merged together in both form and content." See already Y. Yadin, "The Temple Scroll," in *New Directions in Biblical Archaeology*, ed. D. N. Freedman and J. C. Greenfield (Garden City, N.Y.: Doubleday & Co., 1971), pp. 156-166, esp. pp. 159-160.

[15] R. Bultmann (*History of the Synoptic Tradition* [New York: Harper & Row, 1963], p. 125) and E. Lohmeyer (*Das Evangelium des Markus*, MeyerK, 11th ed. [Göttingen: Vandenhoeck & Ruprecht, 1951], pp. 182-183) both treat 9:12c as a post-Markan interpolation, but the statement that the Son of man must suffer many things is strongly reminiscent of the three redactional passion predictions (8:31; 9:31; 10:33-34), especially of 8:31, and the use of ἵνα to express the scriptural necessity of Jesus' death is a Markan characteristic (cf. 14:49). Mark's redactional insertions often create literary awkwardness; see, e.g., 4:31; 9:6; 14:28; 16:7.

[16] Bultmann, *History*, p. 125; Lohmeyer, *Evangelium*, pp. 182-183; Black, "Theological Appropriation," p. 9.

[17] If Mark 9:12c is Markan, so probably is 9:13c. Here are the only two Markan instances of γέγραπται ἐπί + accusative; contrast 14:21, καθὼς γέγραπται περὶ αὐτοῦ, which is probably traditional.

[18] Matthew and Luke certainly realize the difficulties with Mark 9:11-13. Luke omits the passage altogether, and Matt. 17:10 omits Mark 9:12c and 9:13c.

[19] The only evidence for such an expectation is Rev. 11:1-13, where the "two witnesses" are killed. Scholars sometimes identify these witnesses with Elijah and Moses on the basis

9:13bc to be a reference to the ministry of the historical Elijah (1 Kings 19:2–10) and assume that Mark is working with a typology between Elijah's historical and eschatological appearances.[20] In the text itself, however, there is no suggestion of typology; if such were the case, one would expect a conclusion such as, "as they did to him before" (cf. Luke 17:26, 28). Even some of those who cite 1 Kings 19, therefore, do not seem to be very happy with this solution,[21] and overall, as M. Black puts it, the suggestion of a reference to 1 Kings 19 has found only limited acceptance.[22]

There is room, then, for a fresh attempt to solve the problem of the reference to Elijah's violent fate in Mark 9:13. As a preliminary to such an attempt, we first reconsider the form and purpose of 9:11–13 as a whole, starting with close observation of certain grammatical and material details of the passage.

Mark 9:11, 9:12c, and 9:13 all refer to scriptural prophecy. Mark 9:12c introduces the second such reference with the disjunctive words καὶ πῶς γέγραπται, "how then has it been written?" The καί (here = "then") is the counterpart of the μέν (an untranslatable contrastive particle[23]) in 9:12b,[24] and the μέν . . . καί structure suggests a contrast between the scripturally based expectation that the returning Elijah will restore all things (9:12b) and the scripturally based expectation that the Son of man will suffer many things and be rejected (9:12c).

---

of the miracles they perform (cf. Rev. 11:6 with 1 Kings 17:1 and Ex. 7:17–20). The author of Revelation, however, is probably just borrowing a pattern of miracles from the Old Testament without thinking specifically of the figures who performed them; with J. M. Nützel, *Die Verklärungserzählung im Markusevangelium*, FB 6 (Würzburg: Echter Verlag, 1973), pp. 114–118; contra Lohmeyer, *Evangelium*, p. 183.

[20] See, e.g., Cranfield, *Mark*, p. 299; W. Lane, *The Gospel of Mark*, NICNT (Grand Rapids: Wm. B. Eerdmans Publishing Co., 1974), p. 326 n. 35; Pesch, *Markusevangelium* 2:80.

[21] See, e.g., Pesch, who, after citing 1 Kings 19, then goes on to speculate that the reference in Mark 9:13c may be not to the Old Testament at all but to apocalyptic traditions (*Markusevangelium* 2:81).

[22] Black, "Theological Appropriation," p. 10.

[23] On the contrastive nature of μέν in combination with other particles, which can include καί, see H. W. Smyth, *Greek Grammar* (Cambridge, Mass.: Harvard University Press, 1956; orig. 1920) §2903.

[24] With Cranfield, *Mark*, p. 298; contra BAGD (pp. 502–503), which assumes that the μέν in 9:12 is picked up by the ἀλλά ("but") in 9:13. The intervening question in 9:12c is simply too disruptive to allow for this theory (see A. T. Robertson, *A Grammar of the Greek New Testament in the Light of Historical Research* [Nashville: Broadman Press, 1934], p. 1152), though in the pre-Markan form of our passage, which *ex hypothesi* lacked 9:12c, this could have been the case. As for the present form, it is unusual, but not unprecedented, to have a μέν picked up by καί; see Mark 4:4–8//Luke 8:5–8; Acts 26:4, 6; 1 Thess. 2:18 (cf. BAGD, p. 503; Robertson, *Grammar*, p. 1152).

The hypothesis that Mark 9:11–13 presents a contrast between two scriptural expectations is strengthened if, with J. Wellhausen, we read 9:12c as a question:[25]

> He said to them, "Is it true that, when he comes before the Messiah, Elijah will restore all things?[26] How then has it been written of the Son of man, that he should suffer many things and be rejected . . . ?"

Wellhausen's punctuation has the advantage of making sense of the Markan transition between 9:12b ("Elijah restores all things?") and 9:12c ("How then has it been written . . . ?"), whereas that transition makes little sense if 9:12b is declarative. Furthermore, the reading of codex D suggests that at least one ancient scribe understood 9:12b as a question: "If Elijah when he comes restores all things, how then is it written . . . ?"[27] In addition, the parallel in 12:35–37 supports the interrogative reading: as in 9:12 according to Wellhausen, Jesus starts out in 12:35 by *questioning* a scribal expectation: "How do the scribes say that the Christ is the son of David?" He then introduces an apparently contradictory scriptural passage: Ps. 110:1, according to which the Messiah is David's lord.[28] All in all, the arguments for reading Mark 9:12b as a question seem convincing.

The foregoing observations push us toward the conclusion that Mark 9:11–13 is one chapter in the long and fascinating history of Jewish and Christian attempts to reconcile apparent contradictions in scripture, about which N. A. Dahl has written a classic study.[29] Mark confronts the exegetical dilemma posed by two seemingly contradictory scriptural expectations. According to Mal. 3:22, Elijah is to return before the "great and terrible day of the Lord." The scribes interpret this passage to mean that Elijah, when he comes before the Messiah, will "restore all things," that is, heal

---

[25] J. Wellhausen, *Das Evangelium Marci übersetzt und erklärt* (Berlin: Reimer, 1903), p. 76; cf. J. Gnilka, *Das Evangelium nach Markus*, EKKNT 2, 2 vols. (Zurich: Benziger Verlag, 1978, 1979), 2:41–42. The translation of Mark 9:12 here is mine.

[26] The RSV translation, "Elijah comes first and restores all things," obscures the fact that the main thought of the sentence is conveyed by the verb ἀποκαθιστάνει ("restores") and that ἐλθών is only a participle, probably a temporal one. Jesus is questioning not that Elijah comes first but that he restores all things. In Mark's eyes the restoration spoken of in Mal. 3:23, which is specifically a restoration of familial relationships, has not yet taken place. Quite the contrary; see, e.g., Mark 13:12–13a. Therefore, in spite of the fact that the verb "will restore" (ἀποκαταστήσει) is part of the text of Mal. 3:23 LXX, Mark does not see John the Baptist/Elijah as a restorer. In 9:11–13 the Markan Jesus affirms only the central function ascribed to Elijah in Mal. 3:22–23, forerunning, not the restoring function that is also mentioned there.

[27] Cited in BDF §442(8).

[28] On this passage, see chapter 7 below.

[29] N. A. Dahl, "Contradictions in Scripture," in *Studies in Paul* (Minneapolis: Augsburg, 1977), pp. 159–177.

the breach in human relations (9:11–12b).[30] If this is so, however, and humanity is to be renewed *before* the Messiah comes, how can one conceive of a Messiah who is to be rejected by humanity, a Messiah whose suffering and rejection are foretold in the scripture (9:12c)? The two expectations appear to contradict each other.

Scriptural Contradictions in Ancient Judaism

How does Mark work with this apparent contradiction? Contemporary Jewish methods for dealing with such problems provide an illuminating parallel. Dahl describes the procedure later codified in R. Ishmael's thirteenth hermeneutical rule (*middah*) as paradigmatic for many first-century attempts to resolve scriptural contradictions. The *middah* says: "Two scriptural passages which contradict one another until a third passage comes and decides between them." According to Dahl, the crucial step in the application of this *middah* is that each of the two seemingly contradictory passages is upheld, but one is recognized as the central teaching while the other is subordinated to it. As Dahl puts it:

> Thus the task which confronted an exegete when he encountered an apparent contradiction in Scripture was not to find a third passage which could resolve this conflict. It was necessary first to establish which text contained the valid halakhah, the correct statement, or the fundamental teaching. Then it was requisite to find a satisfactory explanation of the conflicting text to maintain its validity.

The third passage does not come in as a *deus ex machina*, but merely confirms the way in which the first two passages have already been reconciled. Indeed, in the original form of this rule, which probably goes back to the time of Hillel, a third passage is not even necessary.[31]

Dahl finds this procedure not only in tannaitic midrashim but also in many New Testament passages. These include Pauline passages such as Gal. 3:10–14 and traditions about Jesus such as Mark 10:1–9 par.; we may add to this list Mark 12:18–27 par. and perhaps a pre-Markan form of 12:35–37. A similar harmonizing procedure is present in the Qumran literature.[32]

Dahl's work on scriptural contradiction can now be supplemented with the results of more recent form-critical investigations by J. Neusner. In several recent works, Neusner has called attention to a form that occurs

---

[30] On this expectation, see J. Jeremias, "'Ἠλ(ε)ίας," *TDNT* (1964; orig. 1935) 2:933–934. It is based on the wording of Mal. 3:23.

[31] Dahl, "Contradictions," in *Studies*, pp. 162–165.

[32] On Mark 12:35–37, see the excursus below. On Qumran, see Schiffman (*Halakhah*, p. 76; cf. pp. 54–60) on the technical term "midrash": "The *midrash* is an exegetical form in which a passage is interpreted in light of a second passage. *Midrash* involves the harmonization of two biblical sources."

in *Pesiqta de Rab Kahana* and that is a variation on a pattern found in *Genesis Rabbah* and *Leviticus Rabbah*.[33] This form consists of: (1) a base verse (the scriptural verse that is of primary interest and that recurs throughout the chapter), (2) a contrastive verse (an intersecting verse that appears to be in conflict with the base verse), and (3) an implicit syllogism that works out the tension by reinterpreting the base verse in terms of the contrastive verse. To apply Dahl's terms to Neusner's analysis, the contrastive verse contains the fundamental teaching, which is in conflict with the apparent sense of the base verse. The implicit syllogism, however, maintains the validity of the base verse by reinterpreting it in terms of the contrastive verse. This implicit syllogism is the real point of the midrash; hence, Neusner calls this pattern the "propositional form."[34]

For example, in *pisqa'* 6 the base verse is Num. 28:1–4, in which God requires certain animal sacrifices. This requirement is in apparent conflict with the contrastive verse, Ps. 50:12, in which God denigrates animal sacrifice. The conclusion resolves the tension, reinterpreting the base verse in terms of the contrastive verse: God does not need the food, but he gets pleasure from the smell. This conclusion is never explicitly stated; it is only an *implicit* syllogism. As Neusner says:

> It is implicit because it is never stated in so many words, yet it is readily recognized. . . . [The implicit syllogism here and the one in another form] are ways of stating in the idiom our authorship has chosen, in the media of expression they have preferred, and through modes of demonstration and evidentiary proof they deem probative, a truth they never spell out but always take for granted we shall recognize and adopt.[35]

The implicit nature of the concluding syllogism is an important point to remember for our further study.

The Refutational Form in the Mekilta *and in* Mark 9:11–13

One tannaitic midrash upon which Neusner has not written extensively is the *Mekilta*.[36] Investigation of this document, however, turns out to be

---

[33] J. Neusner, *Comparative Midrash: The Plan and Program of Genesis and Leviticus Rabbah,* BJS 111 (Atlanta: Scholars Press, 1986); *Midrash as Literature: The Primacy of Documentary Discourse,* Studies in Judaism (Lanham, Md.: University Press of America, 1987); *Pesiqta de Rab Kahana: An Analytical Translation,* BJS 122, 123, 2 vols. (Atlanta: Scholars Press, 1987); *What Is Midrash?,* Guides to Biblical Scholarship (Philadelphia: Fortress Press, 1987).

[34] See Neusner, *Midrash as Literature,* pp. 57, 60–66; idem, *Pesiqta* 2:183, 187–188, 225–226; *What Is Midrash,* pp. 72–73.

[35] Neusner, *Pesiqta* 2:183.

[36] Neusner deliberately leaves the *Mekilta* out of consideration because of the difficulty in dating it; see *Midrash as Literature,* p. 11.

extremely important for our purposes. It contains several examples of a rhetorical pattern very similar to Neusner's "propositional form" and also strikingly parallel to the form of Mark 9:11–13. In his redaction of 9:11–13, I would suggest, Mark is making use of a Jewish exegetical form that we can see more clearly developed in the *Mekilta*.

The *Mekilta* is a tannaitic midrash and hence later than the New Testament, but we have already seen that the basic pattern under discussion can be traced from the Qumran literature to the New Testament and beyond. Furthermore, analysis of the particular form assumed by this pattern in the *Mekilta*, and of its implicit logic, enables us to fill in the otherwise puzzling gaps we have noted in the logic of Mark 9:11–13. The exegete of Mark 9:11–13, therefore, is justified in making cautious use of this form from the *Mekilta*.

I suggest that this form be called the "refutational form." In many ways it is a more compressed version of Neusner's "propositional form"; what requires a whole long chapter in *Pesiqta de Rab Kahana* here usually occurs within the space of a single paragraph. I use the adjective "refutational," rather than Neusner's "propositional," because the form first suggests an inference that might possibly be drawn from the base verse, then refutes that inference with an implicit syllogism derived from the contrastive verse. A typical example is found in Tractate *Pisḥa*, chapter 3:[37]

> "Speak (2 pl.) to all the congregation of Israel" (Ex. 12:3). R. Ishmael says: But is it really so that both of them [i.e., Aaron as well as Moses] spoke? And has it not been said, "Speak (2 sing.) to the children of Israel . . ." (Ex. 31:13)? What then does scripture mean by saying, "Speak" (2 pl.)? Only this: whenever Moses spoke, Aaron inclined his ear to listen with awe, and scripture accounts it to him as if he had heard it directly from the mouth of the Holy One.

The difficulty this passage tries to resolve is the tension between the base verse, Ex. 12:3, which implies that both Moses and Aaron spoke to Israel, and the contrastive verse, Ex. 31:13, which implies that only Moses spoke. This apparent contradiction is resolved by interpreting the base verse in terms of the contrastive verse: Whenever Moses spoke, Aaron listened with awe, and the scripture therefore reckoned him on a par with Moses. This conclusion implies the unexpressed syllogism that is the point of the passage: not Moses and Aaron but only Moses spoke, and the second person plural in Ex. 12:3 refers to Moses' speaking and Aaron's listening.

This more-or-less representative example of the refutational form[38] is

---

[37] All translations of *Mekilta* passages in this chapter have been altered from J. Z. Lauterbach's edition (*Mekilta de-Rabbi Ishmael*, 3 vols. [Philadelphia: Jewish Publication Society, 1961]).

[38] In an appendix to my *ZNW* article ("Mark 9:11–13," pp. 58–63), I have reproduced and commented upon eight examples of this form from the *Mekilta*.

strikingly similar in structure to Mark 9:11–13, as can be seen from the following chart:

Mekilta, Pisha, Chapter 3	*Mark 9:11–13*
Citation of base verse, Ex. 12:3: "Speak (2 pl.) to the congregation of Israel"	Allusion to base verse, Mal. 3:22: "Elijah must come first"
Question about possible inference: "But is it really so that (וכי) both of them spoke?"	Question about possible inference: "But does Elijah, when he comes, restore all things?"
"And has it not been said . . . ?" (והלא כבר נאמר)	"And how has it been written . . . ?" (καὶ πῶς γέγραπται)
Contrastive verse, Ex. 31:13: "Speak (2 sing.) to the children of Israel"	Contrastive scriptural expectation: "The Son of man is to suffer many things and be rejected"
"What then does scripture mean by saying . . . ?" (ומה תלמוד לומר)	
Citation of base verse, Ex. 12:3: "Speak (2 pl.)"	
"Only this" (אלא)	"But (ἀλλά) I say to you . . ."
Interpretation of base verse in terms of contrastive verse: "Whenever Moses spoke, Aaron inclined his ear to listen with awe, and scripture accounts it to him as if he had heard it directly from the mouth of the Holy One"	Interpretation of base verse in terms of contrastive expectation: "Elijah has come, and they did to him whatever they wished"

This chart displays the parallelism between the two forms, not only in overall structure but even in vocabulary at parallel points. Both passages start out with the base verse.[39] Both next raise a question about a possible inference

---

[39] Mark 9:11 does not correspond exactly to Neusner's definition of a "base verse," since it is not the verse that recurs throughout a chapter of an extended midrash. Furthermore, it is, strictly speaking, an allusion to Mal. 3:22 rather than a direct citation of it. Nevertheless, it does correspond generally to Neusner's "base verse" in that it is the starting point of the discussion and an allusion to the verse that must be explained.

from the base verse. The *Mekilta*'s question is introduced by the particle וכי ("but is it really so that . . ."), which indicates that a negative answer is expected;[40] this corresponds to Mark 9:12b, which, if taken interrogatively as we have suggested, obviously expects a negative answer. Next come nearly identical formulas, "and has it not been said . . . ?" (*Mekilta*) and "and how has it been written . . . ?" (Mark), followed by the contrastive verse.[41] At the end of each passage, the conclusion is introduced by single words (אלא; ἀλλά) which mean practically the same thing,[42] conjunctions that even sound alike (*'ella'*, *alla*) and may be etymologically related.[43] In each case this conjunction is followed by a statement that reinterprets the base verse in terms of the contrastive verse.[44]

The forms are not identical; the main difference is that the *Mekilta* passage, immediately before the conclusion, re-cites the base verse, introducing this citation with the formula, "What then does scripture mean by saying . . . ?"[45] This is not a major departure, however. It merely makes explicit what is implicit in Mark 9:11–13. We can readily imagine a slightly expanded form of that pericope, in which a parallel question is interposed between 9:12 and 9:13: "What then does scripture mean by saying, 'Elijah must come first'?" Moreover, at least one passage from the *Mekilta*, *Shirata* 2 (2:19), neglects to re-cite the base verse, and thus forms a perfect parallel to Mark 9:11–13:

---

[40] M. Jastrow, *A Dictionary of the Targumim, the Talmud Babli and Yerushalmi, and the Midrashic Literature* (2 vols. in 1; New York: Judaica, 1982), p. 630.

[41] In the case of Mark 9:12, as we have seen, the "contrastive verse" is actually not an Old Testament citation but an exegetical conclusion from several Old Testament passages. At the end of this chapter I will comment on the significance of this difference.

[42] See Jastrow, *Dictionary*, p. 66; and BAGD, pp. 38–39(3). Both words can be used for logical inferences.

[43] I am suggesting that אלא may be one of the many examples of Greek loanwords in Mishnaic Hebrew; on the general phenomenon, see S. Lieberman, *Greek in Jewish Palestine* (New York: Jewish Theological Seminary, 1942) and S. Levin, *The Indo-European and Semitic Languages* (Albany, N.Y.: State University of New York Press, 1971). Jastrow (*Dictionary*, p. 66) lists אלא as a contraction of אם לא = אן לא "if not"), but even if this derivation is correct, the particular form that the contraction assumes is likely to have been influenced by the Greek word ἀλλά.

[44] That this is the function of Mark 9:13 will be demonstrated below.

[45] Another difference is that the base verse in Mark 9:11–13 is introduced not by Jesus but by the disciples, quoting the scribes, whereas in the examples of this form in the *Mekilta* there is no change of speakers. This difference corresponds to the narrative genre of Mark as well as to the more controversial, less academic nature of the Markan passage; see the remarks of D. Juel on the more scholastic bent of rabbinic as opposed to New Testament exegesis (*Messianic Exegesis: Christological Interpretation of the Old Testament in Early Christianity* [Philadelphia: Fortress Press, 1988], p. 57). It should also be pointed out that the *Mekilta* contains some passages that have controversial elements and are similar to our "refutational form"; see, e.g., *Pisha* 11 (1:81–82). On both points, see the illuminating remarks of D. Daube, *The New Testament and Rabbinic Judaism* (New York: Arno Press, 1973; orig. 1956), pp. 57–59.

"The horse and his rider [God has thrown into the sea] (Ex. 15:1)." But is it really so that there was only one horse and one rider? And has it not been said: "And he took six hundred chosen chariots," etc. (Ex. 14:7), "Pharaoh's chariots," etc. (Ex. 15:4)? But when the Israelites do the will of God, their enemies are before them as but one horse and rider.

The parallel between this passage and Mark 9:11–13 can be diagramed thus:

Mekilta, Shirata, Chapter 2	*Mark 9:11–13*
Base verse, Ex. 15:1: "The horse and his rider"	Base verse, Mal. 3:22: "Elijah must come first"
Question about possible inference: "But is it really so that (וכי) there was only one horse and rider?"	Question about possible inference: "But does Elijah, when he comes, restore all things?"
"And has it not been said . . . ?" (והלא כבר נאמר)	"And how has it been written . . . ?" (καὶ πῶς γέγραπται)
Contrastive verses, Ex. 14:7: "And he took six hundred chosen chariots," etc. and Ex. 15:4: "Pharaoh's chariots," etc.	Contrastive scriptural expectation: "The Son of man is to suffer many things and be rejected"
"But" (אלא)	"But" (ἀλλά)
Interpretation of base verse in terms of contrastive verse: "When the Israelites do the will of God, their enemies are before them as but one horse and one rider"	Interpretation of base verse in terms of contrastive expectation: "Elijah has come, and they did to him whatever they wished"

The correspondence in form between the two passages is complete. It should also be noted that, in the *Mekilta* passage, the base verse is contrasted not with a single text but with a scriptural teaching attested by several texts. This is true in most of the examples found in the *Mekilta*,[46] making even closer the parallel with Mark 9:11–13, in which the "contrastive verse" (9:12c) is an exegetical inference drawn from several passages.

Mark 9:13 as an Exegetical Reconciliation

By a long and circuitous route we have come back to Mark 9:13. If the analysis above is correct, this verse should contain the implicit syllogism

---

[46] See examples ##3–7 in the appendix to Marcus, "Mark 9,11–13."

that reinterprets the base verse (Mal. 3:22: Elijah will come before the Messiah) in terms of the contrastive verse (the scriptural expectation that the Son of man will suffer and be rejected) and thus reconciles them. Is it possible to see Mark 9:13 in this way? Indeed, it is. "Elijah has come, and they did to him whatever they wished." This statement, I suggest, is Mark's way of reinterpreting the concept of Elijah as the Messiah's forerunner in terms of the concept of a suffering Messiah. To combine Dahl's terminology with Neusner's and to apply it to Mark 9:11–13, the correct statement or fundamental teaching is that contained in the contrastive verse, which speaks of the suffering of the Son of man (9:12c). But the centrality of this scriptural teaching does not mean that Mark simply throws out the base verse, which implies that the Messiah is to be preceded by a forerunner (9:11).[47] On the contrary, Mark *reinterprets* the base verse in terms of the contrastive verse. The Messiah *is* preceded by a forerunner, but he proves himself to be that forerunner not by accomplishing great triumphs in the public sphere but precisely by *going before Jesus in the way of suffering and death* (9:13).[48] The nature of the forerunner is drastically qualified by the nature of the Messiah he precedes.[49]

The implicit syllogism becomes clear: Since Jesus is a suffering Messiah, his forerunner must be a suffering Elijah. As in the rabbinic forms cited above, this is an *implicit* syllogism, never spelled out in so many words. The author, however, can take it for granted that his hearers will recognize and adopt this syllogism. Apparently Mark can assume in his hearers a midrashic mind-set similar to that which the authors of the *Mekilta* and other rabbinic midrashim could assume in theirs.

What, then, of the concluding formula in 9:13c, "as it has been written of him"? We return to the question that started us on our search for parallel forms: *Where* has it been written that the returning Elijah should suffer violence?

We note first that the presence of the formula "as it has been written" creates a correspondence between Mark 9:13 and the conclusion of Ishmael's thirteenth *middah* ("until a third passage comes and decides between them") as well as with the conclusion of some examples of the refutational form in the *Mekilta*. Two of the eight examples of the form found in the *Mekilta*[50] conclude with a corroborative scriptural citation, introduced

---

[47] Contra W. Grundmann, *Das Evangelium nach Markus*, THKNT 2, 2nd ed. (Berlin: Evangelische Verlag, 1959), pp. 184–185.

[48] See chapter 2, pp. 41–42 above.

[49] See Wellhausen, *Evangelium*, p. 76; Pesch, *Markusevangelium* 2:79; Gnilka, *Evangelium* 2:41–42. None of these authors, however, relates Mark 9:11–13 to exegetical attempts to reconcile scriptural contradictions.

[50] See Marcus, "Mark 9,11–13," appendix, ##2 and 6.

by the formula "as it has been said" or "thus it says." They are thus, in one way, especially close in form to Mark 9:13.

Yet this formal similarity conceals an important difference. No Old Testament text, as we have seen, speaks of the violent fate of the returning Elijah, so Mark 9:13 cannot be an Old Testament *citation*. Furthermore, as we have also seen, a third scriptural passage is not strictly necessary to reconcile two contradictory texts, despite the literal wording of Ishmael's *middah*. Finally, we need to remind ourselves that in the New Testament "as it has been written" and similar formulas sometimes refer not to a specific scriptural passage but to an exegetical conclusion drawn from several passages.

Putting all these observations together and shaking well, a solution to the conundrum of Mark 9:13c begins to emerge. "As it has been written of Elijah," I would claim, is a reference not to a specific Old Testament text but to 9:13ab as the syllogistic conclusion that reconciles the scriptural expectations expressed in 9:11 and in 9:12c. This exegetical conclusion "has been written," in the sense that it harmonizes the biblical idea of a forerunner with the biblical idea of a suffering Messiah. Like other exegetical conclusions we have studied—for example, 9:12c itself—Mark 9:13 can claim the formula normally reserved for scripture, "it has been written." It can appropriate this formula because, in Mark's view, it brings out the hidden logic that binds together two apparently contradictory passages, thus enabling them both to be maintained. Just as the statement "the Son of man must suffer" is an exegetical conclusion knitting together various streams of biblical expectation (Isaiah 53, the psalms of the Righteous Sufferer, Daniel 7, etc.) and thus itself assuming the mantle of "scripture"; so Mark 9:13 is an exegetical conclusion knitting together the scriptural expectation of the Messiah's forerunner with the scriptural expectation of the suffering of the Son of man—and thus also deserving the name of scripture.

Conclusions: Mark 9:11–13 and the Markan Community

We conclude with some thoughts on the theological ramifications of the foregoing analysis and on the message of Mark 9:11–13 for the Markan community.

The first ramification should be obvious from what has just been said: the line between scripture and exegesis of scripture is not hard and fast in Mark. Mark 9:12 and 9:13, which are exegetical conclusions, are referred to by means of the same verb, γέγραπται ("it has been written"), that is used to refer to scriptural citations in 1:2; 7:6; 11:17; and 14:27. Scriptural authority is claimed for scriptural interpretation.

Indeed, it is striking that, in our passage, the more literal scriptural expectation, of Elijah as the forerunner of the Messiah (9:11), is drastically qualified by the more interpretive, strongly christocentric "scriptural" expectation of the suffering of the Son of man (9:12c), which is actually an exegetical conclusion.[51] Our passage, then, underscores the frequently made but nonetheless vital point that New Testament interpretation of the Old Testament has a christological starting point. The Old Testament is not read in the New Testament in a straight-line continuum from unambiguous expectation to irrefragable fulfillment. Rather, the entire Old Testament is reread through the lens of the crucified Messiah.

It is not the case, however, that Jesus' fate is simply read into the Old Testament. Mark's exegesis of the Old Testament is not merely a massive exercise in dogmatic "eisegesis." Early Christian exegetes such as Mark do not merely exploit the Old Testament; they also *learn something* from it. In the case at hand, Mark, starting from his assumption of the centrality of the scriptural witness to the suffering of the Messiah, reaches an exegetical conclusion about another figure, Elijah/John the Baptist, and his relationship to the crucified Messiah. The movement of thought, then, is not *exclusively* from Christ to the scripture but also from the scripture christologically construed to a deeper understanding of the events surrounding Christ.[52]

Finally, it is important to notice a *difference* between what occurs in Mark 9:11–13 and what occurs in the Jewish examples of the application of Ishmael's thirteenth *middah*. In none of the Jewish examples is the *middah* applied to scriptural conclusions, but only to actual scriptural citations. Similarly, in the examples of the refutational form found in the *Mekilta*, the contrastive verse is always a *verse* (usually several verses), never an exegetical conclusion. In Mark 9:11–13, in contrast, Ishmael's *middah* is used to reconcile a scriptural allusion that functions as the base verse (Mal. 3:22 = Mark 9:11) with an exegetical *conclusion* that functions as the contrastive verse (Mark 9:12c). This exegetical conclusion, indeed, is the fulcrum of the passage.

The amount of authority thus attributed to Mark 9:12c is extraordinary. A hermeneutical rule for the treatment of a biblical *text* is here applied to a Christian midrash. Although we have noted that at Qumran exegetical conclusions can be treated as scripture, there is nothing there comparable

---

[51] There is a certain analogy to this procedure in the fact that half of the examples of the refutational form from the *Mekilta* refute a literal understanding of the base verse; see Marcus, "Mark 9,11–13," appendix, ##1, 4, 6, and 7. (Thanks to N. A. Dahl for pointing this out to me in a letter.)

[52] This point is impressively made in Juel's book *Messianic Exegesis*. It runs counter to the thesis of Suhl that the movement of Mark's thought is *entirely* from New Testament events to postulated Old Testament prophecies (*Zitate*, p. 44).

to Mark 9:11–13; no *pesher* on the *War Scroll* or the *Hodayoth* has come to light, or is likely to. We are, it appears, on our way in Mark 9 toward the concept of Christian scripture, in which Christian exegeses of the Old Testament and other Christian writings themselves become "canonical." Such an end result still lies very far in the future, but the first step has been taken. It is surely significant, and consonant with Mark's overall cross-centered theology, that this initial step is taken by means of this particular exegetical conclusion — the one that speaks of the suffering of the Son of man.

For the members of Mark's community, the knowledge that "they" had done violence both to the Son of man's forerunner, John the Baptist, and to the suffering Son of man himself, would have had a striking resonance in their own situation of persecution for his sake and the gospel's (cf. 8:35; 10:29; 13:9). The successors of the earthly authorities responsible for the execution of John the Baptist and Jesus are now "doing whatever they want" to the Markan community, too, and their apparent omnipotence, in contrast to the apparent powerlessness of the community, is undoubtedly causing some of Mark's hearers to experience grave doubts about the gospel message of the arrival of the kingdom of God in the person of Jesus.[53]

Mark 9:11–13 in its Markan context addresses these doubts in two ways. First, it assures the community that its suffering does not mean that it has slipped out of God's hand. We have seen in an earlier chapter that John, Jesus, and the members of the Markan community all preach and are delivered up, and this parallelism is connected with the communal dimension of the figure of the Son of man, about which we have also remarked.[54] The suffering of the members of the Markan community, then, is not an indication of their abandonment by God but rather a sign that they possess the weighty privilege of participating in the communal identity of Jesus, "as it has been written concerning him" (9:13).

A participation in the suffering experienced by this inclusive figure implies also a participation in the empowerment he receives at his resurrection from the one who has handed him over to suffering and death. The linkage made between the violent deaths of John the Baptist and Jesus in 9:11–13 appears a few short verses after the prophecy of Jesus' suffering, death, *and resurrection* in 8:31. For Mark, the suffering Son of man is also God's beloved son who has been vindicated by him in the resurrection and seated at his father's right hand, and the community now shares in that vindication.

The way in which the community participates in this vindication will become clearer when we study the Old Testament testimony about the

---

[53] See J. Marcus, *The Mystery of the Kingdom of God*, SBLDS 90 (Atlanta: Scholars Press, 1986), pp. 69–71, 121–123.

[54] See chapter 2, pp. 41–42 above; see also pp. 95–96.

exaltation of the rejected stone (Mark 12:10–11//Ps. 118:22–23). That passage is the subject of the following chapter.

Excursus: "Elijah Must Come First"

The question of whether or not there was in the first century A.D. a Jewish expectation that Elijah would come before the Messiah has been fiercely debated in recent scholarship. M. M. Faierstein and J. A. Fitzmyer deny such a Jewish expectation and suggest that it may be a Christian innovation, while C. Milikowsky and D. C. Allison affirm it.[55]

Though this is not the place for a detailed discussion of this debate, we must at least state our agreement with Allison that Mark attributes to "the scribes" a belief that Elijah must come before the Messiah, and that ascription itself is evidence for a first-century Jewish belief in Elijah as the Messiah's forerunner. Fitzmyer argues that 9:11 only implies that Elijah must come before the Son of man rises from the dead. Against this position is that the difficulty with which the disciples are struggling in 9:11 is not the expectation that Elijah must come before the Son of man rises from the dead; there would be no occasion for such an objection at this point in the Markan narrative, since the Son of man has not yet risen. The objection must have to do with something that has *already* happened — namely, the appearance on the scene of Jesus the Messiah, whose messianic dignity (cf. 8:29) has just been confirmed by the transfiguration (9:2–8). Compare the Matthean version (Matt. 17:9–13), where it is even clearer, because of the omission of Mark 9:12c, that the author presupposes a Jewish expectation of Elijah as the Messiah's forerunner.

Fitzmyer says: "There is not even a hint here [in Mark 9:11–13] about a Messiah, and 'Son of man' is not a messianic title." Fitzmyer probably means that "Son of man" is not a messianic title in first-century Judaism. This itself is debatable (see *1 Enoch*); and in any case, *for Mark*, as the coalescence of "Christ" and "Son of man" in 14:61–62 shows, "Son of man" *is* a messianic title.[56]

---

[55] M. M. Faierstein, "Why Do the Scribes Say That Elijah Must Come First?" *JBL* 100 (1981), 75–86; C. Milikowsky, "Elijah and the Messiah," *Jerusalem Studies in Jewish Thought* 2 (1982–83), 491–496 [Hebrew]; D. C. Allison, "Elijah Must Come First," *JBL* 103 (1984), 256–258; J. A. Fitzmyer, "More about Elijah Coming First," *JBL* 104 (1985), 295–296.

[56] See J. D. Kingsbury, *The Christology of Mark's Gospel* (Philadelphia: Fortress Press, 1983), pp. 157–179.

6

Mark 12:10-11

The Rejected and Vindicated Stone

12:10a   Have you not read this scripture:
12:10b   *"A stone which the builders rejected*   A
12:10c   *this one was made the head of the corner* B
12:11a   *from the Lord this came to be*   B'
12:11b   *and it is astonishing in our eyes"?*   A'

The Old Testament Text and Its Context

Mark 12:10–11 consists of an introductory formula, "have you not read this scripture?" followed by a verbatim quotation of Ps. 118:22–23 from the Septuagint. In its Markan context this citation forms a pendant to the parable of the vineyard, which Jesus has enunciated in 12:1–9. The link between the two parts is strengthened by a series of verbal and thematic correspondences: the rejection of the stone corresponds to the rejection of the servants and the son in the parable, its vindication by the Lord corresponds generally to the action of "the lord of the vineyard" in 12:9, and the words "builders" (οἰκοδομοῦντες) and "head" (κεφαλήν) are reminiscent of the building (ᾠκοδόμησεν) of the tower (12:1) and the wounding of one of the servants in the head (ἐκεφαλίωσαν, 12:4). The link between 12:1–9 and 12:10–11 makes it probable that in Mark's mind the main characters in the two parts are to be identified: the wicked tenants are the rejecters of the stone, the stone itself is the son, and the "lord of the vineyard" is God.

On the other hand, there is also some tension between Mark 12:10–11 and the parable that precedes it, for the parable is pessimistic in tone while the Old Testament citation is optimistic.[1] Thematically, the citation of Ps.

---

[1] Cf. C. E. Carlston, *The Parables of the Triple Tradition* (Philadelphia: Fortress Press, 1975), p. 190.

111

118:22–23 forms an A B B′A′ pattern. Mark 12:10c and 12:11a, parts B and
B′, speak of a divine action of vindicating the stone.[2] This divine action is
framed by two human responses in parts A and A′ (12:10b and 12:11b): the
rejection of the stone by the builders and the finding of the stone's vindication to be marvelous by "us." The citation thus gains an optimistic tinge;
the initial human rejection of 12:10b gives way to the positive human reaction of 12:11b after the references to divine vindication in 12:10c, 11a.
Indeed, the theme of human rejection is expressed only in a subordinate
relative clause at the beginning of the citation ("whom the builders
rejected"), whereas the theme of divine and human acceptance is expressed
by the three main clauses that follow it.

In contrast to the Old Testament citation, the parable is pessimistic. Its
focus is the rejection of the servants and of the son as well as the recompense
that is finally meted out to the wicked tenants by the vineyard owner. There
is no hint that the son or the servants are themselves restored to the vineyard;
indeed, this would be impossible in the case of some of them, who have
been killed. The parable is thus primarily a tale of rejection, while the scripture citation is primarily a description of vindication.[3]

This tension suggests that the parable and the Old Testament citation
did not originally belong together,[4] though the parable is already joined
with the first verse of Ps. 118:22–23 in *Gos. Thom.* logia 65–66. We would
reconstruct the tradition history of Mark 12:1–12 as follows:

1. The original form of the parable was close to that found in *Gos. Thom.*
logion 65 and told a simple but shocking three-part story about
unscrupulous tenants who recognized the critical moment in which they
stood and acted decisively—even to the point of committing murder.[5]

2. At some later point, but still in a Semitic milieu, a citation of Ps. 118:22
was added to the parable (cf. *Gos. Thom.* logion 66), and the main focus
switched from the decisive act of the tenants to the murder and vindication of the "son."[6]

---

[2] See the divine passive ἐγενήθη, "was made to be," and παρὰ κυρίου, "from the Lord"; see
J. R. Michaels, *1 Peter*, WBC 49 (Waco, Tex.: Word Books, 1988), p. 105.

[3] See B. Lindars, *New Testament Apologetic: The Doctrinal Significance of the Old Testament Quotations* (Philadelphia: Westminster Press, 1961), p. 174; E. Schweizer, *The Good News
According to Mark* (Atlanta: John Knox Press, 1970), p. 239; contra K. Snodgrass, *The Parable
of the Wicked Tenants: An Inquiry into Parable Interpretation*, WUNT 27 (Tübingen: J. C. B.
Mohr [Paul Siebeck], 1983), pp. 95–96.

[4] See A. Suhl, *Die Funktion der alttestamentlichen Zitate und Anspielungen im Markusevangelium* (Gütersloh: Gerd Mohn, 1965), p. 141; Carlston, *Parables*, pp. 180–181.

[5] See J. D. Crossan, who compares the unscrupulous actions of the unjust steward in Luke
16:1–7 (*In Parables: The Challenge of the Historical Jesus* [New York: Harper & Row, 1973],
pp. 86–96, 111).

[6] In the original parable, according to Crossan, the "son" has no christological significance,
but is merely the third messenger sent to the tenant farmers. The citation of Psalm 118, which

3. Still later, but before Mark, the parable was expanded by the addition of features such as the elaborate description of the construction of the vineyard, the head wound of the second servant and the killing of the third one, the dispatch and mistreatment of "many other" servants, the ejection of the son's body from the vineyard, and the coming of the lord of the vineyard to punish the tenants. All of these traits turned the parable into an allegory of salvation history as understood by the early church. The vineyard was Israel; its owner was God (cf. Isa. 5:1–7);[7] and the servants sent to the vineyard were the prophets,[8] including John the Baptist, who was beheaded. The son thrown out of the vineyard was Jesus, who was killed outside of the city walls of Jerusalem (cf. Heb. 13:12–13), and the destruction of the wicked tenants was a judgment threatened against Israel for this murder.[9]

4. Finally, Mark himself added the "frame" of the passage in 12:1a, 12,[10] the description of the son as "beloved" in 12:6 (cf. 1:11; 9:7), and possibly

---

introduces the christological theme, is probably not an original part of the parable, but its relative antiquity is suggested by the Semitic wordplay בניא/בנים/בן (son/stone/builders; see M. Black, "The Christological Use of the Old Testament in the New Testament," *NTS* 18 [1971], 12). Mark himself is probably not responsible for adding it; see J. Jeremias, *The Parables of Jesus*, 2nd rev. ed. (New York: Charles Scribner's Sons, 1972; orig. 1954), p. 108; and E. Best, *Following Jesus: Discipleship in the Gospel of Mark*, JSNTSup 4 (Sheffield: JSOT Press, 1981), p. 219.

   [7] The elaborate description in Mark 12:1 corresponds closely to Isa. 5:1–2, and the rhetorical question in Mark 12:9a ("what then will the lord of the vineyard do?") roughly to Isa. 5:4–5; therefore, the identification of Israel as God's vineyard in Isa. 5:7 is probably the background for the vineyard image in Mark 12:1–9.

   [8] Cf. the Old Testament expression, "my servants the prophets": Jer. 7:25–26; 25:4; Amos 3:7; Zech. 1:6; see Jeremias, *Parables*, p. 71; W. Lane, *The Gospel of Mark*, NICNT (Grand Rapids: Wm. B. Eerdmans Publishing Co., 1974), p. 418.

   [9] Contra Suhl, according to whom allegorical details are almost completely absent in Mark 12:1–9! (*Zitate*, p. 139). Neither is Snodgrass credible when he argues for the priority of the Synoptic (Matthean!) version of the parable on the basis of an alleged tendency of *Gospel of Thomas* to deallegorize (*Parable*, pp. 52–71); see J. A. Fitzmyer, who finds no such tendency in *Thomas* and adds that the allegorization of a parable in the gospel tradition is a more normal process than a change from allegory to parable (*The Gospel According to Luke*, AB 28, 28A, 2 vols. [Garden City, N.Y.: Doubleday & Co., 1981, 1985], 2:1278–1281). On allegorizing in the pre-Markan stage of the tradition, see the treatment of Mark 4:14–20 in J. Marcus, *The Mystery of the Kingdom of God*, SBLDS 90 (Atlanta: Scholars Press, 1986), pp. 29–31; on the Q (and hence probably pre-Markan) themes of the murder of the prophets, the rejection of John the Baptist and Jesus, and the consequent judgment of Israel, see J. D. Kingsbury, *Jesus Christ in Matthew, Mark, and Luke*, Proclamation Commentaries (Philadelphia: Fortress Press, 1981), pp. 5–7.

   [10] See Carlston (*Parables*, p. 181), J. Gnilka (*Das Evangelium nach Markus*, EKKNT 2, 2 vols. [Zurich: Benziger Verlag, 1978, 1979], 2:142), and Best (*Following*, pp. 218–219), who point to the terms "began" and "in parables" in v. 1 and "to arrest," the γάρ ("for") clause, the theme of fear, and the transitional function of v. 12.

the motif of the transfer of the vineyard to others.[11] He also expanded the reference to Psalm 118 by adding 12:11 (= Ps. 118:23), thus paving the way for the implicitly favorable mention of the crowd in 12:12 by means of the statement that the Lord's doing is "marvelous in our eyes."

The Eschatological Interpretation of Psalm 118

As we have seen, the stone of Mark 12:10–11 corresponds to the beloved son of the parable. This identification is supported by the observation that a heavenly voice has previously identified Jesus as the beloved son at the baptism and the transfiguration (1:11; 9:7); Mark has probably added the word "beloved" to the parable in 12:6 in order to conform it to these passages. Following out the correspondence between the parable and the quotation from the psalm, the rejection of the stone must represent the murder of the son, that is, the execution of Jesus.[12] This identification is cemented by the fact that the verb ἀποδοκιμάζειν ("to reject") occurs in only one other place in Mark, in 8:31, where Jesus uses it to prophesy his own rejection by the Jewish leaders. The raising of the stone to the head of the corner, then, must correspond to the resurrection of Jesus, since the resurrection is presented in the three passion predictions as the reversal of the humiliation of the crucifixion (8:31; 9:31; 10:33–34). In Mark 12:10–11, therefore, Jesus uses Ps. 118:22–23 to prophesy his death and resurrection.

These are events that Mark understands to belong in an eschatological framework, as is already indicated by the linkages between the apocalyptic prophecies of chapter 13 and the passion narrative of chapters 14–16.[13] This eschatological use of the psalm by Mark corresponds to a general tendency in postbiblical Judaism and early Christianity to interpret the psalms eschatologically. We have already seen in chapter 3, for example, that Psalm 2 is interpreted eschatologically in Judaism and that this interpretation provides the background for Mark's citation of it in Mark 1:11. We will see below, in chapters 7 and 8, that Psalm 110 and the Psalms of the Righteous Sufferer are also interpreted eschatologically in Mark and that here also Mark is drawing on Jewish exegetical traditions.

---

[11] This feature parallels the decided Markan emphasis on Jesus' concern for Gentiles or their positive reaction to him; see Best, who refers to 7:24–30; 8:1–9; 11:17; 12:9; 13:10; 14:9; and 15:39 among other passages (*Following*, p. 218). Of these, at least 11:17; 13:10; and 14:9 are probably redactional; see J. Marcus, "The Jewish War and the *Sitz im Leben* of Mark," *JBL* (forthcoming), nn. 33, 39, and 55. This positive Markan attitude toward Gentiles goes beyond that found in Q; see Kingsbury, *Jesus Christ*, pp. 23–24 and n. 9 above.

[12] Contra Suhl, who asserts without argument that the stone is not Christ but what happened to him (*Zitate*, p. 142).

[13] See R. H. Lightfoot, *The Gospel Message of St. Mark* (Oxford: Clarendon Press, 1950), pp. 48–59.

Psalm 118 too is interpreted eschatologically in postbiblical Judaism. In the original psalm the speaker is Israel, as is suggested by the transition between the references to Israel and the house of Aaron in vv. 1–4 and the "I" language of vv. 5–21.[14] This identification is preserved in later Jewish exegesis of the psalm, but in an eschatological context. For example, in the comments on Ps. 118:10–12 in the Midrash on Psalms, the speaker's persecution by "the nations" is exegeted as a reference to the eschatological wars of Gog and Magog against Israel, from which Israel is delivered by God.[15] That such eschatological interpretations of Psalm 118 were already current in Mark's time is suggested by the use of Ps. 118:25–26 in Mark 11:9–10; here the psalm's macarism of pilgrims who come to the Temple is transformed eschatologically by being linked with "the coming kingdom of our father David."[16] It would not be surprising, then, if the background to Mark's other citation of Psalm 118, in Mark 12:10–11, were also provided by Jewish exegetical traditions interpreting the psalm as a prophecy of eschatological victory. As in 1:2–3 and 1:11, the passage would here be making use of the Old Testament picture of God coming in triumphant holy war to save his people.

That this is indeed the context in which Mark understands his citation of Psalm 118 to belong is suggested by the transition from Mark 12:9 to 12:10–11. Right before Mark's citation of Ps. 118:22–23, the parable speaks allegorically of a coming of God to make holy war: "The lord of the vineyard . . . will come and destroy. . . ." In the larger Markan context this would be understood as a reference to the events of the Jewish War, which Mark views as the prelude to the eschaton (see 13:14–26). Thus the theme of eschatological holy war in 12:9 dovetails perfectly with the traditional, eschatological exegesis of Psalm 118, the passage that is cited immediately afterward in 12:10–11.

Mark 12:9 and the Markan Life-Setting

The use made of the traditional picture drawn from Psalm 118 in Mark 12:9, however, is not without its quirks. The psalm speaks of the salvation of Israel through the destruction of the Gentiles: "All nations surrounded me; in the name of the Lord I cut them off" (Ps. 118:10–12). As we have seen, several traditions preserved in the Midrash follow the lead of the original psalm and interpret it as a description of God's eschatological holy

---

[14] M. J. Lagrange, *Évangile selon Saint Marc*, Études bibliques, 2nd ed. (Paris: Lecoffre, 1920), p. 289.

[15] See Snodgrass, *Parable*, p. 99.

[16] See J. Jeremias, *The Eucharistic Words of Jesus* (Philadelphia: Fortress Press, 1966), p. 258; Snodgrass, *Parable*, p. 99.

war against the evil Gentile kingdoms of Gog and Magog. Mark 12:9, on the contrary, speaks of the destruction of *Israel*, or at least of its leaders, and the transfer of the vineyard to "others," that is, the church made up of both Jews and Gentiles, with the stress on the latter.[17] The "transfer" motif, as we have seen, is probably a Markan addition, while the theme of destruction may antedate Mark's editing. The author of our Gospel and the tradition he follows, then, are significantly modifying a traditional interpretation of Psalm 118. God's war is now not *on behalf of* Israel but *against* it, and in that war he does not *destroy* the Gentiles but rather *brings them into* his people.

This is a radical inversion of the traditional holy war pattern associated with the psalm, although it has a certain precedent in the way in which the Old Testament prophets threaten Israel that God will launch a holy war directed not only against their enemies but also against them.[18] It is an inversion that has had tragic consequences for relations between Christians and Jews down through the centuries, especially once Christianity ceased to be a persecuted stepchild of Judaism and became instead the established religion and Judaism's persecutor. Mark appears to be, if not the inventor, then at least an early representative of a Christian view of salvation history that condemns Judaism as a sterile religion standing under God's judgment while it awards to the Gentile church the honorific title "people of God."

The danger posed by the absolutizing of Mark's images and similar New Testament images cannot be overestimated. One way to guard against this danger is to remember that Mark's Gospel, like most of the New Testament writings, is addressed to a particular first-century situation which he has in mind as he formulates his sharp polemic.[19] A faint outline of this situation can be reconstructed from evidence provided by the Gospel itself, and portions of this outline can be filled in further on the basis of historical knowledge gleaned from other sources. The task is not an easy one, nor are its results absolutely certain, but the effort does pay exegetical dividends.

These dividends begin to come into focus when we anticipate the following section of this chapter and suggest that Mark's citation of the "stone" text from Ps. 118:22–23 in 12:10–11 brings into view the theme of the Temple. The conjunction of the Temple theme implied in 12:10–11 with the theme

---

[17] On the identity of "you" and the "others" in 12:9, see the excursus at the end of this chapter.

[18] See G. von Rad, *Old Testament Theology*, 2 vols. (New York: Harper & Row, 1965), 2:124–125. The Markan inversion probably has background in the teaching of John the Baptist and Jesus. The Q sayings Matt. 3:7–10//Luke 3:7–9; Matt. 8:11–12//Luke 13:28–29, for example, speak of a judgment upon Israel and an entry of Gentiles into the kingdom of God.

[19] On the general subject of New Testament polemic against non-Christian Jews, see L. T. Johnson, "The New Testament's Anti-Jewish Slander and the Conventions of Ancient Polemic," *JBL* 108 (1989), pp. 419–444.

of Gentiles introduced (by Mark?) into 12:9 is reminiscent of the similar collocation of those themes a few verses earlier, in 11:17, a verse that melds a citation of Isa 56:7 with an allusion to Jer. 7:11 yet that bears strong traces of Markan redaction.[20] Here Jesus charges that the Temple was intended to be a house of prayer for all the ἔθνη, a word that can mean either "nations" or "Gentiles"; in any event, Gentiles are prominently included in the promise. Instead of becoming a sanctuary for Gentiles, however, the Temple has been turned into a σπήλαιον λῃστῶν, a phrase that is usually translated "den of thieves." The normal word for "thief," however, is not λῃστής but κλέπτης; λῃστής has the much more technical meaning of "brigand" and is the word commonly used by Josephus for the revolutionary bands that were active in the Jewish revolt against the Romans of A.D. 66–74.[21]

Mark's lament that the Temple has become a den of brigands rather than a house of prayer for Gentiles takes on an extraordinarily topical color when certain details of the revolt are remembered.[22] The immediate cause of the war was the refusal of foreign sacrifices in the Temple in A.D. 66 (Josephus, *Jewish War* 2.409), and in the winter of A.D. 67–68 a group of revolutionary "brigands," the core of the Zealot party, moved into Jerusalem under the leadership of Eleazar son of Simon and set up their headquarters in the inner Temple itself, remaining there until the fall of the city in A.D. 70 (see Josephus, *Jewish War* 4.151–157; 5.5). It is likely that there was a link between this action and the anti-Gentile attitude that prevailed among several of the revolutionary groups; hence the Markan antinomy "house of prayer for all peoples/den of brigands." The Zealots probably saw themselves as purifying the Temple from corrupting foreign influence, and their empirically hopeless fight against the Romans was likely fueled by the conviction that God would give to his purified Israel the victory against the heathen. Indeed, it is not farfetched to speculate that scriptures such as Psalm 118 would have been seen by the Zealots and other revolutionaries in besieged Jerusalem as prophecies of precisely this aid:[23]

> All nations compassed me about; in the name of the Lord I cut them off. They compassed me about, indeed they surrounded me; but in the name of the Lord I cut them off. (Ps. 118:10–11, alt.)

It is easy to see why such an attitude would be of concern to Mark and his community when we reflect that Mark's community is probably

---

[20] On the redactional nature of 11:17, see Marcus, "Jewish War," n. 39.

[21] See Marcus, "Jewish War."

[22] For more detailed discussion, see Marcus, "Jewish War."

[23] See M. Hengel's reference to Ps. 118:24 in *The Zealots: Investigations into the Jewish Freedom Movements in the Period from Herod I Until 70 A.D.* (Edinburgh: T. & T. Clark, 1989), p. 302.

composed predominantly of Gentiles[24] and when we combine this probability with our theory that the community is situated somewhere close to
Palestine. As I have shown elsewhere, a mostly Gentile Christian community
in such a location would have had good reasons for fearing the Jewish revolutionary movement.[25] The predominantly Gentile Hellenistic cities on the
borders of Israel had, since Hasmonean times, been engaged in a continuous
struggle with the inhabitants of the Jewish state, and this tension was
probably a major factor in precipitating the Great Revolt. When the war
broke out, this tension burst into armed conflict in these "ring" cities;
massacres of Jews by Gentiles and of Gentiles by Jews became frequent.
Indeed, U. Rappaport has pointed out that most of the fighting in the war's
first year was not between Jews and Romans but between Jews and inhabitants of the Hellenistic cities.[26]

If Mark's community is a predominantly Gentile group situated in one
of these "ring" cities or somewhere nearby, a plausible background is
provided for the sharp polemic against the Jewish leaders in 12:9. Mark
is confronted with an Israel that has taken up the cudgels against the non-
Jewish world in a desperate fight for survival. In the heat of the war, and
fired by apocalyptic visions of victory by a purified Israel (such as Ps.
118:10–11!), some Jews are prepared to take drastic steps against Gentiles
and against Jews who advocate coexistence with them—that is, the sort
of people who make up the Markan community. Such Jews, in their view,
do not deserve the name of "Israel" and must be purged. Mark 12:9 turns
the accusation around, implies that the scriptures foretell that *the purgers*
will be purged, denies the name of Israel to *them*, and asserts that the
inheritance of Israel has now been turned over to a new people that prominently includes Gentiles in its ranks.[27]

---

[24] See the comment in 7:3–4 about what "the Pharisees, and all the Jews" do, which makes
most sense if the audience is predominantly Gentile; cf. the explanatory clauses in 14:12; 15:42.

[25] See Marcus, "Jewish War."

[26] U. Rappaport, "Jewish-Pagan Relations and the Revolt against Rome in 66–70 C.E.,"
Jerusalem Cathedra 1 (1981), 81–95, esp. p. 94.

[27] In Mark 12:1–12 the addressees whom Jesus threatens are the chief priests, scribes (with
whom the Pharisees are closely linked elsewhere in the Gospel: 2:16; 7:1, 5; 9:11), and the
elders (see 11:27). This lineup of opponents may partly reflect the leadership of the Great
Revolt. See H. Schwier, who points out that some priests, including members of the high-
priestly families, and some Pharisees were influential supporters of the revolt (*Tempel und
Tempelzerstörung: Untersuchungen zu den theologischen und ideologischen Faktoren im ersten
jüdisch-römischen Krieg [66–74 n. Chr.]*, NTOA 11 [Göttingen: Vandenhoeck & Ruprecht, 1989],
pp. 128, 139, 162, 176–177, 190–201).

Temple Imagery

THE TEMPLE IN PSALM 118

The upside-down holy war against Israel and on behalf of the Gentiles depicted in Mark 12:9 is linked with the psalm's description of the exaltation of the rejected stone to the head of the corner. We have already seen that the juxtaposition of the two passages makes it probable that Mark views the psalm's rejected stone as the parable's beloved son, who is rejected by the wicked tenants. But how exactly does Mark understand the "stone" imagery that he draws from the psalm and applies to Christ?

In the psalm itself, the stone is, quite literally, a stone, one initially rejected by the builders of the Jerusalem Temple but subsequently made the cornerstone of the Temple. This literal understanding of the psalm verse and its connection with the Temple were not forgotten in the postbiblical period, as is proved by the *Testament of Solomon* (22:7–23:4), a Christian work incorporating Jewish traditions and variously dated from the first to the third century A.D.[28] Here Solomon enlists demonic help to place a gigantic, immovable stone at the corner of the Temple in order to complete its construction; Solomon himself then exclaims in ecstasy, "Truly the Scripture which says, 'It was the stone rejected by the builders that became the keystone,' has now been fulfilled. . . ." Although in this passage the κεφαλὴ γωνίας ("head of the corner") is a keystone or capstone, other passages suggest that the same phrase can be interpreted as a stone at the base of the building; in any case, the image suggests a stone essential to the structure.[29] What is important is the association of the phrase with the Temple.

This association is strengthened by the fact that 1 Peter 2:4–7 preserves the Temple-building associations of the stone image in a passage that alludes to, and later quotes, Ps. 118:22:

> . . . Come to him, a living *stone, rejected* by human beings but *in God's sight* chosen and precious; and like living *stones* be yourselves *built into a spiritual house*, a holy priesthood, to offer spiritual sacrifices acceptable to God through Jesus Christ. . . . To you therefore who believe he [Christ] is precious, but for those who do not believe, "The very stone which the builders rejected has become the head of the corner. . . ."[30]

---

[28] On the *Testament of Solomon*, see D. C. Duling in *OTP* 1:941–942; on its citation of Ps. 118:22, see R. N. Longenecker, *Biblical Exegesis in the Apostolic Period* (Grand Rapids: Wm. B. Eerdmans Publishing Co., 1975), p. 51.

[29] Best, *Following*, p. 225 n. 64.

[30] Translation altered from the RSV.

The words "rejected" and "in God's sight" at the beginning of this passage are allusions to Ps. 118:22, and the verse itself is quoted at its end. The references to being built[31] into a spiritual house, to a holy priesthood, and to spiritual sacrifices are examples of Temple imagery.[32] A very similar association of stone imagery with the Temple is found at Qumran (1QS 8:4; 1QH 6:25–29; 7:8–9), where the elect community is linked with a stone which is the new Temple.[33]

A further argument for seeing Temple imagery in Mark 12:10–11 is the implicit presence of such imagery in the vineyard parable of 12:1–9 that precedes it. C. A. Evans notes that in *Targum Jonathan* and the Tosefta (*Me'il.* 1:16; *Sukk.* 3:15) the tower and the winepress of Isa. 5:2, the passage that underlies Mark 12:1, are interpreted as the Temple and its altar, and he argues that *1 Enoch* 89:73 indicates that the equation "tower = Temple" was already current in the first century.[34] Evans's arguments are corroborated by a recently published Qumran fragment, 4Q500, which seems to be based on Isa. 5:1–7 and which links the wine vat with "the gate of the holy height," an apparent reference to the Temple mount as a tower.[35] Already, therefore, the description of the digging of the wine vat and of the building of the tower in Mark 12:1 may suggest the Temple theme.

It is not necessary, however, to go as far afield as rabbinic literature, Qumran, or even 1 Peter in order to establish the link between the stone imagery of Mark 12:10 and the theme of the Temple. Mark himself confirms this linkage. The setting for our passage is the Temple itself (11:27), and the Temple theme is prominent in the preceding chapter of Mark (11:9–11, 15–18, 27–33). In the very next chapter, moreover, the eschatological discourse is introduced by a short passage in which stone imagery and the Temple theme are interwoven in a manner strikingly reminiscent of our passage:

> And as he came out of *the temple*, one of his disciples said to him, "*Look, Teacher, what wonderful stones* (λίθοι) *and what wonderful buildings* (οἰκοδομαί)!" And Jesus said to him, "*Do you see these great buildings* (οἰκοδομάς)? There will not be left here *a stone upon a stone* (λίθος ἐπὶ λίθον) which will not be thrown down." (Mark 13:1–2, alt.)

---

[31] The verb used here is οἰκοδομεῖσθε, the same verb used in Ps. 118:22 LXX; Mark 12:10.

[32] See J. R. Donahue, *Are You the Christ?* SBLDS 10 (Missoula, Mont.: Society of Biblical Literature, 1973), p. 125.

[33] This link is established at Qumran by means of Isa. 28:16, a "stone" text that is also linked with Ps. 118:22 in 1 Peter 2:4; see B. Gärtner, *The Temple and the Community in Qumran and the New Testament*, SNTSMS 1 (Cambridge: Cambridge University Press, 1965), pp. 133–136.

[34] C. A. Evans, "On the Vineyard Parables of Isaiah 5 and Mark 12," *BZ* 28 (1984), 83–84.

[35] See J. M. Baumgarten, "4Q500 and the Ancient Conception of the Lord's Vineyard," *JJS* 40 (1989), 1–3.

Not only does the word "stone" occur emphatically three times in conjunction with the Temple theme in these two verses, but the passage is also linked with ours by the themes of building (cf. the builders in 12:10) and of seeing (cf. "it is marvelous in our eyes" in 12:11).

These links suggest that the Old Testament context of the psalm quotation, with its references to the Temple liturgy, is in view in Mark 12:10–11 and that Jesus is being portrayed as the cornerstone of a new Temple. This result coheres with the thesis of D. Juel's book *Messiah and Temple:* the "Temple charge" of Mark 14:58; 15:29, though false as Jesus' opponents understand it, is from another point of view ironically true. The old Temple will be destroyed, and a new eschatological Temple, not made with hands, will take its place.[36]

By prefacing the reference to this new eschatological Temple (12:10–11) with a reference to the entry of Gentiles (included in the "others" of the possibly redactional end of v. 9), Mark aligns himself with a strain of Old Testament and postbiblical Jewish expectation that describes the eschatological pilgrimage of Gentiles to the end-time Temple in Jerusalem.[37] This expectation is particularly prominent in Isaiah, as passages such as the following illustrate:

> And it shall come to pass in the latter days that the mountain of the house of the LORD shall be established as the highest of the mountains and shall be raised above the hills; and all the nations shall flow to it, and many peoples shall come, and say: "Come, let us go up to the mountain of the LORD, to the house of the God of Jacob; that he may teach us his ways and that we may walk in his paths." (Isa. 2:2–3)

> And the foreigners who join themselves to the LORD, to minister to him, to love the name of the LORD, and to be his servants, . . . these I will bring to my holy mountain, and make them joyful in my house of prayer; their burnt offerings and their sacrifices will be accepted on my altar; for my house shall be called a house of prayer for all peoples. (Isa. 56:6–7)

Mark's introduction of a citation from the latter passage into the story of Jesus' cleansing of the Temple (11:17) confirms his awareness of this motif of an end-time pilgrimage of the Gentiles to the new Temple. Such awareness is consonant with our results in chapter 2, where we saw that Mark ascribes fundamental importance to Isaiah and interprets Jesus' "way" as the return of Yahweh to Zion (cf. Mark 1:2–3). The thrilling Isaian picture of the Gentiles' eschatological pilgrimage and inclusion in salvation is part of this "return" motif.

---

[36] Juel, *Messiah and Temple: The Trial of Jesus in the Gospel of Mark*, SBLDS 31 (Missoula, Mont.: Scholars Press, 1973), passim.

[37] On this expectation, see J. Jeremias, *Jesus' Promise to the Nations* (Philadelphia: Fortress Press, 1958), pp. 59–62, 65–66.

Mark's use of these Old Testament traditions, however, displays some discontinuity with its Jewish forbears. While the Jewish traditions speak of a *joining* of Gentiles to Israel, Mark 12:9 speaks not only of an inclusion of "others" (prominently Gentiles) in Israel but also of an exclusion of the original tenants from it. As we note in the excursus at the end of this chapter, it is unclear whether Mark restricts these tenants to the leaders of Israel or includes among them also the masses of Jewish people who have rejected the Christian message; he at least does not take pains to guard his text against the latter interpretation. If Mark *is* hinting that not only Israel's leaders but also the great mass of her people have forfeited their status as Israel, his attitude probably reflects the sociological tension of the war situation, as we have described it above. Such a *Sitz im Leben* makes an exclusionary attitude comprehensible, though it does not reduce the deplorable nature of its effects in the twenty centuries that have followed.

THE CHRISTIAN COMMUNITY AS THE NEW TEMPLE

In the preceding section we have seen that 12:10–11 is a reference to Christ as the cornerstone of a new Temple. What is this Temple, in Mark's conception? Here again a look at the original psalm is a good starting place. We have already seen that in the original psalm the "I" who speaks is understood collectively as Israel and that this understanding is reflected in postbiblical Jewish texts. Early Christian exegetes seem to have been aware of this collective interpretation of the "I" of Psalm 118; we have already noted, for example, 1 Peter 2:4–7, in which the stone of Ps. 118:22 is linked with other stones, that is, the Christian community as the new Temple. A similar collective interpretation of "stone" texts is already found in 1QH 6:25–29; 7:8–9; and 1QS 8:4. It would not be surprising, therefore, to find that Mark thought of the Christian community collectively as the eschatological Temple whose cornerstone is Christ, the rejected stone.

This does indeed seem to be Mark's interpretation, as the transition from the parable in Mark 12:1–9 to the citation of the psalm in 12:10–11 suggests. At the end of the parable, in a verse that may have been significantly edited by Mark, Jesus prophesies that the lord of the vineyard will come and destroy the wicked vineyard workers and give the vineyard to others. For Mark's readers this prophecy would probably awaken echoes of the tragic conclusion of the Jewish Revolt that began in A.D. 66 and that climaxed in the conquest of Jerusalem in 70. The destruction of Jewish sovereignty in Israel (the vineyard) is understood as a judgment against the Jewish people or their leaders (the vineyard workers) on the part of God (the lord of the vineyard). The vineyard, Israel, is now transferred to others, the predominantly Gentile church as the new Israel. This allegorical prophecy leads immediately into the citation of Ps. 118:22–23, which is viewed as confirming the point just made.

The best way of understanding this transition is to say that the church, to which allusion has been made by means of the word "others" of 12:9, is the new Temple of which Jesus is the cornerstone in 12:10–11. Only such an understanding can explain how the scripture citation can be viewed as confirming the point of the parable. As we have already noted, in the parable the son himself is not delivered; the last glimpse we get of him is in v. 8, where he is killed and cast out of the vineyard. The only note of vindication comes in the transfer of the vineyard from its former murderous tenants to the new tenants. We may say, then, that the son, the heir of the vineyard, is vindicated by the transfer of the vineyard to the "others" who are collectively associated with him.

Mark, in other words, views Christ's resurrection, the exaltation of the rejected stone to the head of the corner, as the creation of a new Temple composed of the resurrected Lord in union with his eschatological community of "others." This Markan reinterpretation of the Temple and association of it with the eschatological community of "others" probably reflects his community's encounter with the Jewish revolutionaries; his implicit denial of the ultimate significance of the Jerusalem Temple and linkage of the Temple theme with Gentiles is in part at least a polemic against the revolutionaries' pro-Temple, anti-Gentile zeal. As we have seen, these Markan themes are foreshadowed by the citation of Isa. 56:7 in 11:17, a citation that is probably Markan redaction. Here Jesus claims the Temple as his own house (ὁ οἶκος μου, "*my* house") and states that its purpose was to become a house of prayer for *all nations*.[38]

This linkage of Christ with the new community created by his death and resurrection reflects an important Markan emphasis. As we have already noted in chapter 5, and as we shall emphasize again in chapter 8, Mark pictures Jesus not just as an individual but as a figure with collective dimensions. In 2:27–28, for example, Jesus defends his disciples' act of plucking grain on the Sabbath by saying, "The sabbath was made for man . . . , therefore the Son of man is lord of the sabbath" (alt.). Here the title "Son of man" seems to associate Jesus with other human beings, those for whom the Sabbath came into being. In 3:14, Jesus appoints twelve disciples "to be with him," and this "being with him" is probably paradigmatic for all disciples.[39] The church is the community of those chosen to be with Jesus

---

[38] See Best, *Following*, p. 218: "In Isa 56:7 the μου of 'my house' refers to God but in the Christian context which Mark provides and in the context of Jesus as speaker it probably belongs to Jesus. The new community belongs to Jesus; it is not just any 'new community' but his community, 'his house.'"

[39] See K. Stock, *Boten aus dem Mit-Ihm-Sein: Das Verhältnis zwischen Jesus und den Zwölf nach Markus*, AnBib 70 (Rome: Biblical Institute Press, 1975), passim.

in the way of the cross (8:34) but also in the new life of empowerment that is found as they tread that difficult and treacherous path.[40] In 13:11 Jesus prophesies that when his disciples are called upon to bear witness to him, it will not be they who speak but the Holy Spirit, a spirit which the reader of the Gospel knows to be bestowed by Jesus himself (1:8). Finally, in 14:22–25 the disciples are given Jesus' body to eat and his blood to drink; although the implication is not drawn out explicitly, it is hard to escape the inference that in the Eucharist Jesus' life is mediated to the Christian community.[41] Jesus Christ and the Christian community, therefore, are not separable realities in Mark's eyes. For this reason the eschatological creation alluded to in 12:9, the transfer of the vineyard to "others," represents one aspect of the vindication of the rejected stone that is spoken of in 12:10–11.

The Builders and the Builder

The agent of both community creation and stone vindication is God, who is represented in the parable itself as the lord of the vineyard who transfers it to the "others" and in the scripture citation as the Lord from whom the exaltation of the stone comes. God's action of vindicating the stone is the reversal of the action of a group identified as "the builders," who reject it.

Both Markan contextual clues and history-of-religions background suggest that these "builders" are to be identified as the scribes and other Jewish leaders with whom Jesus has been engaged in polemical dialogue since 11:27. In that verse the chief priests, scribes, and elders come to Jesus and pose the question about authority. Immediately after Jesus enunciates the parable of the vineyard and its accompanying scriptural citation, these Jewish leaders try to arrest him because they perceive that the parable is *spoken against them* (12:12). In Mark's conception, then, they are represented in the parable by the wicked tenants and in the scripture by the builders who reject the stone.

This Markan clue concerning the identity of the "builders" dovetails with evidence from rabbinic traditions, in which "builders" is a common term for scribes or scholars.[42] The scholars, in this rabbinic self-understanding, are those who "build Jerusalem" by applying God's original revelation at Sinai to contemporary problems and by educating the people:

---

[40] See, e.g., 6:6–13, where the disciples receive from Jesus the power to preach, exorcise, and heal.

[41] See Stock, *Boten*, pp. 162–163.

[42] See E. Lohmeyer, *Das Evangelium des Markus*, MeyerK, 11th ed. (Göttingen: Vandenhoeck & Ruprecht, 1951), p. 247 n. 5; S-B 1:876; J. D. M. Derrett, "The Stone that the Builders Rejected," in *Studies in the New Testament*, 5 vols. (Leiden: E. J. Brill, 1977, 1978), 2:64–65.

[In Cant 1:5] do not read "daughters" (בנות) but "builders" (בונות) of Jerusalem; the great Sanhedrin of Israel is meant, who sit and build her through every question and answer. (*Midr. Cant.* 1:5)

Or, to switch the metaphor slightly, the scholars are בונים בתורה, those who "build in the Torah" by elucidating its meaning for contemporary audiences.[43] The scribes, therefore, are "edifiers" who increase the joy of the world because they add to the house of Torah, upon which the happiness of Israel and indeed of the entire world depends.

The Markan version of the parable of the vineyard utilizes this Jewish equation of builders with scribes in a polemical fashion that shatters the continuity between the building activity of God and that of the scribes. In the Jewish understandings just described, the interpretive activity of the scribes joyfully builds upon the foundational action of God in giving the Torah to his people, but in Mark the building of the scribes *opposes* that of God and brings his judgment down upon them. God's act of building the vineyard (see ᾠκοδόμησεν in 12:1) is negated by the scribal "builders" (οἰκοδομοῦντες, 12:10), who are linked with the wicked tenants. The latter oppose God when they beat and kill the servants whom he has sent into the vineyard.

Instead of building the vineyard, then, the scribes render it unfit for anything but transfer to another group of tenants. Similarly, instead of bringing out the true sense of the scripture through authoritative exegesis, they and the other Jewish leaders are shown to be ignorant of the scripture's true meaning (see 12:10a, "Have you never read this scripture?"). The contradiction to the self-understanding of the Jewish scribes is similar to that enshrined in 7:1–13, where the Markan Jesus, in direct opposition to the self-understanding of the scribes, denounces their exegesis as a merely human tradition that makes the word of God void.

"The Lord Is for Me. What Will Man Do to Me?"

In spite of Mark's opposition to some of the results of scribal exegesis of the scriptures, it is obvious that his own exegesis often takes off from Jewish traditions of biblical interpretation. We have seen several examples of this dependence already. One other example may illuminate Mark 12:1–12 further. The problems of dating this tradition are severe, but it raises some interesting interpretive possibilities.

---

[43] See the texts cited by Derrett (previous note). The "builders" are sometimes referred to as "understanders," an identification that is facilitated by the closeness between the verbs בנה ("to build") and הבין ("to understand").

Yalkut Shimoni on Ps. 118:6 ascribes to the Midrash the following comment on that verse:

> "The Lord is for me; what will man do to me?" (Ps. 118:6). A parable. What is the matter like? It is similar to a king who had *a servant*, and he *loved him* more than all his servants, and the other servants *were jealous* of him. He said, *my lord has compassion on me*, what can man do to me?[44]

This exegesis contains some striking points of contact with Mark 12:1–12, as the italicized portions show. A passage from Psalm 118 is linked with a parable in which God is compared to a "lord" who has a beloved servant. Mark similarly links his citation of Psalm 118 (12:10–11) with a parable in which *God*, the *lord* of the vineyard, sends various *servants* and finally his *beloved* son into it (12:1–9). The jealousy of the other servants in the *Yalkut* passage, moreover, corresponds to the hostility of the tenants toward the son in Mark; physical harm seems to be a possibility, although it is a possibility that is averted ("What can man do to me?").

The correspondence is so close that it seems distinctly possible that Mark 12:1–12 is drawing on some version of this exegesis of Ps. 118:6. If this is so, however, the Markan use of this exegetical tradition reflects a characteristic Christian modification of the Jewish pattern. In the *Yalkut* passage, the beloved servant can confidently trust that his "lord" will deliver him from the hostile intentions of his jealous fellow servants. In the Markan parable, in contrast, the beloved son is not protected from the murderous plans of the wicked tenants; rather, they are able to kill him. The same sort of contrast is evident when the Markan passage is compared to a passage in *Sipre* on Deuteronomy which has been dubbed "the rabbinic parable of the wicked tenants."[45] Here a king lets out a field to wicked tenants who steal from it; when a son is born to him, therefore, he evicts them from the field in favor of his son. As in the *Yalkut* passage, no violence is done to the son, and the parable reflects a serene confidence that God will protect from the wicked tenants the one whom he favors.

If Mark 12:1–9 is drawing on Jewish traditions similar to those found in *Sipre* and *Yalkut*, the Markan tradition alters them in a way that reflects not only Jesus' original parable of the vineyard but also early Christian memories of the violent fate of Jesus. Unlike the speaker in Psalm 118, Jesus is *not* delivered from the deadly hostility of his enemies. The psalm's hope

---

44 The translation of the passage is mine. I have been unable to locate it in the standard Hebrew and English editions of the Midrash. Burton Visotzky has suggested to me in conversation the possibility that *Yalkut* knows of a manuscript of the Midrash that includes the tradition, but that this reading has been lost in the transmission of the Midrash text.

45 *Sipre Deut.* 32:9, par. 312; cited, for example, in S-B 1:874; Jeremias, *Parables*, p. 73 n. 88; Evans, "Vineyard Parables," p. 84 n. 17.

for divine protection, therefore, becomes one that is fulfilled only in Jesus' resurrection and in the eschatological creation of Christian communities that live their life in union with him.

Conclusions: Mark 12:10–11 and the Markan Community

Mark's community knows that it owes its very existence as part of God's Israel to the vindication of the rejected stone, that stone's exaltation to the head of the corner. In a very real way, the members of the community share in the stone's reversal. They too know what it means to be rejected by Israel's scribal builders, relegated to the status of "others," "alienated from the commonwealth of Israel, and strangers to the covenants of promise, having no hope and without God in the world" — to use the words of Eph. 2:12. They too have been rejected stones, but contrary to all expectation they now find themselves incorporated into a living sanctuary that pulses with the very life of God. Their entry into this sanctuary is an eschatological miracle, the fulfillment of the ancient scriptural hope that in the time of the end God's house will become a house of prayer for all peoples (see 11:17). The confession of 12:11, "this is the Lord's doing, and it is astonishing in our eyes," is their confession, not only in view of the resurrection of Christ but also in view of their own incorporation into the sphere of life.

But this incorporation does not mean that the Markan community has entered once and for all into a serene heavenly realm where it is untroubled by the agitation of life on earth. Quite the contrary, the story of the violence done to God's servants in 12:1–8 would unmistakably echo, for Mark's readers, the sayings about taking up one's cross and losing one's life for the sake of the gospel (8:34–35), as well as the daily reality of persecution they are confronting (see 13:9–13). True, the Markan Christians can joyfully confess their eschatological awareness that the first have become last and the last first, and that as part of this revolution they have been incorporated into a new fellowship whose communal existence is a foretaste of eternal life; but all of this eschatological blessing comes only "with persecutions" (10:29–31).

In the midst of these persecutions, of this rejection, which continues the rejection experienced by Jesus, the Markan community also experiences the vindication of Jesus. While on one level, therefore, the rejection and the vindication described in 12:10 are sequential, speaking of the crucifixion and resurrection of Jesus, it is also true to Mark's theology to say that the vindication comes *in the midst* of the rejection.[46] Already at the

---

[46] See further our discussion below in chapter 8 of Mark's use of the Isaian Suffering Servant figure to express this motif of victory in the midst of suffering.

crucifixion of Jesus the centurion confesses him as the Son of God (15:39); already in *their* crucifixion the Markan Christians experience the eschatological power that bursts forth at the exaltation of the rejected stone. This paradox of vindication in the midst of rejection is, from the world's point of view, a logical impossibility, but it becomes possible in the unearthly logic of the new age that comes from the Lord and is marvelous in human eyes.

Excursus: "You" and the "Others" in Mark 12:9

The referent of the "you" threatened with destruction in 12:9 is unclear. On the one hand, in the Markan context there are reasons for identifying the original tenants not with the Jewish people as a whole but with its leaders. According to 11:27 Jesus is addressing the scribes and elders, not the people as a whole, and he links the wicked tenants of 12:1–9 with the builders of 12:10. As we show in the body of this chapter, "builders" is a common rabbinic term for scribes, and Mark himself seems to distinguish the builders' negative reaction to Jesus from the positive reaction of the presumably Jewish crowd in 12:12.

On the other hand, later in Mark, in the passion narrative, the crowd joins with the Jewish leaders in condemning Jesus (15:11–15), thus implicitly shouldering part of the responsibility for his death, which is what the tenants accomplish in 12:8. In the Old Testament, moreover, the prophets were sent to, and rejected by, the people as a whole, not just its leaders; therefore in 12:2–5 the rejecters of the servants/prophets may be the people rather than just the leaders.[47] More important, New Testament passages tend to put the blame for the persecution of the prophets on the people as a whole.[48] If, as we think, the reference in 12:9 ("he will destroy the tenants") is to the tragic end of the Jewish Revolt, this might also point in the direction of a general reference, since it was not only the leaders but also the Jewish people in Palestine as a whole who suffered the havoc of the war.

The question of the identity of "you" is inextricable from that of the identity of the "others." If "you" were the leaders of Israel, then the "others" to

---

[47] See Carlston, *Parables*, p. 189; Best, *Following*, p. 219; contra Snodgrass, who argues that the prophets often directed their message against the leaders (*Parable*, p. 77). Against Snodgrass, they more often directed it against the people, and the Old Testament references to the persecution and murder of the prophets, a vital element in Mark 12:4–5, are about evenly divided between those that blame the leaders (1 Kings 18:4, 13; 22:27; 2 Chron. 16:10; Jer. 20:2; 26:20–23; 37:15–16; 38:4–6) and those that include the people or blame them solely (1 Kings 19:10, 14; 2 Chron. 24:21; Neh. 9:26; Jer. 2:30; 11:21; 26:8–11). References from G. Friedrich et al., "προφήτης, κτλ.," *TDNT* (1968; orig. 1959), 6:834 n. 348.

[48] See 1 Thess. 2:15; Matt. 5:12; Luke 6:23; Luke 13:33–34//Matt. 23:37; Acts 7:52; contrast references to leaders in Matt. 23:31, 34//Luke 11:47–49. References from Friedrich, "προφήτης," pp. 834–835.

whom their privileges were given should logically be the apostles, the new leaders of Israel, as Origen already suggested. As Carlston puts it, this would indeed be startling evidence of "early Catholicism" in Mark.[49] In view of the lack of other support for such a view of the apostles in Mark and the constant Markan emphasis on the Gentile mission (see n. 11 above), it is better to take the "others" as the members of the church, especially its Gentile component.[50] This in turn makes it more likely that the "you" from whom the "others" are distinguished are the Jewish people as a whole, though 11:27; 12:10–12 are still strong witnesses for identifying "you" as the leaders.

---

[49] Carlston, *Parables,* p. 188 n. 54.
[50] See Carlston, *Parables,* p. 189; Best, *Following,* pp. 219–220.

7

Mark 12:35-37

David's Son and David's Lord

12:35a	And answering, Jesus said, teaching in the Temple,	A
12:35b	How do the scribes say that the Christ is the Son of David?	B
12:36a	David himself said in the Holy Spirit,	C
12:36b	*The Lord said to my lord,*	
12:36c	*Sit at my right hand,*	D
12:36d	*Until I put your enemies*	
12:36e	*under your feet.*	
12:37a	David himself calls him "lord";	C'
12:37b	How then is he his son?	B'
12:37c	And the large crowd heard him gladly.	A'

The Old Testament Text

Mark 12:35-37 is beautifully arranged around a quotation of Ps. 110:1 (12:36b-e), which is cited according to the Septuagint with the single exception of the word "under" (ὑποκάτω), where the Septuagint has "footstool" (ὑποπόδιον). The Markan word "under"[1] probably reflects the influence of Ps. 8:7 LXX, "You have subordinated all things under (ὑποκάτω) his feet." These two psalm verses are often coupled in early Christianity.[2]

---

[1] Although there are only four Greek manuscripts that read ὑποκάτω, the parallel in the preferred reading of Matt. 22:44 supports it, while the Septuagintal reading ὑποπόδιον is followed in Luke 20:43 and Acts 2:44. Knowing the Septuagint and the Lukan passages, copyists would have tended to substitute the "correct" reading ὑποπόδιον for ὑποκάτω, a tendency also found in some manuscripts of Matt. 22:44; see B. M. Metzger, *A Textual Commentary on the Greek New Testament* (London and New York: United Bible Societies, 1971), p. 111.

[2] See D. M. Hay, *Glory at the Right Hand: Psalm 110 in Early Christianity* (Nashville: Abingdon Press, 1973), pp. 35–36; J.-G. Mudiso Mbâ Mundla, *Jesus und die Führer Israels:*

This conflated Old Testament citation stands at the center (D) of a chiasm[3] in which the outer parts (AA′) comprise the frame of the story, introducing Jesus' direct speech and recording the crowd's reaction to it (vv. 35a, 37c).[4] The next step into the chiasm (BB′) consists of introductory and concluding questions about Christ as the Son of David (vv. 35b, 37b), and the third step (CC′) consists of a notice that "David himself" (αὐτὸς Δαυίδ) said something (vv. 36a, 37a).

What is Mark's direct role in shaping this passage? It seems essentially to be limited to fashioning the frame of the passage, Mark 12:35a, 37c.[5] Mark 12:35a, "and answering Jesus said, teaching in the Temple," is replete with Markan vocabulary.[6] The word "teaching," for example, indicates a favorite theme of Markan redactional verses,[7] and the mention of the Temple links our passage with the overarching redactional framework of the entire section 11:27–13:1.[8] As for v. 37c, "large crowd" is a characteristic term for Markan redaction (5:21, 24; 6:34; 8:1; 9:14), and the fact that this crowd hears Jesus gladly creates a striking parallel with the description of Herod in 6:20. The entire sentence, moreover, forms a transition to the following pericope.

Aside from this redactional frame, however, the rest of the passage seems to be basically traditional, an impression confirmed by the apparently independent version in *Barn.* 12:10–11:

> Since therefore they are going to say that the Christ is David's son, David himself prophesies, fearing and understanding the error of the sinners: "The Lord said to my lord, Sit at my right hand, until I make your enemies

---

Studien zu den sog. Jerusalemer Streitgesprächen, NTAbh N.F. 17 (Münster: Aschendorff, 1984), p. 241; M. C. de Boer, *The Defeat of Death: Apocalyptic Eschatology in 1 Corinthians 15 and Romans 5,* JSNTSup 22 (Sheffield: Sheffield Academic Press, 1988), pp. 114–120.

[3] Cf. the analysis of the structure of the Matthean parallel, Matt. 22:41–46, by S. P. Saunders in " 'No One Dared Ask Him Anything More': Contextual Readings of the Controversy Stories in Matthew" (Ph.D. diss., Princeton Theological Seminary, 1990), pp. 436–447.

[4] G. Schneider ("Die Davidssohnfrage [Mk 12.35–37]," *Bib* 53 [1972], 65 n. 3) rightly rejects K. Aland's inclusion of 12:37c in the following pericope 12:38–40, comparing 6:20, where "he heard him gladly" ends a passage, and adding that καὶ . . . ἔλεγεν ("and . . . he said") in 12:38a is an introductory formula (cf. 4:2; 9:31; 11:17; 12:35).

[5] See J. Gnilka, *Das Evangelium nach Markus,* EKKNT 2, 2 vols. (Zurich: Benziger Verlag, 1978, 1979), 2:169; and Mudiso Mbâ Mundla, *Führer,* pp. 236–237.

[6] Although the pattern καὶ ἀποκριθείς ("and answering") + verb of speaking commonly occurs in Mark's traditional material, the form elsewhere is either καὶ ἀποκριθείς . . . λέγει ("and answering . . . he says," 3:33; 8:29; 9:5; 11:22, 33) or καὶ ἀποκριθείς . . . εἶπεν ("and answering . . . he said" [aorist], 10:51; 11:14; 14:48); Mark 12:35a is the only instance of καὶ ἀποκριθείς . . . ἔλεγεν ("and answering . . . he said" [imperfect]). Cf., however, 15:12 ὁ δὲ Πιλᾶτος πάλιν ἀποκριθείς ἔλεγεν αὐτοῖς, "but Pilate again answering said [imperfect] to them. . . ."

[7] See its appearance in the "framework" passages 1:21–22; 2:13; 4:1–2; 6:2, 6, 30, 34; 8:31; 9:31; 10:1; 11:17. It is probably traditional in 7:7 and 12:14, but 14:49 may represent Markan redaction.

[8] Cf. the references to the Temple in 11:27b; 12:35; 12:41; and 13:1.

your footstool" (ἕως ἂν θῶ τοὺς ἐχθρούς σου ὑποπόδιον τῶν ποδῶν σου) . . .
See how David calls him "lord" and does not say "son."[9]

Like Mark 12:35–37 par., this passage uses Ps. 110:1 to highlight a problem
with the designation "Son of David." It does not, however, seem to be directly
dependent on any of the Synoptic passages; its introduction ("Since they
are going to say that the Christ is David's son") is closest to Mark 12:35,
but the form in which the psalm verse is cited ("make your enemies your
footstool," in dependence on the Septuagint) is closest to Luke 20:43. Since
apart from these features it manifests no particular relatedness to any one
of the Synoptic passages, it is best to view it as an independent version of
the tradition found in Mark 12:35–37 par.[10] The fact that this independent
version does not ascribe the tradition to Jesus, coupled with our observation above of the redactional nature of the Markan frame, suggests strongly
that our pericope may have originally circulated as an unascribed exegetical
saying.

It is possible that Mark himself is responsible for the introduction of the
allusion to Ps. 8:7 by the substitution of "under" for "footstool," since
Barnabas attests the latter reading and we have seen in previous chapters
that conflation is a typical Markan technique. If *Barnabas* is any guide, Mark
may also be responsible for the transformation of what was originally a
midrashic discussion without "opponents" into something resembling a
controversy story;[11] such a transformation would make good sense in the
controversial atmosphere of Mark 11:27–12:40.[12]

Psalm 110 as an Eschatological Prophecy

The introduction to the citation of Ps. 110:1 in Mark 12:36 asserts that
David spoke these words "in the Holy Spirit." As E. Lohmeyer has noted,
this introduction already suggests that the psalm verse is to be understood
eschatologically, since elsewhere in the New Testament words of the Holy

---

[9] Translation altered from that of K. Lake in *The Apostolic Fathers*, LCL, 2 vols. (Cambridge, Mass.: Harvard University Press, 1912), 1:387.

[10] See H. Köster, *Synoptische Überlieferung bei den apostolischen Vätern*, TU 65 (Berlin:
Akademie-Verlag, 1957), pp. 145–146; C. Burger, *Jesus als Davidssohn: Eine traditionsgeschichtliche Untersuchung*, FRLANT 98 (Göttingen: Vandenhoeck & Ruprecht, 1970), pp. 57–58.

[11] Our story is difficult to categorize form-critically, since a scribal opinion is opposed but
the scribes themselves do not present it, as in the typical controversy story; see Mudiso Mbâ
Mundla, *Führer*, pp. 243–245.

[12] Mark 11:27–33; 12:13–17; and 12:18–27 are all controversy stories. Formally 12:1–12 and
12:28–34 are not controversy stories, but they both belong in the context of Jesus' confrontation with the Jewish leaders.

Spirit are usually prophetic words concerning coming eschatological events.[13]

In understanding Psalm 110 as a prophecy of eschatological events, Mark is in line with a stream of interpretation of the psalm that can be traced from the Old Testament through intertestamental Judaism and into the New Testament. Although in the original *Sitz im Leben* of the psalm "my lord" was the reigning Davidic monarch whose exaltation took place on the day of his coronation, already by the time of the psalm's incorporation into the Psalter in the postexilic period its horizon had been transformed into the eschatological hope that the kingship of Yahweh would become universally effective at the end of days.[14]

A similar eschatological orientation is visible in 11QMelchizedek, a document whose title figure is probably drawn from Ps. 110:4. In the Qumran document we are presented with a description of a judgment "at the end of days" (2:4) by Melchizedek, a figure who has been exalted to God's right hand (2:9–11). In this judgment Melchizedek becomes the agent of God's vengeance on Belial and the spirits of his lot (2:9, 13, 24), and the document's prophecy of judgment is explicitly linked with the good news of the earthly epiphany of God's kingship through two citations of Isa. 52:7, "Your God has become king!" (2:16, 24).[15] Although some scholars have rejected the hypothesis of a direct link between Psalm 110 and 11QMelch, the combination of themes found in both documents (Melchizedek, exaltation to God's right hand, divine kingship, victory over enemies, and judgment) is too close to be fortuitous. Hence the depiction in 11QMelch of the eschatological battle between the spirits, in which the kingly power of God is manifested through Melchizedek, should be considered a chapter in the history of the interpretation of Psalm 110.[16] The Midrash on Psalms, similarly, interprets Ps. 110:1 as a reference to the way in which God will fight on

---

[13] E. Lohmeyer, *Das Evangelium des Markus*, MeyerK, 11th ed. (Göttingen: Vandenhoeck & Ruprecht, 1951), p. 262. See Acts 1:16; 4:25; Heb. 3:7; 9:8; 10:15; 2 Peter 1:21; see under πνεῦμα, BAGD, p. 677 (6c). On rabbinic parallels, see E. Schweizer, "πνευμα, πνευματικός," *TDNT* (1968; orig. 1959), 6:382–383.

[14] See chapter 3 above, p. 59; and J. A. Fitzmyer, "'Now This Melchizedek . . .' (Heb. 7:1)," in *Essays on the Semitic Background of the New Testament*, Sources for Biblical Study 5 (Missoula, Mont.: Scholars Press, 1974), pp. 224–225.

[15] As P. J. Kobelski points out, the theme of kingship is probably drawn from Ps. 110:2, which speaks of the exalted figure of v. 1 as a king who rules in the midst of his enemies (*Melchizedek and Melchireša'*, CBQMS 10 [Washington, D.C.: Catholic Biblical Association, 1981], p. 54).

[16] See the discussion by Kobelski, *Melchizedek*, pp. 152–155; also D. Flusser, "Melkizedek and the Son of Man," *Christian News from Israel* 17 (1966), 23–29; cf. C. Gianotto, *Melchisedek e la sua tipologica: Tradizioni giudaiche, cristiane e gnostiche (sec.II a.C. - sec. III d.C.)*, Supplementi alla Rivista Biblica 12 (Brescia: Paideia, 1984), p. 84 n. 118; contra J. A. Fitzmyer, "Further Light on Melchizedek from Qumran Cave 11," in *Essays*, p. 254.

behalf of the Messiah: "The Holy One, blessed be he, declared, 'He will sit, and I will make war'" (*parasha* 4).

This trajectory of exegesis of Psalm 110, which interprets it as a description of a divine victory in apocalyptic holy war, is continued in the New Testament in passages that seem to be tradition-historically related to Mark 12:35–37. We noted above that in the citation of Ps. 110:1 in Mark 12:36 the word ὑποκάτω ("under"), which displaces ὑποπόδιον ("footstool") from the Septuagint, is probably drawn from Ps. 8:7 and that the two passages are frequently conflated in the New Testament. As M. C. de Boer has pointed out, the two psalm verses also come together in 1 Cor. 15:25–27; Eph. 1:20–23; and 1 Peter 3:21b–22. In all of these cases, de Boer shows, the conflated passages are used apocalyptically to speak of the resurrection of Christ as a victory, or the beginning of a victory, over demonic powers. De Boer concludes that the conflation of the two psalm verses in these passages reflects an apocalyptic tradition of their interpretation that had entered into early Christian liturgies or creeds.[17]

The apocalyptic trajectory of interpretation of Psalm 110 evident in these New Testament passages and in 11QMelch seems to have exerted an influence on the shaping of the entire section of which Mark 12:35–37 is a part. If Mark's only purpose in quoting Ps. 110:1 had been to establish that David called the Messiah "Lord," he could have contented himself with citing the first words of the verse, "The Lord said to my lord." He has *not* so contented himself, however, but has gone on to cite the latter half of the verse, which speaks, in his interpretation, of the Messiah's exaltation to God's right hand and of God's victory on his behalf over enemies. If Mark's psalm citation includes these themes, it is reasonable to assume that they are important to him. But why are they important?

The words from the psalm quoted in Mark 12:36c, "Sit at my right hand," imply that the figure so addressed—in Mark's interpretation, Jesus the Messiah—is invited to take a seat in the heavenly throne room and, in that position, to "rule in the midst of your enemies," as the continuation of the psalm exhorts him to do (Ps. 110:2). This continuation, which is not quoted by Mark, only makes explicit what is implicit in the part that *is* quoted, the description of the co-regent who is invited to sit himself at the right hand of the divine monarch. That sitting itself implies an entry into the sphere of God's power and a participation in his victorious rule.[18] As we have seen, 11QMelch, through its citation of Isa. 52:7, explicitly develops this theme of participation in God's kingly power.

---

[17] De Boer, *Defeat*, pp. 114–120.
[18] See H.-J. Kraus, *Psalmen*, BKAT 15, 2 vols. (Neukirchen-Vluyn: Neukirchener Verlag, 1960), 2:757.

The theme of God's kingly power is sounded not only in the context of Ps. 110:1 and its later interpretations but also in the immediately preceding Markan passage, 12:28–34. Here the scribe who has publicly recognized the wisdom of Jesus' reply hears himself praised in return: "You are not far from the kingly rule of God" (alt.) (βασιλεία τοῦ θεοῦ). It is likely that Mark himself has introduced the theme of the βασιλεία τοῦ θεοῦ into the discussion of the great commandment (note its absence from the Matthean and Lukan parallels),[19] and he has done so, I suggest, to prepare for the allusion to the same theme in 12:36//Ps. 110:1. The scribe is not far from the βασιλεία because he is close in spirit to Jesus, whose exaltation to God's right hand, spoken of in the psalm, will mark the definitive first act in the extension of the βασιλεία from heaven to earth.

Beyond suggesting Jesus' *future* (i.e., postresurrectional) participation in God's kingly power, the juxtaposition of 12:28–34 and 12:35–37 may also hint that Jesus' earthly activity already foreshadows the βασιλεία. The perspicacious scribe, in contrast to the other scribes who have questioned Jesus' authority (11:28) and ascribed it to Satan (3:22), recognizes that Jesus speaks and acts in a way that is consonant with divine revelation. By this recognition the scribe stands on the brink of acknowledging the truth foretold by David in Ps. 110:1, that the Messiah will speak and act as God's righthand man. The dialogue with the scribe thus hints that Jesus is already anticipating his office of divine co-regent and that the βασιλεία is proleptically present in his authority.

Immediately after Jesus' praise of the scribe, moreover, and immediately before our passage, Mark notes, in what is almost certainly an editorial comment,[20] that "nobody any longer dared to ask him a question" (alt.) (οὐδεὶς οὐκέτι ἐτόλμα αὐτὸν ἐπερωτῆσαι, end of 12:34). The emphatic use of the double negative (οὐδεὶς οὐκέτι) drives home the point that the sovereign power of God is already being manifested as Jesus silences his opponents. Jesus' teaching, as we know from 1:27 and other passages, represents an explosion of divine power; through it — to use the terms of Ps. 110:2 — the Lord is sending a scepter out from Zion and causing his Messiah to rule in the midst of his enemies. This next verse of the psalm is so apropos to

---

[19] See D. Lührmann, who ascribes 12:32–34 to Markan redaction, noting its absence in the Matthean and Lukan parallels and adding that agreements between Matthew and Luke against Mark (the designation of the scribe as a νομικός and of his motive as "testing" Jesus) suggest that they may have access to a parallel tradition similar to the pre-Markan one (*Das Markusevangelium*, HNT 3 [Tübingen: J. C. B. Mohr (Paul Siebeck), 1987], pp. 205–206).

[20] See Lührmann, *Markusevangelium*, p. 205; and J. Gnilka, who says that the comment is "anchored in the macrotext" of Mark and therefore probably represents Markan redaction (*Das Evangelium nach Markus*, EKKNT 2, 2 vols. [Zurich: Benziger Verlag, 1978, 1979], 2:163). The double negative, moreover, is a characteristic of Markan style; see V. Taylor, *The Gospel According to Saint Mark*, 2nd ed. (Grand Rapids: Baker Book House, 1981), p. 46.

the context that it seems probable that Mark actually has it in mind in 12:34 as he prepares the way for the pericope in which he will cite v. 1. Indeed, although it is not explicitly cited, "rule in the midst of your enemies" would make a fitting caption for the entire section beginning in 11:1 and extending to the end of chapter 12, replete as it is with Jesus' imperious actions and his controversies with the Jewish leaders.[21] There seem to be good grounds, then, for assuming that Mark is aware of the theme of eschatological kingship and victory found in Psalm 110 and that he has shaped the context of 12:35–37 accordingly.

This hypothesis is supported by the way in which Mark follows the question about the Son of David with the denunciation of the scribes in 12:38–40.[22] While the redactional connection between Mark 12:28–34 and 12:35–37 hints that there is an anticipation of the psalm's fulfillment in Jesus' earthly ministry and a decisive beginning of its realization in his resurrection, the fact that 12:35–37 is followed by the denunciation of the scribes points to its complete fulfillment at the parousia, when the scribes "will receive greater condemnation" from God himself (12:40). For Mark, this divine judgment probably represents the final step in the realization of the scriptural prophecy that God will put the Messiah's enemies under his feet and thus bring the βασιλεία τοῦ θεοῦ into effective existence (12:36de// Ps. 110:1).[23]

The enemies spoken of in Mark 12:36//Ps. 110:1, therefore, must at least include Jesus' human opponents such as the scribes.[24] But it is probably a mistake to limit the Markan understanding of this verse to a judgment of human enemies; demonic forces are probably also included. We have already seen in this chapter that both the Qumranic exegesis of Psalm 110 and the other New Testament passages that conflate Ps. 110:1 with Ps. 8:7 link the psalm with a victory over demonic powers. Such a link makes sense in the Markan case also, since throughout the Gospel the opposition of Jesus' human enemies is portrayed in a way that makes it clear that it reflects the opposition of Satan and the demons.[25] In our specific context, Jesus' silencing of his human opponents (12:34) recalls his earlier silencings of

---

[21] See also the mention of the Temple in 12:35, which is superfluous in view of 11:27. This may be partially intended to remind the scripturally trained reader of the promise to send a scepter *out of Zion* (Ps. 110:2) and of the decree, "You are a *priest* forever" (Ps. 110:4).

[22] On the basis of the varied forms of the material found in Mark 11–12, Gnilka argues against the assumption that Mark is incorporating a pre-Markan collection of controversy stories here; the arrangement of the material, rather, is his own work (*Evangelium* 2:172).

[23] On the periodization of the kingdom in Mark, see J. Marcus, *The Mystery of the Kingdom of God*, SBLDS 90 (Atlanta: Scholars Press, 1986), pp. 185–199.

[24] E. Best compares Mark 14:62, where Ps. 110:1 is reused to speak of the judgment of Jesus' human enemies at the eschaton (*The Temptation and the Passion: The Markan Soteriology*, SNTSMS 2 [Cambridge: Cambridge University Press, 1965], pp. 87–88).

[25] Contra Best, *Temptation*, pp. 87–88; see chapter 3 above, p. 71.

demons (1:25, 34; 3:12), and his prophecy of the scribes' eschatological condemnation (12:40) is reminiscent of the prescient question posed by the unclean spirit in the Capernaum synagogue, "Have you come to destroy us?" (1:24).[26]

The citation of Ps. 110:1 in its Markan context, therefore, leaves us with the strong impression that Mark, like other Jewish and Christian interpreters before him, views the psalm as a prophecy of eschatological events that have warlike contours and cosmic proportions. Despite a modern reader's first impression of God's invitation to the Messiah to *sit*, the scene is anything but a static one. Rather, the assumption of the sitting posture symbolizes an entry into power,[27] a power which is already beginning to manifest itself in the submission of human and demonic opponents to the divine will embodied in Jesus, and which will become totally and publicly effective at the parousia.

Jesus as Son of David

Our discernment of a cosmic dimension in the battle implied in Mark 12:35–37 has relevance for the christological point made by the passage, that the title "Son of David" does not do full justice to Jesus' messiahship. In order to secure this point, however, it will be necessary to review the usage of the title "Son of David" in chapters 10–12 of Mark, noting the ways in which a Davidic typology is both constructed and disrupted in the Markan story.

As G. Schneider and C. Burger have noted, the material on Davidic sonship in Mark is not strewn throughout the Gospel but concentrated in these three connected chapters that deal with Jesus' way to his passion in Jerusalem.[28] The first instance occurs in the healing of blind Bartimaeus (10:47–48), which takes place in Jericho on the way to Jerusalem (cf. ὁδός in 10:46, 52). The second occurs in the triumphal entry to Jerusalem (11:9–10), and the third occurs in the Temple, which stands at the very theological center of the city (12:35–37).[29]

---

[26] It is significant, in the overall Markan context, that this first exorcism story in the Gospel takes place *in a synagogue*. The demon's opposition to Jesus in the Capernaum synagogue (1:23–24) is mirrored by that of the Pharisees and Herodians in the next story that takes place in a synagogue, the healing of the man with the withered hand (3:1–6). Note also the demonic ring of the description of the scribes as people "who devour widows' houses" (12:40).

[27] Cf. 14:62, in which Jesus' sitting at the right hand of power is linked with his coming with the clouds of heaven; also Jesus' sitting to teach in 4:1; 9:35; and 13:3, which is an implicit claim to magisterial authority (see Marcus, *Mystery*, p. 14).

[28] Schneider, "Davidssohnfrage," pp. 87–88; Burger, *Davidssohn*, p. 59.

[29] For Mark, the motifs "Jerusalem" and "Temple" exist in the closest possible connection with each other, as is graphically illustrated by the parallel construction in 11:11, καὶ εἰσῆλθεν εἰς Ἱεροσόλυμα εἰς τὸ ἱερόν, "and he entered *into Jerusalem into the Temple*. . ." (alt.).

The geographical localizations of these traditions seem to be connected with the Davidic hope and to carry some theological weight for Mark. In the Bartimaeus pericope Mark highlights both the localization in Jericho and the "Son of David" title: the localization by a redactional repetition of the city's name (10:46),[30] the title by introducing an unsuccessful effort by the bystanders to suppress it, which literarily has the reverse effect (10:48).[31] Similarly, in the narrative of the triumphal entry, Mark links the Davidic thrust of the crowd's acclamation (11:9–10) with Jerusalem and the Temple by juxtaposing the acclamation with the redactional verse 11:11.[32] Finally, Mark seems to have taken some trouble to situate the *Davidssohn-frage* itself in the Temple through the redactional verse 12:35a.

These localizations begin to unfold their significance when it is remembered that early Jewish traditions posit a strong connection between the Davidic Messiah on the one hand and Jerusalem and the Temple on the other. *Psalms of Solomon* 17:22, 30–31, for example, includes as part of its hope for the coming of "their king, the Son of David" (17:21), the expectation that God will

> undergird him with strength to destroy the unrighteous rulers,
> to purge Jerusalem from Gentiles who trample her to destruction. . . .
> He will purge Jerusalem (and make it) holy as it was even from the
>   beginning,
> (for) nations to come from the ends of the earth to see his glory, . . .
> to see the glory of the LORD with which God has glorified her.

The divine glory referred to here is most likely that of the Temple;[33] thus, the "Son of David" comes to Jerusalem in order to purify the Temple and to cause the glory of God to return to it. Similarly, the fourteenth benediction of the Eighteen Benedictions (Palestinian recension) conjoins prayers for Jerusalem, the Temple, and the kingdom of the Davidic Messiah:

> Be merciful, Lord our God, with thy great mercies, to Israel thy people
> and to Jerusalem thy city; and to Zion, the dwelling-place of thy glory;

---

[30] Burger, *Davidssohn*, pp. 43–45, 62–63. Codex Vaticanus has eliminated the awkwardness of the repetition of the reference to Jericho by omitting 10:46a.

[31] Burger, *Davidssohn*, pp. 59–62. The literary boomerang effect of the attempt to silence Bartimaeus makes it unlikely that Mark is uninterested in the "Son of David" title, as is suggested by E. Best ("Mark's Preservation of the Tradition," in *The Interpretation of Mark*, ed. W. Telford, IRT 7 [Philadelphia: Fortress Press; London: SPCK, 1985], pp. 120–121). Nor does Bartimaeus's use of *rabbouni* for Jesus (10:51) impugn his christological discernment (contra A. Suhl, *Die Funktion der alttestamentlichen Zitate und Anspielungen im Markusevangelium* [Gütersloh: Gerd Mohn, 1965], p. 93; and Hay, *Glory*, p. 114), since in 10:52 Jesus praises his faith; see J. D. Kingsbury, *The Christology of Mark's Gospel* (Philadelphia: Fortress Press, 1983), pp. 105–106.

[32] On the redactional character of 11:11, see Lührmann, *Markusevangelium*, p. 187.

[33] See R. B. Wright in *OTP* 2:645, 667.

and to thy Temple and thy habitation; and to the kingship of the house
of David, thy righteous Messiah. Blessed art thou, Lord, God of David,
who buildest Jerusalem.[34]

It is thus no accident that Mark conjoins the "Son of David" title with the
descriptions of the healing on the way to Jerusalem[35] and the entry into
Jerusalem. As G. Schneider puts it:

> On the basis of the healing of the blind man the group of disciples can
> conclude that, since Jesus really is the Son of David, the "kingdom of
> David" will break in, and indeed at the point at which Jesus enters
> Jerusalem.[36]

The themes of the Son of David, Jerusalem, and the Temple belong
together.

The Insufficiency of the Title "Son of David"

If these three motifs belong together, it is curious that Mark proceeds
to disrupt them in 12:35-37. Here, as we have seen, the Temple setting
is redactionally emphasized, as is another feature associated with the Son
of David in some traditions, his teaching (12:35a; cf. *Pss. Sol.* 17:24, 35-37,
43).[37] The "Son of David" title itself, however, is explicitly challenged (12:35b,
37ab). The implicit logic of our passage is that no father refers to his own

---

[34] Translation from E. Schürer, *The History of the Jewish People in the Age of Jesus Christ
(175 B.C.–A.D. 135)*, revised and edited by G. Vermes et al., 3 vols. (Edinburgh: T. & T. Clark,
1979), 2:461–462. The text given is the Palestinian recension, which has a good claim to
originality since it does not imply the destruction of the Temple, as the Babylonian recension
does (though Vermes prefers the Babylonian recension). In any event, both recensions are
probably not later than the first century A.D.; see G. Vermes, *Jesus the Jew: A Historian's
Reading of the Gospels* (Philadelphia: Fortress Press, 1981), pp. 131–132. On the relevance of
this prayer for the Markan *Davidssohnfrage*, see Mudiso Mbâ Mundla, who also cites *b. Ber.*
48b, where R. Eliezer (second-generation Tanna) says that he who does not mention the
kingdom of David in the blessing "who builds Jerusalem" has not fulfilled his obligation
(*Führer*, pp. 270–272).

[35] On the theory that Mark 10:47–48 reflects a Solomonic typology, see the excursus at
the end of this chapter.

[36] See Schneider, "Davidssohnfrage," pp. 87–88.

[37] Cf. M. de Jonge, "The Use of the Word 'Anointed' in the Time of Jesus," *NovT* 8 (1966),
136; and R. A. Horsley and J. S. Hanson, *Bandits, Prophets, and Messiahs: Popular Movements
at the Time of Jesus*, New Voices in Biblical Studies (San Francisco: Harper & Row, 1985),
pp. 106, 119.

son as "my lord";[38] therefore it is a misnomer to speak of Jesus as David's son.[39]

This challenge to the title "Son of David" is a problem not only because the previous chapters of Mark seem to affirm the title but also because of broader considerations from the history of religions. As E. Lövestam points out, the Davidic descent of the Messiah is extraordinarily well-attested in the Old Testament,[40] and we may add that this attestation continues in first-century Jewish texts (*Psalms of Solomon* 17, the Qumran literature, and the fifteenth benediction of the Eighteen Benedictions [fourteenth benediction in Palestinian recension]).[41] In early Christian sources outside of Mark 12:35–37 par. and *Barn.* 12:10–11, this descent is not contested;[42] on the contrary, the Messiah's Davidic sonship is presumed in christological formulas (Rom. 1:3) and is used as a known fact upon which other arguments may be based (Acts 2:30–31; 13:22–23). The apparent denial in Mark 12:35–37 that the Messiah is the son of David, therefore, represents a puzzling piece of christology that is at home neither in first-century Judaism, nor in first-century Christianity, nor in the flow of Mark's story. Altering the wording of Mark 12:35b, then, it might be more correct to ask: How can our author say that the Messiah is *not* the Son of David?

Our solution to this conundrum takes its point of departure from C.

---

[38] This plain sense of the passage is recognized even by some who assert that it *cannot* mean that in its Markan context; see, e.g., F. J. Matera, *The Kingship of Jesus: Composition and Theology in Mark 15*, SBLDS 66 (Chico, Calif.: Scholars Press, 1982), pp. 86–89. Matera and also Kingsbury (*Christology*, pp. 102–114), in trying to press 12:35–37 into the mold of 10:47–48 and 11:9–10, exhibit the perils of "the paradigm on which composition and narrative critics have come to rely: a monologic gospel text in which conflicting perspectives are synthesized, canceled, or harmonized by the assignation of some masterful overriding purpose" (S. D. Moore, *Literary Criticism and the Gospels: The Theoretical Challenge* [New Haven, Conn.: Yale University Press, 1989], p. 34).

[39] On the theory that Mark 12:35–37 is a reconciliation of scriptural contradictions, see the excursus at the end of this chapter.

[40] E. Lövestam, "Die Davidssohnfrage," *SEÅ* 27 (1962), pp. 72–73; cf. M. de Jonge, "Jesus, Son of David and Son of God," in *Intertextuality in Biblical Writings: Essays in Honour of Bas van Iersel*, ed. S. Draisma (Kampen: Kok, 1989), p. 97.

[41] See B. D. Chilton, "Jesus *ben David*: Reflections on the *Davidssohnfrage*," *JSNT* 14 (1982), 100. Even at Qumran, where two Messiahs are expected, a Davidic Messiah ("the Messiah of Israel") and a priestly Messiah ("the Messiah of Aaron"), the term "*the* Messiah," used absolutely, refers to the Davidic figure; see J. Marcus, "Mark 14:61: Are You the Messiah-Son-of-God?" *NovT* 31 (1988), 128 nn. 10–11.

[42] In John 7:42 some members of the crowd object to Jesus' messiahship because the scripture has prophesied that the Messiah will be of the seed of David and from Bethlehem, "the city where David was." This may, however, be a case of "Johannine misunderstanding"; the reader of the Gospel may know that the objection is invalid because Jesus really was a Davidide and from Bethlehem. See R. E. Brown, *The Gospel According to John*, AB29, 29A, 2 vols. (Garden City, N.Y.: Doubleday & Co., 1966, 1970), 1:330.

Burger's observation that chapters 10–12 of Mark present a progression of thought on the subject of Jesus' Davidic sonship:[43]

10:47–48:   An *individual* hails Jesus as the "Son of David."
11:9–10:   A *crowd* identifies Jesus as the "Son of David," but in an indirect manner.
12:35–37:   *Jesus himself* takes up the question of his Davidic sonship, and implicitly denies it.

Of these three presentations of the Davidic motif, the third, in which Jesus himself addresses the question of his Davidic sonship, is obviously the most authoritative; yet it cannot wipe out the positive typology that has certainly though subtly been established. We will return later to the problem of reconciling 10:47–48 and 11:9–10 with 12:35–37; at the moment we will investigate why Mark presents Jesus as questioning the adequacy of the "Son of David" title in the latter.

One aspect of the reply to this question is that for Mark Jesus is not just the "Son of David"; another title, "Son of God," does more justice to his identity. This is certainly how *Barn.* 12:10 interprets the parallel tradition; the introduction to the discussion of the "Son of David" reads: "See again Jesus, not as Son of man but as Son of God."[44] Although, contrary to *Barn.* 12:10, Mark does not specifically mention Jesus' status as "Son of God" in 12:35–37, there are good arguments for saying that in view of the overall Markan context its presence is implied. As W. Wrede already pointed out, the emphatic placement of αὐτοῦ in 12:37b ("how is he then *his*, i.e., David's, son?")[45] implies that Jesus is the son of someone other than David. The logical candidate is God, an impression confirmed by the presence of the title "Son of God" in key pericopes at the Gospel's beginning, middle, and end (1:1?, 11; 9:7; 15:39).[46]

Indeed, the connection between the title "Son of God" and Psalm 110 may be traditional, since in the Septuagint version of the psalm God continues his address to the one whom he has exalted by saying, "From the womb, before the dawn, I have begotten you" (ἐκ γαστρὸς πρὸ ἑωσφόρου ἐξεγέννησά σε, Ps. 109:3 LXX). In the Septuagint, then, God himself is the father of the one whom the psalmist calls "my Lord," and this Septuagintal reading may reflect the original Hebrew better than the Masoretic Text, which is virtually unintelligible.[47]

---

[43] Burger, *Davidssohn*, pp.58–59.
[44] Hay thinks that the association of "Son of God" with Ps. 110:1 in *Barn.* 12:10 comes from a tradition that predates Barnabas (*Glory*, p. 119).
[45] See Marcus, "Messiah-Son-of-God," p. 135, citing Wrede and Hay.
[46] See Gnilka, *Evangelium* 2:171.
[47] See Hay, *Glory*, pp. 21–22.

Against this argument that Mark 12:35–37 implicitly contrasts the titles "Son of God" and "Son of David" it might be objected that in the Old Testament and later Jewish traditions, as well as the New Testament, these titles complement rather than compete against each other. In Rom. 1:2–3, for example, "from the seed of David" and "Son of God" are complementary categories, and this complementarity has roots in the prehistory of the epithets. E. Schweizer, as a matter of fact, goes so far as to say that in the Old Testament the titles "Son of God" and "Son of David" are identical.[48] Although Schweizer's statement is an exaggeration, the Old Testament background of the title "Son of God" lies in conceptions of Davidic kingship. Psalm 110 itself, for example, was originally an oracle concerning the enthronement of the Davidic monarch, and Psalm 2, 2 Sam. 7:12–16, and 1 Chron. 17:11–14 similarly speak of a descendant of David who becomes God's son. From the postbiblical period, 4QFlor 1:10–11 applies the divine promise of 2 Sam. 7:14, "I will be his father, and he shall be my son," to the Davidic Messiah. With this background in mind, D. Juel and F. J. Matera have recently interpreted the title "Son of God" in Mark in terms of "royal messianism,"[49] by which they appear to mean that its chief background lies in the Old Testament and postbiblical Jewish picture of the Davidic king, and this interpretation would militate against our suggested exegesis of Mark 12:35–37, in which Jesus is not just the "Son of David" because he is the "Son of God."

In chapter 3, I have already expressed reservations about this exclusively Davidic interpretation of the title "Son of God" in some streams of early Christianity, including Mark. To the arguments there adduced I would now add that in Rom. 1:3–4, as Schweizer himself points out, the epithets "of the seed of David" and "Son of God" succeed each other as two stages, so that discontinuity as well as continuity between them is implied.[50] Luke 1:32–35, moreover, seems to demonstrate two different interpretations of divine sonship, a Davidic interpretation (1:32–33) and a quasi-physical interpretation (1:35).[51]

Mark 14:62 confirms that Mark himself thinks that divine sonship carries a nuance transcending Davidic sonship. As I have argued elsewhere,[52] in this Markan passage the high priest asks Jesus whether or not he is the

---

[48] E. Schweizer, "υἱός, υἱοθεσία," *TDNT* (1972), 8:366–367.

[49] D. Juel, *Messiah and Temple: The Trial of Jesus in the Gospel of Mark*, SBLDS 31 (Missoula, Mont.: Scholars Press, 1973), pp. 108–114; Matera, *Kingship*, pp. 140–145, 149.

[50] Schweizer, "υἱός," pp. 366–367; cf. J. D. G. Dunn, *Romans*, WBC 38, 2 vols. (Dallas: Word Books, 1988), 1:11–13.

[51] See Marcus, "Messiah-Son-of-God," p. 140 n. 58 for discussion and references to secondary literature.

[52] Ibid.

Messiah-Son-of-God, that is, the Messiah understood as the Son of David or as the son of any other human being but as the Son of God. Jesus' reply conjoins a reference to Dan. 7:13 with an allusion to Ps. 110:1, and it is the resultant implication that, as Son of God and Son of man, Jesus will sit at God's right hand and come in glory as the eschatological judge, which leads the high priest to label Jesus a blasphemer. Here, then, in what has been rightly labeled a comprehensive summary of Markan christology,[53] the title "Son of God" is brought into close connection with Ps. 110:1, and the title is thus seen as implying commensurability with God ("sitting on the right hand of power"). The association of divine sonship with Ps. 110:1 in Mark 14:61–62 supports the previous assertion that Jesus' divine sonship is also at issue in the citation of the psalm verse in Mark 12:35–37.[54] The relatively high christology associated with divine sonship in passages like Mark 12:35–37 and 14:61–62 goes beyond what is normally associated with the "Son of David" in Judaism, and it is probably the openness of "Son of God" to such higher interpretations that drives a wedge between it and "Son of David" and causes it not to develop as a significant messianic title in Jewish traditions.[55]

Although the origin of the title "Son of God," therefore, may lie in Old Testament pictures of the Davidic king that are painted in vividly mythological colors, in the subsequent development of Jewish messianism the Davidic hope often splits off from the hint of transcendence implied by the notion of divine sonship.[56] "Son of David" and similar characterizations tend to indicate a figure who will restore the Davidic monarchy and raise Israel to a position of preeminence in the world. He may be a human being granted extraordinary wisdom and even miraculous powers by God (see *Pss. Sol.* 17:25, 36–37, 43), but he remains a human being, one made in the image and likeness of his ancestor David[57] and especially stamped by

---

[53] See Lührmann, *Markusevangelium*, p. 250.

[54] See F. Neugebauer, who argues that the question posed in Mark 12:35–37 about the "Son of David" is definitively answered in the hearing before the Sanhedrin in 14:61–62 ("Die Davidssohnfrage [Mark xii. 35–37 parr.] und der Menschensohn," *NTS* 21 [1974], 84, 88, 90). Contrary to Neugebauer, however, the "Son of man" title that appears in 14:61–62 should not be emphasized to the exclusion of the "Son of God" title.

[55] See above, chapter 3, excursus on the disuse of the title "Son of God" in ancient Judaism.

[56] On G. Vermes's theory about the relation of the "Son of God" title to talmudic traditions about Hanina ben Dosa and R. Meir, see above, chapter 3, p. 78.

[57] See E. Lohse, "υἱὸς Δαυίδ," *TDNT* (1972), 8:482; Schürer, *History* 2:504; Neugebauer, "Davidssohnfrage," p. 89 n. 4, pp. 91–92. The picture is admittedly more complicated in the case of 4 Ezra, in which one passage specifically identifies the Messiah as a Davidide (12:32), while other passages seem to associate him with the "Son of man" from Daniel 7 (4 Ezra

David's role as a military leader and righteous ruler.[58] The transcendent aura of the Davidic king in royal psalms such as Psalm 2 and Psalm 110, on the other hand, tends to emerge in later biblical and Jewish traditions not in conjunction with the title "Son of David"[59] but in conjunction with other titles such as "Son of man"[60] — a title, by the way, whose fountainhead passage, Daniel 7, may have originated as a midrash on Psalm 110.[61]

For Mark, therefore, a messianic hope that has been fashioned along strictly Davidic lines is simply not big enough to embrace the one whose resurrection to God's right hand implies his participation in the divine majesty. As God's son, moreover, Jesus is his filial plenipotentiary, who is empowered by him to subdue not only human enemies but also their demonic puppet masters (3:11; 5:7; cf. 1:24). The supernatural nature of the opposition against which Jesus the Son of God does battle and the cosmic nature of his victory mean that "Son of David" cannot adequately express his identity. When Jesus quells the power of the sea, strides in triumph across the waves, and announces his presence to the disciples with the sovereign self-identification formula "I am he" (4:35–41; 6:45–52), he is speaking in and acting out the language of Old Testament divine warrior theophanies, narratives in which Yahweh himself subdues the demonic

---

13) and still others imply his preexistence (7:28–29; 12:32–34; see M. E. Stone, "The Question of the Messiah in 4 Ezra," in *Judaisms and Their Messiahs at the Turn of the Christian Era*, ed. J. Neusner et al. [Cambridge: Cambridge University Press, 1987], pp. 210–211). Elsewhere Stone acknowledges the exceptional nature of this cosmic portrayal of the Davidic Messiah ("Apocalyptic Literature," in *Jewish Writings of the Second Temple Period*, ed. M. E. Stone, CRINT 2 [Philadelphia: Fortress Press, 1984], pp. 413–414).

58 On the military aspect of the Davidic expectation, see S. Mowinckel, *He That Cometh* (Nashville: Abingdon Press, 1954), pp. 311–321; see also the discussion of evidence from Josephus in the following section of the present study and of 1QSb 5:27–28, in which it is implied that the royal Messiah will lead the battle against the nations, in D. Dimant, "Qumran Sectarian Literature," in *Jewish Writings*, ed. Stone, p. 540. De Jonge is right to emphasize that the Messiah in *Psalms of Solomon* 17 is not *just* a military figure ("Use," p. 136), but J. Klausner (*The Messianic Idea in Israel: From Its Beginning to the Completion of the Mishnah* [New York: Macmillan Co., 1955], p. 323) and J. H. Charlesworth ("The Concept of the Messiah in the Pseudepigrapha," *ANRW* 2.19.1, p. 199) exaggerate when they deny the military aspect altogether; see *Pss. Sol.* 17:22, 24, 26, 28–30 (see de Jonge, "Use," p. 136 n. 2). *Psalms of Solomon* 17:33 does not portray a pacifistic Messiah. It emphasizes, rather, that it is God who wins the battle for him, a holy war motif that harks back to the Goliath story (1 Sam. 17:45–47) and is used to similar effect in 1QM 11:1–3.

59 A possible exception occurs in *b. Sanh.* 38b (discussed in Marcus, "Messiah-Son-of-God," pp. 140–141).

60 See, e.g., Stone's discussion of the "Son of man" in the Similitudes of Enoch ("Apocalyptic Literature," in *Jewish Writings*, ed. Stone, p. 402): "The characteristics of such a figure extend beyond those normally attributed to the Davidic Messiah."

61 See Hay, who points out that Psalm 110 and Daniel 7 are the only scriptural passages that explicitly speak of someone enthroned beside God (*Glory*, p. 26).

forces of chaos in a saving, cosmos-creating act of holy war.[62] While Mark
stops short of taking such stories to their logical conclusion and calling Jesus
God, these suggestive narratives do place his Jesus in a category that cannot be adequately grasped by an epithet that restricts him to the dimensions of David.

Mark 12:28–37, the Shemaʿ, *and "Two Powers in Heaven"*

The preceding paragraphs have presented a very lofty picture of Markan
christology; Jesus, as a result of his exaltation to God's right hand, seemingly attains a status close to that of God himself. Yet, it is important to
add, Mark's high christology does not, in his opinion, compromise the unity
of God. Mark 12:35–37 is significantly placed immediately after the discussion of the great commandment in 12:28–34, and the passages are tied
together not only by their proximity but also by verbal links ("teacher,"
"teaching," 12:32, 35; repetition of "lord" in both 12:29 and 12:36). These
links make it significant for the interpretation of 12:35–37 that in 12:28–34
Jesus affirms the statement of the *Shemaʿ* from Deut. 6:4 that there is one
God. The scribe drives home the point by adding, "There is no other beside
him" (cf. Deut. 4:35; Isa. 45:21).

The juxtaposition in 12:28–37 of the citation of the *Shemaʿ* with the allusion to a figure enthroned beside God is reminiscent of a series of rabbinic
debates about the relation between God's oneness and heavenly inter-
mediaries. In many of these debates Deut. 6:4, which A. Segal calls "the
very center of the synagogue liturgy," is marshaled against heretical notions
of "two powers in heaven."[63] It is probable that Deut. 6:4 performs a similar
function in Mark 12:28–37, warding off any misunderstanding of Ps. 110:1
in the sense of bitheism. In Mark's eyes, apparently, the picture of the figure
enthroned at God's right hand does not refute the statement that God is
one because the enthroned figure is still subordinate to God.

This combination of exalted status with subordination to God is consonant

---

[62] See Pss. 65:7; 77:16, 20; 107:25–30; Isa. 43:16; Nah. 1:3–4; and the "I am" formula that
is especially prominent as a divine self-identification in Deutero-Isaiah; see H. C. Kee, "The
Terminology of Mark's Exorcism Stories," *NTS* 14 (1967–68), 232–246; W. Lane, *The Gospel
of Mark,* NICNT (Grand Rapids: Wm. B. Eerdmans Publishing Co., 1974), pp. 176–177; and
Gnilka, *Evangelium* 1:269–270. There is a certain analogy between this theophanic portrait
of Jesus and the presentation of the man from the sea in 4 Ezra 13. The latter is "described
with symbolic language drawn largely from biblical descriptions of epiphanies of God,
particularly as warrior" (Stone, "Messiah in 4 Ezra," in *Judaisms,* ed. Neusner et al., p. 213).
[63] A. F. Segal, *Two Powers in Heaven: Early Rabbinic Reports About Christianity and
Gnosticism,* SJLA 25 (Leiden: E. J. Brill, 1977), p. 139; see the passages he cites on pp. 89,
137–140, 148–149, 152, and 232.

with Mark's overall christology. We have already observed in chapter 2 the way in which Mark ties Jesus closely with God, yet often maintains a distinction between them (see above, pp. 37–41). Two examples that are linked with the *Shema*' deserve special attention. In 10:18 Jesus rejects the rich young man's epithet "good teacher" and adds that no one is good except God alone. Jesus' terminology here, "except one, God" (εἰ μὴ εἷς ὁ θεός) recalls that of the *Shema*'[64] and tends to distance Jesus from God. In 2:7, on the other hand, the scribes use precisely the same evocative phrase (εἰ μὴ εἷς ὁ θεός) to accuse Jesus of arrogating to himself the prerogative of God to forgive sins. Jesus replies that the Son of man has the authority to forgive sins *on earth* (2:10). This reply *links* Jesus with the activity of the one God, and it probably indicates that in Mark's mind it is not a violation of monotheism for Jesus to represent in the earthly sphere the heavenly God's gracious forgiveness of sins. Jesus is God's divine agent, to whom he has delegated much of his own authority.[65] Though such a role falls short of equality with God, it transcends the usual associations of "Son of David."

Throughout his Gospel, then, and particularly through his juxtaposition of 12:28–34 with 12:35–37, Mark maintains a delicate balance between the somewhat discordant scriptural notions that there is no other beside God, on the one hand, and that he has chosen to exalt his anointed king to a position at his right hand, on the other.

The Davidic Messiah and the Markan Life Setting

The exaltation motif of Mark 12:36 certainly implies a high christology, and the lower christology frequently associated with "Son of David" goes a long way toward explaining Mark's reserve regarding the title. One other reason may be suggested for this reserve. Throughout this study we have traced evidence that Mark is aware of the events of the Jewish Revolt of A.D. 66–74, indeed that he and some of the members of his community have suffered as a result of the revolutionaries' attempt to purify Israel from Gentile influence. It now becomes relevant to recall that this same revolt was probably led by messianic figures of Davidic stripe.[66]

Reconstruction of the messianic dimension in the revolt is complicated by the fact that Josephus, our main source, consistently attempts to play down for his Roman audience the catalytic effect of Jewish religious

---

[64] See R. Pesch, *Das Markusevangelium*, HTKNT 2, 2 vols. (Freiburg: Herder, 1978), 1:139.

[65] See L. W. Hurtado (*One God, One Lord: Early Christian Devotion and Ancient Jewish Monotheism* [Philadelphia: Fortress Press, 1988]) on the Jewish roots of the Christian idea of Jesus' divine agency.

[66] For interaction with secondary literature on the Jewish War in substantiation of the position outlined here, see the section on Davidic messianism in J. Marcus, "The Jewish War and the *Sitz im Leben* of Mark," *JBL* 111 (1992) 441–462.

traditions in precipitating the insurrection. In spite of this apologetic white-washing, however, significant evidence of the major part Davidic messianic expectations played can be gleaned from his account. In *Jewish War* 6.313, for example, Josephus writes that what more than all else incited his country-men to war "was an ambiguous oracle, likewise found in their sacred scrip-tures, to the effect that at that time one from their country would become ruler of the world." Although the scriptural basis of this oracle is unclear,[67] it at least shows the vital role of messianic expectation in fueling the revolt.

Elsewhere Josephus permits us to glimpse that Davidic hopes crystal-lized around two revolutionary leaders, Menachem the son of Judas the Galilean and Simon bar Giora. Menachem is the more shadowy figure, but it is sufficiently clear that he aroused messianic expectations. In *Jewish War* 2.433–434 Josephus describes the way in which Menachem broke into Herod's arsenal at Masada in August of 66 and armed a group of brigands, adding that he then "returned to Jerusalem as a king"[68] and became a leader of the insurrection. In *Jewish War* 2.444, moreover, Menachem appears in the Temple in royal robes. The language of kingship links Menachem with the Davidic hope, and we may note also the association with Jerusalem and the Temple that was evident in the portrait of the "Son of David" in *Psalms of Solomon* 17 and the fourteenth of the Eighteen Benedictions.

The Davidic hope is even closer to the surface in Josephus's account of Simon bar Giora, whose rise to power paralleled that of David in some remarkable ways, a fact that was probably not lost on his contemporaries.[69] Josephus, as is his custom, reinterprets Simon's Davidic image in a polemical fashion, writing that "it was clear from the start that he was bent on tyranny" and that his entourage "included many citizens who obeyed him like a king" (*Jewish War* 2.652; 4.510).

That Simon also viewed *himself* in a messianic light is demonstrated in the manner of his capture by the Romans (*Jewish War* 7.29–31). After the destruction of the Temple and the looting of the city, Simon, in a last, desperate move, "put on white tunics with a purple cape fastened over them, and popped up out of the ground at the very place where the temple had once stood." Simon's royal garments here imply a messianic claim, and Josephus's phrase "popped up out of the ground" (ἐκ τῆς γῆς ἀνεφάνη) suggests a miracle. In response to Simon's "epiphany," the Romans were

---

[67] See the differing opinions of P. Billerbeck (S-B 4:1002) and R. Meyer (*Der Prophet aus Galiläa: Studie zum Jesusbild der drei ersten Evangelien* [Darmstadt: Wissenschaftliche Buch-gesellschaft, 1970; orig. 1940], pp. 52–54), who argue for Dan. 7:13–14, and M. Hengel (*The Zealots: Investigations into the Jewish Freedom Movements in the Period from Herod I Until 70 A.D.* [Edinburgh: T. & T. Clark, 1989], pp. 237–240), who argues for Num. 24:17.

[68] Translation of Josephan passages in this section are from Horsley and Hanson, *Bandits*, pp. 114–115.

[69] Ibid., pp. 121–122.

temporarily dumbfounded, but they quickly recovered their composure and took him into custody. Although Josephus presents Simon's action as an attempt to deceive the Romans by creating consternation, it is more likely that this "epiphany" was not just a ruse; Simon may have hoped that at the last moment God would act through his anointed one to save the city and miraculously restore the ruined Temple. This incident suggests not only Simon's messianic self-consciousness but also its intimate connection with a hope for a divine action with regard to the Temple, the same combination of ideas that we have noted in connection with Menachem and have linked to first-century Jewish texts—as well as to Mark 10–12.

For the purposes of our inquiry, the conclusion that Jewish revolutionary leaders like Menachem and Simon bar Giora understood themselves and were understood by their contemporaries to be bearers of the Davidic messianic hope has far-reaching implications. When Jesus is hailed as "Son of David" on the way to Jerusalem and when the enthusiastic populace of Jerusalem greets him as the coming one who will restore David's kingdom, he is marching along a path that will later be trodden by other messianic claimants. Indeed, it is easy to imagine that at least some of Mark's hearers might have seen Jesus' triumphal entry into Jerusalem as the antitype to Simon's entry in April-May 69.[70] Josephus (*Jewish War* 4.574–578) describes how the inhabitants of the city implored Simon to enter Jerusalem and how he, "arrogantly consenting to rule," entered it "and was greeted as savior and guardian by the people," thereafter becoming master of the city and attacking the Temple to drive out a rival group of revolutionaries. The parallels with Mark's account of Jesus' entry are striking. In both, the Davidic figure makes an implicit claim to kingship by entering the city, and in both he is hailed as one who saves (see "Hosanna" = "save us" in Mark 11:9–10). In both, moreover, he immediately drives home his claim by launching an attack on the Temple, which has fallen into the hands of a group that is perceived to be corrupting it.

Given our understanding of the Markan life setting, these parallels suggest that Mark has fashioned the "Davidic" section of his narrative (10:46–12:37) with the claims of figures like Simon and Menachem before his eyes. Such a background would go a long way toward explaining the ambivalent attitude his Gospel displays toward Davidic expectations. On the one hand, it is important for him to affirm that the true "Son of David" already appeared in Jerusalem many years before Menachem and Simon,

---

[70] Chronologically, of course, it is the other way around; Jesus' entry prefigures that of Simon. But if the events of the Jewish Revolt were fresh in the minds of Mark's readers, that more immediate event would provide the background for Mark's narration of the historically more distant one.

manifesting his kingship to the acclaim of the crowds and the accompaniment of miracles. Jesus was the authentic fulfillment of the Davidic hope, a holy warrior sent by God to free his people from an alien rule and to liberate the Temple from the degradation into which it had sunk. Menachem and Simon, who came after him, were only pale imitations.[71] In this sense Mark's portrayal of Jesus manifests a positive relation to the Davidic typology.

On the other hand, partly because Mark knows, perhaps through bitter experience, that the revolutionary claimants to the Davidic hope have channeled some of their nationalistic religious fervor into purges of foreign elements such as the Gentile members of his community, he sees that there is a negative, even a demonic, potentiality in Davidic messianism.[72] Because of this potentiality, his embrace of that sort of messianism cannot be unequivocal. Where messianism is defined dominantly by the militantly nationalistic features of the Davidic image, those who have felt the sting of the zealotry such messianism provokes and feeds upon will naturally be inclined to deny the ultimacy of that image and to ask with the Markan Jesus how it can be claimed that the Messiah is David's son.

Conclusions: Mark 12:35-37 and the Markan Community

Mark does not simply reject the warlike features associated with the Davidic hope. Indeed, our investigation up to this point leads us to suspect that it is precisely those features that have *attracted* him to the figure of David and that have caused him to *affirm* a Davidic typology in 10:47-48 and 11:10-11. Mark is not merely responding defensively to features of Jewish messianism when he has Bartimaeus hail Jesus as the "Son of David" and has the crowd link his coming with that of the kingdom of David. For Mark, Jesus *is* a warrior, and his entrance into Jerusalem is a decisive campaign in God's holy war of eschatological liberation, a war that Mark 1:1-3 already established as the theme of the Gospel. Jesus' way is the way of the Lord; in his entrance into the holy city the Lord returns to Zion to redeem it from an alien rule.

Paradoxically, however, the Davidic image turns out to be both too triumphant and not triumphant enough to encompass the sort of Messiah whom

---

[71] Cf. John 5:43: "I have come in my Father's name, and you do not receive me; if another comes in his own name, him you will receive." This passage has been taken by some scholars as a reference to Bar Kochba (see Brown, *John* 1:226). This is improbable on chronological grounds, but a reference to a figure such as Menachem or Simon is not out of the question.

[72] Cf. the contrast in John 10:8, 10: The thief (= the brigand?), who appears to be a messianic pretender, comes only to steal and to kill and to destroy. Already some of the church fathers saw here a reference to Jewish revolutionaries such as Judas the Galilean and Theudas, and they have been followed by some modern commentators; see R. Schnackenburg, *The Gospel According to St. John,* 3 vols. (New York: Crossroad, 1968-1982), 2:291 and 2:507 n. 62.

Mark wishes to portray to his community. It is not triumphant enough, as we have seen, because Jesus is victor not only over his earthly enemies but also, as his entire earthly ministry reveals, over their supernatural masters. In Jewish traditions roughly contemporary with Mark, "Son of David" almost invariably designates a human fighter who triumphs over human enemies, not a heavenly warrior who vanquishes heavenly foes. The heavenly dimension of Jesus' victory is vital to Mark's christological thought, and hence he cannot remain satisfied with the "Son of David" title, which by comparison with "Son of God" and "Son of man" has a rather quaint sound and a diminished horizon. A modern-day English speaker would not normally refer to the Taj Mahal as a "house," though that in fact is what it was originally intended to be; no more is Mark content to let Jesus' messiahship be conclusively defined by the restrictive Davidic image.

That image, on the other hand, is too triumphant because the manner in which Jesus wins his definitive victory over his enemies is through his suffering and death. For Mark, a messianism that is not informed by the notion of Jesus' suffering is one that is woefully inadequate — as Peter learns to his discomfiture (8:27–33). Mark's messianic secret motif withholds from the human characters in his story the revelation of Jesus as Messiah-Son-of-God and Son of man until the point at which he is brought to trial, condemned to death, crucified, and killed (14:61–62; 15:39), because only these events display the distinctive nature of Jesus' messiahship.[73] Jesus, moreover, is not called a king until chapter 15, the chapter in which he is interrogated by Pilate, beaten and mocked by the soldiers as "the king of the Jews," crucified under the same name, and derided by the Jewish leaders for being a king of Israel who cannot save himself (15:2, 9, 12, 18, 26, 32). By this timing Mark suggests that Jesus' kingship is revealed only in his passion and death.[74] The Temple theme, which we have seen to be associated with the Davidic hope, reappears in this context of condemnation, mockery, and death (14:58; 15:29, 38).[75] Similarly, the crowd's cry of "Hosanna" ("Save us!"), which hails Jesus as the one whose advent marks the coming of David's kingdom (11:9–10), is ironically echoed in the Jewish leaders' mockery of Jesus as a Messiah and king of Israel who saves others but cannot save himself (15:31). The way of the Lord, then, is Jesus' way of suffering and death.

The manner in which Mark consecutively affirms and qualifies the Davidic image should occasion no surprise. For Mark, Jesus *is* a royal figure and a holy warrior. But in what way is he a king, and what sort of warrior is he? What is the nature of the alien rule from which he redeems his people,

---

[73] See chapter 3, n. 32 above.
[74] See Matera, *Kingship*, pp. 147–149.
[75] On the role played by this theme in the passion narrative, see Juel, *Messiah and Temple*, passim.

and how does he win his battle? The answers to these questions necessitate a stretching of the Davidic mold to the breaking point.

The degree to which Jesus fits or breaks the Davidic mold is not just an academic question for Mark and his community. As we can gather from chapter 13, that community is being loudly assailed by the cries of other claimants to the Davidic throne, people whom Mark calls false messiahs but whom he acknowledges are deceiving many (13:6, 21–22). The epistemological question of how the true Messiah is to be discerned, therefore, is a critical one. If, as our previous analysis has suggested, the "false messiahs" to whom Mark refers are linked with the messianic excitement of the Jewish War and if our reconstruction of the relation of Mark's community to that upheaval has merit, then the full gravity of the epistemological crisis facing that community becomes apparent. Its members find themselves caught up in the vortex of the war and surrendered to the mercy of men whose pretensions to David's throne seem to be borne out by their repetition of David's near-miraculous feats of national liberation. Who then is a false messiah? A person such as Simon bar Giora, who seems to fit the Davidic pattern so well? Or Jesus, whose claim to messiahship seems at first glance to be negated by his ignominious death at the hands of Gentile sinners and the subsequent persecution of his followers?

In response to this pressing question, the Markan Jesus poses a question of his own, the conundrum about Davidic sonship that has been the subject of this chapter. In questioning the adequacy of the Davidic image of the Messiah, the Markan Jesus points to divine sonship and cosmic exaltation as the true horizons of the Messiah's identity. In Mark's eyes, Jesus is indeed the consummation of the centuries-old hope for a coming king from the line of David, a hope that Simon and all the other "messiahs" have falsely claimed to fulfill. But he is more than that because he has ascended not only the road to Jerusalem but also the way to the heavenly throne room, there to be enthroned at God's right hand and invited to wait until he has seen God put all his enemies under his feet. And in the end his messianic kingship is infinitely more secure than the short-lived rule of Simon and the other "messiahs," since it is not threatened but rather advanced when he and his followers are persecuted, arrested, and driven to death.

In order to understand how that can be so, we must turn to the final section of Mark's work, the section that it is most difficult at first to see as "gospel."

Excursus: Two Theories About the "Son of David" Title

B. D. Chilton, taking up a suggestion by D. C. Duling, discusses the possibility that "Son of David" in 10:47–48 reflects not a messianic hope but a conception of David's son Solomon as an exorcist and a healer. In 12:35–37, therefore, Jesus "presupposes his identification as David's son, and denies that this is a messianic claim."[76] As M. de Jonge points out, however, in 12:35–37 "the issue is not whether the healing 'Son of David' is the Messiah, but whether the Messiah is the 'Son of David.'" He adds that in Mark we do not find a clear connection between Jesus and Solomon as exorcist and that Chilton moves too quickly from the Solomonic connection with exorcism in particular to healing in general. Mark 14:61–62, moreover, poses insuperable difficulties for Chilton's thesis, since here Jesus affirms his messiahship.[77] I would add that, in the immediate Markan context of 10:47–48, the "Son of David" title is closely linked with the messianic hope for "the coming kingdom of our father David" in 11:10 not only by the reference to David but also by the parallel between the meanings of ἐλέησον με ("have mercy on me") in 10:47–48 and ὡσαννά ("save us") in 11:9–10.

E. Lövestam draws on the work of D. Daube to claim that Mark 12:35–37 is an example of the sort of ancient Jewish method of reconciling apparent scriptural contradictions that we have studied in chapter 5. In the present case, according to Lövestam, the contradiction between the scriptural expectation that the Messiah is to be the "Son of David" and the scriptural inference from Ps. 110:1 that he is to be David's lord is reconciled by the implicit assertion that the "Son of David" expectation refers to the earthly stage of the Messiah's career while the "lord of David" expectation refers to his postresurrectional exaltation to God's right hand.[78] As Suhl objects, however, "There is no indication of this in the text!"[79] While admitting that at some stage in its pre-Markan development Mark 12:35–37 may have represented a reconciliation of scriptural contradictions, I find it difficult to see it as such *in its present form.* As Bultmann already pointed out, two scriptural passages are *not* counterposed in our text; only Psalm 110 is cited, and its foil is not another scriptural passage but a scribal opinion that is not referred to a biblical text.[80] In contrast to the three examples from *b. Nid.* 70b on which Daube bases his argument, the reconciliation of the two scriptural expectations is not explicitly stated or even clearly implied. On the contrary, the most natural reading of the concluding question of Mark 12:37 is that it expects a negative answer.

[76] D. C. Duling, "Solomon, Exorcism, and the Son of David," *HTR* 68 (1975), pp. 235–252; Chilton, "Jesus ben David," pp. 92–97.

[77] De Jonge, "Son of David," in *Intertextuality,* ed. Draisma, pp. 100–101.

[78] D. Daube, *The New Testament and Rabbinic Judaism* (New York: Arno Press, 1973; orig. 1956), pp. 158–169; Lövestam, "Davidssohnfrage," pp. 72–82; cf. D. Juel, *Messianic Exegesis: Christological Interpretation of the Old Testament in Early Christianity* (Philadelphia: Fortress Press, 1988), pp. 142–144.

[79] Suhl, *Zitate,* p. 90.

[80] R. Bultmann, *History of the Synoptic Tradition* (New York: Harper & Row, 1963), p. 407; cf. de Jonge, "Son of David," in *Intertextuality,* ed. Draisma, p. 96 n. 11.

8

Mark 14–16

The Passion Narrative

Mark's account of Jesus' suffering, death, and resurrection in chapters 14–16 is suffused with Old Testament citations and allusions to an extent unparalleled in the rest of his narrative, a frequency that reflects the primitive Christian conviction that Christ died and was raised on the third day in accordance with the scriptures (see 1 Cor. 15:3–4).[1] Only one citation, however, the reference to Zech. 13:7 in Mark 14:27, is introduced with a quotation formula, ὅτι γέγραπται, "for it has been written." In two other instances, 14:21 and 14:49, there are references to fulfillment of the scriptures,[2] but these references are not linked with the citation of specific texts, but only with the conviction that Jesus' betrayal and death are prophesied in scripture. The rest of the scriptural echoes are citations of or allusions to Old Testament texts that are built into the narrative without being singled out as biblical references; their identification as such depends on the readers' knowledge of the scriptures and their ability to relate those scriptures to the Markan narrative.

This chapter will concentrate on four bodies of Old Testament literature that appear to play a decisive role in the Markan narrative: Zechariah 9–14; Daniel 7; the Psalms of the Righteous Sufferer; and the Deutero-Isaian Servant Songs, especially Isaiah 53. The influence of Zechariah 9–14 and Daniel 7 seems to be limited to small sections of Mark's passion account, whereas the influence of the Righteous Sufferer Psalms and the Isaian Servant Songs extends throughout the account. The Old Testament passages with more limited influence, those from Zechariah and Daniel, will be

---

[1] See D. Lührmann, *Das Markusevangelium*, HNT 3 (Tübingen: J. C. B. Mohr [Paul Siebeck], 1987), p. 230.

[2] 14:21: the Son of man goes as it has been written concerning him (καθὼς γέγραπται περὶ αὐτοῦ); 14:49: but in order that the scriptures might be fulfilled (ἀλλ᾿ ἵνα πληρωθῶσιν αἱ γραφαί).

considered first here, then the passages from Psalms and Isaiah that seem to have affected Mark's narrative more globally.

Zechariah 9–14

Old Testament Citation and Allusions

Zechariah 9–14 is a recognizable unit that is distinguished from the rest of the prophetic book by its eschatological content, its literary and thematic unity, and distinct characters and vocabulary (e.g., the evil shepherds, *the* shepherd, and the flock). The fact that the New Testament has numerous references to five of the six chapters of Zechariah 9–14[3] but no clear references to Zechariah 1–8 outside of Revelation suggests that the early Christians read Zechariah 9–14 as a unit.[4] This conclusion applies to Mark, who in 14:22–28 draws together numerous allusions to Zechariah 9–14. We begin with the most obvious example.

Mark 14:27 contains an explicit citation of Zech 13:7, introduced by the formula "for it has been written" (ὅτι γέγραπται): "I will strike the shepherd, and the sheep will be scattered." Except for the first-person "*I* will strike" (πατάξω), the text is identical with the Q text of the Septuagint, a text that J. de Waard characterizes as the bearer of a Palestinian Septuagint tradition.[5] The reference to Zech. 13:7 is probably part of the tradition as it has come down to Mark, since John 16:32 preserves an allusion to the Zecharian verse in a similar context but the Johannine text seems to be independent of the Markan one.[6]

The following verse, Mark 14:28, is probably a Markan contribution to the pericope. The prophecy of the scattering of the sheep (= disciples) in 14:27 leads logically into Peter's protest in 14:29 that *he* will not desert Jesus, whereas the prophecy of Jesus' postresurrectional leading of the disciples in 14:28 disrupts the context, reveals Mark's characteristic preoccupation

---

[3] Chapter 10 is the exception; see the summary of allusions in M. C. Black, "The Rejected and Slain Messiah Who Is Coming with the Angels: The Messianic Exegesis of Zechariah 9–14 in the Passion Narratives" (Ph.D. diss., Emory University, 1990), p. 6.

[4] Ibid., pp. 35–48.

[5] J. de Waard, *A Comparative Study of the Old Testament Text in the Dead Sea Scrolls and in the New Testament* (STDJ 4; Leiden: E. J. Brill, 1965), pp. 37–38.

[6] See Black, "Rejected," p. 196; on the relation between the Markan passion narrative and the Johannine one, see n. 87 below. Contra A. Suhl (*Die Funktion der alttestamentlichen Zitate und Anspielungen im Markusevangelium* [Gütersloh: Gerd Mohn, 1965], pp. 62–64) and M. Wilcox ("The Denial-Sequence in Mark xiv. 26–31, 66–72," *NTS* 17 [1970–1971], pp. 429–430), according to whom the Zecharian citation in Mark 14:27b itself comes from Mark's hand. As Suhl himself admits, 14:27b and 14:28 move in two rather different directions, and the assertion that Mark is responsible for both of them is therefore rather difficult to believe.

with Galilee, and foreshadows 16:7, a verse that disrupts *its* context and also speaks of Galilee.[7]

Since 14:28 probably comes from Mark's hand, it is particularly interesting to observe that it seems to allude to the wider context of the verse from Zechariah just quoted. The verb "to lead" (προάγειν) continues the shepherd metaphor from 14:27, and this metaphor receives emphasis not only in Zech. 13:7 but throughout Zechariah 9–14 (see Zech. 9:16; 10:3; 11:4–17; 13:7). The restoration of the disciples implied in 14:28 corresponds to Zechariah's prophecy of the restoration of Israel after judgment. Two verses after Zech. 13:7, in 13:9, we read about a "refining" of Israel in which a third of the nation will perish. The third that is left, however, will call on the Lord's name, and he will answer them, so that the covenant is restored: "I [God] will say, 'They are my people,' and they will say, 'The Lord is my God.'" Again, this prophecy of Israel's restoration is not an isolated instance within Zechariah 9–14; see, for example, 9:11–12; 10:6–9.[8]

But the Zecharian connections of the redactional verse Mark 14:28 do not end here. Jesus' reference to his resurrection connects this verse with some ancient Jewish exegeses of Zech. 14:1–5. The latter passage speaks of an earthquake on the Mount of Olives during the final, eschatological battle of the nations against Jerusalem. In the Jewish exegeses referred to, the events on the Mount of Olives are connected with the general resurrection of the dead. The Targum on Zech. 14:4 in Codex Reuchliniansus, for example, announces that the Lord will blow ten blasts on a great trumpet to revive the dead. *Targum of Canticle of Canticles* 8:5, in an obvious allusion to Zech. 14:4, says that "when the dead rise, the Mount of Olives will be cleft, and all Israel's dead will come up out of it."[9] Several midrashim interpret the coming of Yahweh with his holy ones in Zech. 14:5 as a reference to his arrival with the resurrected prophets.[10] Though none of these references can be dated with certainty to the pre-Christian era, their wide distribution at least raises the possibility that the resurrectional reading of Zech. 14:1–5 was known and used by Mark in 14:28.

---

[7] See E. Lohmeyer, *Das Evangelium des Markus*, MeyerK, 11th ed. (Göttingen: Vandenhoeck & Ruprecht, 1951), p. 311; V. Taylor, *The Gospel According to Saint Mark*, 2nd ed. (Grand Rapids: Baker Book House, 1981), p. 549; Black, "Rejected," pp. 188–189, 192–193.

[8] See C. F. Evans, "I Will Go Before You into Galilee," *JTS* n.s. 5 (1954), 8–10; F. F. Bruce, "The Book of Zechariah and the Passion Narrative," *BJRL* 43 (1960), 344–345; Wilcox, "Denial-Sequence," pp. 426–436; Black, "Rejected," pp. 193–194.

[9] For references and discussion, see Black, "Rejected," pp. 141–150. The extensiveness and relative antiquity of this interpretation are witnessed by the north wall of the Dura-Europos synagogue, which shows a mountain with a huge split in its middle and dead bodies within the mountain; subsequent pictures depict the raising of these bodies by angels.

[10] *Ruth Rab.* 2; *Eccl. Rab.* 1.11; *Cant. Rab.* 4.11; cited by Black, "Rejected," pp. 148–149.

The previous Markan passage, the Lord's Supper pericope in 14:22–26, also seems to allude to Zech. 14:1–5. Mark 14:26, which forms a transition between the two passages, describes a movement to the Mount of Olives by Jesus and his disciples. We have just noted the reference to the Mount of Olives in Zech. 14:4; this is one of only two Old Testament references to the mount (the other is 2 Sam. 15:30). The Zecharian passage is a prophecy that at the eschaton Yahweh will go forth to do battle against Israel's enemies, and "on that day his feet will stand on the Mount of Olives." Although Yahweh is the subject here, Josephus and rabbinic traditions provide evidence that the passage was read as a reference to the advent of the Messiah; the Markan placement of Jesus on the Mount of Olives may therefore be christologically significant.[11] The Zecharian context of eschatological war at first seems to be remote from the Markan one of Jesus' last night on earth, but as we have already seen in our study of Mark 12:35–37, the notion of Jesus' passion as an eschatological battle is highly consistent with Markan eschatology. The reference to the Mount of Olives in Mark 14:26, then, is likely to be an allusion to messianic expectations that arose from Zech. 14:1–5.

The Zecharian allusion in the reference to the Mount of Olives is probably part of the tradition that has come down to Mark, so we cannot credit him with creating the Old Testament association. He does, however, seem to be aware of it, as is apparent from Mark 13:3–4, a passage that is probably redactional and in which the reference to the Mount of Olives fits precisely the context of judgment found in Zech. 14:1–5.[12]

The eschatological prophecy of which Zech. 14:4 is a part culminates in Zech. 14:9: "And Yahweh will become king over all the earth; on that day Yahweh will be one and his name one" (alt.). The phrases "Yahweh will become king" and "on that day" in Zech. 14:9 provide links with Mark 14:25 ("until *that day* when I drink it new in *the kingdom of God*"), since the Zecharian verse is one of only two Old Testament passages that link the phrase "on that day" with the establishment of God's eschatological kingship (cf. Micah 4:6). The Targum on Zechariah 14:9, moreover, speaks specifically of the revelation of "the kingdom of Yahweh" (מלכותא דייי), and the verse was one of ten "kingship verses" (מלכיות) that were recited on Rosh

---

[11] See Black, "Rejected," pp. 144–147. The texts from Josephus (*Jewish War* 2.261–263; *Antiquities* 20.170) speak of an Egyptian "prophet" who gathered his forces on the Mount of Olives around A.D. 56 and promised them a miraculous conquest of Jerusalem, after which he proposed to "set himself up as a tyrant of the people." The rabbinic texts cited by Black specifically link Zech. 14:1–5 with the coming of the Messiah.

[12] See J. Gnilka, *Das Evangelium nach Markus*, EKKNT 2, 2 vols. (Zurich: Benziger Verlag, 1978, 1979), 2:182–183, 243. As evidence of the redactional nature of Mark 13:3–4 he mentions Jesus' sitting position, which corresponds to that in the redactional introduction to the parable chapter (4:1), and the isolation motif (κατ᾽ ἰδίαν, "privately"), which is typically Markan.

Hashanah in ancient synagogues.[13] The theme of Yahweh's universal sovereignty, furthermore, brackets the whole of Zechariah 9–14, since it first
appears in Zech. 9:1–8, where it is linked with the prophecy in 9:9–10 of
the coming of the messianic king whose dominion will extend to the ends
of the earth. The phrase "on that day," similarly, appears throughout Zechariah 9–14.[14] The Markan reference to the Mount of Olives, then, following
immediately upon Jesus' prophecy that "on that day" (a phrase that links
Zech. 14:4 with 14:9) he will drink new wine in the kingdom of God, creates
a strong link with Zechariah 14 and with Zechariah 9–14 in general.

There is probably a further allusion to Zechariah 9–14 in Mark 14:24,
"This is my blood of the covenant." Although the primary background to
this part of the "cup word" in Mark is Moses' pronouncement in Ex. 24:8,
"Behold the blood of the covenant," the influence of Zech. 9:11, "the blood
of my covenant," is evident in the insertion of the personal pronoun "my."[15]
Further evidence for a connection with Zech. 9:11 is provided by the fact
that the Targum on this verse links it with the deliverance from Egypt: "You
also, for whom a covenant was made by blood, I have delivered you from
bondage to the Egyptians. . . ." This allusion to the exodus in the Targum
on Zech. 9:11 parallels the Passover setting of the allusion to Zech. 9:11
in Mark.[16]

The allusions to Zechariah 9–14 in Mark 14:24–28 can be summed up
as follows:

Mark		*Zechariah*
14:24	my blood of the covenant	9:11
14:25	that day, kingdom of God	14:4, 9
14:26	Mount of Olives	14:4
14:27	strike the shepherd, and	13:7
	sheep will be scattered	
14:28	resurrection	14:4
	restoration of scattered sheep	13:8–9

---

[13] For the modern form of the "kingship verses," see S. Tal, ed., *Rinnat Yisrael Prayerbook*
(Jerusalem: Moreshet, 1982), pp. 450–451; on their history, see I. Elbogen, *Der jüdische Gottesdienst in seiner geschichtlichen Entwicklung* (Leipzig: Fock, 1913), pp. 140–142; A. Z. Idelsohn,
Jewish Liturgy and Its Development (New York: Henry Holt, 1932), pp. 213–214. According
to the latter, the recitation of the מלכיות probably goes back to Second Temple times. This
is logical, given the association of Rosh Hashanah with God's kingship from the origin of the
holiday; see J. Gray, *The Biblical Doctrine of the Reign of God* (Edinburgh: T. & T. Clark, 1979),
pp. 7–38.

[14] Black, "Rejected," pp. 48, 53–54. He notes the repetition of "on that day" in Zech. 9:16;
12:3–4, 6, 8–9, 11; 13:1–2, 4; 14:4, 6, 8, 13, 20.

[15] See Bruce, "Book of Zechariah," p. 347.

[16] See Black, "Rejected," pp. 180–182.

The Zecharian allusions in the Last Supper pericope seem to be embedded in the pre-Markan narrative. We have noted, however, that Mark has apparently penned verses with Zecharian allusions in 13:3–4 and 14:28. A proper understanding of the triumphal entry passage in 11:1–11, moreover, depends on a knowledge of Zech. 9:9–10.[17] It seems reasonable, therefore, that Mark and at least some of his readers would have recognized the Zecharian allusions in 14:24–28.

ZECHARIAH 9–14 AND THE ESCHATOLOGICAL INTERPRETATION OF JESUS' PASSION

The context of Zechariah 9–14 in the Old Testament is "wholly forward-looking and eschatological,"[18] and this orientation has profound ramifications for Mark's use of it. The eschatological context of Zechariah 9–14 is preserved in postbiblical exegesis of these chapters, as we have already seen from examples drawn from the Targum and rabbinic traditions. The Qumran literature provides an earlier illustration. In CD B 19:7–9 there is a quotation of Zech. 13:7, the passage whose beginning is cited in Mark 14:27, and the passage is then interpreted to refer to "the poor of the flock" who "will be saved at the time of visitation." This motif of the flock's salvation is drawn from the immediately following Zecharian verses, 13:8–9, even though they are not quoted; the Qumran text is thus structurally similar to Mark 14:27–28, which first quotes part of Zech. 13:7–9, then alludes to its continuation. The eschatological orientation of the Qumran text is obvious from the reference to the eschatological time of visitation.[19] A further contact between the Qumran document and Mark 14:27–28 is that in the former the "poor of the flock" who receive the Zecharian promise of restoration are the faithful members of the elect community, just as in Mark they are the stumbling but ultimately faithful disciples of Jesus. Both passages, then, reflect a "sectarian" exegesis that restricts the application of the Zecharian

---

[17] Contra Suhl, who denies any special connection of Mark 11:1–11 with Zech. 9:9–10 (*Zitate*, p. 57); with Black, who notes the common elements in the two passages: entry into Jerusalem, riding on an ass, and the rejoicing of the crowd ("Rejected," pp. 163–164). As Black further notes, there is a particular contact with the Septuagint, which describes the animal as νεός ("new"); cf. Mark 11:2, ἐφ' ὃν οὐδεὶς οὔπω ἀνθρώπων ἐκάθισεν, lit., "upon which no one of human beings never yet sat." The use of double negatives is a characteristic of Markan style (see Taylor, *Mark*, p. 46), so that Mark himself may have made the connection with Zechariah clearer in this verse.

[18] Black, "Rejected," p. 44; see also P. D. Hanson, *The Dawn of Apocalyptic: The Historical and Sociological Roots of Jewish Apocalyptic Eschatology*, rev. ed. (Philadelphia: Fortress Press, 1979), pp. 280–401.

[19] See R. T. France, *Jesus and the Old Testament: His Application of Old Testament Passages to Himself and His Mission* (Downers Grove, Ill.: Inter-Varsity Press, 1971), pp. 176–177; Black, "Rejected," pp. 117–120.

oracle of promise more than is done in the original text, where the restored group is the third of the nation left alive after two thirds have perished. These contacts between the Qumran and Markan passages that quote Zech. 13:7, in combination with the eschatological context of Zechariah 9–14 in the Old Testament itself—a context of which Mark seems to be aware—suggest that the events spoken of in Mark 14:22–28 are to be viewed as eschatological happenings. For Mark, the occurrences of Jesus' last night on earth inaugurate the time of eschatological testing spoken of by Zechariah, a time in which the shepherd of God's people will be struck and the people themselves will be tested to the breaking point. Mark knows, however, that Zechariah also points forward to a restoration of the covenant with this apostate people "on that day" in which the kingdom of God is revealed and, according to current exegesis, the dead are resurrected. Thus the arrest, execution, and resurrection of Jesus, as well as the apostasy, dispersal, and restoration of the disciples, are set within an eschatological context through the echoes of Zechariah that resound in this portion of the Markan narrative.[20]

ZECHARIAH 9–14 AND THE MARKAN COMMUNITY SETTING

Mark's use of the eschatological prophecies of Zechariah 9–14 in his passion narrative may have a special resonance for his audience, because those prophecies are playing an important role in the Jewish Revolt, which forms the backdrop to Mark's composition of the Gospel.

We have alluded in a note (n. 11) to texts from Josephus describing an Egyptian prophet who gathered his forces on the Mount of Olives around A.D. 56 and promised them a miraculous conquest of Jerusalem, and we have suggested that this action should be seen against the backdrop of the promise found in Zech. 14:1–5 of a divine deliverance of Jerusalem. It seems inherently likely that such trust in the scriptural promises of miraculous deliverance continued in the Jewish Revolt that began ten years later, and indeed Josephus himself admits that what drove the Jews to revolt more than anything else was an unspecified scriptural oracle. Though this particular oracle was probably not from Zechariah,[21] M. Hengel specifically mentions Zech. 12:2–6 and 14:2–5 as the sort of passage that led the defenders of the city "to hope with unshakable certainty for a miraculous intervention on the part of God."[22]

Mark's awareness of the catalytic role played by Zechariah 9–14 in the

---

[20] See C. F. Evans, "I Will Go," p. 8.

[21] On the oracle, see chapter 7, n. 67 above.

[22] M. Hengel, *The Zealots: Investigations into the Jewish Freedom Movements in the Period from Herod I Until 70 A.D.* (Edinburgh: T. & T. Clark, 1989), p. 242.

Jewish Revolt may be indicated by his retelling of the story of Jesus' cleansing of the Temple in Mark 11:15–17. In a previous chapter we have discussed v. 17, which contrasts God's intention that the Temple should be a house of prayer for all peoples with the charge that Jesus' enemies have made it "a den of brigands." We argued that this verse represents Markan redaction and that it refers to the events of the Jewish War, in which the revolutionary parties attempted to cleanse Palestine, and especially Jerusalem, from Gentile contamination and to set up in the Temple itself their headquarters for the climactic battle in the holy war against the Romans.

It may now be added that one of the probable scriptural justifications for this purge and takeover of the Temple lay in the eschatological prophecies of Zechariah 14. As C. Roth has pointed out, the very last verse of Zechariah, 14:21, literally says that "on that day" there will no longer be a *Canaanite* in the house of the Lord.[23] Later rabbinic interpretations argue against taking the word "Canaanite" literally, saying that it should be interpreted, rather, to refer to traders. This interpretation, Roth argues, coheres with Jesus' action of expelling the traders from the Temple in Mark 11:15. But the revolutionaries of the First Revolt apparently followed a different, more nationalistic tradition of interpretation, one that took the Zecharian verse literally as forbidding any Gentile presence in the Temple.

If Roth's line of reasoning is correct, then Zech. 14:21 probably played a crucial role in the events reflected in Mark 11:17, the revolutionaries' purge of Gentiles and takeover of the Temple. Mark, it may be surmised, has probably shaped 11:17 to reflect his knowledge of these events,[24] and it is likely that this knowledge includes an awareness of the importance of the Zecharian text. This is especially plausible since the earlier portion of the same Markan chapter, the account of the triumphal entry in 11:1–11, echoes Zech. 9:9–13 not only in the description of Jesus' entry into Jerusalem on an ass but also in the crowd's linkage of this entry with "the coming kingdom of our father David."[25]

The allusions to Zechariah 9–14 in Mark 14:22–28, then, may well be read by Mark and his audience in such a way that they provide a contrast to the interpretation of those passages circulating in Jewish revolutionary circles known to them. Instead of seeing the arrival of the kingdom of God in the appearance of a triumphant Messiah figure on the Mount of Olives,

---

[23] C. Roth, "The Cleansing of the Temple and Zechariah xiv.21," *NovT* 4 (1960), 174–181; for a summary of his arguments and their relevance for Mark, see J. Marcus, "The Jewish War and the *Sitz im Leben* of Mark," *JBL* (forthcoming).

[24] As Black notes ("Rejected," p. 229), Roth's study does not reflect the results of redaction criticism. Roth traces the Zecharian echoes in Mark 11:15–17 to Jesus himself, but they fit better into a *Sitz im Leben* in the time of Mark—that is, during the Jewish War—when the revolutionaries actually did transform the Temple into a "den of brigands."

[25] See Zech. 9:10, which speaks of the worldwide dominion of the messianic king.

a miraculous deliverance of Jerusalem from the Gentile armies that sur-
round it, and a resanctification of the Temple through its cleansing from
pagan influence, Mark would see the arrival of the kingdom of God, paradoxically, in the deliverance of Jesus to his Jewish enemies on the Mount
of Olives, his humiliating death at the hands of Gentiles in Jerusalem, and
the proleptic act of Temple destruction that accompanies that death (see
15:38).[26] He also would see its arrival, however, in the resurrection that
follows Jesus' death, the restoration of the community of disciples, and the
spread of the gospel to all the nations (see 13:10), so that the prophecy of
Zech. 14:9 is fulfilled: "And the LORD will become king over all the earth;
on that day the LORD will be one and his name one."

ZECHARIAH 9–14 AND MARKAN CHRISTOLOGY

Our comments above about Mark's reading of Zechariah 9–14, which contrasts with the reading given those chapters by the Jewish revolutionaries,
should not be taken to mean that the idea of a warrior Messiah is anathema
to Mark. As we have seen in the preceding chapter of this study, Mark both
affirms and qualifies the idea of a militant Davidic Messiah in 10:46–52;
11:9–10; and 12:35–37. A similar process of affirmation with qualification
is visible in the present instance.

Mark 14:27–28 makes prominent use of military imagery. In the quotation from Zech. 13:7 in Mark 14:27, the motif of the sheep and their
shepherd draws on several Old Testament passages that use the image to
speak of an army and its general or a nation and its leader.[27] In Zechariah
9–14 itself, all of the references to the shepherd and his sheep (Zech. 9:16;
10:3; 11:4–17; 13:7) appear in contexts that speak of battle. The verb "to
lead" (προάγειν), moreover, which the Markan Jesus uses in the redactional
v. 28, following the citation of Zech. 13:7, can itself be a military term both
in classical Greek (Thucydides 7:6) and in the Septuagint (2 Macc. 10:1).[28]
Mark 14:27–28, therefore, draws on Old Testament images that suggest the
injury of a leader who is also the commander in chief of an army, a consequent scattering of his army, and its later regroupment under the revived
leader. This military imagery is coherent with an important aspect of the
messianic oracles in Zechariah 9–14. Zechariah 9:9–13, for example, which
we have seen to lie in the background of Jesus' triumphal entry in Mark

---

[26] On Mark 15:38 as a foreshadowing of the destruction of the Temple, see D. Juel, *Messiah
and Temple: The Trial of Jesus in the Gospel of Mark*, SBLDS 31 (Missoula, Mont.: Scholars
Press, 1973), pp. 138–139.
[27] See Bruce ("Book of Zechariah," p. 344), citing Jer. 23:1–6; Ezek. 34:23–24; 37:24;
Zechariah 9–14.
[28] See C. F. Evans, "I Will Go," p. 9.

11:1–11, speaks of a victorious king who imposes his military will on the
entire world. This passage contains Davidic imagery[29] and was frequently
interpreted messianically in rabbinic traditions.[30]

There are other aspects of the messianism of Zechariah that qualify the
triumphalism of 9:9–13. Within the passage itself, the king is described not
only as "triumphant and victorious" but also as "humble and riding on an
ass," a description that a later rabbinic tradition opposes to the glorious
messianic expectation of Dan. 7:13.[31] In Zech. 12:10–13:1, moreover, we find
a reference to the inhabitants of Jerusalem mourning when "they look on
him whom they have pierced," and in Zech. 11:4–17 and 13:7–9 God calls
for a sword to strike his shepherd, "the man of my association." Although
it is impossible to say with certainty whether or not these four passages
refer to one person,[32] all suggest the suffering of the people's leader and
seem to have been influenced by the figure of the Servant of the Lord in
Isaiah.[33]

Mark's own version of Zech. 13:7 moves even further in this direction.
We have previously noted that the one divergence of Mark's text from the
Q form of the Septuagint is in the first person singular "I will strike" (πατάξω),
as opposed to the second person plural imperative "Strike!" (πατάξατε) of
the Septuagint. Although God, who issues the command for the sword to
strike the shepherd, is ultimately behind this action in the Masoretic Text
and the Septuagint as well as in Mark,[34] the change to ascribing direct agency
to God calls for explanation. J. Jeremias has plausibly argued that this change
reflects the influence of Isa. 53:6b, "The LORD has laid on him the iniquity
of us all."[35] Here God becomes the direct agent in causing the Servant's
suffering, and this direct agency is even more strongly emphasized in a later
verse: "It pleased the LORD to bruise him; he has put him to grief" (Isa.
53:10, alt.). Nor is this the only place in which the Markan text conflates
an allusion to Isaiah 53 with one to Zechariah 9–14; in Mark 14:24, as we

---

[29] The riding of an ass and the contrast with chariots and horses recall details of David's
flight from Absalom in 2 Samuel 15–19 (see 2 Sam. 16:1; 15:1). It is also significant that in
this story David ascends the Mount of Olives (2 Sam. 16:30), suffers various humiliations (2 Sam.
16:5–8), and is betrayed by his counselor Ahithophel, who later commits suicide by hanging
himself (2 Sam. 17:23). These details provide points of contact with the Synoptic accounts
of Jesus' passion, as R. E. Brown has emphasized to me in conversation; see Black, "Rejected,"
pp. 68–69.

[30] See Black, "Rejected," pp. 105–110.

[31] See the citation of R. Joshua (a second-generation Tanna) by R. Alexandri (a second-
generation Amora) in *b. Sanh.* 98a; see Black, "Rejected," pp. 107, 179.

[32] They are not so read in rabbinic traditions; see Black, "Rejected," pp. 131–132, 141.

[33] Ibid., pp. 63–88.

[34] See C. F. Evans, "I Will Go," p. 5.

[35] J. Jeremias, "ποιμήν, κτλ.," *TDNT* (1968), 6:493 n. 78; see also Black, "Rejected,"
pp. 186–187.

shall see below, the Zecharian allusion "my blood of the covenant" is immediately followed by an allusion to Isa. 53:12, "which is poured out for many."

In Mark 14:27–28, then, the text seems to preserve both the militant dimension of the shepherd figure in Zech. 13:7–9 and its nuance of suffering. The militant dimension, implied especially by the verb προάγειν ("to lead"), is consonant with the fact that Mark sets his entire story in the context of Deutero-Isaiah's picture of apocalyptic holy war (1:1–3). For Mark, God is on the march into the world. He has led his people once more into the desert in order to renew them (see 1:4–5; 6:31–35; 8:4); now he is leading them back to Jerusalem for the decisive battle against the gathering forces of darkness, with the "man of his association" (Zech. 13:7) standing in for him as the shepherd of the flock. But the prophecy of the "striking" of this shepherd raises the question of exactly *how* the apocalyptic battle is to be won. We will return to this question later when we consider Mark's references to the Deutero-Isaian Servant of the Lord in his passion narrative.

THE COLLECTIVE DIMENSION IN THE IDENTITY OF THE "SHEPHERD"

One more dimension of the shepherd figure drawn from Zechariah 9–14 may be important for understanding the Markan passion narrative. This figure has a collective dimension, as is suggested in the passage cited in Mark 14:27: "I will strike the shepherd, and the sheep will be scattered" (Zech. 13:7, alt.). Here the divine action against the shepherd also involves the sheep in his fate.[36] Similarly, there is a certain parallel between the suffering of the pierced figure in Zech. 12:10 and that of the flock doomed to slaughter in 11:4–7, 15. Although this collective dimension of the shepherd is not extensively developed in Zechariah 9–14, it is interesting to note its presence here, since the other Old Testament backgrounds used by Mark in the passion narrative have a collective dimension that is significant for Markan christology.

CONCLUSIONS

Allusions to Zechariah 9–14 in the Markan passion narrative are concentrated in the consecutive pericopes that describe the Last Supper (14:22–26) and Jesus' prophecy of the apostasy and restoration of the disciples (14:27–31). Although most of these allusions stem from pre-Markan tradition, Mark himself has probably introduced the allusion in 14:28, and he

---

[36] This collective dimension is implied also in John 10:11, a New Testament passage that is at least partly based on Zech. 13:7–9 (see R. Schnackenburg, *The Gospel According to St. John*, 3 vols. [New York: Crossroad, 1968–1982], 2:295).

seems to be aware of the Zecharian background of this section of his Gospel. The eschatological orientation of Zechariah 9–14 in the Old Testament and in later Jewish exegesis also seems to apply to Mark's use of the chapters, and Mark's application of them may partly be a response to the catalytic role they played in the Jewish Revolt. Mark does not efface the military lineaments of the "shepherd" described by Zechariah, but he emphasizes the paradox that this shepherd's victory involves an element of divinely willed suffering—a suffering in which the "sheep" are also involved.

Daniel 7

MARK'S USE OF DANIEL 7:13

Daniel 7:13 is cited in Mark 14:62, where Jesus answers the high priest's question whether or not he is the Messiah-the-Son-of-the-Blessed[37] by saying, "I am; and you will see the Son of man sitting at the right hand of Power, and coming with the clouds of heaven." The phrases "Son of man" and "coming with the clouds of heaven" are obviously dependent on the Danielic passage: "Behold, with *the clouds of heaven* there came one like a *son of man*."

The motif of power is probably also an echo of Daniel 7. In 7:9–10, the Ancient of Days is described in awe-inspiring fashion, and in 7:14 this figure imparts his glory to the one like a son of man. Mark 13:26, another direct Markan citation of Dan. 7:13,[38] introduces the word "power" into the citation, and Mark 8:38–9:1, which is probably also an allusion to Dan. 7:13–14,[39] links the coming of the Son of man in glory with the coming of the kingdom of God in power. The word "power" in 14:62 therefore probably reflects a targumizing of Dan. 7:13–14.

The verbal relation of the three Markan passages to Daniel 7 may be charted as follows:

Daniel 7:13–14	*Mark 8:38–9:1*	*Mark 13:26*	*Mark 14:62*
angels (7:10)	with the angels		
with clouds of heaven		in clouds	with clouds of heaven
came	when he comes	coming	coming
one like a son of man . . .	the Son of man	the Son of man	the Son of man
to him was given . . . glory	in the glory of his father	glory	
and a kingdom	kingdom of God come in power	great power	right hand of power

[37] On this translation of the high priest's question in Mark 14:61, see J. Marcus, "Mark 14:61: Are You the Messiah-Son-of-God?" *NovT* 31 (1988), 125–141.
[38] On the Danielic citation here, see France, *Jesus and the Old Testament*, p. 140.
[39] See France, who cites the Son of man imagery, the verb "to come," the motif of glory, the angelic retinue, and the mention of the kingdom (*Jesus and the Old Testament*, p. 139).

We may add that, although the phrase "sitting at the right hand" in 14:62 is most directly an allusion to Ps. 110:1, it is also consonant with the picture in Dan. 7:13-14 of the humanlike figure being presented to the Ancient of Days and made his co-regent.

Daniel 7:13 seems to be an important verse for Mark; we have just seen that he alludes to it three times in the course of his narrative. There are good reasons for thinking that Mark has introduced the Danielic allusions in 8:38; the verb "to come," the motif of the angels, and the phrase "in the glory of his father" are lacking in the Q version of the saying (Matt. 10:33//Luke 12:9), and the theme of eschatological glory forms a neat transition to 9:1 and the story of the transfiguration, which immediately follows.[40] It is more difficult to decide whether or not Mark has also introduced the Danielic allusions in 14:62b,[41] but even if he has not, the evidence of redactional activity in 8:38 suggests strongly that he is aware of them.

THE LARGER CONTEXT OF DANIEL 7 AND THE MARKAN TRIAL SCENE

The scene of which Dan. 7:13 is a part describes four beasts that arise out of the sea and represent the four world empires that have oppressed Israel (Dan. 7:1-8; cf. v. 18). Opposed to them is the God of Israel, who is pictured as a numinous "one that was ancient of days" surrounded by millions of angels (7:9-12). A humanlike figure, the "one like a son of man," is presented before this venerable figure and given a share in his dominion (7:13-14); later in the chapter the same dominion is granted to "the saints of the Most High" (7:18) and "the people of the saints of the Most High" (7:27). Correspondingly, dominion is taken away from the final beast (7:26), an act that is interpreted as a judgment upon it. The theme of judgment, indeed, pervades the latter half of the chapter: "the court sat in judgment, and the books were opened" (7:10); "judgment was given to (or for)[42] the saints of the Most High" (7:22); "the court shall sit in judgment" (7:26). The "one like a son of man" is not himself described as a judge, but judgment is given to or for the "saints of the Most High," who are associated with him (7:22). Drawing on this Danielic background, the Similitudes of Enoch

---

[40] See M. Horstmann, *Studien zur markinischen Christologie: Mk 8,27–9,13 als Zugang zum Christusbild des zweiten Evangeliums*, NTAbh 6, 2nd ed. (Münster: Aschendorff, 1973), pp. 45–47; Lührmann, *Markusevangelium*, p. 152.

[41] Lührmann argues that he has, since 14:61b–62 brings together the three crucial Markan titles Messiah, Son of God, and Son of man (*Markusevangelium*, p. 250). Gnilka, however, argues for 14:62b being a *pre-Markan* expansion of an original answer that was limited to the assertion "I am" (*Evangelium* 2:276–277).

[42] On this ambiguity, see A. Lacocque, *The Book of Daniel* (Atlanta: John Knox Press, 1979), p. 153.

present the Son of man himself as a judge (*1 Enoch* 45:3, etc.), and this picture of the judging Son of man is probably reflected in New Testament passages such as Matthew 25 and John 5:27.[43]

The figure of the judging Son of man drawn from Daniel 7 is reflected also in Mark 8:38, a passage whose developed Danielic allusion, as we have seen, is most likely a result of Mark's own redactional work. When he comes in his father's glory with the angels, we read there, the Son of man will be ashamed of those who now deny Jesus. The word "to be ashamed" (ἐπαισχύ-νεσθαι) here carries a nuance of eschatological judgment, as in the Septuagint.[44]

Since Mark 8:38 shows that Mark is aware of the larger context of Dan. 7:13–14, which has to do with judgment, we should not be surprised to observe that the citation of Dan. 7:13 in Mark 14:62 also carries a nuance of judgment.[45] This nuance is conveyed in Mark 14:62b through the use of the word ὄψεσθε ("you will see"). That this word has a special nuance is suggested by its awkwardness in the context; after Jesus' reply "I am" in 14:62a, one would expect him to support his claim to be the Messiah-Son-of-God by continuing, "and I (or the Son of man) will sit down at the right hand of Power and come with the clouds of heaven." The reference to "seeing" seems gratuitous; why is it there?

Naturally enough, some have seen this word as the remnant of a preexistent tradition that has been appropriated by Mark. N. Perrin, for example, has argued for a background in Zech. 12:10, "they will look (LXX ἐπι-βλέφονται) upon him whom they have pierced . . . and they will mourn over him."[46] The present context, however, does not support the idea of repentance suggested by such an allusion, and in fact another set of backgrounds makes more sense in the context. R. Pesch has noted the presence of the motif of seeing in martyrological traditions, in which the persecutors of the righteous *see* that those whom they have persecuted have been vindicated by God, while they themselves are condemned.[47] Such a background coheres with the setting of Mark 14:62 within the narrative of Jesus' martyrdom. Pesch also notes the parallel in *1 Enoch* 62:3–5. This passage is particularly

---

[43] See Schnackenburg, *John* 2:113; Collins, *Apocalyptic Imagination*, 210. The date of the Similitudes of Enoch is a vexed question; for recent defenses of their pre-Christian provenance, see J. J. Collins, *The Apocalyptic Imagination: An Introduction to the Jewish Matrix of Christianity* (New York: Crossroad, 1984), pp. 142–143; M. Black, *The Book of Enoch or 1 Enoch: A New English Edition*, SVTP 7 (Leiden: E. J. Brill, 1985), pp. 181–188.

[44] See R. Bultmann, "αἰσχύνω, κτλ.," *TDNT* (1964; orig. 1933), 1:189–190.

[45] See R. Pesch, *Das Markusevangelium*, HTKNT 2, 2 vols. (Freiburg: Herder, 1978), 2:439.

[46] N. Perrin, *Rediscovering the Teaching of Jesus* (New York: Harper & Row, 1976; orig. 1967), pp. 181–185. The Septuagint of this verse, however, does not speak of piercing.

[47] Pesch (*Markusevangelium* 2:438), citing Wisd. Sol. 5:2; Rev. 11:2 [apparently a mistake for 11:12]; and *Apoc. Elijah* 35:17 [Eng. in Charlesworth, *OTP*, 5:28].

close to Mark 14:62 because it speaks of an eschatological *seeing* of *the Son of man* by the worldly leaders who have opposed his will:

> On the day of judgment, all the kings, the governors, the high officials, and the landlords *shall see and recognize him* — how he sits on the throne of his glory, and righteousness is judged before him. . . . They shall be terrified and dejected; and pain shall seize them *when they see that Son of man* sitting on the throne of his glory. . . .

We have previously noted the closeness of the Markan conception of the Son of man to the development of that Danielic figure in *1 Enoch*, in that both writings go beyond Daniel 7 in ascribing judgment to the Son of man. The motif of seeing is an additional point of contact, and the conclusion seems justified that Mark 14:62 is drawing on the sort of tradition present in *1 Enoch* 62:3–5, perhaps even on this passage itself, as well as on the martyrological motif of seeing the vindication of the righteous. In both backgrounds, seeing is associated with judgment.

The context of judgment in these backgrounds fits very well into the trial scene of which Mark 14:62 forms the climax. In a characteristic example of Markan irony, however, Jesus, the Son of man, is here *being judged* rather than judging. He is arraigned before the Sanhedrin (14:53), confronted with witnesses (14:55–59), questioned directly by the high priest (14:60–61), and finally condemned unanimously by the whole Sanhedrin (14:63–64). Yet because of the Danielic background to this scene, as mediated by *1 Enoch* and as qualified by the martyrological motif, it becomes plain that Jesus' condemnation is not the last word in the story. Mark's use of Daniel implies that in the long run it is Jesus' judges who will be judged; they, who today are scandalized by him and his words, will be condemned by him when they see him coming with the clouds at the eschaton (see 8:38).

THE SON OF MAN AND THE MARKAN COMMUNITY

The threat of judgment against Jesus' persecutors would probably strike a chord among the members of Mark's persecuted community. Implicit in it is the promise that their persecutors too will be judged at the parousia.

Mark's use of Daniel 7 in Mark 14:62 and elsewhere probably reflects his community situation in two other ways as well. First, it is likely that Daniel 7–12 was playing a significant role in the Jewish Revolt, which formed an important part of the backdrop to Mark's Gospel. P. Billerbeck and R. Meyer, indeed, think that Dan. 7:13–27 is the unspecified Old Testament oracle that according to Josephus (*Jewish War* 6.312–313) sparked the revolt, and Hengel, although disagreeing that Daniel 7 was initially so vital, argues that Daniel's prophecies assumed increasing importance during the siege of Jerusalem, when the hopes of the revolutionaries became concentrated "on the Temple as the place of God's saving revelation at the moment of greatest distress."[48] This situation would have created conditions strikingly reminiscent of Daniel's prophecies, in which the threat to the Temple and God's deliverance of it play such an important role (see Dan. 9:26–27; 11:31; 12:11). Hengel cites as evidence Josephus's report (*Jewish War* 6.285–286) that on the tenth of Av in A.D. 70 a Zealot prophet proclaimed to the inhabitants of Jerusalem that God had commanded them to go up to the sanctuary to receive there the signs of redemption; six thousand people thereupon stormed the burning Temple and perished in it. Hengel argues that this suicidal action was motivated by the belief that the seventy weeks of years prophesied in Dan. 9:24–27 were at an end and that the heavenly redeemer would now appear on the clouds of heaven (Dan. 7:13–27) until the decreed end was poured out on the desolator (9:27; cf. 11:45).[49]

Although Hengel's argument involves a good deal of educated guesswork, it is plausible that the eschatological prophecies of Daniel 7–12 were mined in the final desperate days of the Jewish Revolt. Mark himself links the Danielic prophecy of the "abomination of desolation" (Dan. 9:27; 11:31; 12:11; cf. Mark 13:14), which he apparently interprets as the desecration of the Temple,[50] with the prophecy of the coming of the Son of man (Dan. 7:13–14; cf. Mark 13:26), and it is conceivable that in so doing he is drawing on a connection already established in Jewish exegesis and appropriated by the Jewish revolutionaries, among others.[51]

If so, Mark's use of Daniel 7 retains the association of the coming of the Son of man with the destruction of the Temple, but severs it from the destruction of the *Gentile* kingdom envisaged in Daniel 7–12 (see Dan. 7:11, 26; 9:27; 11:45). Rather, it is the *Jewish* leaders responsible for Jesus' death (and by extension the revolutionary Jewish leaders of the Markan present?)

---

48   S-B 4:1002; R. Meyer, *Der Prophet aus Galiläa: Studie zum Jesusbild der drei ersten Evangelien* (Darmstadt: Wissenschaftliche Buchgesellschaft, 1970), pp. 52–54; Pesch, *Markusevangelium* 2:291; Hengel, *Zealots,* p. 245.
49   Hengel, *Zealots,* pp. 242–243.
50   See Marcus, "Jewish War."
51   H. Schwier mounts a strong argument that the Jewish Revolt was sparked in large measure by a concern about the Roman profanation of the Temple (*Tempel und Tempelzerstörung: Untersuchungen zu den theologischen und ideologischen Faktoren im ersten jüdisch-römischen Krieg (66–74) n. Chr.,* NTOA 11 [Göttingen: Vandenhoeck & Ruprecht, 1989], pp. 55–74, 90–101); this concern would have made a link with the Danielic prophecies about the "abomination of desolation" likely. Compare the resilient theory originated by T. Colani in 1864 that Mark 13:14 and 13:26 were part of a Jewish apocalypse related to the events of A.D. 40 or 66–70 and subsequently reshaped by Mark; see G. Hölscher, "Der Ursprung der Apokalypse Markus 13," *TBl* 12 (1933), 193–202; R. Bultmann, *History of the Synoptic Tradition* (New York: Harper & Row, 1963), p. 122; R. Pesch, *Naherwartungen: Tradition und Redaktion in Mk 13,* Kommentare und Beiträge zum Alten und Neuen Testament (Düsseldorf: Patmos Verlag, 1968), passim (though cf. the different position in Pesch's *Markusevangelium* 2:264–318).

who are warned, by means of the citation of Dan. 7:13 in Mark 14:62, of the condemnation awaiting them when the Son of man returns. In this connection, it may be significant that twice in the brief narrative of Mark 14:55–64 we read about enemies of Jesus *standing up* (ἀναστάντες, ἀναστάς) to accuse and oppose him (14:57, 60). This same verb and similar ones are used frequently in Daniel 7 as well as elsewhere in the book for the arising of evil Gentile rulers who oppose and are finally shattered by the power of God.[52] Mark's use of the verb in 14:57 and 14:60 may partly be intended to echo these Danielic passages and to reapply them polemically to *Jewish* leaders.[53]

The second way in which Mark's use of Daniel 7 reflects the situation of his community has to do with the inclusive nature of the Son of man figure. The coming of Jesus as Son of man at the eschaton, as described with Danielic imagery in Mark 14:62, vindicates the one who in the Markan passion narrative is judged, condemned to death, and executed. Jesus the Son of man performs a similar function in Mark 13:26, but this time he vindicates not himself but the community of disciples who, like him and because of him, are hated by all, brought to trial before the authorities, judged to be guilty, and condemned to death (13:9–12).[54] Jesus' trial scene in 14:53–65 thus anticipates — and perhaps in some ways reflects — the trial of Christians described in 13:9–12,[55] and in Mark's conception the glorious Son of man vindicates both the suffering Son of man and the suffering Markan community.

This overlap between the vindication of Jesus and that of the Markan community is a throwback to Daniel 7, where the figure of the "one like a son of man" has a collective dimension. As we have previously noted, Daniel's "one like a son of man" bears a functional similarity both to "the holy ones of the Most High" (7:18, 21–22, 25) and to "the people of the saints of the Most High" (7:27), in that he is given everlasting dominion. Whether the "holy ones" are meant to be understood as angels or as human beings, and whether the "one like a son of man" is intended to be the people's transcendent symbol, their heavenly representative, or their angelic leader, Daniel 7 still establishes a homology between the glorious humanlike figure

---

[52] Dan. 2:39; 7:3, 5, 8, 17, 20, 24; 8:22–23; 11:2–3, 4, 7, 14–15, 20–21, 31; 12:11.

[53] As we shall see below, the use of ἀναστάντες in Mark 14:57 also has Old Testament background in Pss. 27:12 and 35:11.

[54] See Collins, *Apocalyptic Imagination,* p. 210.

[55] The historical difficulties of the Sanhedrin trial in Mark 14:53–65 and the doublets (both internally and with the trial before Pilate in 15:1–20) suggest that it may be far removed from historical fact and reflect later Christian theological interests to a great extent; see Bultmann, *History,* pp. 269–271; J. R. Donahue, *Are You the Christ?* SBLDS 10 (Missoula, Mont.: Society of Biblical Literature, 1973), pp. 12–30, 222–223, 238–239; E. P. Sanders, *Jesus and Judaism* (Philadelphia: Fortress Press, 1985), pp. 296–301.

and the people of the holy ones.[56] On the other hand, there is also a distinction between him and the holy ones/people of the holy ones. The latter are said to be at war with the "horn" and to be worn out by him (7:21, 25; cf. 8:24; 12:7), while the "one like a son of man" is not said to be in direct confrontation with the beasts or the "horn," or to suffer.[57]

The homology between the people of God and the Son of man continues in *1 Enoch*, though here it is clearer that the Son of man is a distinct figure and not just a symbol of the people. The intimate relationship between them, however, is emphasized in numerous ways. Almost every time the Son of man is mentioned, the elect community is also mentioned.[58] He and they share various epithets, such as "righteous" and "elect"; in *1 Enoch* 40:5, for example, Enoch hears a voice blessing "the Elect One [= the Son of man] and the elect ones [= the community of righteous people]." The hiddenness of the Son of man, furthermore, parallels the sufferings of this community, and the ultimate hope of the righteous is that "with that Son of man they shall eat and lie down and rise up for ever and ever" (*1 Enoch* 62:14).[59] For *1 Enoch*, the divine side of the apocalyptic war includes three forces that interpenetrate one another in the closest possible way: the community of the human righteous, the community of the angels, and the mysterious head of both communities, the Son of man.[60]

At the same time, in *1 Enoch* as in Daniel 7 the figure of the Son of man preserves a measure of distinctiveness in that he does not suffer, while the righteous community does. This distinction is not accidental; as Collins trenchantly observes:

> The fact that he is preserved from their sufferings makes him a figure of pure power and glory and an ideal embodiment of the hopes of the persecuted righteous. The efficaciousness of the "Son of Man" figure requires that he be conceived as other than the community, since he must possess the power and exaltation which they lack.[61]

Despite this necessary distinction, the many analogies between the Enochic Son of man and the elect community point toward a collective dimension to the Son of man figure in *1 Enoch*.

In Mark, the analogy between the Son of man and the elect community is even more fully developed than it is in Daniel 7 and *1 Enoch*, in that

---

[56] See Collins, *Apocalyptic Imagination*, pp. 81–85; J. Schaberg, "Daniel 7–12 and the New Testament Passion-Resurrection Predictions," *NTS* 31 (1985), 208.

[57] See Schaberg, "Daniel 7–12," p. 208.

[58] See M. D. Hooker, *Jesus and the Servant: The Influence of the Servant Concept of Deutero-Isaiah in the New Testament* (London: SPCK, 1959), p. 145.

[59] Translation of R. H. Charles, *APOT*, altered.

[60] See Collins, *Apocalyptic Imagination*, pp. 147–150.

[61] Ibid., p. 150; see Hooker, *Jesus and the Servant*, p. 146.

the Son of man *is* said to suffer (see Mark 8:31; 9:12, 31; 10:33, 45; 14:21, 41). J. Schaberg points to the fact that each of the three predictions of the passion and resurrection of the Son of man is followed by teaching on the subject of discipleship (8:31–38; 9:31–37; 10:32–45), as though the destiny of the Son of man extended beyond himself to include those who followed him, and she plausibly sees this extension as a development of the corporate dimension of the figure in Daniel 7.[62]

Why does Mark extend the homology between the elect community and the Son of man to include not just the vindication but also the suffering of the latter, while Daniel and *1 Enoch* do not? Plainly this extension reflects the centrality of Jesus' suffering and death in Mark's story, but it also says something about the different way in which Mark's community experiences its life in the present. Whereas in Daniel and *1 Enoch* the Son of man figure makes up for the power and exaltation that the community lacks, in Mark the community shares in Jesus' sufferings and *at the same time* and *through* those sufferings shares in the apocalyptic power that erupts in the midst of the community. The members of Mark's community already receive in the present time new houses, family members, and fields—with persecutions (10:30). When they are hailed before magistrates and beaten in synagogues, the Holy Spirit speaks through their unpremeditated witness (13:11). Indeed, since the giving of the kingdom to "others" in 12:9 parallels the exaltation of the rejected stone in 12:10–11 (see chapter 6 above), there is a certain sense in which the community already participates in the life of the risen Christ who "sits at the right hand of Power" according to 14:62 (cf. 12:36). Mark's community, then, finds grounds for hope not only in the promise of its vindication in the near future but also in a mysterious empowerment that it experiences now in the very midst of tribulation.

CONCLUSIONS

Whether or not he is responsible for the allusions to Dan. 7:13 in Mark 14:62, Mark seems to be aware of their source and context. The context of judgment found in Daniel 7 is carried over to Mark 14:53–65, though with a characteristic Markan twist: the Son of man who, in Jewish appropriations of Daniel 7, will condemn the ungodly, is here condemned by them. Mark's use of Daniel 7 may reflect the prominence of that passage in the Jewish Revolt of A.D. 66–74, and Mark displays an awareness of the collective dimension of the Son of man figure in the original Danielic context and in *1 Enoch*. He goes beyond these sources, however, in linking the Son of man not only with the vindication experienced by the elect community but also with their suffering.

---

[62] Schaberg, "Daniel 7–12," pp. 215–217.

The Psalms of the Righteous Sufferer

ALLUSIONS AND CITATIONS

The most pervasive source for Old Testament allusions and citations in the Markan passion narrative is a group of psalms in which the speaker laments the persecution that he suffers from his enemies, protests his innocence, and calls upon God to deliver him.[63] These "Psalms of the Righteous Sufferer" correspond to H. Gunkel's form-critical category of "laments of the individual,"[64] but the designation "Psalms of the Righteous Sufferer" will be retained here as more descriptive of the actual content of the psalms.

Echoes of these psalms extend throughout Mark's passion narrative. The very first verse of that narrative, 14:1, speaks of a plot on the part of the chief priests and the scribes to arrest Jesus by cunning (ἐν δόλῳ) and to kill (ἀποκτεῖναι) him. Cunning, δόλος, is frequently mentioned in the Psalms of the Righteous Sufferer as a characteristic of that figure's persecutors,[65] and in Ps. 10:7–8 (LXX 9:28–29) a reference to the δόλος of the enemy is immediately followed by a description of his intention to kill (ἀποκτεῖναι) his innocent victim.

The next allusion comes in 14:18, at the Last Supper, where Jesus prophesies to his disciples, "Truly I say to you that one of you will betray me, the one eating with me" (alt.) (ὁ ἐσθίων μετ' ἐμοῦ). The phrase "the one eating with me" has often been identified as an allusion to Ps. 41:9:[66]

> For even my bosom friend (lit., the man of my peace), in whom I trusted,
> the one eating my bread (ὁ ἐσθίων ἄρτους μου), has lifted up his heel against
> me (alt.).

The very awkwardness of the belated phrase "the one eating with me" supports such an identification.[67] Were the narrative not intent on echoing Psalm 41, a smoother sentence, such as "one of you who are eating with me will betray me," could have been employed.[68]

---

[63] See H. C. Kee, who contrasts the preference for the psalms in Mark 14–15 to the situation in the rest of Mark 11–16, where references to the prophets are more frequent ("The Function of Scriptural Quotations and Allusions in Mark 11–16," in *Jesus und Paulus: Festschrift für Werner Georg Kümmel zum 70. Geburtstag*, ed. E. E. Ellis and E. Grässer [Göttingen: Vandenhoeck & Ruprecht, 1975], p. 183).

[64] See D. J. Moo, *The Old Testament in the Gospel Passion Narratives* (Sheffield: Almond Press, 1983), pp. 225–227.

[65] See Pss. 10:7 (LXX 9:28); 35:20; 36:3; 52:2; 55:11; cf. Gnilka, *Evangelium* 2:220. (Psalm versification in this chapter follows the English translations. For Psalms 11 and following, subtract one to obtain the chapter numbers in the Septuagint.)

[66] See, e.g., Moo, *Old Testament*, pp. 237–238, and the literature cited there.

[67] See Suhl, *Zitate*, p. 51.

[68] Matthew apparently felt the awkwardness of ὁ ἐσθίων μετ' ἐμοῦ, since he omitted it; Luke lacks the entire prophecy of betrayal.

This allusion is particularly important because of its linkage with 14:21, in which Jesus says that "the Son of man is going as it has been written concerning him" (alt.) (καθὼς γέγραπται περὶ αὐτοῦ). Although Mark introduces none of the allusions and citations to the Psalms of the Righteous Sufferer with a citation formula, at this point he comes close to doing so, for the juxtaposition of 14:18 and 14:21 implies that Jesus is going to his death as it has been written concerning him in the psalm that predicts his betrayal.[69]

Other allusions to the Psalms of the Righteous Sufferer are not difficult to find in Mark 14–16. In 14:34, for example, Jesus' confession that his soul is very sad (περίλυπος) recalls the refrain of Pss. 42:5, 11; 43:5, "Why are you so very sad (περίλυπος), O my soul?" (alt.).[70] In 14:41, Jesus' announcement that he is about to be *delivered* (παραδίδοται)[71] into the *hands* of sinners reflects Ps. 140:8, in which the psalmist pleads not to be delivered to a sinful man; v. 4 of the same psalm speaks of protection from the *hand* of a sinful man.[72] The language of 14:55, "they sought testimony against Jesus in order to put him to death" (alt.), is reminiscent of Ps. 37:32, "he seeks to put him to death" (alt.); see also Ps. 54:3.[73] In 14:57 the somewhat incongruous description of the rising up of false witnesses (rising up from where?) probably reflects Pss. 27:12 and 35:11,[74] and in 14:61 and 15:4–5 the silence of Jesus may reflect Ps. 38:13–15.[75]

The most concentrated collection of allusions to a psalm of the Righteous Sufferer comes in the account of Jesus' crucifixion in chapter 15. Here

[69] See Moo, *Old Testament*, p. 238. John 13:18 clearly cites Ps. 41:9 in a similar context, and uses a fulfillment formula ("in order that the scripture might be fulfilled" [alt.]) to do so.

[70] Moo notes the rarity of περίλυπος in the Septuagint and the New Testament and its absence from Philo, Josephus, and the papyri, so that "its presence here [in Mark 14:34], along with ψυχή, confirms the allusion" (*Old Testament*, p. 240).

[71] The verb παραδιδόναι appears ten times in Mark 14–16 (14:10–11, 18, 21, 41–42, 44; 15:1, 10, 15; cf. also the christological usages in 3:19; 9:31; 10:33). It also appears frequently in the Psalms of the Righteous Sufferer (27:12; 41:2; 74:19; 88:8; 140:8). In these psalms, however, the implied or actual subject is God, whereas in the Markan passion narrative, except in 14:41, the subject is Jesus' enemies. While the psalmic usages of παραδιδόναι, therefore, may have colored the other Markan passages, we cannot really speak of an allusion except in 14:41.

[72] Gnilka, in his commentary on 14:41 (*Evangelium* 2:263), mentions that in Pss. 36:11; 71:4; and 82:4 the pious person prays to be delivered from the hand of a sinner or of sinners, but he strangely fails to mention 140:8.

[73] See Gnilka, *Evangelium* 2:279.

[74] See Donahue, *Christ*, pp. 74–76. Moo regards this allusion only as "possible" (*Old Testament*, pp. 247–248), but the combination of the motif of false witness with the verb ἀνίστημι in both the psalm passages and in Mark, as well as the incongruity of the verb in the Markan passage, suggests that his conclusion is too weak. There may be a secondary echo of Danielic passages that speak of the arising of God's enemies; see above, p. 169.

[75] See also Ps. 39:9; Isa. 53:7; *T. Benj.* 5:4; see Gnilka, *Evangelium* 2:281. More doubtful, because of differences in vocabulary, are Gnilka's references to Ps. 27:12 in relation to Mark 15:1 and to Ps. 109:3 in relation to 15:3 (2:299, 301).

allusions to Psalm 22 play a central role in the narrative.[76] The dividing of
Jesus' garments in v. 24 (Ps. 22:18), the mockery and head shaking of v. 29
(Ps. 22:7),[77] and the cry of dereliction in v. 34 (Ps. 22:1) are the most obvious
examples. More distant echoes are the demand that Jesus save himself in
vv. 30–31 (Ps. 22:8)[78] and the motif of derision in v. 32 (Ps. 22:6),[79] but in
view of the pervasiveness of the influence of the psalm elsewhere in the
narrative allusions to it in vv. 30–32 seem likely.[80]

After these numerous allusions to Psalm 22, the bystander's action in giving Jesus vinegar to drink in 15:36 recalls Ps. 69:21,[81] and the perhaps
unhistorical detail of the women standing "at a distance" (μακρόθεν) from
Jesus in 15:40 probably echoes Ps. 38:11.[82]

The following chart of allusions to the Psalms of the Righteous Sufferer
in Mark's passion narrative may thus be compiled:[83]

Mark		*Psalms*
14:1	by cunning, to kill	10:7–8
14:18	the one eating with me	41:9
14:34	very sad	42:5, 11; 43:5
14:41	delivered to the hands of sinners	140:8
14:55	sought to put him to death	37:32
14:57	false witnesses rising up	27:12; 35:11

---

[76] See F. J. Matera (*The Kingship of Jesus: Composition and Theology in Mark 15*, SBLDS 66 [Chico, Calif.: Scholars Press, 1982], pp. 128–129), summarizing the works of C. D. Peddinghaus and J. Oswald.

[77] Moo thinks that the reference to passersby is probably due to the influence of Lam. 2:15 but that the evangelists were led to the latter passage because of its similarity to the primary Old Testament background, Ps. 22:6–8 (*Old Testament*, p. 258).

[78] Moo argues against a reference to Psalm 22 here, pointing out that Mark speaks of self-deliverance while the psalm speaks of divine deliverance (*Old Testament*, p. 259).

[79] Mark 15:32 speaks of the brigands who were crucified with Jesus reviling (ὠνείδιζον) him; Ps. 22:6 uses the cognate noun ὄνειδος (cf. Ps. 31:11; see Gnilka, *Evangelium* 2:321). Moo notes that the verb ὀνειδίζειν appears in Pss. 42:10 and 69:9, which are sources of testimonia, but he thinks the verb is too common to speak of an allusion, and he does not even mention Ps. 22:6 (*Old Testament*, p. 262).

[80] But an allusion to Ps. 22:15 in Mark 15:36, as suggested by Matera (*Kingship*, pp. 128–129), seems unlikely; the immediate background for the Markan verse is Ps. 69:21 (see below), and there is no mention of thirst in Mark.

[81] Moo, *Old Testament*, pp. 278–279.

[82] The allusiveness of this detail is supported by its incongruity in the Markan context: Why should the women stand at a distance from the crucified Jesus, rather than nearby as in John 19:25–26? See R. E. Brown, who argues for the historicity of the Johannine account and notes that the Synoptic picture has an orientation toward fulfilling the psalm verse (*The Gospel According to John*, AB 29, 29A, 2 vols. [Garden City, N.Y.: Doubleday & Co., 1966, 1970], 2:904).

[83] Compare the chart in Moo, *Old Testament*, pp. 285–286.

14:61; 15:4-5	silence before accusers	35:13-15
15:24	division of garments	22:18
15:29	mockery, head shaking	22:7
15:30-31	Save yourself!	22:8
15:32	reviling	22:6
15:34	cry of dereliction	22:1
15:36	gave him vinegar to drink	69:21
15:40	looking on at a distance	38:11

PRE-MARKAN TRADITION AND MARKAN REDACTION

Is Mark himself aware of these allusions? This question is rendered crucial by the evidence that Mark made use of a pre-Markan narrative of Jesus' passion.[84] Given this preexistent source, it would be theoretically conceivable that Mark took over the allusions from the source without being aware of their Old Testament basis or, if he was aware of it, without attaching much theological weight to it.

Indeed, most of the allusions to the Psalms of the Righteous Sufferer probably *were* already present in the pre-Markan passion narrative. Almost all of them are integral parts of the pericopes to which they belong, and two of them, the allusions to Pss. 41:9 and 22:18 (Mark 14:18; 15:24), have parallels in John in similar contexts (John 13:18; 19:23-25).[85] John 12:27, moreover, contains language similar to that of Ps. 42:6, a verse that follows the refrain of 42:5, which is alluded to in a similar context in Mark 14:34.[86] All of this suggests strongly that allusions to Psalms of the Righteous Sufferer

---

[84] Although there have been several recent challenges to the hypothesis of a pre-Markan passion narrative (see the summary in *The Interpretation of Mark*, ed. W. Telford, IRT 7 [Philadelphia: Fortress Press, 1985], pp. 13-14), it is still safe to say that it represents the critical consensus. For a particularly careful argument for its existence, see the sections by R. Scroggs in W. Kelber et al., "Reflections on the Question: Was There a Pre-Markan Passion Narrative?" in *Society of Biblical Literature 1971 Seminar Papers* (Chico, Calif.: Society of Biblical Literature), pp. 503-585. The attempt of Matera (*Kingship*, pp. 7-55) to prove that Mark himself is responsible for the linking of the originally independent pericopes now found in chapter 15 runs aground on the difficulty of imagining that some of these passages could ever have been told apart from a larger connected story of Jesus' crucifixion. For a survey of attempts to isolate the pre-Markan narrative, see M. L. Soards, "The Question of A Pre-Markan Passion Narrative," *Bible Bhashyam* 11 (1985), 144-169.

[85] The overlap between Mark 14:18 and John 13:18 in alluding to Ps. 41:9 vitiates the argument of Suhl (*Zitate*, pp. 51-52) that this allusion is Markan redaction.

[86] Moo notes this similarity, but he adds that Ps. 6:3-4 is a closer parallel to John 12:27 (*Old Testament*, pp. 241-242). But the use of language similar to that of Psalm 42 in a Gethsemane-like scene (see Brown, *John* 1:475) is still a remarkable parallel to Mark 14:34. This observation makes unlikely Suhl's suggestion that Mark himself has introduced 14:34 into its present context (*Zitate*, p. 132).

were part of the common narrative that was used by both Mark and John.[87] With the exception of 15:40, moreover, the allusions in Mark 15 are all identified by the vast majority of scholars as belonging to the pre-Markan passion narrative.[88] The consensus is not so overwhelming with regard to the allusions in Mark 14, but this is because there is controversy among scholars about the extent to which the pericopes in chapter 14 were part of the pre-Markan narrative. The traditional nature of the vast majority of them, however, is scarcely in question.

The allusions to the Psalms of the Righteous Sufferer, therefore, seem to be predominantly pre-Markan. They are not, however, exclusively so. In at least one case, the allusion to Ps. 10:7–8 in Mark 14:1, there exists strong evidence that Mark himself is responsible for the echo of the Old Testament text. J. Gnilka has argued that Mark 14:1 is a redactional verse, citing as Markan traits the united front of chief priests and scribes, the time notice, and several stylistic features.[89] Not all of these arguments are equally convincing,[90] and John does have a parallel for the basic action in Mark 14:1, the decision by Jesus' enemies to put him to death (John 11:47–52).[91] This parallel, however, lacks the echo of Ps. 10:7–8, so at least the crucial words in Mark 14:1 may reflect Markan editing. This possibility becomes a probability when two other verses, both of which are part of the Markan "framework" and therefore probably redactional, are compared with 14:1b:

> 11:18   καὶ ἐζήτουν πῶς αὐτὸν ἀπολέσωσιν
> and they sought how they might destroy him
>
> 12:12   καὶ ἐζήτουν αὐτὸν κρατῆσαι
> and they sought to arrest him
>
> 14:1   καὶ ἐζήτουν . . . πῶς αὐτὸν ἐν δόλῳ κρατήσαντες
> ἀποκτείνωσιν
> and they sought . . . how they might arrest him with cunning and kill him

The structural similarity demonstrates with a high degree of probability that the allusion to Ps. 10:7–8 is Mark's own doing and that therefore it

---

[87] The Johannine passion narrative seems to be literarily independent of those in the Synoptics; their similarities are probably due to their common use of a pre-Gospel passion source. See Brown, *John* 2:787–791; G. Schneider, "Das Problem einer vorkanonischen Passionserzählung," *BZ* 16 (1972), pp. 229–231; Lührmann, *Markusevangelium*, pp. 227–231.

[88] See the helpful charts in Soards, "Question," pp. 153–160.

[89] Gnilka, *Evangelium* 2:219. The stylistic features are the beginning of a new section with δέ ("and"; cf. 1:14; 7:24; 10:32), the use of μετά ("after") to indicate time (1:14; 9:2; 10:34; 13:24), and the words ἀποκτείνειν ("to kill") and κρατεῖν ("to arrest").

[90] Some scholars see time notices as evidence for a pre-Markan passion narrative (see, e.g., K. L. Schmidt, "Die literarische Eigenart der Leidensgeschichte Jesu," *Die christliche Welt* 32 [1918], 114–116), and 10:32 and 13:24 are probably traditional.

[91] See Lührmann, *Markusevangelium*, p. 227.

is not unreasonable to surmise that he would recognize many of the other allusions to "Righteous Sufferer" psalms and expect at least some of his readers to do likewise.

THE ESCHATOLOGICAL TRAJECTORY IN THE INTERPRETATION OF THE PSALMS OF THE RIGHTEOUS SUFFERER

Assuming that Mark and at least some of his readers would have recognized the allusions to the Psalms of the Righteous Sufferer in his passion narrative, the question remains how he and they would have interpreted these allusions.

In attempting to answer this question, it is relevant to observe that by the first century many of these psalms, and the motif of the Righteous Sufferer that arose from them, were being interpreted in an eschatological manner. Mark, as we shall see, follows this trajectory of eschatological interpretation of the Righteous Sufferer psalms.[92]

L. Ruppert has argued convincingly that the most direct history-of-religions background for the New Testament descriptions of Jesus' suffering is provided by transformations of the Righteous Sufferer motif that reflect an apocalyptic eschatology growing out of the experience of martyrdom. According to Ruppert, the basic picture in the Psalms of the Righteous Sufferer is of a person suffering *in spite of* his righteousness and calling for God to vindicate him by destroying his enemies *in this life*. In contrast, such apocalyptic sources as Wisd. Sol. 2:12–20; 5:1–7;[93] 4 Ezra, and 2 Apoc. Bar., as well as the New Testament, present the idea that the righteous one *must suffer on account of* his righteousness but that he will be *glorified at the eschaton*.[94] The New Testament picture, then, reflects an apocalyptic transformation of the Righteous Sufferer motif.

This analysis is confirmed by some of the interpretations of Righteous Sufferer psalms in postbiblical Judaism. Already, for example, the Septuagint translates the enigmatic heading of most of the Righteous Sufferer psalms, למנצח,[95] with the words εἰς τὸ τέλος, "to [or "for"] the end," a rendering that may indicate that these psalms were understood eschatologically by the

---

[92] On Mark's eschatological interpretation of the psalms in chapters 11–16, see Kee, "Function," in *Jesus und Paulus*, ed. Ellis and Grässer, p. 171; cf. chapter 3 above, pp. 59–62; chapter 6, pp. 114–115; chapter 7, pp. 132–137.

[93] According to L. Ruppert, these two passages are an apocalyptic Palestinian source that has been incorporated into Wisdom of Solomon (*Jesus als der leidende Gerechte? Der Weg Jesu im Lichte eines alt- und zwischentestamentlichen Motivs*, SB 59 [Stuttgart: Katholisches Bibelwerk, 1972], pp. 23–24).

[94] Ibid., pp. 42–43.

[95] All of the psalms alluded to by Mark (see the chart above, pp. 174–175) bear this inscription except Psalms 10, 27, and 35.

Septuagint translators.⁹⁶ This interpretation is supported by *b. Pesaḥ.* 117a,
which interprets למנצח eschatologically.⁹⁷

The Qumran literature, moreover, provides clear evidence of eschatological readings of the Righteous Sufferer psalms. For example, Psalm 37,
which, as we have seen, is alluded to in Mark 14:55, is interpreted in
4QpPs37 as speaking of the tribulation and subsequent glorification
experienced by the elect community in the end time (3:10–13).⁹⁸ The
Thanksgiving Hymns, too, presents numerous pictures of eschatological
tribulation, and sometimes this tribulation is described in language borrowed from the Psalms of the Righteous Sufferer. In 1QH 8:32, for example,
the hymnist cites Ps. 42:5 in his suffering, just as the Markan Jesus cites
it to refer to his agony in Gethsemane in Mark 14:34. 1QH 5:23–24,
moreover, affords a remarkable parallel to the use of Ps. 41:9 in Mark 14:18:

> And [all who a]te my bread lifted the heel against me. And all who joined
> my assembly spoke evil of me with a perverse tongue. And the men of
> my [counc]il rebelled and murmured round about.⁹⁹

Not only is the psalm's reference to a betrayer referred to a person within
the elect community, as in Mark 14:18–21, but the hymn goes on to imply
that this act of treachery is a result both of divine providence and of human
sinfulness.¹⁰⁰ The same combination of seemingly contradictory explana-
tions is found in Mark 14:21, where Judas's betrayal of Jesus is portrayed
both as an act that "has been written" and is therefore preordained and
as a deed whose terrible responsibility he himself will bear ("It would have
been better for that man if he had not been born").

Equally illuminating are the eschatological interpretations of Psalm 22
that are found in early Jewish texts. In 1QH 5:31, for example, Ps. 22:15
is cited. From the context, it is apparent that the sufferings described in

⁹⁶ L. C. L. Brenton translates εἰς τὸ τέλος consistently as "for the end" (*The Septuagint with Apocrypha: Greek and English* [Grand Rapids: Zondervan Publishing House, 1982; orig. 1851]); cf. K. Bornhäuser, *The Death and Resurrection of Jesus Christ* (Bangalore: C.L.S., 1958; orig. 1946), Excursus I, 1–5; and H. D. Preuss, "Die Psalmenüberschriften in Targum und Midrasch," ZAW 71 (1959), 45–46. For another interpretation, see P. R. Ackroyd, "נצח – εἰς τέλος," *ExpT* 80 (1968–1969), 126.
⁹⁷ ניצוח וניגון לעתיד לבא, "Niṣûaḥ and nîgûn [introduce psalms] relating to the future"; see Preuss, "Psalmenüberschriften," pp. 45–46.
⁹⁸ See Ruppert, *Jesus*, pp. 22, 27.
⁹⁹ See Moo, *Old Testament*, pp. 237, 242. Translation of 1QH 5:23–24 is from A. Dupont-Sommer, *The Essene Writings from Qumran*, trans. G. Vermes (Gloucester, Mass.: Peter Smith, 1973).
¹⁰⁰ 1QH 5:25–26: "But it is in order that my [wa]y might be exal[ted], and it is because of their sin that Thou hast hidden the fount of understanding and the secret of truth" (trans. Dupont-Sommer).

the psalm are being reinterpreted as the distresses of the end time.[101] Similarly, 4QPs^f begins with a citation of Ps. 22:14–17, followed by quotations from Psalms 107 and 109 and then by three apocryphal compositions: the Apostrophe to Zion (= 11QPs22), an Apocryphal Psalm, and the Apostrophe to Judah. The text as a whole is in its present form, according to H.-J. Fabry, an expansion of Ps. 22:14–17. All three apocryphal compositions present a vision of the eschatological consummation, and the sufferings described in Psalm 22 are viewed as the prelude to that consummation, the tribulations experienced by the community in the eschatological war.[102]

This military interpretation of the sufferings described in Psalm 22 reflects the end of the psalm, which speaks of Yahweh's dominion over the nations (Psalm 22:28). Such passages in the individual lament psalms are probably a throwback to the origin of the Righteous Sufferer motif in the Davidic king's complaints about the murderous attacks of pagan armies (see Psalm 18 = 2 Samuel 22). This motif is later "democratized" in the individual lament psalms, yet these psalms still retain passages such as Pss. 7:8 and 9:5 that reflect their origin in the tradition of the attack by the nations.[103]

The eschatological interpretation of Psalm 22 continues in later Jewish texts. The Targum on Psalm 22:31, for example, inserts a reference to the proclamation of Yahweh's might *to the final generation,* and the Targum on the preceding verse interprets it as a reference to the eschatological event of the resurrection of the dead. The resurrectional interpretation of vv. 30–31 is also assumed in many traditions preserved in the Midrash on Psalms, and Billerbeck summarizes the situation by saying that vv. 26–31 of the psalm are often taken in Targum and Midrash in an eschatological sense, although the person of the Messiah is never mentioned.[104]

It is fair to say, then, that Psalm 22 and other Psalms of the Righteous Sufferer are often interpreted in the postbiblical period as references to eschatological events, and we would present it as a working hypothesis that these psalms bring a similar eschatological context along with them in Mark.

---

[101] See H.-J. Steichele, *Der leidende Sohn Gottes: Eine Untersuchung einiger alttestamentlicher Motive in der Christologie des Markusevangeliums,* Biblische Untersuchungen 14 (Regensburg: Pustet, 1980), p. 246.
[102] See H.-J. Fabry, "Die Wirkungsgeschichte des Psalms 22," in *Beiträge zur Psalmenforschung: Psalm 2 und 22,* ed. J. Schreiner, FB 60 (Würzburg: Echter Verlag, 1988), p. 298. For the text, see J. Starcky, "Psaumes Apocryphes de la Grotte 4 de Qumrân," *RB* 73 (1966), 353–371. See the references to eschatological battle in the Apostrophe to Zion (lines 10–11) and the Apostrophe to Judah (lines 11–12).
[103] Ruppert, *Jesus,* pp. 17, 33–35.
[104] S-B 2:574.

THE LARGER CONTEXTS OF PSALM 22 AND MARK 15

The later, triumphal portion of Psalm 22 is not cited in the Markan passion narrative. How relevant is it, therefore, that Jewish texts interpret this portion eschatologically? This question brings up the larger issue of attention to context in Mark's citation of Old Testament texts.

In previous parts of this study, we have argued that Markan citations of verses from Old Testament texts often bring into view the larger contexts of those texts. We would make a similar claim for the citations of Psalm 22 in Mark 15. In so doing we are following the lead of H. Gese, who argues that not only the psalm's description of innocent suffering but also its promise of vindication are essential background for understanding the Gospel accounts of the crucifixion of Jesus.[105] Gese points out that the entire psalm is framed by references to the kingship of Yahweh (vv. 3, 28; the Septuagint translates v. 29a τοῦ κυρίου ἡ βασιλεία, "kingship belongs to the Lord"). He notes, moreover, that the psalm speaks of a proclamation to the ends of the earth (v. 27) and asserts that it hints at the resurrection of the dead (v. 29). Understood against this background, the psalm is used in the passion narratives not only to provide Old Testament background for Jesus' suffering but also to hint at a deliverance from death that is the revelation of the kingdom of God to all, including the Gentiles.

Some scholars have reacted with skepticism to Gese's thesis, complaining that the latter, triumphant part of Psalm 22 is never explicitly cited in the passion narratives, that it is not clear that the psalm really refers to the resurrection of the dead, and that Gese, in his concentration on the form and meaning of the original psalm, does not pay sufficient attention to the way in which biblical texts were interpreted in the first century.[106]

These objections, however, are not as telling as they might at first seem. We have seen in the preceding section that, no matter what it meant *in the original*, Psalm 22 was often interpreted *in later Judaism* as a description of eschatological events, including resurrection. We have also seen that in 1QH 5:31 and 4QPs^f the psalm's description of the suffering of the righteous is wedded closely to its hope for eschatological vindication in God's kingdom. This line of interpretation seems to have left its mark on New Testament passages independent of the passion narratives as well. F. Matera calls attention to Heb. 2:12–13, which weaves together Ps. 22:22

---

[105] H. Gese, "Psalm 22 und das Neue Testament: Der älteste Bericht vom Tode Jesu und die Entstehung des Herrenmahles," in *Vom Sinai zum Zion: Alttestamentliche Beiträge zur biblischen Theologie*, BETTA 64 (Munich: Chr. Kaiser Verlag, 1974), pp. 192–196.

[106] Steichele, *Leidende Sohn*, p. 256 n. 230; J. Reumann, "Psalm 22 at the Cross," *Int* 28 (1974), 47; D. Juel, *Messianic Exegesis: Christological Interpretation of the Old Testament in Early Christianity* (Philadelphia: Fortress Press, 1988), p. 100.

("I will declare your name to my brothers, in the midst of the assembly
I will hymn you" [alt.]) with Isa. 8:17–18 ("I will trust in him . . . I and the
children whom God has given me" [alt.]).[107] The missing link that binds
these Old Testament texts together seems to be that both of them, in their
contexts, speak of a God who hides his face from righteous sufferers. In
Hebrews, then, the psalm's triumphant declaration of eschatological victory
is implicitly linked with its description of suffering.

A similar unitary reading of Psalm 22 that weds the motif of suffering
to that of eschatological victory is reflected in 2 Tim. 4:17–18, a passage
that is dependent on the psalm to an extent not heretofore realized. Notice
the italicized segments in the following translation:[108]

> *The Lord stood by me* and *empowered me,* in order that through me *the
> message might be fully proclaimed* and *all the nations might hear,* and
> *I was delivered from the mouth of the lion.* And the Lord will deliver me
> from every evil work and *will save me for his heavenly kingdom. To him
> be the glory* for ever and ever!

The reference to deliverance from the lion's mouth is the most obvious allusion to Psalm 22, but it is only a part of a network of such allusions. The
chart below summarizes the links between the two passages:

Psalm 22

presence and empowerment of God	vv. 1, 11, 19, 24, 26
proclamation	vv. 22, 25, 30–31
the nations	v. 27
deliverance from lion's mouth	vv. 13, 21
trust that God will deliver	vv. 4–5, 8, 20–21, 31
God's kingdom	vv. 3, 28
praise of God	vv. 3, 22–23, 25

While most of these motifs can be found in other biblical texts, the *combination* of them here suggests that 2 Tim. 4:17–18 as a whole should be
viewed as a midrash on Psalm 22. Hebrews 2:12–13 and 2 Tim. 4:17–18,
then, continue the trajectory of Jewish interpretation of Psalm 22 that links
the sufferings described in the psalm with the eschatological revelation of
God's kingdom. A close look at Mark 15 reveals that a similar linkage is
made there. The clear echoes of Psalm 22 in Mark 15:24, 29, and 34 alternate with references to Jesus as the king of the Jews (vv. 18, 26, 32) and
with the royal title "Son of God" (v. 39). The citations of the psalm, then,
are interwoven with the theme of Jesus' kingship; the latter, in turn, is

---

[107] Matera, *Kingship,* pp. 130–131.

[108] My translation. In their commentary on the passage, M. Dibelius and H. Conzelmann
suggest only a possible allusion to Ps. 22:21 (*The Pastoral Epistles,* Hermeneia [Philadelphia:
Fortress Press, 1972; orig. 1955], p. 124 n. 17).

redactionally linked by Mark with the theme of the kingdom of God. In v. 43 we hear that Joseph of Arimathea was "one who was himself waiting for the kingdom of God." This relative clause is probably redactional, since it contains a typical Markan periphrasis and characterizes Joseph in a way similar to the description of the "good" scribe in 12:28–34 ("not far from/ waiting for the kingdom of God").[109] Mark uses this insertion to make a characteristically ironic point: Joseph should no longer be waiting, since the kingdom of God has now been revealed with the revelation of the kingship of the crucified Jesus.

We have seen, then, that Mark 15 links the sufferings of Jesus, which are described with language borrowed from Psalm 22, to the eschatological revelation of God's kingship, a theme that is also linked with the sufferings described in the psalm in early Jewish and Christian exegesis.[110] It is likely that these two links are related, that is, that Mark has introduced the theme of the kingdom of God because of the traditional exegesis of Psalm 22. Already 15:39 might have turned his attention to the latter part of the psalm, since Ps. 22:27 speaks in terms strikingly reminiscent of the picture of the Gentile centurion's acknowledgment of Jesus:

> All the ends of the earth shall remember and turn to the LORD, and all the families of the nations shall worship before him.

It would not be surprising if from reflection on Ps. 22:27 Mark passed to reflection on the very next verse, 22:28, which speaks of God's kingship, and introduced an allusion to it at an appropriate place in his own narrative, four verses later. Indeed, we may note in passing that the narrative from Mark 15:20b to the end of the Gospel follows the course of the psalm in many significant details:

	Psalm 22	*Mark*
Suffering	vv. 1–21	15:20b–37
Worship of Gentiles	v. 27	15:39
Kingdom of God	v. 28	15:43
Resurrection	v. 29	16:6
Proclamation to God's people	vv. 30–31	16:7

---

[109] See M. Ambrozic, *The Hidden Kingdom: A Redaction-Critical Study of the References to the Kingdom of God in Mark's Gospel*, CBQMS 2 (Washington, D.C.: Catholic Biblical Association, 1972), p. 242; I. Broer, *Die Urgemeinde und das Grab Jesu*, SANT (Munich: Kösel, 1972), pp. 160–161. The positive evaluation of the scribe is not present in the Matthean and Lukan parallels to Mark 12:28–34 (cf. Matt. 22:34–40 and Luke 10:25–28), and it is possible that it and the related reference to the kingdom of God represent Markan redaction.

[110] This analysis, of course, is light-years removed from the claim that Jesus himself had the triumphant end of the psalm in mind when he cited its first verse on the cross. For a critique of the latter view, see G. Rossé, *The Cry of Jesus on the Cross: A Biblical and Theological Study* (Mahwah, N.J.: Paulist Press, 1987), pp. 103–107.

ATTENTION TO CONTEXT IN OTHER MARKAN CITATIONS
OF THE PSALMS OF THE RIGHTEOUS SUFFERER?

Having seen that Mark's citation of verses from Psalm 22 brings into view
the larger context of that psalm, we are entitled to ask whether the same
may not be true of his citation of other psalms in the passion narrative. Of
course, none of the other psalms cited in the passion narrative is as pervasive as Psalm 22, so it would not be surprising if this psalm were a special
case in its possession of a large contextual penumbra. Nevertheless, three
possible instances of wider vision will be suggested.

1. The very first psalm alluded to in the passion narrative, Psalm 10 (Mark
14:1//Ps. 10:7–8), ends like Psalm 22 with a reference to God's kingship.[111]
It is possible, then, that Mark is deliberately bracketing his entire passion
narrative with echoes of biblical passages that deal with the kingdom of God.

2. The citation of Ps. 41:9 in Mark 14:18 is true to the wider context of
the psalm since it not only speaks of betrayal but also situates this betrayal
in the context of a *meal.*[112] The continuation of the psalm, moreover, fits
extremely well into the immediate Markan context and the larger flow of
Mark's story:

> But you, O LORD, be gracious to me, and raise me up (והקימני; καὶ
> ἀνάστησόν με), that I may requite them! By this I know that you are pleased
> with me, in that my enemy has not triumphed over me. But you have
> upheld me because of my integrity, and have set me in your presence
> forever (alt.).

The psalmist's confidence that God will not allow his enemies to triumph
over him and that he will enable him to requite them coheres well with
Jesus' statement in 14:21 that it would have been better for Judas had he
never been born. The psalmist's prayer that God "raise him up"[113] and place
him in his presence, similarly, is consonant with the larger Markan story,
in which Jesus' resurrection is viewed as his deliverance from the evil plots
of his enemies and his exaltation to God's right hand (cf. 8:31; 9:31; 10:33–34;
12:36; 14:62).

3. Psalm 69 is alluded to in Mark 15:36, where a bystander fills a sponge
with vinegar and offers it to the crucified Jesus (see Ps. 69:21). Two verses
later in the psalm we encounter the declaration, "Let their eyes be dark-
ened so that they cannot see" (Ps. 69:23), an imprecation that forms an ironic

---

[111] Ps. 10:16: "The Lord will reign for ever and ever" (alt.).

[112] See Ruppert, *Jesus,* p. 50.

[113] I am not suggesting that the original psalm has in view the idea of resurrection, only
that by Mark's time it would have been read in that way. On the early Christian reinterpretation of the Old Testament language of "raising up" to refer to Jesus' resurrection, see D. C.
Duling, "The Promises to David and Their Entrance into Christianity—Nailing Down a Likely
Hypothesis," *NTS* 68 (1973), pp. 55–77.

counterpoint to the subsequent statement of the Markan bystander, "*Let us see* (ἴδωμεν) if Elijah will come and take him down" (alt.). In the overall Markan context, the bystander's comment echoes the mockery of the chief priests four verses earlier, "Let the Christ, the King of Israel, descend now from the cross, *that we might see* (ἵνα ἴδωμεν) and believe" (15:32, alt.), as well as the judgment on the "outsiders" in 4:12, "that looking they might look and not see" (ἵνα βλέποντες βλέπωσιν καὶ μὴ ἴδωσιν; see also 8:18). The "seeing" spoken of in 15:36b, then, is really a form of blindness.[114] It would thus be perfectly consonant with Markan theology if the reference to Ps. 69:22 in Mark 15:36a were meant to include the psalm's later reference to a curse of blindness as well.

Jesus as Righteous Sufferer and the Markan Community

Apart from these contextual connections, one other aspect of the Psalms of the Righteous Sufferer is important for understanding their use in the Markan passion narrative. The figure of the Righteous Sufferer in the psalms is an individual, yet one who has communal dimensions.[115] As M. Hooker puts it in her discussion of "the familiar problem of the 'I' in the psalms":

> To the question "Who is this 'I'? Are the Psalms 'collective' or 'individual'?" the answer is probably that they are both; the individual's experience was bound up with that of the community, and even when the psalmist was being most intensely personal, his words remained true for others.[116]

The justice of this interpretation is shown by the large overlap of language and theme between the psalms of individual suffering and other psalms of communal lament;[117] we have already noted, for example, that the individual laments of Psalms 7 and 9 contain the anomalous motif of the judgment and defeat of the nations (Pss. 7:8; 9:5) and that Psalms 10 and 22, which are incorporated into Mark's passion narrative, end with the proclamation of God's kingship (Pss. 10:16; 22:28).

This communal dimension of the speaker in the Old Testament lament psalms is continued in some of the literature from Qumran, especially the *Hodayoth* (1QH), compositions which, as we have seen, belong on an exegetical trajectory that leads from the Old Testament motif of the

---

[114] See J. Marcus, *The Mystery of the Kingdom of God*, SBLDS 90 (Atlanta: Scholars Press, 1986), p. 147.

[115] See F. J. Leenhardt, who compares the "I" style in Rom. 7:7–25 (*L'Épître de St. Paul aux Romains*, CNT 6, 2nd ed. [Geneva: Labor et Fides, 1981; orig. 1957], p. 106).

[116] Hooker, *Jesus and the Servant*, p. 43.

[117] See the discussion in Gray, *Biblical Doctrine*, pp. 85–106.

Righteous Sufferer to its appropriation in the Markan passion narrative.[118] Ruppert thinks that the "Righteous Sufferer" motif found in the original *Hodayoth* of the Teacher of Righteousness is transferred to the members of his community in some later *Hodayoth;* he thus postulates a process similar to the democratization of the motif in the development of the Old Testament Psalter.[119] The result is that there are passages in the *Hodayoth* that clearly refer to the personal experiences of the founder (e.g., 1QH 2:8–9; 4:5–39), but these passages are placed in the context of the similar experiences of his followers (e.g., 1QH 2:20–30). H. Bardtke concludes that in the overall context of the *Hodayoth* the Teacher of Righteousness becomes the first in a series of people who have undergone the same experiences in the battle for the truth.[120] The "I" who speaks in the *Hodayoth* thus attains a certain measure of universality.[121]

This communal dimension also seems to be present in Mark's picture of Jesus as a Righteous Sufferer. He too is an inclusive figure and the first in a series of suffering but ultimately triumphant warriors in the apocalyptic battle. Jesus calls the disciples to be with him (3:14),[122] and he twice speaks of their suffering loss for his sake, even to the point of joining him in death (8:35; 10:29). It is also clear, however, that those who join themselves with Jesus will participate in his charismatic endowment by God (13:11). As Son of man, moreover, Jesus gives his life as a ransom for many (10:45) and pours out his blood for many (14:24).[123] All of these passages imply a suprapersonal dimension to Jesus' personality. We have already seen that there is a germ of the idea of collective personality in Zechariah 9–14 and that it is more fully developed in Daniel 7 and the later exegesis of that passage. We must now add that the figure of the Righteous Sufferer in the psalms and in later Jewish interpretation has a similar dimension. As we shall see below, the Deutero-Isaian Servant of the Lord is also a figure with a collective dimension, and he, too, seems to have left an imprint on the Markan passion narrative.

---

[118] See K. G. Kuhn, who speaks of the "I" style in 1QS 11:7–10 and the *Hodayoth* as a development of that found in the Old Testament psalms ("New Light on Temptation, Sin, and Flesh in the New Testament," in *The Scrolls and the New Testament,* ed. K. Stendahl [New York: Harper & Brothers, 1957; orig. 1952], pp. 102–103).

[119] See L. Ruppert, *Der leidende Gerechte: Eine motivgeschichtliche Untersuchung zum Alten Testament und zwischentestamentlichen Judentum,* FB 5 (Würzburg: Echter Verlag, 1972), pp. 123–131.

[120] H. Bardtke, "Considerations sur les cantiques de Qumran," *RB* 63 (1956), 232–233.

[121] See Leenhardt, *Romains,* p. 106 n. 4.

[122] See chapter 6 above, pp. 123–124.

[123] Of course, other history-of-religions backgrounds such as conceptions of atonement play an important role in explicating passages such as 10:45 and 14:24, and these two passages specifically reflect Isaiah 53, as we shall see below.

It might be urged against the collective interpretation of the citations
of the Righteous Sufferer psalms that the Markan passion narrative presents
Jesus as a character *sui generis,* one who dies a unique and solitary death,
abandoned by the Twelve in his hour of agony (14:32–42), forsaken by them
at his arrest (14:50), and only observed "from afar off" by the women at
his death (15:40). Yet, as we have already seen in our discussion of the Son
of man in Daniel, *1 Enoch,* and Mark, the fact that Jesus in some sense
stands over against the community of his disciples does not necessarily
negate his representative function. It is hard to imagine, moreover, that
readers familiar with the idiom of the Old Testament lament psalms, and
especially the members of Mark's suffering community, would have failed
to recognize in his application of those psalms to Jesus' passion an echo
of their own brutal experience.

CONCLUSIONS

Although Mark himself is not the source of most of the allusions to the
Psalms of the Righteous Sufferer in his account of Jesus' suffering and death,
he is aware of their scriptural basis. He is, moreover, the heir of an interpretive tradition that takes these psalms as prophecies of eschatological
tribulation and of the establishment of the kingdom of God, which includes
the resurrection of the dead. Jesus' suffering, death, and resurrection thus
become, in his interpretation, eschatological events prophesied in the scriptures. These scriptures speak of the suffering and vindication of an inclusive
figure who incorporates in his own person the experience of the people
of God. They are thus an appropriate palette from which to mix the pigments
for the Markan picture of Jesus, for the story of Jesus' martyrdom and
glorification is also the story of the persecuted but divinely empowered
Markan community that takes up its cross and follows him on the way.

The Deutero-Isaian Servant Songs

ALLUSIONS TO THE SERVANT SONGS

Closely related to the Psalms of the Righteous Sufferer is the picture
of Yahweh's Suffering Servant in Isa. 50:4–9 and 52:13–53:12. Indeed, L.
Ruppert describes the Isaian Servant as a prophetic adaptation of the
Righteous Sufferer motif.[124] Although this adaptation has some unique
features that justify separate treatment, it is important to remember its
genetic closeness to the psalms we have just investigated, especially since,
as we shall see, Mark interweaves allusions to the two sets of scriptures.

---

[124] See Ruppert, *Jesus,* pp. 19–20.

Isaiah 50:4–9 and 52:13–53:12 are the third and fourth of the Servant Songs in Deutero-Isaiah, which also include Isa. 42:1–4 and 49:1–6.[125] The Servant Songs, and especially Isaiah 53, are extensively cited in later Christian "passion apologetic," and C. Maurer claims that they already play a decisive role in the Markan passion narrative.[126]

The most obvious instance of an allusion is in the "cup word" of Mark 14:24. Although, as we have seen, the term "my blood of the covenant" at the beginning of the saying probably reflects Zech. 9:11, its completion, "which is poured out on behalf of many" (alt.), seems to have been influenced by the Hebrew text of Isa. 53:12, where we read that the Lord's servant "poured out his soul to death" and "bore the sin of many."[127] The combination of the motifs of "pouring out" and "the many," together with the nuance of vicariousness expressed by the word ὑπέρ ("on behalf of"), secures the link with Isa. 53:12.[128] An allusion to Isa. 53:12 here is further supported by the probable presence of an allusion to it in Mark 10:45, which like 14:24 speaks of Jesus dying for "many."[129]

It is also probable that some of the details in the accounts of Jesus' trial before the Sanhedrin and Pilate have been influenced by the Isaian Servant Songs. Jesus' silence before his accusers in 14:61 and 15:5, for example, is similar to that of the Servant in Isa. 53:7,[130] though we have seen above that it is also similar to the behavior of the sufferer in Ps. 38:13–15. Two of the elements in the torture of 14:65, the spitting and the slapping, probably echo Isa. 50:6.[131] In 15:5, the amazement (θαυμάζειν) at Jesus' silencing

---

[125] On the legitimacy of treating these passages as a recognizable unit within Deutero-Isaiah, see France, *Jesus and the Old Testament*, pp. 110–111 n. 102; and Moo, *Old Testament*, pp. 79–80; contra Hooker, *Jesus and the Servant*, pp. 156–158.

[126] C. Maurer, "Knecht Gottes und Sohn Gottes im Passionsbericht des Markusevangeliums," *ZTK* 50 (1953), 1–38. The phrase "passion apologetic" is borrowed from B. Lindars, *New Testament Apologetic: The Doctrinal Significance of the Old Testament Quotations* (Philadelphia: Westminster Press, 1961), pp. 75–137; see, e.g., Acts 8:32–33; 1 Peter 2:22–25; *1 Clement* 16:3–14; *Barn.* 5:2; Justin, *Apology* 50; *Dialogue* 13, 43, 63, 97, 108, 111, 114; Origen, *Celsus* 1.54, 6.75; Cyprian, *Treatises* 13; Lactantius, *Institutes* 16.

[127] See Maurer, "Knecht Gottes," p. 18; and Moo, *Old Testament*, pp. 130–132. The Markan phrasing is dependent on the Masoretic Text rather than the Septuagint, which has "he was delivered to death" instead of "he poured out his soul to death."

[128] Contra Suhl, who denies a link with Isaiah 53 and instead advances the unlikely hypothesis that the background to the "cup word" lies in a Gnostic conception (*Zitate*, pp. 114–120).

[129] With Moo, *Old Testament*, pp. 122–126, 132 n. 1; contra Suhl, who asserts unconvincingly that Mark would not have compared 10:45 with 14:24 (*Zitate*, pp. 118–119). Suhl also argues that the motifs of "the many" and "ransom" are not restricted to Isaiah 53, but he fails to note that their combination *is* peculiar to that passage and to Mark 10:45.

[130] See Maurer, "Knecht Gottes," p. 9; Moo, *Old Testament*, pp. 148–151.

[131] Contra Suhl, *Zitate*, p. 58; with Moo, who points out that ῥάπισμα ("slap") occurs only in Isa. 50:6 in the Septuagint and only in contexts related to the mockery of Christ in the

of Pilate, who is both a ruler and a Gentile, verbally echoes the Septuagint of Isa. 52:15, "Thus many nations shall wonder (θαυμάσονται) at him, and kings shall shut their mouths" (alt.).¹³² The other Gentile who plays a role in the passion narrative, the centurion, also expresses awe at the sight of the crucified Jesus (15:39), and this too may echo Isa. 52:15. The general plot of the Barabbas episode — a criminal is saved, while an innocent man is handed over to be murdered — as well as the prominence of the verb παρα-διδόναι ("to hand over," Mark 15:10, 15) may mirror Isa. 53:6, 12.¹³³

The verb παραδιδόναι, however, occurs not only in the Barabbas episode but throughout the passion narrative (14:10–11, 18, 21, 41–42, 44; 15:1, 10, 15). It also features prominently in the foreshadowing of Judas's betrayal in 3:19 and in two of the three passion predictions (9:31; 10:33 [twice]).¹³⁴ As we have noted above, some of these passages (14:18, 21, 41) have background in the Psalms of the Righteous Sufferer, in which the verb παραδιδό-ναι is also prominent. But the combination in Mark 10:33–34 of παραδιδόναι in the passive voice with language recalling Isa. 50:6 (spitting, scourging) supports an allusion to the Isaian Servant Songs in that passage,¹³⁵ and it is even possible that the reference to Jesus' resurrection there would have recalled to biblically literate readers the exaltation of the Servant in Isa. 52:13. Generalizing from the case of 10:33–34, we may cautiously assert that the use of παραδιδόναι elsewhere in Mark is probably intended to awaken echoes of Isaiah 53.¹³⁶

The allusions to the Deutero-Isaian Servant Songs in the Markan passion narrative may be charted as follows:¹³⁷

New Testament, and that ἐμπτύειν ("to spit") and its cognates occur only three times in the Septuagint and only in the New Testament in predictions or descriptions of Jesus' mockery (*Old Testament*, pp. 88, 139).

¹³² See Moo, who notes that the Masoretic Text differs here (*Old Testament*, p. 148 n. 2).

¹³³ See Gnilka, *Evangelium* 2:303.

¹³⁴ Schaberg thinks that the verb παραδιδόναι in the Synoptic passion predictions is drawn from Dan. 7:25 ("Daniel 7–12," p. 210). This suggestion is unconvincing, however, since the subject of the passive verb in Daniel is the evil "horn," to whom power will be given (παραδοθήσεται) for a limited time. Similarly dubious is Schaberg's suggestion that the background of "after three days" in the passion predictions lies in the Danielic reference to "a time, two times, and half a time."

¹³⁵ See Moo, *Old Testament*, pp. 88–89, 92–96. The word used for scourging in 10:34, μαστιγοῦν, is a cognate of the noun used for scourges, μαστίγας, in Isa. 50:6. Mark uses a different verb for scourging, φραγελλοῦν, in 15:15. The choice of words in 10:34, therefore, seems to echo Isa. 50:6 deliberately.

¹³⁶ We would feel better about this conclusion if the word were combined with other language drawn from Isaiah 53, which is not the case in any of the Markan texts.

¹³⁷ Maurer suggests many other links between the Markan passion narrative and the Deutero-Isaian Servant Songs, but none of them is impressive. Mark 14:21 is better explained as an allusion to Ps. 41:9, which is referred to in 14:18, than as an allusion to Isa. 53:12 (contra Maurer, "Knecht Gottes," p. 9; see above, pp. 172–173). The arrest of Jesus as a λῃστής, a brigand,

Mark		Isaiah
14:10–11, 18, 21,	handing over	53:6, 12
41–42, 44; 15:1, 10, 15		
14:24	blood poured out for many	53:12
14:61; 15:5	silence before accusers	53:7
14:65	spitting, slapping	50:6
15:5, 39	amazement of nations and kings	52:15
15:6–15	criminal saved, innocent man	53:6, 12
	delivered to murder	

These allusions to the Servant Songs seem to be predominantly traditional. Only two of the passages, 14:10–11 and 15:10, show clear signs of Markan redaction,[138] and in these passages the only link with the Servant Songs is the rather tenuous one of the word παραδιδόναι ("to hand over"). All the rest of the allusions appear to be integral parts of the traditional pericopes to which they belong. The Suffering Servant typology of the Markan passion narrative, then, is probably an inheritance from pre-Markan tradition.

Is it possible, then, that Mark has simply taken over this typology from tradition without attaching much importance to it, perhaps without even recognizing it? This seems doubtful. As we have seen, Mark 10:33–34 contains apparent echoes of Isa. 50:6 (scourging, spitting) and of the παραδιδόναι language that we have argued reflects Isa. 53:6, 12. This passage, however, is generally recognized as a redactional creation because of its striking linguistic contacts with the passion narrative itself.[139] It is noteworthy, moreover, that while both Mark 10:34 and 14:65 allude to Isa. 50:6 when they speak of spitting, 10:34 adds a reference to scourging while 14:65 adds a reference to slapping—both elements that are found in Isa. 50:6 LXX. The relation between the three verses is illustrated in the following chart:

---

in 14:48–49 reflects neither the Masoretic Text nor the Septuagint of Isa. 53:12 (contra Maurer, pp. 8–9). If an allusion to the Isaian servant by way of Wisd. Sol. 2:13–18 were intended in Mark 14:61, then παῖς ("servant") rather than υἱός ("son") would have been used (contra Maurer, pp. 24–28; with Ruppert, *Jesus*, pp. 53–54; Moo, *Old Testament*, pp. 156–158). An echo of Isa. 53:9 is present in Matt. 27:57 but not in Mark 15:43–46, where Joseph of Arimathea is described as a respected member of the council rather than as a rich man (contra Maurer, p. 9). In general, A. Suhl's methodological criticism of Maurer (*Zitate*, p. 60) is forceful: the influence of Old Testament texts on Mark can only be assumed when the correspondence between them is not only material but also linguistic, and many of Maurer's examples fail this test.

138 See Gnilka, *Evangelium* 2:228–229, 297–298.
139 See Taylor, *Mark*, pp. 436–438; Gnilka, *Evangelium* 2:95–96; Lührmann, *Markusevangelium*, p. 178. Mark 10:33–34 is much fuller than the two previous passion predictions (8:31; 9:31), which probably enshrine pre-Markan tradition, and the correspondence in vocabulary with the passion narrative is much closer. Gnilka (2:96 n. 3) lists κατακρίνειν ("to condemn," 14:64); ἐμπαίζειν ("to mock," 15:20, 31); ἐμπτύειν ("to spit on," 14:65; 15:19).

Isaiah 50:6 LXX	*Mark 10:34*	*Mark 14:65*
scourging	scourging	
slapping		slapping
spitting	spitting	spitting

In combination with each other, therefore, the two Markan passages contain the three essential elements of Isa. 50:6. The possibility thus presents itself that Mark formulated 10:34 in such a way as to supply the element missing from 14:65, scourging. It seems likely, then, that he recognizes Suffering Servant typology when he sees it and expects his readers to do the same.

THE SERVANT SONGS IN THE OLD TESTAMENT AND IN POSTBIBLICAL JUDAISM

But what does this typology mean to Mark? In attempting to answer this question, it is again helpful to look at the original context of the passages in question and at Jewish exegesis of them. We will find that, as was the case with Daniel 7 and the Psalms of the Righteous Sufferer, these passages were often interpreted eschatologically in postbiblical Judaism and seen to have communal dimensions.

As we have seen, the suffering dimension of the Servant's "biography" probably reflects the influence of the Psalms of the Righteous Sufferer. Other features of the Servant figure, however, seem to represent a democratization and transformation of the figure of the king as holy warrior that is presented in some of the Royal Psalms.[140] Like the king in Psalms 2 and 110, the Deutero-Isaian Servant triumphs over the hostile nations through the power of Yahweh. He wins this victory, however, not by defeating the nations in battle but by establishing justice among them (Isa. 42:1–4), becoming a light to them (Isa. 49:6), and discomfiting them through his suffering on their behalf (Isa. 52:13–53:12).[141] The figure of the Servant seems to oscillate between an individual reference and a collective one,[142] and

---

140 These two backgrounds are related, since as we have seen the Psalms of the Righteous Sufferer probably developed out of the Royal Psalms. We may schematize some of the Old Testament background of Mark's picture of Jesus' suffering as follows:

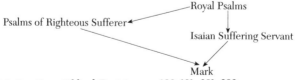

141 See Gray, *Biblical Doctrine,* pp. 180–181, 281–293.
142 See C. H. Dodd, *According to the Scriptures: The Sub-structure of New Testament Theology* (London: Nisbet, 1952), pp. 118–119. J. Jeremias notes that, aside from three verses in which

the Servant has a universal task that is conceived of eschatologically.[143] Both of the latter features unfold further in the postbiblical interpretation of the Servant figure.

As J. Jeremias points out, for example, the Septuagint extends to other passages the collective understanding of the Isaian Servant already offered by some passages in the Masoretic Text.[144] This process continues in the Wisdom of Solomon, which depicts the righteous man's fate along the lines of Isa. 52:13–53:12.[145] According to L. Ruppert, Wisd. Sol. 2:12–20 and 5:1–7 reflect a Palestinian source that actualized the Isaian passage to speak of the martyrdom of a particular individual figure. The author of Wisdom, however, has given this figure a collective reference, transforming the source's account of a suffering individual into an account of the suffering of righteous *people* in general.[146]

Contrary to Jeremias, however, this collective interpretation of the Isaian Servant is not limited to the productions of diaspora Judaism.[147] It occurs, for example, in two passages from the Qumran literature:

[The twelve men and three priests in the Council of the Community] shall *expiate iniquity by upholding the righteous cause* and *bearing the anguish* of the refiner's furnace. . . . [They are] *true witnesses* in judgment, *the elect ones of God's favor, to make propitiation* for the land and to requite the wicked with their recompense. . . . They will be *objects of God's favor,* so as *to make propitiation* for the land and to execute judgment upon wickedness, that perversity may be no more. (1QS 8:3–7, 10)

This is the Rule for the whole congregation of Israel *in the latter days.* . . . [The members of the community] are the men of God's counsel who kept

---

historical personages are referred to as "my servant" by God, the singular "servant of God" occurs in Isaiah only in chapters 41–53, and here nineteen times: 41:8–9; 42:1, 19 (twice); 43:10; 44:1, 2, 21 (twice), 26; 45:4; 48:20; 49:3, 5, 6; 50:10; 52:13; 53:11. Of these he lists nine as having a collective referent: 41:8–9; 44:1, 2, 21 (twice); 45:4; 48:20; 49:3 ("παῖς θεοῦ," *TDNT* 5:682–684); cf. Moo, *Old Testament,* p. 81.
[143] The mission of the Servant is to establish justice in the whole earth (Isa. 42:4) and to extend Yahweh's salvation to the ends of the earth (49:6).
[144] Jeremias, "παῖς θεοῦ," pp. 683–684, listing 42:1, 19; 44:26; 48:20.
[145] Jeremias ("παῖς θεοῦ," p. 684) lists the following contacts between the two passages:

Wisdom of Solomon	Isaiah
2:13	52:13; 53:11
2:19–20	53:7–8
4:18	53:3
4:20; 5:3	53:2–4
5:5 (κλῆρος)	53:12 (κληρονομήσει)
5:6–7	53:6

[146] Ruppert, *Jesus,* pp. 23–24.
[147] Jeremias, "παῖς θεοῦ," pp. 683–684.

His covenant in the midst of wickedness, so as *to make propiti[ation* for
the lan]d. (1QSa 1:1–3)[148]

In these passages the reference to the community as God's witnesses recalls
Isa. 43:10, 12 ("you are my witnesses"), and the description of them as the
elect ones of God's favor recalls Isa. 42:1 ("my elect one in whom my soul
delights" [alt.]). The references to expiating iniquity by upholding the
righteous cause, making propitiation, and bearing anguish reflect the ideas
if not the language of Isaiah 53.[149] In a manner very similar to Mark
10:33–34, then, these passages conflate central concepts from Isaiah 53
with language drawn from other Deutero-Isaian passages that mention the
"Servant of the Lord" (cf. Isa. 42:1; 43:10).[150] They do so, moreover, in a
context that makes clear the setting in "the latter days" and the communal
interpretation of the Isaian Servant.[151] The communal interpretation is
attested also by the Targum, which extends the collective reference of Isa.
49:3 to 49:5–6. Origen, furthermore, relates that he disputed with Jews who
interpreted Isaiah 53 to refer collectively "to the people, understood as a
single person, which had been dispersed and tormented" (*Celsus* 1.55), and
these disputations probably took place in the Palestinian city of Caesarea.[152]

As for the eschatological interpretation of the Servant Songs, it is attested
in *Targum Jonathan* and in certain rabbinic traditions which interpret the
Servant messianically, although other rabbinic traditions refer the Servant
passages to the prophets (including Isaiah himself), the righteous, and the
scribes, without an eschatological reference.[153] As we have seen above,
however, the antiquity of the eschatological interpretation is confirmed by
the Qumran evidence. Additional support for it comes from the Son of man
figure in the Similitudes of Enoch. The latter is an eschatological Messiah
whose description is at least partly shaped by the Deutero-Isaian Servant
passages, although he is not portrayed as suffering.[154] Indeed, there is no

---

[148] Translation altered from F. F. Bruce, *Biblical Exegesis in the Qumran Texts*, Exegetica
3 (The Hague: Uitgeverij van Keulen, 1959), pp. 50–58.

[149] M. Black, "Servant of the Lord and Son of Man," *SJT* 6 (1953), 7–8; cf. Bruce, *Biblical
Exegesis*, p. 53.

[150] This is further evidence for the discreteness of the "Servant" passages in Deutero-Isaiah;
cf. above, n. 125.

[151] Contra Jeremias, whose denial of the communal dimension displays an uncharacteristic
exegetical finickiness and reflects his desire to force the evidence into a neat schema: collective interpretations in the Diaspora, individual interpretations in Palestine ("παῖς θεοῦ,"
pp. 682–685).

[152] The disputations are mentioned by Jeremias ("παῖς θεοῦ," p. 684); on their setting in
Caesarea, see L. Levine, *Caesarea under Roman Rule*, SJLA 7 (Leiden: E. J. Brill, 1975), pp. 83,
113.

[153] See Jeremias, "παῖς θεοῦ," pp. 684–700.

[154] See Jeremias, "παῖς θεοῦ," pp. 687–688; Hooker, *Jesus and the Servant*, p. 54.

conclusive evidence that the Messiah was interpreted as the *Suffering Servant* of the Lord anywhere in pre-Christian Judaism.[155]

Later Jewish interpreters of the Servant Songs, then, often preserve the eschatological and communal dimensions of the original.

MARK'S USE OF THE SUFFERING SERVANT MOTIF

Mark's appropriation of the Suffering Servant motif picks up some of the lines of Jewish exegesis just sketched. Like the death of the Servant, the death of Jesus is presented as an eschatological event. For example, the references in 14:25 to "that day" and the kingdom of God place the "cup word" in 14:24, with its allusion to Isa. 53:12, in an eschatological context. The death scene itself, moreover, is accompanied by eschatological indications and portents: the three-hour scheme in 15:25, 33, and 34; the darkening of "the whole earth" in 15:33; and the ripping of the Temple veil in 15:38.[156]

The corporate dimensions of the Suffering Servant in Jewish exegesis also seem to be reflected in the Markan narrative. As we have seen in our section on Daniel 7, the way in which the Markan passion predictions are followed by instruction on discipleship suggests that the Suffering Son of man is a figure who in some way includes the Markan community. In that section we noted that part of the background for this figure lies in Daniel 7, but we have seen in the present section that he also has strong roots in Isaiah's Suffering Servant passages.

We have also remarked in this section that the Markan use of the verb παραδιδόναι ("to hand over") in the passion predictions and the passion narrative seems to reflect Isa. 53:6, 12. The verb παραδιδόναι, however, also features prominently in the reference to John the Baptist's arrest in 1:14 and in the prophecies of the disciples' betrayal in 13:9, 11–12. As we have already twice noted, on Mark's time line first John preaches and is delivered up (1:7, 14); then Jesus preaches and is delivered up (1:14; 9:31; 10:33); and finally the disciples preach and are delivered up (13:9–13).[157] Jesus' forerunner and his disciples, then, participate in his fate of "being delivered up" (παραδοθῆναι), and this inclusion in his destiny

---

[155] Contra Jeremias, "παῖς θεοῦ," pp. 684–700; with Hooker, *Jesus and the Servant*, pp. 53–58; Moo, *Old Testament*, pp. 82–86.

[156] To the three-hour scheme compare the eschatological hour scheme in 13:32, 35 and 4 Ezra 6:23–24; to the darkening of the earth compare Amos 8:9; to the ripping of the Temple veil compare the prophecy of eschatological Temple destruction in 13:1–3, 14; see R. H. Lightfoot, *The Gospel Message of St. Mark* (Oxford: Clarendon Press, 1950), pp. 48–59; J. Schreiber, *Theologie des Vertrauens: Eine redaktionsgeschichtliche Untersuchung des Markusevangeliums* (Hamburg: Furche, 1967), pp. 33–40; Gnilka, *Evangelium* 2:317.

[157] See chapter 2 above, p. 41; and chapter 5, p. 109.

is consistent with the corporate dimensions of the Isaian Servant, whose soul is "delivered up (παρεδόθη) to death" (Isa. 53:12 LXX).

The Saving Significance of Jesus' Death

The foregoing analysis of the influence of the Isaian Servant Songs on the Markan passion narrative diverges conspicuously from the opinion of H. C. Kee, who has written:

> No explanation is offered of the means by which suffering accomplishes redemption; all that is asserted is its divine necessity as recorded in the scriptures (9:13; 14:21; 14:49). . . . There are no sure references to Isaiah 53 and none of the distinctive language of the Suffering Servant is evident. Rather, the closest analogy to the understanding of suffering implicit in the Markan passion narrative is in the canonical psalms referred to and in the Hodayoth. . . . There is no explicit doctrine of atonement in the Hodayoth, nor is there any in the Markan passion narrative. In both cases, suffering is viewed as an inevitable, divinely ordained, and therefore necessary stage on the way to vindication of the elect and fulfillment of the divine redemptive plan.[158]

It should be clear by now that the Markan text poses serious problems for Kee's assertions. The Psalms of the Righteous Sufferer and their imitations in the Qumran *Hodayoth* should not be played off against the Isaian Servant passages; both are part of the background for Mark's narrative. Although the allusions to the Deutero-Isaian Servant Songs in the Markan passion narrative are not as pervasive as the allusions to the Psalms of the Righteous Sufferer, we have seen that they *are* present and that Mark and at least some of his readers would probably have recognized them. A comparison of the charts on pp. 174–175 and 189 reveals that the Markan passion narrative interweaves allusions to the Righteous Sufferer from the psalms and the Suffering Servant from Isaiah in chapters 14–15; indeed, it is probably a mistake to think of them as two totally distinct figures in Mark's mind.

There is one important feature that the Isaian Servant Songs add to the picture of the Righteous Sufferer in the Psalms. As the quotation from Kee highlights, the psalms present a sequential movement: *first* suffering at the hands of one's enemies, *then* victory over them through the power of God. Although this sequence is not totally absent from Isa. 52:13–53:12 (see, e.g., 52:13; 53:10–12), it is mixed in with the idea that *already in his suffering* the Servant accomplishes a salvific purpose and thus wins an eschatological victory. As we have noted, this idea is a striking modification of the psalmic pattern of divine victory through defeat of the nations; in the Isaian passage

---
[158] Kee, "Function," in *Jesus und Paulus*, ed. Ellis and Grässer, pp. 182–183.

the Servant triumphs by dying *on behalf of* the Gentiles as well as his own
people.

This seems to be Mark's idea also. Contrary to Kee, it is not merely the
case that the Markan Jesus' suffering is a *necessary stage on the way to*
apocalyptic vindication; rather, in a certain sense Jesus' death already *is*
an apocalyptic victory over the oppressive cosmic power of sin. We have
seen that, contrary to Kee, passages such as Mark 10:45 and 14:24 imply
the atoning value of Jesus' death through allusions to Isaiah 53. This accent
on the saving power of Jesus' death is consonant with a general Markan
emphasis visible in the apocalyptic signs that accompany the crucifixion,
in the centurion's confession at the moment of Jesus' death, and in the
omission of a specific narrative of resurrection appearances. Resurrection
appearances are certainly *implied* by 14:28 and 16:7, and in Mark's overall
context as in Isa. 52:13–53:12 the salvific power of the death is confirmed
by exaltation/resurrection. But in both cases the emphasis falls proportionally
more on the death than is true in other streams of tradition.[159]

We have argued in the preceding section that the Suffering Servant figure
in Mark, as in Deutero-Isaiah itself and in some Jewish exegesis, has collective dimensions. The present argument for the saving significance of the
Servant's death therefore raises the question whether Mark and his community would have seen their own suffering, like that of Jesus, as salvific.
Does Mark's community, like the community of Qumran, see itself as "making propitiation for the land" by "upholding the righteous cause and bearing
anguish"? Would its members agree with the author of Colossians that they
were completing what was lacking in the afflictions of Christ for the sake
of his body, the church (Col. 1:24; cf. 2 Cor. 1:6)?

Although Mark's Gospel provides no unequivocal indication that they
would, Mark 8:34 does speak of taking up one's cross and following Jesus,
thus implying a participation in his sufferings. Mark 13:9–13, moreover, portrays the persecution and suffering experienced by the community as the
arena in which its proclamation of the gospel manifests the power of God.
If, as seems likely, the martyr church's proclamation of the gospel leads
some of its hearers to cast in their lot with Jesus and thus to "save their
lives" (see 8:35–38), then we may say that, indirectly, Mark's community
is giving its life as a ransom for many (see 10:45) and pouring out its blood
for their sake (see 14:24). We should emphasize, however, that if indeed
the idea of the vicarious suffering of the community is present in Mark,
that suffering is only efficacious because of its linkage with the sufferings
of Jesus, because it is a suffering "for his sake and the gospel's" (see
again 8:34–35).

---

[159] See A. Lindemann, "Die Osterbotschaft des Markus: Zur theologischen Interpretation
von Mark 16.1–8," *NTS* 26 (1980), 298–317.

CONCLUSIONS

Allusions to the Deutero-Isaian Servant Songs are present in the Markan passion narrative and elsewhere in the Gospel, and these allusions bring with them eschatological and collective nuances that relate the Markan Jesus to the Suffering Servant motif in Deutero-Isaiah and in early Judaism. Mark and at least some of his readers, moreover, would probably have recognized these allusions. This awareness of the Isaian context is what might be expected in a Gospel that begins by presenting its entire story as the fulfillment of the prophecy of holy war victory announced by the prophet Isaiah (1:1–3; cf. Isa. 40:3). For Mark, however, as already in a way for Deutero-Isaiah, God's apocalyptic invasion of the earth is seen above all in the suffering of his righteous servant, by whose stripes his people are healed and at whose tortured countenance the raging of nations is shocked into silence (see Isa. 53:5; 52:14–15).[160]

Summary: The Old Testament in the Passion Narrative and the Markan Community

The various elements of the Old Testament background to the Markan passion narrative examined in this chapter—Zechariah 9–14, Daniel 7, the Psalms of the Righteous Sufferer, and the Deutero-Isaian Servant Songs—reinforce and complement one another in filling out Mark's picture of Jesus. In all four cases Mark's use of the Old Testament passages reflects the Jewish exegesis of the time. All four portray a figure whose fate is set in an eschatological context and has a collective dimension. All four share a pattern of suffering and vindication.

Each element, however, also adds its own particular hue to the Markan canvas. Zechariah 9–14 provides Old Testament background for the site of an important part of the drama, the Mount of Olives, and for the prophecy of the restoration of the disciples. Daniel 7 speaks of Jesus' coming role as judge at the parousia and hints that the scene in Mark 14, in which the Jewish authorities presume to judge him, is tremendously ironic—*he* will soon judge *them*. The Psalms of the Righteous Sufferer supply graphic details of Jesus' suffering and death, down to the division of his garments, his words on the cross, and the vinegar he is offered in his last moments. The Isaian Servant Songs suggest that this suffering is not just the prelude to God's eschatological victory but already in a sense *is* that victory.

---

[160] See W. H. Brownlee, who links the Qumran allusions to the Isaian Servant of the Lord with the community's retreat to the wilderness based on Isa. 40:3 ("The Servant of the Lord in the Qumran Scrolls," *BASOR* 135 [1954], 33).

Another element shared by the four Old Testament backgrounds we have highlighted is their linkage with the concept of the kingdom of God. We have noted that Zechariah 14, which is alluded to in this section, contains one of the "kingship verses" that were recited in ancient synagogues on Rosh Hashanah and that Zechariah 9 also speaks of God's worldwide dominion. Psalm 22:28, which is part of a psalm that is central to the narrative of Jesus' crucifixion, is another of the kingship verses, and Psalm 10, which is alluded to at the beginning of the passion narrative, ends with a reference to God's kingship. Daniel 7 and Deutero-Isaiah are also classic Old Testament texts for the concept of the kingdom of God.[161] In his passion narrative, then, Mark makes use of texts that exercised a formative influence on first-century conceptions of God's kingship.

Those conceptions were important not only for the early Christians but also for their Jewish contemporaries, and they seem to have played a significant role in the revolutionary disturbances that culminated in the revolt of A.D. 66–72. A central tenet of the "fourth philosophy" described by Josephus, and one which he ascribes to Jewish revolutionaries from Judas the Galilean, the leader of a revolt in 4 B.C., to Eleazar ben Ari, the commander of the last-ditch Jewish resistance at Masada that ended in A.D. 72, is that the Jews should have no ruler but God. One of the sources for this tenet seems to have been a radical and synergistic interpretation of Old Testament traditions about the kingdom of God, one which promised that God would bring in his eschatological kingdom if the Jews would do their part by refusing allegiance to the Romans and battling aggressively against them.[162]

We have previously argued that the Jewish Revolt against the Romans is a major element in the *Sitz im Leben* of Mark's community, and if this is so it is plausible that Mark's use of the Old Testament in his passion narrative and elsewhere is in part a response to the revolutionaries' interpretation of the scriptures having to do with the kingdom of God. This response is characterized by continuity and discontinuity with the revolutionaries' exegesis. Mark joins the revolutionaries in their single-minded concentration on the hope that God will establish his kingship through a saving act of eschatological warfare. He is also at one with them in their recognition that the sufferings of the present time do not contradict but rather intensify that hope. But he parts company with them over the nature of God's

---

[161] On Daniel 7, see O. Camponovo, *Königtum, Königsherrschaft und Reich Gottes in den frühjüdischen Schriften*, OBO 58 (Göttingen: Vandenhoeck & Ruprecht, 1984), pp. 122–125; on Deutero-Isaiah, see R. Schnackenburg, *God's Rule and Kingdom* (Freiburg: Herder, 1963), pp. 36–38; E. Zenger et al., "Herrschaft Gottes/Reich Gottes," *TRE* 15 (1986), 182–183.

[162] See *Jewish War* 2.117–119; 2.433; 7.323, 410, 418; *Antiquities* 18.23; see also Marcus, "Jewish War."

battle and over the role that human beings play in it. He envisages the apocalyptic war not as a campaign against Gentiles but as an assault on cosmic powers of evil, and a decisive part of this assault is the extension of the good news about it to the Gentiles (see 13:10). He sees the decisive victory in this war not in a miraculous deliverance of Jerusalem from the Romans but in Jesus' divinely willed suffering and death in Jerusalem and in the promise of a mysterious encounter with him in Galilee. He describes human participation in this victory not as a picking up of the spear but as a taking up of the cross.

Mark and the Jewish revolutionaries concur in their call for stringent self-sacrifice in the face of the momentous challenge of the eschatological crisis; they agree that those who save their lives will lose them, while those who lose them in God's cause will find them in his apocalyptic triumph (see Mark 8:35). But when will that triumph be seen, and where? Instructed by his Gospel, the members of Mark's community will believe that they can already see God's triumph in the present, that they can discern its contours in a form bespeaking suffering love and vindication, which seems to rise above the smoke of the ruined city, that they can hear the strains of the hallelujah song in a voice that cuts through the groaning caused by war, social ostracism, and persecution, and that speaks a word of insistent and empowering presence uniting the Markan now with the bygone story of Jesus' life on earth: "Come, follow me."[163]

---

[163] Mark 1:17–18; 2:14; 6:1; 8:34; 10:21, 28, 32, 52.

9

Conclusions

Continuity and Discontinuity with Jewish Exegesis

Mark's use of the Old Testament to express aspects of his Christology has its background in the Old Testament exegesis of his Jewish contemporaries. This exegesis reflects the eschatological expectation that gripped the Jewish world in the period leading up to and including the Jewish War of A.D. 66–74. Spurred on by the conviction that God was about to act decisively to fulfill his ancient promises to his people, throw off the hated yoke of pagan rulers, and establish his worldwide rule through a purified Israel, Jews were rereading their ancient writings as prophecies of this hoped-for act of saving holy war. It is also true, however, that the influence moved in the other direction, as well, that is, that the Old Testament prophecies fed eschatological fervor. In many cases, indeed, eschatological interpretation required little reworking of the ancient texts. Old Testament passages such as Isaiah 40–66, Zechariah 9–14, and Daniel 7–12 were already eschatological in their orientation, and Psalms 2, 22, 110, and 118 could easily be interpreted as such, since they spoke of God's defeat of the massed enemies of Israel and the establishment of his sovereignty to the ends of the earth. Mark's eschatological interpretation of these passages, then, continues a trajectory begun in the texts themselves and in Jewish exegesis.[1]

In addition to eschatological interpretation, other Markan exegetical strategies also have their background in Jewish interpretation of the Old Testament. The conjuring up of the larger context of a passage through the

---

[1] On the eschatological exegesis of the New Testament and its background in apocalyptic Judaism, see E. E. Ellis, "Biblical Exegesis in the New Testament Church," in *Mikra: Text, Translation, Reading and Interpretation of the Hebrew Bible in Ancient Judaism and Early Christianity*, CRINT 2.1, ed. M. J. Mulder (Philadelphia: Fortress Press, 1988), pp. 710–713.

citation of a specific verse or two is, as we have seen, a consistent Markan practice, and this practice corresponds to a method of citation found in rabbinic literature. Other Markan techniques that seem to be borrowed from Jewish exegesis include the choice of a particular Old Testament version because it is theologically serviceable,[2] the adjustment of the Old Testament text to make it more applicable to the Markan situation and useful for Markan theology,[3] the conflation of Old Testament texts,[4] the reconciliation of scriptural contradictions,[5] and the blurring of the line between scripture and interpretation.[6]

In other ways, however, Mark's interpretation of the Old Testament departs from the Jewish exegesis of the time even as it builds upon it. Mark, for example, sets his whole story in a Deutero-Isaian framework through the citation of "Isaiah the prophet" in 1:1–3, and crucial background for his picture of Jesus' "way" up to Jerusalem is provided by Deutero-Isaiah's picture, in Isa. 40:3 and elsewhere, of Yahweh's triumphal march through the wilderness to Zion in a saving act of holy war on behalf of his people. This Markan emphasis is in continuity with Jewish exegesis of Deutero-Isaiah. We know from 1QS 8:12–16, for example, that the Dead Sea community's expectation, based on Isa. 40:3, of an eschatological victory following a divine march through the wilderness, played a major role in motivating its migration to the arid and forbidding region of Khirbet Qumran. But that this victory was to be achieved through the Messiah's death and confirmed by his resurrection was an expectation apparently unknown in the Judaism of Mark's time.[7]

---

[2] In the Old Testament citations and allusions we have studied, Mark seems to reflect the Septuagint in 1:3 (Isa. 40:3); 1:11 (Ps. 2:7); 9:7 (Deut. 18:15); 9:12 (Mal. 3:23); 12:10–11 (Ps. 118:22–23); 12:35–37 (Pss. 110:1/8:7); 14:1 (Ps. 10:7–8); 14:18 (Ps. 41:9); 14:34 (Pss. 42:5, 11; 43:5); 14:41 (Ps. 140:4, 8); 14:55 (Ps. 37:32); 14:57 (Pss. 27:12; 35:11); 14:65 (Isa. 50:6); 15:5 (Isa. 52:15); 15:24 (Ps. 22:18); 15:29 (Ps. 22:7); 15:30–31 (Ps. 22:7); 15:32 (Ps. 22:6); 15:36 (Ps. 69:21); and 15:40 (Ps. 38:11); also the word παραδιδόναι in the passion narrative (Isa. 53:6, 12). He seems to be giving a Greek rendering of the Masoretic Text independent of the Septuagint in 1:2 (Ex. 23:20/Mal. 3:1); 1:10 (Isa. 63:19); 14:24 (Isa. 53:12); 14:62 (Dan. 7:13); and 15:34 (Ps. 22:1). In 14:27 he cites Zech. 13:7 according to the Q text of the Septuagint, a text that reflects a Palestinian Septuagint tradition. For evidence of a similar textual eclecticism at Qumran, see W. H. Brownlee, "Biblical Interpretation among the Sectaries of the Dead Sea Scrolls," *BA* 14 (1951), p. 61.

[3] Examples include Mark 1:2–3 and 14:62. On the use of this technique at Qumran, see especially Brownlee, "Biblical Interpretation."

[4] See Mark 1:2–3 (Ex. 23:20/Mal. 3:1/Isa. 40:3); 1:11bc (Ps. 2:7/Isa. 42:1); 12:36 (Ps. 110:1/Ps. 8:7); 14:24 (Ex. 24:8/Zech. 9:11/Isa. 53:12); 14:27 (Zech. 13:7/Isa. 53:6, 10); 14:62 (Ps. 110:1/Dan. 7:13).

[5] See Mark 9:11–13.

[6] See especially our comments on the phrase "as it has been written" in Mark 9:13.

[7] There is, however, as we have seen, a foreshadowing of it in Deutero-Isaiah itself, where Yahweh's Suffering Servant wins a holy war victory not by defeating the foreign kings and people but by suffering on their behalf and Israel's.

Similarly, we find both continuity and discontinuity between Mark and some Jewish exegetes in the way in which they bring out the parallelism between the human and the cosmic dimensions of the eschatological war. For Jewish exegetes such as the Qumran sectarians, the end-time battle is not only against the children of darkness but also against their demonic leaders; for Mark, similarly, the eschatological victory foretold in passages such as Psalm 2 (cf. Mark 1:11) expresses itself in a proleptic defeat of Satan and a routing of his minions (1:13, 21–28). But the degree to which Mark effaces the standard motif of the defeat of the Gentiles, at times even replacing it with promises of salvation for Gentiles and warnings of judgment against Jewish leaders,[8] is unprecedented,[9] and the changed emphasis perhaps reflects a Markan *Sitz im Leben* in which the members of the community are suffering persecution from revolutionary Jewish leaders whose complaints against them include their openness to non-Jews.

Again, Mark is following Jewish precedents when he portrays Jesus, the Son of man, as a corporate figure whose fate somehow includes that of the elect community. He breaks with those precedents, however, when he ascribes to that Son of man not only the vindication for which the community yearns but also the suffering by which it is now assaulted. We have suggested that this extension of the corporate dimension of the Son of man reflects both the indelible memory of Jesus' end and the community's experience of divine sustenance in the midst of its travail, so that suffering is seen not to contradict but rather to provide the arena for divine empowerment.

Most important for Mark's christology, we find in his Gospel both continuity and discontinuity with Jewish conceptions of the interrelation between the kingdom of God and the kingship of his Messiah. This interrelation is seen in Mark in many ways. The description of God's royal road in Mark 1:2–3 draws a parallel between the way of the Lord and the way of Jesus. The three architechtonic appearances of the royal title "Son of God" at the Gospel's beginning, middle, and end (1:11; 9:7; 15:39) are redactionally placed in proximity to references to the kingdom of God. The second of these appearances, Mark 9:7, is part of a passage whose mountain setting and description of transfiguration are reminiscent of contemporary Jewish accounts of Moses' enthronement. The allusions to Ps. 110:1 in Mark

---

[8] See, e.g., the use of Psalm 118 in Mark 12:9–12 and the use of Daniel 7 in Mark 14:53–65; cf. 13:10.

[9] It is true that for the Qumran sectarians the "children of darkness" include Jews who have not joined themselves to the elect community, and particularly Jewish leaders such as the "Wicked Priest" and his allies "the seekers after smooth things" (= the Pharisees; on the identities of these figures, see G. Vermes, *The Dead Sea Scrolls: Qumran in Perspective* [Philadelphia: Fortress Press, 1977], pp. 150–152). But they still look forward to an eschatological war against the Kittim—that is, the Romans—and thus interpret the eschatological war differently from Mark.

12:35–37 and 14:62, similarly, imply that after the resurrection Jesus will be enthroned at God's right hand. The four bodies of Old Testament literature that are crucial for the christology of the passion narrative— Zechariah 9–14, Daniel 7, the Psalms of the Righteous Sufferer (especially Psalm 22), and Deutero-Isaiah—all have strong traditional connections with the notion of the kingdom of God. Indeed, it is likely that these scriptures, with their interconnected notions of the kingdom of God and the kingship of the Messiah, played a major role in touching off and sustaining the Jewish Revolt that had as its rallying cry "no ruler but God."

Mark, then, is following in the footsteps of some of his Jewish contemporaries when he makes the motif of the kingdom of God of central importance and binds it intimately to the notion of the kingship of the Messiah. Again, however, there seems to be no Jewish parallel for Mark's thought that the Messiah's kingship and the kingdom of God are manifest already and in a definitive way in his suffering and death.

The Substructure of New Testament Theology?

This Markan combination of continuity and discontinuity with Jewish interpretations of the Old Testament and even with the Old Testament itself raises a question—with which we shall conclude this study—about the implicit claim made by the subtitle of C. H. Dodd's justly famous book about New Testament biblical exegesis, *According to the Scriptures*.

Dodd subtitles his book "The Sub-structure of New Testament Theology." Certainly some support could be found for the claim that the Old Testament provides the substructure for New Testament theology in the way in which Mark starts his Gospel by saying that "the beginning of the good news of Jesus Christ" is "as it has been written in Isaiah the prophet" (1:1–2). This beginning implies that the good news about Jesus is in accordance with the prophecies of Isaiah and, by implication, of the other seers whose works are collected in the scriptures of Israel. A major thesis of our study, similarly, has been that Mark takes up patterns and themes from the Old Testament and uses them to make clear to his biblically literate readers various aspects of Jesus' identity and of his relation to the community whose existence was inaugurated by his life, death, and resurrection. It makes sense to conclude that these Old Testament motifs have also played a considerable role in shaping Mark's own conception of Jesus.

On the other hand, Mark is in some ways similar to the author of the *Habakkuk Commentary* at Qumran, who asserts that God told Habakkuk to write down the words of his prophecy but withheld from him the mysterious meaning of those words, which had to await its revelation through the Teacher of Righteousness (1QpHab 7:1–5). For Mark, similarly, the unexpected significance of the Old Testament prophecies has now been revealed, and they are seen to point to a figure who fills the Old Testament molds in surprising ways that threaten to break the molds themselves. In Mark's exegesis the Old Testament prophecies of national tribulation and exaltation at the eschaton are focused in an unprecedented and astonishing way on the individual figure of Jesus the Messiah, though as we have seen that figure has communal dimensions. In a manner apparently unexpected in contemporary Jewish exegesis, moreover, this Messiah suffers and dies rather than triumphing by force of arms, though he retains a militant dimension as God's holy warrior against the forces of cosmic evil. The Old Testament patterns and themes used by Mark have thus suffered an alchemical transformation based on a logically prior belief, the good news of the arrival of the eschaton in the event of Jesus Christ.

The logical priority of the word of the gospel over ancient tradition in a way goes back to Deutero-Isaiah himself. The latter's sense of the eschatological newness of the divine action for which he longs is so great that in one passage he stretches to the breaking point his commitment to the sacred traditions of Israel by exhorting his hearers *not* to remember the former things or to call them to mind. At the same time and paradoxically, however, he portrays the awaited divine action in this same passage in terms borrowed from Israelite traditions about creation and exodus (Isa. 43:16–21).

A similar grasp on both ancient tradition and eschatological newness is found in Mark's narrative. In Mark 12:24 Jesus diagnoses the spiritual malady of the Sadducees: "Is not this why you go wrong—because you know *neither the scriptures nor the power of God?*" (alt.). For Mark, the scriptures and the power of God are two separate but inseparable realities. Despite the order of the terms "scripture" and "power of God" in 12:24, there is no doubt that in Mark's mind knowledge of the power of God has a logical priority over knowledge of the scriptures.[10] Knowing the scriptures without knowing the vivifying power of God causes faith to deteriorate into a moribund traditionalism that is so separated from the wellsprings of its life that it does not even know it is honoring God with its lips while keeping its heart far from him (see Mark 7:6–7//Isa. 29:13). But Mark would also reject a presumptuous and one-sided claim to know the power of God directly without reference to the scriptures, a claim that blithely ignores the tradition that imparts, however fragmentarily and imperfectly, a sense for the shape that the grace and the judgment of God assume in human history.

In Mark's Gospel, in other words, a commitment to the "old, old story" is retained at the same time that the story itself is transformed by being read in a new way. Mark has certainly learned much of what he knows about Jesus Christ from the scriptures. He would never have learned it, however, if he had not already known that Jesus Christ is the key to the scriptures.

---

[10] The order in 12:24 reflects the fact that the Sadducees begin the controversy with a reference to a scriptural law (Mark 12:19//Deut. 25:5–6).

Works Cited

Ackroyd, P. R. "נצח – εἰς τέλος." *ExpT* 80 (1968–1969), 126.

Allen, L. C. "The Old Testament Background of (ΠΡΟ)‛ΟΡΙΖΕΙΝ in the New Testament." *NTS* 17 (1970–71), 104–108.

Allison, D. C. "Elijah Must Come First." *JBL* 103 (1984), 256–258.

Ambrozic, A. M. *The Hidden Kingdom: A Redaction-Critical Study of the References to the Kingdom of God in Mark's Gospel.* CBQMS 2. Washington, D.C.: Catholic Biblical Association, 1972.

Anderson, A. A. *Psalms.* NCB. 2 vols. London: Oliphants, 1972.

Anderson, B. W. "Exodus Typology in Second Isaiah." In *Israel's Prophetic Heritage: Essays in Honor of James Muilenburg,* edited by B. W. Anderson and W. Harrelson, pp. 177–195. New York: Harper & Row, 1962.

Anderson, G. W. "Isaiah xxiv–xxvii Reconsidered." In *Congress Volume: Bonn, 1962,* pp. 118–126. VTSup 9. Leiden: E. J. Brill, 1963.

Anderson, H. "The Old Testament in Mark's Gospel." In *The Use of the Old Testament in the New and Other Essays: Studies in Honor of William Franklin Stinespring,* edited by J. M. Efird, pp. 280–306. Durham, N.C.: Duke University Press, 1972.

Auerbach, E. *Mimesis: The Representation of Reality in Western Literature.* Princeton, N.J.: Princeton University Press, 1953.

Bacher, W. *Die älteste Terminologie der jüdischen Schriftauslegung.* 2 vols. Leipzig: Hinrichs, 1899, 1905.

Bacon, B. W. "Notes on New Testament Passages." *JBL* 16 (1897), 136–139.

———. "Supplementary Note on the Aorist *eudokēsa,* Mark i. 11." *JBL* 20 (1901), 28–30.

Bardtke, H. "Considérations sur les cantiques de Qumran." *RB* 63 (1956), 220–233.

Barrett, C. K. "The Allegory of Abraham, Sarah, and Hagar in the Argument of Galatians." In *Rechtfertigung: Festschrift für Ernst Käsemann,* edited by J. Friedrich et al., pp. 1–16. Tübingen: J. C. B. Mohr (Paul Siebeck), 1976.

Baumgarten, J. M. "4Q500 and the Ancient Conception of the Lord's Vineyard." *JJS* 40 (1989), 1–6.

Bellinzoni, A. J., ed. *The Two-Source Hypothesis: A Critical Appraisal.* Macon, Ga.: Mercer University Press, 1985.

Best, E. *Following Jesus: Discipleship in the Gospel of Mark.* JSNTSup 4. Sheffield: JSOT Press, 1981.

———. "Mark's Preservation of the Tradition." In *The Interpretation of Mark,* edited by W. Telford, pp. 119–133. IRT 7. Philadelphia: Fortress Press; London: SPCK, 1985. Orig. 1974.

———. "The Role of the Disciples in Mark." *NTS* 23 (1977), 377–403.

———. *The Temptation and the Passion: The Markan Soteriology.* SNTSMS 2. Cambridge: Cambridge University Press, 1965.

Betz, O. "Jesu heiliger Krieg." *NovT* 2 (1957–58), 116–137.

Black, C. C. *The Disciples according to Mark: Markan Redaction in Recent Debate.* Sheffield: JSOT Press, 1989.

———. "The Quest of Mark the Redactor: Why Has It Been Pursued, and What Has It Taught Us?" *JSNT* 33 (1988), 19–39.

———. Review of J. Marcus, *The Mystery of the Kingdom of God. JBL* 107 (1988), 542–545.

Black, M. *The Book of Enoch or 1 Enoch: A New English Edition.* SVTP 7. Leiden: E. J. Brill, 1985.

———. "The Christological Use of the Old Testament in the New Testament." *NTS* 18 (1971), 1–14.

———. "Servant of the Lord and Son of Man." *SJT* 6 (1953), 4–8.

———. "The Theological Appropriation of the Old Testament by the New Testament." *SJT* 39 (1986), 1–17.

Black, M. C. "The Rejected and Slain Messiah Who is Coming with the Angels: The Messianic Exegesis of Zechariah 9–14 in the Passion Narratives." Ph.D. diss. Emory University Press, 1990.

Boring, M. E. "The Christology of Mark: Hermeneutical Issues for Systematic Theology." *Semeia* 30 (1984), 125–153.

Bornhäuser, K. *The Death and Resurrection of Jesus Christ.* Bangalore: C.L.S., 1958. Orig. 1946.

Boyarin, D. *Intertextuality and the Reading of Midrash.* Bloomington, Ind.: Indiana University Press, 1990.

Bratcher, R. G. *Old Testament Quotations in the New Testament.* Helps for Translators. 2nd ed. London, New York, and Stuttgart: United Bible Societies, 1984.

Brenton, L. C. L. *The Septuagint with Apocrypha: Greek and English.* Grand Rapids: Zondervan Publishing House, 1982. Orig. 1851.

Bretscher, P. G. "Exodus 4:22–23 and the Voice from Heaven." *JBL* 87 (1968), 301–311.

Breytenbach, C. *Nachfolge und Zukunftserwartung nach Markus: Eine methodenkritische Studie.* ATANT 71. Zurich: Theologischer Verlag, 1984.

Broer, I. *Die Urgemeinde und das Grab Jesu.* SANT. Munich: Kösel, 1972.

Brown, R. E. *The Gospel According to John.* AB 29, 29A. 2 vols. Garden City, N.Y.: Doubleday & Co., 1966, 1970.

Brownlee, W. H. "Biblical Interpretation among the Sectaries of the Dead Sea Scrolls." *BA* 14 (1951), pp. 54–76.

———. "The Servant of the Lord in the Qumran Scrolls." *BASOR* 132, 135 (1953–1954), 8–15, 33–38.

Bruce, F. F. *Biblical Exegesis in the Qumran Texts.* Exegetica 3. The Hague: Uitgeverij van Keulen, 1959.

———. "The Book of Zechariah and the Passion Narrative." *BJRL* 43 (1960), 336–353.

Bultmann, R. "αἰσχύνω, κτλ." *TDNT* 1:189–190. 1964. Orig. 1933.

———. *History of the Synoptic Tradition.* New York: Harper & Row, 1963. Orig. 1931.

Burger, C. *Jesus als Davidssohn: Eine traditionsgeschichtliche Untersuchung.* FRLANT 98. Göttingen: Vandenhoeck & Ruprecht, 1970.

Burton, E. D. W. *Syntax of the Moods and Tenses in New Testament Greek.* Grand Rapids: Kregel, 1976. Orig. 1900.

Buse, I. "The Markan Account of the Baptism of Jesus and Isaiah LXIII." *JTS* n.s. 7 (1956), 74–75.

Caird, G. B. Review of M. Pesce, *Paolo e gli arconti a Corinto. JTS* 29 (1978), pp. 543–544.

Camponovo, O. *Königtum, Königsherrschaft und Reich Gottes in den früh-jüdischen Schriften.* OBO 58. Göttingen: Vandenhoeck & Ruprecht, 1984.

Carlston, C. E. *The Parables of the Triple Tradition.* Philadelphia: Fortress Press, 1975.

Carroll, J. T. "The Uses of Scripture in Acts." In *Society of Biblical Literature 1990 Seminar Papers,* edited by D. J. Lull, pp. 512–528. Atlanta: Scholars Press, 1990.

Carson, D. A., and H. G. M. Williamson, eds. *It is Written: Scripture Citing Scripture: Essays in Honour of Barnabas Lindars.* Cambridge: Cambridge University Press, 1988.

Charlesworth, J. H. "The Concept of the Messiah in the Pseudepigrapha." *ANRW* 2.19.1, pp. 188–218.

———. *The New Testament Apocrypha and Pseudepigrapha: A Guide to Publications.* ATLA Bibliography Series. Metuchen, N.J.: Scarecrow Press, 1987.

Chevallier, M. A. *L'Esprit et le Messie dans le bas-Judaïsme et le Nouveau Testament.* Paris: Presses universitaires de France, 1958.

Chilton, B. D. *A Galilean Rabbi and His Bible: Jesus' Own Interpretation of Isaiah.* London: SPCK, 1984.

———. *God in Strength: Jesus' Announcement of the Kingdom.* StudNT-Umwelt, Serie B, Band 1. Freistadt: Plöchl, 1979.

———. *The Isaiah Targum: Introduction, Translation, Apparatus and Notes.* The Aramaic Bible 11. Wilmington, Del.: Michael Glazier, 1987.

———. "Jesus *ben David:* Reflections on the *Davidssohnfrage.*" *JSNT* 14 (1982), 88–112.

———. "The Transfiguration: Dominical Assurance and Apostolic Vision." *NTS* 27 (1980), 115–124.

Collins, J. J. *The Apocalyptic Imagination: An Introduction to the Jewish Matrix of Christianity.* New York: Crossroad, 1984.

Coutts, J. "Ephesians I.3–14 and I Peter I.3–12." *NTS* 3 (1956–1957), 115–127.

Craigie, P. C. *Psalms 1–50.* WBC 19. Waco, Tex.: Word Books, 1983.

Cranfield, C. E. B. *The Gospel According to Saint Mark.* CGTC. Cambridge: Cambridge University Press, 1974. Orig. 1959.

Cross, F. M. *Canaanite Myth and Hebrew Epic: Essays in the History of the Religion of Israel.* Cambridge, Mass.: Harvard University Press, 1973.

Crossan, J. D. *In Parables: The Challenge of the Historical Jesus.* New York: Harper & Row, 1973.

Dahl, N. A. "Contradictions in Scripture." In *Studies in Paul,* pp. 159–177. Minneapolis: Augsburg, 1977. Orig. 1969.

———. "The Crucified Messiah." In *The Crucified Messiah and Other Essays,* pp. 10–36. Minneapolis: Augsburg, 1974. Orig. 1960.

Daube, D. *The New Testament and Rabbinic Judaism.* New York: Arno Press, 1973. Orig. 1956.

Davenport, G. L. "The 'Anointed of the Lord' in Psalms of Solomon 17." In *Ideal Figures in Ancient Judaism,* edited by J. J. Collins and G. W. E. Nickelsburg, pp. 67–92. SBLSCS 12. Chico, Calif.: Scholars Press, 1980.

de Boer, M. C. *The Defeat of Death: Apocalyptic Eschatology in 1 Corinthians 15 and Romans 5.* JSNTSup 22. Sheffield: Sheffield Academic Press, 1988.

———. "Paul and Jewish Apocalyptic Eschatology." In *Apocalyptic and the New Testament: Essays in Honor of J. Louis Martyn,* edited by J. Marcus and M. L. Soards, pp. 169–190. JSNTSup 24. Sheffield: Sheffield Academic Press, 1989.

de Jonge, M. "Jesus, Son of David and Son of God." In *Intertextuality in Biblical Writings: Essays in Honour of Bas van Iersel,* edited by S. Draisma, pp. 95–104. Kampen: Kok, 1989.

———. "The Use of the Word 'Anointed' in the Time of Jesus." *NovT* 8 (1966), 132–148.

Derrett, J. D. M. *The Making of Mark: The Scriptural Bases of the Earliest Gospel.* 2 vols. Shipston-on-Stour: P. Drinkwater, 1985.

——. "The Stone That the Builders Rejected." In *Studies in the New Testament,* 2:60–67. 5 vols. Leiden: E. J. Brill, 1977–1978.

de Waard, J. *A Comparative Study of the Old Testament Text in the Dead Sea Scrolls and in the New Testament.* STDJ 4. Leiden: E. J. Brill, 1965.

Dibelius, M. *From Tradition to Gospel.* Cambridge: James Clarke & Co., 1971. Orig. 1933.

——. *Die Geisterwelt im Glauben des Paulus.* Göttingen: Vandenhoeck & Ruprecht, 1909.

Dibelius, M., and H. Conzelmann. *The Pastoral Epistles.* Hermeneia. Philadelphia: Fortress Press, 1972. Orig. 1955.

Dimant, D. "Qumran Sectarian Literature." In *Jewish Writings of the Second Temple Period,* edited by M. E. Stone, pp. 483–550. CRINT 2. Philadelphia: Fortress Press, 1984.

Dodd, C. H. *According to the Scriptures: The Sub-structure of New Testament Theology.* London: Nisbet, 1952.

Donahue, J. R. *Are You the Christ?* SBLDS 10. Missoula: Society of Biblical Literature, 1973.

——. "A Neglected Factor in the Theology of Mark." *JBL* 101 (1982), 563–594.

Draisma, S., ed. *Intertextuality in Biblical Writings: Essays in Honour of Bas van Iersel.* Kampen: Kok, 1989.

Duling, D. C. "The Promises to David and Their Entrance into Christianity—Nailing Down a Likely Hypothesis." *NTS* 68 (1973), 55–77.

——. "Solomon, Exorcism, and the Son of David." *HTR* 68 (1975), 235–252.

——. "Testament of Solomon." *OTP* 1.935–987.

Dunn, J. D. G. *Romans.* WBC. 2 vols. Dallas: Word Books, 1988.

Dupont-Sommer, A. *The Essene Writings from Qumran.* Translated by G. Vermes. Gloucester, Mass.: Peter Smith, 1973.

Eaton, J. H. *Kingship and the Psalms.* 2nd ed. Sheffield: JSOT Press, 1986.

Efird, J. M., ed. *The Use of the Old Testament in the New and Other Essays: Studies in Honor of William Franklin Stinespring.* Durham: Duke University Press, 1972.

Elbogen, I. *Der jüdische Gottesdienst in seiner geschichtlichen Entwicklung.* Leipzig: Fock, 1913.

Elliger, K. *Jesaja II (41,17–42,9).* BKAT. Neukirchen-Vluyn: Neukirchener Verlag, 1971.

Ellis, E. E. "Biblical Exegesis in the New Testament Church." In *Mikra: Text, Translation, Reading and Interpretation of the Hebrew Bible in Ancient Judaism and Early Christianity,* edited by M. J. Mulder, pp. 691–725. CRINT 2.1. Philadelphia: Fortress Press, 1988.

——. "Midrash, Targum, and New Testament Quotations." In *Prophecy and Hermeneutic in Early Christianity: New Testament Essays,* pp. 188–197. Grand Rapids: Wm. B. Eerdmans Publishing Co., 1978. Orig. 1969.

Ernst, J. *Das Evangelium nach Markus.* RNT. Regensburg: Pustet, 1981.

Evans, C. A. "On the Vineyard Parables of Isaiah 5 and Mark 12." *BZ* 28 (1984), 82–86.

• Evans, C. F. "I Will Go Before You into Galilee." *JTS* n.s. 5 (1954), 3–8.

Fabry, H.-J. "Die Wirkungsgeschichte des Psalms 22." In *Beiträge zur Psalmenforschung: Psalm 2 und 22,* edited by J. Schreiner, pp. 279–318. FB 60. Würzburg: Echter Verlag, 1988.

Faierstein, M. M. "Why Do the Scribes Say That Elijah Must Come First?" *JBL* 100 (1981), 75–86.

Fishbane, M. *Biblical Interpretation in Ancient Israel.* Oxford: Clarendon Press, 1985.

Fitzmyer, J. A. "'4Q Testimonia' and the New Testament." In *Essays on the Semitic Background of the New Testament,* pp. 59–89. Sources for Biblical Study 5. Missoula, Mont.: Scholars Press, 1971.

——. "The Aramaic Language and the Study of the New Testament." *JBL* 99 (1980), 5–21.

——. "The Contribution of Qumran Aramaic to the Study of the New Testament." In *A Wandering Aramean: Collected Aramaic Studies,* pp. 85–113. SBLMS 25. Missoula, Mont.: Scholars Press, 1979.

——. "Further Light on Melchizedek from Qumran Cave 11." In *Essays on the Semitic Background of the New Testament,* pp. 245–267. Sources for Biblical Study. Missoula, Mont.: Scholars Press, 1971. Orig. 1967.

——. *The Gospel According to Luke.* AB 28, 28A. 2 vols. Garden City, N.Y.: Doubleday & Co., 1981, 1985.

——. "More about Elijah Coming First." *JBL* 104 (1985), 295–296.

——. "'Now This Melchizedek . . .' (Heb 7:1)." In *Essays on the Semitic Background of the New Testament,* pp. 221–243. Sources for Biblical Study 5. Missoula, Mont.: Scholars Press, 1974. Orig. 1963.

——. "The Semitic Background of the New Testament *Kyrios*-Title." In *A Wandering Aramean: Collected Aramaic Essays.* pp. 115–142. SBLMS 25. Missoula, Mont.: Scholars Press, 1979. Orig. 1971.

——. "The Use of Explicit Old Testament Quotations in Qumran Literature and in the New Testament." In *Essays on the Semitic Background of the New Testament,* pp. 3–58. Sources for Biblical Study. Missoula, Mont.: Scholars Press, 1971. Orig. 1961.

Flusser, D. "Melchizedek and the Son of Man." *Christian News from Israel* 17 (1966), 23–29.

France, R. T. "The Formula Quotations of Matthew 2 and the Problem of Communication." *NTS* 27 (1981), 233–251.

———. *Jesus and the Old Testament: His Application of Old Testament Passages to Himself and His Mission.* Downers Grove, Ill.: Inter-Varsity, 1971.

Frei, H. W. *The Eclipse of Biblical Narrative: A Study in Eighteenth and Nineteenth Century Hermeneutics.* New Haven, Conn.: Yale University Press, 1974.

Friedrich, G., et al. "Προφήτης, κτλ." *TDNT* 6:781–861. 1968. Orig. 1959.

Frye, N. "The Story of All Things." In *Paradise Lost,* edited by S. Elledge, pp. 405–422. Norton Critical Editions. New York: W. W. Norton & Co., 1975. Orig. 1965.

Gärtner, B. *The Temple and the Community in Qumran and the New Testament.* SNTSMS 1. Cambridge: Cambridge University Press, 1965.

Gese, H. "Natus ex virgine." *Vom Sinai zum Zion: Alttestamentliche Beiträge zur biblischen Theologie,* pp. 130–146. BETTA 64. Munich: Chr. Kaiser Verlag, 1974.

———. "Psalm 22 und das Neue Testament: Der älteste Bericht vom Tode Jesu und die Entstehung des Herrenmahles." In *Vom Sinai zum Zion: Alttestamentliche Beiträge zur biblischen Theologie,* pp. 180–201. BETTA 64. Munich: Chr. Kaiser Verlag, 1974.

Gianotto, C. *Melchisedek e la sua tipologica: Tradizioni giudaiche, cristiane e gnostiche (sec. II a.C. - sec. III d. C.).* Supplementi alla Rivista Biblica 12. Brescia: Paideia, 1984.

Glasson, T. F. *Moses in the Fourth Gospel.* SBT 40. London: SCM, 1963.

Gnilka, J. *Das Evangelium nach Markus.* EKKNT 2. 2 vols. Zurich: Benziger Verlag, 1978, 1979.

Grässer, E. "Review of A. Suhl, *Die Funktion der alttestamentlichen Zitate und Anspielungen im Markusevangelium.*" *TLZ* 91 (1966), 667–669.

Gray, J. *The Biblical Doctrine of the Reign of God.* Edinburgh: T. & T. Clark, 1979.

Greeven, H. "Περιστερά." *TDNT* 6:63–72. 1968. Orig. 1959.

Gross, H. "Der Messias im Alten Testament." *Bibel und Zeitgemässer Glaube. Band I, Altes Testament,* edited by K. Schubert, pp. 239–261. Vienna: Klosterneuburger, 1965.

Grundmann, W. *Das Evangelium nach Markus.* THKNT 2. 2d ed. Berlin: Evangelische Verlag, 1965.

Guelich, R. A. "'The Beginning of the Gospel': Mark 1:1–15." *BR* 27 (1982), 5–15.

———. *Mark 1–8:26.* WBC 34A. Dallas: Word Books, 1989.

Gundry, R. H. *The Use of the Old Testament in St. Matthew's Gospel.* NovTSup 18. Leiden: E. J. Brill, 1967.

Hahn, F. *Christologische Hoheitstitel: Ihre Geschichte im frühen Christentum.* FRLANT 83. Göttingen: Vandenhoeck & Ruprecht, 1963.

Hanson, A. T. *Jesus Christ in the Old Testament.* London: SPCK, 1965.

Hanson, P. D. "Apocalypse, Genre"; "Apocalypticism," *IDBSup*, pp. 27–34.

———. *The Dawn of Apocalyptic: The Historical and Sociological Roots of Jewish Apocalyptic Eschatology.* Rev. ed. Philadelphia: Fortress Press, 1979.

Harrington, D. J. "Pseudo-Philo." *OTP* 2.297–377.

Harris, R. *Testimonies.* 2 vols. Cambridge: Cambridge University Press, 1916, 1920.

Hartman, L. *Prophecy Interpreted: The Formation of Some Jewish Apocalyptic Texts of the Eschatological Discourse Mark 13 Par.* ConBNT 1. Lund: Gleerup, 1966.

Hay, D. M. *Glory at the Right Hand: Psalm 110 in Early Christianity.* Nashville: Abingdon Press, 1973.

Hays, R. B. *Echoes of Scripture in the Letters of Paul.* New Haven, Conn.: Yale University Press, 1989.

Hengel, M. *Studies in the Gospel of Mark.* Philadelphia: Fortress Press, 1985.

———. *The Zealots: Investigations into the Jewish Freedom Movement in the Period from Herod I Until 70 A.D.* Edinburgh: T. & T. Clark, 1989. Orig. 1961.

Hölscher, G. "Der Ursprung der Apokalypse Markus 13." *TBl* 12 (1933), 193–202.

Hooker, M. D. *Jesus and the Servant: The Influence of the Servant Concept of Deutero-Isaiah in the New Testament.* London: SPCK, 1959.

———. "Mark." In *It Is Written: Scripture Citing Scripture: Essays in Honour of Barnabas Lindars,* edited by D. A. Carson and H. G. M. Williamson, pp. 220–230. Cambridge: Cambridge University Press, 1988.

Horsley, R. A., and J. S. Hanson. *Bandits, Prophets, and Messiahs: Popular Movements at the Time of Jesus.* New Voices in Biblical Studies. San Francisco: Harper & Row, 1985.

Horstmann, M. *Studien zur markinischen Christologie. Mk 8,27–9,13 als Zugang zum Christusbild des zweiten Evangeliums.* NTAbh 6. 2nd ed. Münster: Aschendorff, 1973.

Hultgren, A. J. *Christ and His Benefits: Christology and Redemption in the New Testament.* Philadelphia: Fortress Press, 1987.

Hurtado, L. W. *One God, One Lord: Early Christian Devotion and Ancient Jewish Monotheism.* Philadelphia: Fortress Press, 1988.

Idelsohn, A. Z. *Jewish Liturgy and Its Development.* New York: Henry Holt, 1932.

Iser, W. *The Implied Reader: Patterns of Communication in Prose Fiction from Bunyan to Beckett.* Baltimore: Johns Hopkins University Press, 1974.

Jastrow, M. *A Dictionary of the Targumim, the Talmud Babli and Yerushalmi, and the Midrashic Literature.* 2 vols. in 1. New York: Judaica, 1982.

Jeremias, J. *The Eucharistic Words of Jesus*. Philadelphia: Fortress Press, 1966.

———. "Ἡλ(ε)ίας." *TDNT* 2:928–941. 1964. Orig. 1935.

———. *Jesus' Promise to the Nations*. Philadelphia: Fortress Press, 1958.

———. "Μωϋσῆς." *TDNT* 4:848–873. 1967.

———. "παῖς θεοῦ." *TDNT* 5:654–717. 1967. Orig. 1954.

———. *The Parables of Jesus*. 2nd rev. ed. New York: Charles Scribner's Sons, 1972. Orig. 1954.

———. "ποιμήν, κτλ." *TDNT* 8:485–502. 1968.

Johnson, L. T. "The New Testament's Anti-Jewish Slander and the Conventions of Ancient Polemic." *JBL* 108 (1989), 419–444.

Juel, D. *Messiah and Temple: The Trial of Jesus in the Gospel of Mark*. SBLDS 31. Missoula, Mont.: Scholars Press, 1973.

———. *Messianic Exegesis: Christological Interpretation of the Old Testament in Early Christianity*. Philadelphia: Fortress Press, 1988.

Kazmierski, C. R. *Jesus, the Son of God: A Study of the Markan Tradition and Its Redaction by the Evangelist*. FB 33. Würzburg: Echter Verlag, 1979.

Kee, H. C. "The Function of Scriptural Quotations and Allusions in Mark 11–16." In *Jesus und Paulus: Festschrift für Werner Georg Kümmel zum 70. Geburtstag*, edited by E. E. Ellis and E. Grässer, pp. 165–188. Göttingen: Vandenhoeck & Ruprecht, 1975.

———. Review of W. Roth, *Hebrew Gospel*. *JBL* 109 (1990), 538–539.

———. "The Terminology of Mark's Exorcism Stories." *NTS* 14 (1967–68), 232–246.

———. "The Transfiguration in Mark: Epiphany or Apocalyptic Vision?" In *Understanding the Sacred Text: Essays in Honor of Morton S. Enslin on the Hebrew Bible and Christian Beginnings*, edited by J. Reumann, pp. 135–152. Valley Forge, Pa.: Judson Press, 1972.

Keel, O. *The Symbolism of the Biblical World: Ancient Near Eastern Iconography and the Book of Psalms*. New York: Seabury Press, 1978.

Kelber, W. "Kingdom and Parousia in the Gospel of Mark." Ph.D. diss. University of Chicago, 1970.

Kelber, W., A. Kolenkow, and R. Scroggs. "Reflections on the Question: Was There a Pre-Markan Passion Narrative?" In *Society of Biblical Literature 1971 Seminar Papers*, pp. 505–585. Chico, Calif.: Society of Biblical Literature.

Kertelge, K. *Die Wunder Jesu im Markusevangelium: Eine redaktionsgeschichtliche Untersuchung*. SANT 23. Munich: Kösel, 1970.

Kingsbury, J. D. *The Christology of Mark's Gospel*. Philadelphia: Fortress Press, 1983.

———. *Conflict in Mark: Jesus, Authorities, Disciples*. Minneapolis: Fortress Press, 1989.

———. "The 'Divine Man' as the Key to Mark's Christology—The End of an Era?" *Int* 35 (1981), 243–257.

———. *Jesus Christ in Matthew, Mark, and Luke.* Proclamation Commentaries. Philadelphia: Fortress Press, 1981.

Kittel, G. "δοκέω, κτλ." *TDNT* 2:232–255. 1964. Orig. 1935.

Klausner, J. *The Messianic Idea in Israel: From Its Beginning to the Completion of the Mishnah.* New York: Macmillan Co., 1955.

Klein, H. "Zur Auslegung von Psalm 2: Ein Beitrag zum Thema: Gewalt und Gewaltlosigkeit." *TBei* 10 (1979), 63–71.

Kobelski, P. J. *Melchizedek and Melchireša'.* CBQMS 10. Washington, D.C.: Catholic Biblical Association, 1981.

Koch, D.-A. *Die Bedeutung der Wundererzählungen für die Christologie des Markusevangeliums.* Berlin and New York: Walter de Gruyter, 1975.

Köster, H. *Synoptische Überlieferung bei den apostolischen Vätern.* TU 65. Berlin: Akademie-Verlag, 1957.

Kraus, H.-J. *Die Königsherrschaft Gottes im Alten Testament.* BHT 13. Tübingen: J. C. B. Mohr (Paul Siebeck), 1951.

———. *Psalmen.* BKAT 15. 2 vols. Neukirchen-Vluyn: Neukirchener Verlag, 1960.

Kugel, J. L., and R. A. Greer. *Early Biblical Interpretation.* Library of Early Christianity. Philadelphia: Westminster Press, 1986.

Kuhn, K. G. "Γὼγ καὶ Μαγώγ." *TDNT* 1:789–791. 1964. Orig. 1933.

———. "New Light on Temptation, Sin, and Flesh in the New Testament." In *The Scrolls and the New Testament,* edited by K. Stendahl, pp. 94–113. New York: Harper & Brothers, 1957. Orig. 1952.

Kümmel, W. G. *Introduction to the New Testament.* Nashville: Abingdon Press, 1975.

Lacocque, A. *The Book of Daniel.* Atlanta: John Knox Press, 1979.

Lagrange, M. J. *Évangile selon Saint Marc.* Études bibliques. 2nd ed. Paris: Lecoffre, 1920.

Lake, K. *The Apostolic Fathers.* LCL. 2 vols. Cambridge, Mass.: Harvard University Press, 1912–1913.

Lane, W. *The Gospel of Mark.* NICNT. Grand Rapids: Wm. B. Eerdmans Publishing Co., 1974.

Lauterbach, J. Z. *Mekilta de-Rabbi Ishmael.* 3 vols. Philadelphia: Jewish Publication Society, 1961. Orig. 1933–1935.

Leenhardt, F. J. *L'Épître de St. Paul aux Romains.* CNT 6. 2nd ed. Geneva: Labor et Fides, 1981. Orig. 1957.

Lentzen-Deis, F. *Die Taufe Jesu nach den Synoptikern.* Frankfurter Theologische Studien 4. Frankfurt: Knecht, 1970.

Levin, S. *The Indo-European and Semitic Languages.* Albany, N.Y.: State University of New York, 1971.

Levine, L. *Caesarea under Roman Rule.* SJLA 7. Leiden: E. J. Brill, 1975.

Lieberman, S. *Greek in Jewish Palestine.* New York: Jewish Theological Seminary, 1942.

Lightfoot, R. H. *The Gospel Message of St. Mark.* Oxford: Clarendon Press, 1950.

Lindars, B. *New Testament Apologetic: The Doctrinal Significance of the Old Testament Quotations.* Philadelphia: Westminster Press, 1961.

Lindemann, A. "Die Osterbotschaft des Markus: Zur theologischen Interpretation von Mark 16.1–8." *NTS* 26 (1980), 298–317.

Ling, T. "A Note on I Corinthians II,8." *ExpT* 68 (1956–57), 26.

Lipinski, E. *La Royauté de Yahwé dans la Poésie et le Culte de l'Ancien Israël.* Brussels: Paleis der Academiën, 1965.

Lohmeyer, E. *Das Evangelium des Markus.* MeyerK. 11th ed. Göttingen: Vandenhoeck & Ruprecht, 1951. Orig. 1937.

Lohse, E. *Die Texte aus Qumran. Hebräisch und Deutsch.* Munich: Kösel, 1964.

———. "υἱὸς Δαυιδ." *TDNT* 8:478–488. 1972.

———, et al. "υἱός, υἱοθεσία." *TDNT* 8:334–399. 1972.

Longenecker, R. N. *Biblical Exegesis in the Apostolic Period.* Grand Rapids: Wm. B. Eerdmans Publishing Co., 1975.

———. *The Christology of Early Jewish Christianity.* SBT n.s. 17. Naperville, Ill.: Alec R. Allenson, 1970.

Lövestam, E. "Die Davidssohnfrage." *SEÅ* 27 (1962), 72–82.

———. *Son and Saviour: A Study of Acts 13,32–37.* ConNT 18. Lund: Gleerup, 1961.

Lührmann, D. *Das Markusevangelium.* HNT 3. Tübingen: J. C. B. Mohr (Paul Siebeck), 1987.

Magness, J. L. *Sense and Absence: Structure and Suspension in the Ending of Mark's Gospel.* SBLSS. Atlanta: Scholars Press, 1986.

Maier, J. *The Temple Scroll: An Introduction, Translation, and Commentary.* JSOTSup 34. Sheffield: JSOT Press, 1985.

Mann, J. *The Bible as Read and Preached in the Old Synagogue.* 1940. Reprint. New York: KTAV, 1971.

Marcus, J. "Entering into the Kingly Power of God." *JBL* 107 (1988), 663–675.

———. "The Jewish War and the *Sitz im Leben* of Mark." *JBL* 111 (1992), 441–462.

———. "Mark 14:61: Are You the Messiah-Son-of-God?" *NovT* 31 (1988), 125–141.

———. "Mark 9,11–13: As It Has Been Written." *ZNW* 80 (1989), 42–63.

———. *The Mystery of the Kingdom of God.* SBLDS 90. Atlanta: Scholars Press, 1986.

———. "'The Time Has Been Fulfilled!' (Mark 1:15)." In *Apocalyptic and the New Testament: Essays in Honor of J. Louis Martyn,* edited by J. Marcus and M. L. Soards, pp. 49–68. JSNTSup 24. Sheffield: Sheffield Academic Press, 1989.

Martyn, J. L. *History and Theology in the Fourth Gospel.* 2nd ed. Nashville: Abingdon Press, 1979. Orig. 1968.

Matera, F. J. *The Kingship of Jesus: Composition and Theology in Mark 15.* SBLDS 66. Chico, Calif.: Scholars Press, 1982.

———. "The Prologue as the Interpretative Key to Mark's Gospel." *JSNT* 34 (1988), 3–20.

———. *What Are They Saying About Mark?* Mahwah, N.J.: Paulist Press, 1987.

Maurer, C. "Knecht Gottes und Sohn Gottes im Passionsbericht des Markusevangelium." *ZTK* 50 (1953), 1–38.

Mauser, U. *Christ in the Wilderness: The Wilderness Theme in the Second Gospel and Its Basis in the Biblical Tradition.* SBT 39. Naperville, Ill.: Alec R. Allenson, 1963.

Meeks, W. A. "Moses as God and King." In *Religions in Antiquity: Essays in Memory of Erwin Ramsdell Goodenough,* edited by J. Neusner, pp. 354–371. Studies in the History of Religions 14. Leiden: E. J. Brill, 1968.

———. *The Prophet-King: Moses Traditions and the Johannine Christology.* NovTSup 14. Leiden: E. J. Brill, 1967.

Mettinger, T. *King and Messiah: The Civil and Sacral Legitimation of the Israelite Kings.* ConBOT 8. Lund: Gleerup, 1976.

Metzger, B. M. *A Textual Commentary on the Greek New Testament.* London and New York: United Bible Societies, 1971.

Meyer, R. *Der Prophet aus Galiläa: Studie zum Jesusbild der drei ersten Evangelien.* Darmstadt: Wissenschaftliche Buchgesellschaft, 1970. Orig. 1940.

Michaelis, W. "ὁδός, κτλ." *TDNT* 5:42–114. 1968. Orig. 1954.

———. "σκηνή, κτλ." *TDNT* 7:368–394. 1971. Orig. 1964.

Michaels, J. R. *1 Peter.* WBC 49. Waco, Tex.: Word Books, 1988.

Milikowsky, C. "Elijah and the Messiah." *Jerusalem Studies in Jewish Thought* 2 (1982–83), 491–496 [Hebrew].

Millar, W. R. *Isaiah 24–27 and the Origin of Apocalyptic.* HSM 11. Missoula, Mont.: Scholars Press, 1976.

Miller, D., and P. Miller. *The Gospel of Mark as Midrash on Earlier Jewish and New Testament Literature.* Studies in the Bible and Early Christianity 21. Lewiston, N.Y.: Edwin Mellen Press, 1990.

Moessner, D. P. *Lord of the Banquet: The Literary and Theological Significance of the Lukan Travel Narrative.* Minneapolis: Fortress Press, 1989.

Moo, D. J. *The Old Testament in the Gospel Passion Narratives.* Sheffield: Almond Press, 1983.

Moore, S. D. *Literary Criticism and the Gospels: The Theoretical Challenge.* New Haven, Conn.: Yale University Press, 1989.

Moulton, J. H., et al. *A Grammar of New Testament Greek.* 4 vols. Edinburgh: T. & T. Clark, 1908–65.

Mowinckel, S. *He That Cometh.* Nashville: Abingdon Press, 1954.

Mudiso Mbâ Mundla, J.-G. *Jesus und die Führer Israels: Studien zu den sog. Jerusalemer Streitgesprächen.* NTAbh N.F. 17. Münster: Aschendorff, 1984.

Mulder, M. J., ed. *Mikra: Text, Translation, and Reading and Interpretation of the Hebrew Bible in Ancient Judaism and Early Christianity.* CRINT 2.1. Assen and Maastricht: Van Gorcum; Philadelphia: Fortress Press, 1988.

Mussner, F. "Gottesherrschaft und Sendung Jesu nach Mk 1,14f.: Zugleich ein Beitrag über die innere Struktur des Markusevangeliums." In *Praesentia Salutis: Gesammelte Studien zu Fragen und Themen des Neuen Testaments,* pp. 81–98. Düsseldorf: Patmos Verlag, 1967.

Nardoni, E. "A Redactional Interpretation of Mark 9:1." *CBQ* 43 (1981), 365–384.

Neugebauer, F. "Die Davidssohnfrage (Mark xii. 35–37 parr.) und der Menschensohn." *NTS* 21 (1974), 81–108.

Neusner, J. *Comparative Midrash: The Plan and Program of Genesis and Leviticus Rabbah.* BJS 111. Atlanta: Scholars Press, 1986.

——. *Midrash as Literature: The Primacy of Documentary Discourse.* Studies in Judaism. Lanham, Md.: University Press of America, 1987.

——. *Pesiqta de Rab Kahana: An Analytical Translation.* BJS 122, 123. 2 vols. Atlanta: Scholars Press, 1987.

——. *What Is Midrash?* Guides to Biblical Scholarship. Philadelphia: Fortress Press, 1987.

——, et al. *Judaisms and Their Messiahs at the Turn of the Christian Era.* Cambridge: Cambridge University Press, 1987.

Nickelsburg, G. W. E., Jr. *Resurrection, Immortality, and Eternal Life in Intertestamental Judaism.* HTS 26. Cambridge, Mass.: Harvard University Press, 1972.

Nineham, D. E. *Saint Mark.* Pelican New Testament Commentaries. Middlesex: Penguin, 1963.

Nützel, J. M. *Die Verklärungserzählung im Markusevangelium.* FB 6. Würzburg: Echter Verlag, 1973.

Otto, R. *The Kingdom of God and the Son of Man: A Study in the History of Religion.* Boston: Starr King, 1957. Orig. 1934.

Perrin, N. "The Christology of Mark: A Study in Methodology." In *The Interpretation of Mark,* edited by W. Telford, pp. 95–108. IRT 7. Philadelphia: Fortress Press; London: SPCK, 1985. Orig. 1971, 1974.

——. *Rediscovering the Teaching of Jesus.* New York: Harper & Row, 1976. Orig. 1967.

Perrin, N., and D. C. Duling. *The New Testament: An Introduction: Proclamation and Parenesis, Myth and History*. 2nd ed. New York: Harcourt Brace Jovanovich, 1982.

Pesce, M. *Paolo e gli arconti a Corinto: Storia della ricerca (1888–1975) ed esegesi di 1 Cor 2,6–8*. Brescia: Paideia, 1977.

Pesch, R. *Das Markusevangelium*. HTKNT 2. 2 vols. Freiburg: Herder, 1976–1977.

———. *Naherwartungen: Tradition und Redaktion in Mk 13*. Kommentare und Beiträge zum Alten und Neuen Testament. Düsseldorf: Patmos Verlag, 1968.

Preuss, H. D. "Die Psalmenüberschriften in Targum und Midrasch." *ZAW* 71 (1959), 44–54.

Proksch, O. "ἅγιος, κτλ." *TDNT* 1:88–115. 1964. Orig. 1933.

Pryke, E. J. *Redactional Style in the Marcan Gospel: A Study of Syntax and Vocabulary as Guides to Redaction in Mark*. Cambridge: Cambridge University Press, 1978.

Quell, G., et al. "ἐκλέγομαι." *TDNT* 4:144–176. 1967. Orig. 1942.

Quesnell, Q. *The Mind of Mark: Interpretation and Method Through the Exegesis of Mark 6:52*. AnBib 38. Rome: Pontifical Biblical Institute, 1969.

———. Review of J. D. M. Derrett, *The Making of Mark. CBQ* 48 (1986), 559–560.

Rappaport, U. "Jewish-Pagan Relations and the Revolt against Rome in 66–70 C.E." *Jerusalem Cathedra* 1 (1981), 81–95.

Reploh, K.-G. *Markus, Lehrer der Gemeinde*. SBM 9. Stuttgart: Katholisches Bibelwerk, 1969.

Reumann, J. "Psalm 22 at the Cross." *Int* 28 (1974), 39–58.

Rhoads, D., and D. Michie. *Mark as Story: An Introduction to the Narrative of a Gospel*. Philadelphia: Fortress Press, 1982.

Robertson, A. T. *A Grammar of the Greek New Testament in the Light of Historical Research*. Nashville: Broadman Press, 1934.

Robertson, R. G. "Ezekiel the Tragedian." *OTP* 2.803–819.

Robinson, J. M. *Das Geschichtsverständnis des Markus-Evangeliums*. ATANT 30. Zurich: Zwingli Verlag, 1956.

———. *The Problem of History in Mark and Other Marcan Studies*. 1957. Reprint. Philadelphia: Fortress Press, 1982.

Rossé, G. *The Cry of Jesus on the Cross*. Mahwah, N.J.: Paulist Press, 1987.

Roth, C. "The Cleansing of the Temple and Zechariah xiv.21." *NovT* 4 (1960), 174–181.

Roth, W. *Hebrew Gospel: Cracking the Code of Mark*. Oak Park, Ill.: Meyer-Stone Books, 1988.

Ruppert, L. *Jesus als der leidende Gerechte? Der Weg Jesu im Lichte eines alt- und zwischentestamentlichen Motivs.* SB 59. Stuttgart: Katholisches Bibelwerk, 1972.

———. *Der leidende Gerechte: Eine motivgeschichtliche Untersuchung zum Alten Testament und zwischentestamentlichen Judentum.* FB 5. Würzburg: Echter Verlag, 1972.

Russell, D. S. *The Method and Message of Jewish Apocalyptic.* Philadelphia: Westminster Press, 1964.

Sanders, E. P. *Jesus and Judaism.* Philadelphia: Fortress Press, 1985.

Sasson, V. "The Language of Rebellion in Psalm 2 and in the Plaster Texts from Deir 'Alla." *AUSS* 24 (1986), 147–154.

Saunders, S. P. "'No One Dared Ask Him Anything More': Contextual Readings of the Controversy Stories in Matthew." Ph.D. diss. Princeton Theological Seminary, 1990.

Schaberg, J. "Daniel 7–12 and the New Testament Passion-Resurrection Predictions." *NTS* 31 (1985), 208–222.

Schenke, L. *Die Wundererzählungen des Markusevangeliums.* SBB 5. Stuttgart: Katholisches Bibelwerk, 1974.

Schiffman, L. H. *The Halakhah at Qumran.* SJLA 16. Leiden: E. J. Brill, 1975.

Schmidt, K. L. "Die literarische Eigenart der Leidengeschichte Jesu." *Die christliche Welt* 32 (1918), 114–116.

Schnackenburg, R. *God's Rule and Kingdom.* Freiburg: Herder, 1963.

———. *The Gospel According to St. John.* 3 vols. New York: Crossroad, 1968–1982.

Schneider, G. "Die Davidssohnfrage (Mk 12.35–37)." *Bib* 53 (1972), 65–90.

———. "Das Problem einer vorkanonischen Passionserzählung." *BZ* 16 (1972), 222–244.

Schneider, J. "βαίνω, κτλ." *TDNT* 1:518–523. 1964. Orig. 1933.

Schoeps, H.-J. *Theologie und Geschichte des Judenchristentums.* Tübingen: J. C. B. Mohr (Paul Siebeck), 1949.

Schreiber, J. *Theologie des Vertrauens: Eine redaktionsgeschichtliche Untersuchung des Markusevangeliums.* Hamburg: Furche, 1967.

Schreiner, J., ed. *Beiträge zur Psalmenforschung: Psalm 2 und 22.* FB 60. Würzburg: Echter Verlag, 1988.

Schulz, S. "Markus und das Alte Testament." *ZTK* 58 (1961), 184–197.

Schürer, E. *The History of the Jewish People in the Age of Jesus Christ (175 B.C.–A.D. 135),* revised and edited by G. Vermes et al. 3 vols. Edinburgh: T. & T. Clark, 1973–1987.

Schürmann, H. *Das Lukasevangelium.* HTKNT 3/1. Freiburg: Herder, 1969.

Schwartz, D. R. "Wilderness and Temple: On Religion and State in Judea in the Second Temple Period [Hebrew]." In *Priesthood and Kingship* [Hebrew], pp. 61–78. Jerusalem: Zalman Shezer Center for the History of Israel, 1987.

Schweizer, E. *The Good News According to Mark*. Atlanta: John Knox Press, 1970.

———. "υἱός, υἱοθεσία." *TDNT* 8:363–392. 1972.

———. *The Letter to the Colossians: A Commentary*. Minneapolis: Augsburg, 1982. Orig. 1976.

———. "πνευμα, πνευματιχος." *TDNT* 6:332–454. 1968. Orig. 1959.

Schwier, H. *Tempel und Tempelzerstörung: Untersuchungen zu den theologischen und ideologischen Faktoren im ersten jüdisch-römischen Krieg (66–74 n. Chr.)*. NTOA 11. Göttingen: Vandenhoeck & Ruprecht, 1989.

Segal, A. F. *Two Powers in Heaven: Early Rabbinic Reports About Christianity and Gnosticism*. SJLA 25. Leiden: E. J. Brill, 1977.

Seitz, C. R. "The Divine Council: Temporal Transition and New Prophecy in the Book of Isaiah." *JBL* 109 (1990), 229–247.

Senior, D. *The Passion of Jesus in the Gospel of Mark*. Passion Series 2. Wilmington, Del.: Michael Glazier, 1984.

Signer, M. A. "King/Messiah: Rashi's Exegesis of Psalm 2." *Prooftexts* 3 (1983), 273–284.

Smith, D. M. "The Use of the Old Testament in the New." In *The Use of the Old Testament in the New and Other Essays: Studies in Honor of William Franklin Stinespring*, edited by J. M. Efird, pp. 3–65. Durham, N.C.: Duke University Press, 1972.

Smyth, H. W. *Greek Grammar*. Cambridge, Mass.: Harvard University Press, 1956. Orig. 1920.

Snodgrass, K. *The Parable of the Wicked Tenants: An Inquiry into Parable Interpretation*. WUNT 27. Tübingen: J. C. B. Mohr (Paul Siebeck), 1983.

Snodgrass, K. R. "Streams of Tradition Emerging from Isaiah 40:1–5 and Their Adaptation in the New Testament." *JSNT* 8 (1980), 24–45.

Soards, M. L. "The Question of a Pre-Markan Passion Narrative." *Bible Bhashyam* 11 (1985), 144–169.

Soggin, J. A. "Zum zweiten Psalm." In *Wort-Gebot-Glaube: Walter Eichrodt zum 80. Geburtstag*, edited by H. J. Stoebe, pp. 191–207. ATANT 59. Zurich: Zwingli Verlag, 1970.

Starcky, J. "Psaumes Apocryphes de la Grotte 4 de Qumrân." *RB* 73 (1966), 353–371.

Stegner, W. R. *Narrative Theology in Early Jewish Christianity*. Louisville, Ky.: Westminster/John Knox Press, 1989.

Steichele, H.-J. *Der leidende Sohn Gottes: Eine Untersuchung einiger alttestamentlicher Motive in der Christologie des Markusevangeliums*. Biblische Untersuchungen 14. Regensburg: Pustet, 1980.

Stendahl, K. *The School of St. Matthew and its use of the Old Testament*. 2nd ed. Philadelphia: Fortress Press, 1968. Orig. 1954.

Stevens, B. A. "'Why "Must" the Son of Man Suffer?' The Divine Warrior in the Gospel of Mark." *BZ* 31 (1987), 101–110.

Stock, K. *Boten aus dem Mit-Ihm-Sein: Das Verhältnis zwischen Jesus und den Zwölf nach Markus.* AnBib 70. Rome: Biblical Institute Press, 1975.

Stone, M. E. "Apocalyptic Literature." In *Jewish Writings of the Second Temple Period,* edited by M. E. Stone, pp. 383–441. CRINT 2. Philadelphia: Fortress Press, 1984.

———. "Features of the Eschatology of IV Ezra." Ph.D. diss., Harvard University Press, 1965.

———. "The Question of the Messiah in 4 Ezra." In *Judaisms and Their Messiahs at the Turn of the Christian Era,* edited by J. Neusner et al., pp. 209–224. Cambridge: Cambridge University Press, 1987.

Strack, H. L., and P. Billerbeck. *Kommentar zum Neuen Testament aus Talmud und Midrasch.* 6 vols. Munich: Beck, 1922–65.

Strauss, D. F. *The Life of Jesus Critically Examined.* Philadelphia: Fortress Press, 1972. Orig. 1840.

Stuhlmacher, P. *Das paulinische Evangelium.* Vol. 1, *Vorgeschichte.* FRLANT 95. Göttingen: Vandenhoeck & Ruprecht, 1968.

Stuhlmann, R. "Beobachtungen und Überlegungen zu Markus 4:26–29." *NTS* 19 (1973), 153–162.

———. *Das eschatologische Mass im Neuen Testament.* FRLANT 132. Göttingen: Vandenhoeck & Ruprecht, 1983.

Suhl, A. *Die Funktion der alttestamentlichen Zitate und Anspielungen im Markusevangelium.* Gütersloh: Gerd Mohn, 1965.

Sundberg, A. C. "On Testimonies." *NovT* 3 (1959), 268–281.

Swartley, W. M. "The Structural Function of the Term 'Way' in Mark." In *The New Way of Jesus: Essays Presented to Howard Charles,* edited by W. Klassen, pp. 73–76. Newton, Kans.: Faith and Life Press, 1980.

Swete, H. B. *The Apocalypse of St. John: The Greek Text with Introduction Notes and Indices.* London: Macmillan Publishers, 1906.

Tabor, J. D. "'Returning to the Divinity': Josephus's Portrayal of the Disappearances of Enoch, Elijah, and Moses." *JBL* 108 (1989), 225–238.

Tal, S., ed. *Rinnat Yisrael Prayerbook.* Jerusalem: Moreshet, 1982.

Tannehill, R. C. "The Disciples in Mark: The Function of a Narrative Role." In *The Interpretation of Mark,* edited by W. Telford, pp. 134–157, IRT 7. Philadelphia: Fortress Press; London: SPCK, 1985. Orig. 1977.

———. "The Gospel of Mark as Narrative Christology." *Semeia* 16 (1979), 57–95.

Taylor, V. *The Gospel According to Saint Mark.* 2nd ed. Grand Rapids: Baker Book House, 1981. Orig. 1950.

Teeple, H. M. *The Mosaic Eschatological Prophet.* SBLMS 10. Philadelphia: Society of Biblical Literature, 1957.

Telford, W., ed. *The Interpretation of Mark.* IRT 7. 1977. Reprint. Philadelphia: Fortress Press, 1985.

Theissen, G. *Lokalkolorit und Zeitgeschichte in den Evangelien: Ein Beitrag zur Geschichte der synoptischen Tradition.* NTOA 8. Freiburg: Universitätsverlag; Göttingen: Vandenhoeck & Ruprecht, 1989.

Tolbert, M. A. *Sowing the Gospel: Mark's World in Literary-Historical Perspective.* Philadelphia: Fortress Press, 1989.

Tuckett, C., ed. *The Messianic Secret.* IRT 1. Philadelphia: Fortress Press, 1983.

Tuckett, C. M. *The Revival of the Griesbach Hypothesis: An Analysis and Appraisal.* SNTSMS 44. Cambridge: Cambridge University Press, 1983.

Tyson, J. B. "The Blindness of the Disciples in Mark." *JBL* 80 (1961), 261–268.

van der Loos, H. *The Miracles of Jesus.* NovTSup 9. Leiden: E. J. Brill, 1965.

Vermes, G. *The Dead Sea Scrolls: Qumran in Perspective.* Philadelphia: Fortress Press, 1977.

——. *Jesus the Jew: A Historian's Reading of the Gospels.* Philadelphia: Fortress Press, 1981. Orig. 1973.

——. *Scripture and Tradition in Judaism: Haggadic Studies.* SPB 4. Leiden: E. J. Brill, 1971.

Vielhauer, P. "Erwägungen zur Christologie des Markusevangeliums." In *Zeit und Geschichte: Dankesgabe an Rudolf Bultmann zum 80. Geburtstag,* edited by E. Dinkler, pp. 155–169. Tübingen: J. C. B. Mohr (Paul Siebeck), 1964.

Vögtle, A. Review of F. Lentzen-Deis, *Die Taufe Jesu nach den Synoptikern. BZ* 17 (1973), 115–123.

——. "Die sogenannte Taufperikope Mk 1,9–11: Zur Probelmatik der Herkunft und des ursprünglichen Sinns." In *EKKNT: Vorarbeiten 4,* pp. 105–139. Zurich: Benziger Verlag, 1972.

Volz, P. *Die Eschatologie der jüdischen Gemeinde im neutestamentlichen Zeitalter nach den Quellen der rabbinischen, apokalytpischen und apokryphen Literatur.* 2nd ed. Tübingen: J. C. B. Mohr (Paul Siebeck), 1934.

von Rad, G. *Old Testament Theology.* 2 vols. New York: Harper & Row, 1965.

Vorster, W. S. "The Function of the Use of the Old Testament in Mark." *Neotestamentica* 14 (1980), 62–72.

Weeden, T. J. "The Heresy That Necessitated Mark's Gospel." In *The Interpretation of Mark,* edited by W. Telford, pp. 64–77. IRT 7. Philadelphia: Fortress Press, 1985. Orig. 1968.

——. *Mark: Traditions in Conflict.* Philadelphia: Fortress Press, 1971.

Weiser, A. *The Psalms.* OTL. Philadelphia: Westminster Press, 1962.

Wellhausen, J. *Das Evangelium Marci übersetzt und erklärt.* Berlin: Reimer, 1903.

Wilcox, M. "The Denial-Sequence in Mark xiv. 26–31, 66–72." *NTS* 17 (1970–1971), 426–436.

Wright, R. B. "Psalms of Solomon." *OTP* 2:639–70.

Yadin, Y. "The Temple Scroll." In *New Directions in Biblical Archaeology*, edited by D. N. Freedman and J. C. Greenfield, pp. 156–166. Garden City, N.Y.: Doubleday & Co., 1971.

Zenger, E. "'Wozu tosen die Völker . . .': Beobachtungen zur Entstehung und Theologie des 2. Psalms." In *Freude an der Weisung des Herrn: Beiträge zur Theologie der Psalmen: Festgabe zum 70. Geburtstag von Heinrich Gross*, edited by E. Haag and F.-L. Hossfeld, pp. 495–511. Stuttgart: Katholisches Bibelwerk, 1986.

———, et al. "Herrschaft Gottes/Reich Gottes." *TRE* 15 (1986), 172–244.

Zimmerli, W. "Der 'neue Exodus' in der Verkündigung der beiden grossen Exilspropheten." In *Gottes Offenbarung: Gesammelte Aufsätze zum Alten Testament*, pp. 192–204. TBü 19. Munich: Chr. Kaiser Verlag, 1963.

Zmijewski, J. "Die Sohn-Gottes Prädikation im Markusevangelium. Zur Frage einer eigenständigen markinischen Titelschristologie." *Studien zum Neuen Testament und Seiner Umwelt* 12 (1987), 5–34.

Index of Texts

Index of Modern Authors

Kee, H. C., 3, 5, 12, 15, 53, 63, 81, 84, 87, 145, 172, 177, 194–195
Keel, O., 70
Kelber, W., 32–33, 175
Kertelge, K., 34
Kingsbury, J. D., 6–7, 29, 37, 47, 49–50, 57–58, 69, 110, 113–114, 138, 140
Kittel, G., 91
Klassen, W., 33
Klausner, J., 144
Klein, H., 59–60, 70–71
Klostermann, E., 53
Kobelski, P. J., 133
Koch, D.-A., 32, 34
Köster, H., 132
Kraus, H.-J., 51, 62, 64, 70, 134
Kugel, J. L., 4
Kuhn, K. G., 63, 185
Kümmel, W. G., 15
Kuss, O., 53

Lacocque, A., 165
Lagrange, M., 115
Lake, K., 132
Lane, W., 40, 56, 83, 98, 113, 145
Lauterbach, J. Z., 102
Leenhardt, F. J., 184
Lentzen-Deis, F., 49, 57
Levin, S., 104
Levine, L., 192
Lieberman, S., 104
Lightfoot, R. H., 193
Lindars, B., 4, 51, 112, 187
Lindemann, A., 195
Ling, T., 63
Lipinski, E., 69
Lohmeyer, E., 31, 56–57, 74–75, 83, 93, 97–98, 124, 132–133, 155
Lohse, E., 30, 78, 143
Longenecker, R. N., 4, 13, 16, 82, 119
Lövestam, E., 59, 61–62, 70, 72, 140, 152
Lührmann, D., 38, 39, 135, 138, 143, 153, 165, 176, 189
Lull, D. J., 21

Magness, J. L., 89
Maier, J., 97
Mann, J., 13, 25
Marcus, J., 2, 10, 20, 28, 31, 33, 39–40, 42, 44–46, 57, 66–67, 78, 87, 94, 102, 106, 108–109, 113–114, 117–118,

136–137, 140–142, 146, 160, 164, 168, 184, 197
Martyn, J. L., 82, 93
Marxsen, W., 2
Matera, F. J., 20, 42–43, 51, 70–72, 140, 142, 150, 174–175, 180–181
Maurer, C., 72, 187–188
Mauser, U., 3, 22–27, 35, 37
Meeks, W. A., 81, 84–86, 88, 90–91
Mettinger, T., 64, 70–71
Metzger, B. M., 54, 130
Meyer, R., 147, 167–168
Michaelis, W., 84
Michaels, J. R., 112
Michie, D., 40
Milikowsky, C., 110
Millar, W. R., 76
Miller, D. and P., 4–5, 18, 21
Moessner, D. P., 82
Moo, D. J., 3, 95, 172–175, 178, 187–189, 191, 193
Moore, S. D., 8–9, 140
Moulton, J. H., 73, 81
Mowinckel, S., 144
Mudiso Mbâ Mundla, J.-G., 130–131, 139
Mulder, M. J., 4, 199
Mussner, F., 20

Nardoni, E., 67, 87
Neugebauer, F., 143
Neusner, J., 84–86, 90, 100–101, 103, 106, 144–145
Nickelsburg, G. W. E., 65, 88
Nineham, D. E., 22, 75
Norden, E., 7
Nützel, J. M., 81, 83–84, 98

Oswald, J., 174
Otto, R., 41

Peddinghaus, C. D., 174
Percy, E., 55
Perrin, N., 6, 41, 166
Pesce, M., 63
Pesch, R., 13, 20, 38, 48–50, 95, 98, 106, 146, 166, 168
Preuss, H. D., 178
Proksch, O., 71
Pryke, E. J., 40

Quell, G., 73
Quesnell, Q., 5, 44

Index of Subjects

apocalyptic eschatology, 10–11, 18–20, 26–29, 36, 40–41, 56–63, 74–75, 83–84, 87, 92, 134, 155–159, 163, 170–171, 177–179, 185–186, 194–198, 200, 203

Aqedah, 52

atonement, 194–195

baptism, 31, 74

blindness, healing of, 34–35

citation formulas, 8, 17–18

conflation of OT passages, 12, 15, 25, 54, 96–97, 132, 200

context, attention to in NT citations of OT, 20–21, 46, 81–82, 135–136, 155, 164–167, 180–184, 196, 199–200

contradictions in scripture, 99–107, 127, 152, 200

corporate figures, 95, 109, 115, 122–124, 163–164, 169–171, 184–186, 190–196, 201, 203

David, Davidic monarch, 7, 132, 142–144, 147, 162, 179, 190

death of Jesus, saving significance of, 194–195

demons, 62–63, 76–77, 134, 136–137, 150, 198, 201

disciples and discipleship, 6, 42–45, 158–159, 196

divine man, 6–7

Dura-Europos synagogue, 155

Eleazar son of Simon, 117

Elijah, 4–5, 57, 83–84, 92, 93, 94–110

Elisha, 4–5

eschatological interpretation of OT, 10, 21–23, 59–62, 114–115, 132–137, 158–159, 164, 177–182, 190–193, 196–197, 199, 201

ethics, 29–33

exegesis: cited as scripture, 95–97, 107–109, 200; and eisegesis, 107–108, 202–203; Jewish, 10, 21–23, 59–62, 114–115, 125–127, 132–137, 158–159, 164–171, 177–182, 186, 190–193, 195–203

exodus, new, 24–26

fulfillment of scripture, 2–3

Gentiles, 11, 69, 114–118, 121–123, 129, 149, 160–161, 168, 180, 182, 188, 190, 194–196, 198, 201

gezerah shavah, 16

God, relation of Jesus to, 37–41, 72, 90–92, 143–146

Gospel, 18–20, 45–46

holy war, 11, 22–23, 27–29, 33–34, 36–37, 40–41, 46, 62–63, 75–77, 92, 115–116, 134, 137, 144–145, 149–151, 155–157, 160–164, 170, 179, 185, 190, 194–201, 203

human and divine action, 26, 29–33, 42–45, 198, 201